Other books by Max R. Terman

Earth Sheltered Housing: Principles in Practice (Chapman and Hall)
Messages From An Owl (Princeton University Press)

Praise for

"Dr. Terman takes the reader o ...... traces the steps of his ancestor thr ...... reader experiences both combat and co ...... and brutal reality. Writing in the first person as though he were his great uncle, the author provides a unique perspective to a familiar subject thereby adding a new dimension to the genre and making his reader the beneficiary. From the numbing terror of the battlefield to the grinding misery of the prison camps—in this riveting first person account, you are there."
-Neil E. Veydt, Ph.D. *Veydt and Associates, Educator and Consultant*

"Dr. Terman has, in a manner, done what most Civil War enthusiasts would like to do, that is, to go back in time and see what it was really like. The journey was, it is obvious, an eye opener. I roundly applaud his effort and am convinced that Hiram would do the same."
-Richard Fink, *Chronicler, History of the 82nd Ohio Volunteer Infantry, Kenton, Ohio*

"*Hiram's Honor* tells the fascinating story of an ordinary Union soldier's experience of the greatest drama in American history, the Civil War. It is a novel full of adventure, suffering, friendship, and in the end, hope."
-Dr. William Kostlevy, *historian, Tabor College*

ROANOKE PUBLIC LIBRARY
706 S JEFFERSON STREET
ROANOKE, VA 24016-5104

Union soldiers *(Library of Congress)*. Each has a story. What would it be like to go back in time and walk in their footsteps?

Civil War Numbers and Losses, 1861-1865 (from Price, W. H. 1961. The Civil War Handbook. L. B. Prince and Company, Fairfax, Va. This handbook was written for the 100 year anniversary of the Civil War).

	Union	Confederate
Soldiers in war	2,213,400	1,003,600
Peak strength 1863	962,300	450,200
Total hit in battle	385,100	320,000
Killed in battle	67,100	54,000
Died of wounds	43,000	40,000
Not mortal wounds	275,000	226,000
Captured	211,400	462,000
Died in Prison	30,200	26,000
Died of Disease	224,000	60,000
Discharged	426,500	57,800
Surrendered 1865		174,223

"…they did not love life too much to shrink from death."
-Revelation 12:11

HIRAM'S HONOR

Reliving Private Terman's Civil War

Max R. Terman

Copyright © 2009 by Max R. Terman
Revised Edition

All rights reserved. No part of this book shall be reproduced, stored in a retrieval system, or transmitted by any means without written permission from the author.

ISBN 978-0-615-27812-4
Library of Congress Control Number 2009923675

TESA BOOKS
Hillsboro, Ks. 67063

With the exception of members of the Terman family, military officers, and prominent historical figures, all characters are fictitious. The personal relationships and dialogue, while based on letters and first-hand accounts, are products of the author's imagination. The emotions and understandings experienced as I relived my ancestor's Civil War are as genuine as I could make them.

0 1195 04662212

This book is dedicated to the descendants of Civil War soldiers, present and future, who wonder what it might have been like.

F
TERM

The author at the gravesite of his ancestor, Private Hiram Terman of the 82nd Ohio Volunteer Infantry, Company F.

The firmest friendships have been formed in mutual adversity, as iron
is most strongly united by the fiercest flame.
- Charles Caleb Colton

The beauty of the soul shines out when a man bears with composure
one heavy mischance after another, not because he does not feel them,
but because he is a man of high and heroic temper.
- Aristotle

The story as told by Civil War era drawings.
Unless otherwise noted, illustrations in the novel are photos taken as the author retraced his ancestor's steps and relived the war of Private Terman.

The numbing terror of the battlefield (*Battles and Leaders of the Civil War*).

The fear and humiliation of capture (*The Florence Military Prison Series*).

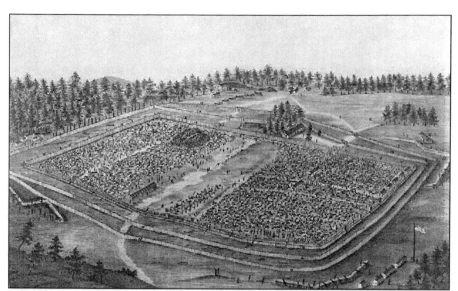

The grinding misery of the prison camp (*Library of Congress*).

The anticipation and exhilaration of exchange and release (*The Florence Military Prison Series*).

INTRODUCTION

Each of our lives is a fragile flower, a bud blooming briefly in the ceaseless seasons of time. We exist at the branch tip of a generational tree of ancestors, who though long dead, still live in the cores of our beings. In many ways, we are what they have been and experiencing their lives enriches our own.

Few trials surpassed those of the American Civil War and fewer yet exceeded the rough waters of the life of my ancestor, Private Hiram Terman, 82nd Ohio Volunteer Infantry. Back in that perilous upheaval, he experienced combat, capture, and prison. What would that have been like? This book is my attempt to go back in time and relive my ancestor's life in that great cataclysm of one hundred and fifty years ago.

I discovered a wealth of information to fuel my imagination. Motivated by our common ancestry, I retraced his steps on the battlegrounds, camps, and prisons. I uncovered official governmental records, regimental accounts, diaries and letters from comrades, and many eyewitness accounts that gave abundant witness to the adventures and trials Hiram experienced and endured. The Historical Notes and Acknowledgements at the end of this book hint at the depth and breadth of information that is available. The Civil War, beyond doubt, is an endless fountain.

This book is both factual and fictional. The train trips, camps, marches, battles, and prison confinements actually happened. The personal and emotional drama Hiram experienced, however, is unknown, lost in the depths of time with him and his Civil War comrades. How do I create this? While Hiram's records are the skeleton and flesh of this resurrection, its soul and spirit comes from "stepping into Hiram's shoes". I must actually become my ancestor, a Civil War Private. That is why I wrote this novel in the first person.

What was it like to be caught up in the whirlwind of a war so personal and vicious, a war fought against fellow citizens and relatives? When I was a boy, my father told stories of our relatives, long dead, who participated in the Great Armageddon of our country's existence.

I remember my father's arm around my shoulder as we settled on the living room couch. "Max, let me tell you about my uncle Hiram in the Civil War. He lived in a time when our country's future was very uncertain. A great war broke out and, son, Hiram was right in the thick of it."

"What kind of things happened to him, Dad?"

"Well, we know from his records and the few stories he and his pards told at the G.A.R. reunion that those old boys went through a lot—Gettysburg, Andersonville, places like that." My father rubbed my head and tousled my hair. "I was not much older than you when grandpa and I went to see those old Civil War vets at Shiloh, just north of here." Dad then looked out in the distance as if trying to measure the years. "I wish Hiram would have said more. He was a quiet man, reserved, didn't say much. The stories he did tell were really something, though." His arm tightened around me. "Maybe someday somebody will be able to piece together his story."

Oh Lord, what they went through! How can I, a man of a different age and time, naïve to the wickedness of war, experience these thoughts and emotions? Help me feel the excitement, the sense of honor, and the absolute will to survive of my ancestor, Private Hiram Terman, that I may experience again his story through the exciting, glorious, yet terrible, filthy, and cruel war in America from 1861-1865. Amen

Some military records for Private Hiram Terman *(National Archives).*

Prisoner of war record. Hiram was captured at Gettysburg July 1, 1863, sent to Belle Island (Richmond), then to Andersonville, followed by prisons in Savannah; Camp Lawton (Millen, Georgia), and then to Camp Parole in Annapolis, Maryland.

Muster sheet and one of Hiram's hospital records.

CHAPTER 1
REUNION

A smile crossed his face and met a tear coursing down his cheek. The gentle swaying of the car and the rhythm of the wheels on the rails rocked him to sleep as the train chugged on through the night. The morning sun then woke the old Civil War veteran as it climbed the horizon and cast its golden rays through the window. His weary eyes surveyed the rolling Ohio countryside. The train was slowing down. *Almost there, not long now.* He had traveled many miles in the heat of summer to attend a reunion advertised in a Grand Army of the Republic newsletter. Relaxing on the soft seat, he reminisced about the old days. *This is a sight better than those dirty boxcars.*

The brakes screeched and jets of steam clouded the veteran's view as the train stopped at the depot of a small town, a mere whistle stop in the north central part of the state. Something about the small station house evoked a worried look. He examined his train ticket a second time. Adjusting his spectacles, he again looked out the window of the plush railroad car at the old faded sign above the depot door. With difficulty, he deciphered the words, "Salem, Ohio". *Oh Lord, am I in the wrong place? The newsletter said Shiloh. Did I get on the right train?*

He stood, leaned on his cane, and grimaced. The scurvy acquired many years ago in the filthy prison camps still clawed at his aged muscles. He hobbled up the aisle to the conductor who stood near the door of the passenger car. The conductor, a tall distinguished man with clear empathetic eyes, turned as he heard the "thump, thump" of the cane on the polished wooden floor. For some reason, the appearance of the old man now arrested his attention. Was this man a survivor of the Great War of the Rebellion, now more than fifty years past?

The old veteran wobbled. The conductor at once extended his hand and with great care supported the aged soldier. The eyes of the old veteran looked up and were underlined by a thin smile. "Thank you, my legs aren't what they used to be."

"Yes sir, what can I do for you?" His eyes continued to scan his subject as if he were a valuable relic. A scar, maybe from a burn, blemished the old soldier's neck above his collar. The conductor's eyes next fell on a gold pin of a large riverboat on the wrinkled lapel of his suit coat. The name Sultana provoked a gasp. *My Lord, this man is a Sultana survivor. The last out of Andersonville—he had to survive that horrendous explosion. My God, my God!*

The old man reached inside his blue suit coat and removed an article about the reunion of Civil War veterans of Richland County, Ohio. "Am I on the right train? This newsletter says the reunion is in Shiloh but the sign there says Salem. Is this town Salem or Shiloh? I must get to this reunion!"

The conductor looked at the paper then at the old veteran. "Sir, you are at the right place. The reunion is indeed here at Salem...I mean Shiloh. The town was renamed in 1862. Too many towns named Salem in Ohio I guess." The conductor looked again at the faded letters on the weathered boards of the station. "You'd think that in fifty years that sign would have been painted over but folks hate to see the old name forgotten."

"Some things should always be remembered," replied the old soldier as he looked at the American flags flapping in the breeze. He paused as if in a trance. *Sweet Jesus, who could ever tell the tale?* His hand stroked his white beard as his mind moved back through the years. He began to sway and reached for the handrail. The conductor placed a gentle hand on the stooped shoulders.

"What you men have done will never be forgotten. The new name of this town is proof of that. Shiloh, what a battle that was! What a sacrifice! And Fredericksburg…" The old man's eyes widened.

"Now I remember! Of course! Salem is now Shiloh, after the famous battle led by General Grant. Hiram told me about Salem in winter quarters after that terrible slaughter at Fredericksburg." *Good Lord, at least I was spared that—but not my will but Thine be done.*

The conductor, beguiled, then asked the short, grizzled veteran, "May I ask why this particular reunion is so important to you? Are you expecting to see some old friends?" A carriage with three more old Union veterans pulled up to the depot, parting a gathering of relatives and well-wishers. A small band began playing the "Battle Hymn of the Republic" in the background. The voices of the gathering crowd grew stronger as they sang the old tune.

"Oh yes, I hope they haven't forgotten about me after all these years." *Glory, Glory, Hallelujah!* The music was getting louder as the band members and the crowd found the rhythm. The conductor raised his voice.

"I am sure they will remember you. Godspeed to you old friend! Watch your step." *Glory, Glory, Hallelujah!*

The veteran smiled and chuckled as he made his way down the steps out of the car and onto the platform. *The Lord has watched my steps. Oh, those battles—and Belle, Andersonville. Lord, blown off that boat, finding that log in that cold river.*

The conductor noticed the other Union veterans begin their climb up the platform. Step by step, the silver-haired soldiers drew nearer to each other. The passengers getting off the train stopped in hushed silence and watched the unfolding drama.

An elderly black man stepped out of the last car with his granddaughter and listened to the singing. They looked down the track and saw the old soldiers walking across the platform. "Grandpa Jim, what's everybody lookin' at up there?" The former slave smiled widely and caressed the head of the little girl as they walked toward the flags fluttering and snapping in the breeze above the depot.

"The last of Mr. Linkum's gun men, honey, the last lightning bolts of dat mighty storm dat blew me up here from Richmond." *His truth is marching on!*

As the comrades met, the band stopped, and the air filled with howls of joy, and then, sobs of sorrow. Tears filled the conductor's eyes and a lump formed in his throat as he watched the old soldiers embrace. A passenger stopped, stared at the aged veterans, and remarked to the conductor. "My Lord, what would it have been like? Don't you wonder what those men have seen?"

"Indeed I do. Indeed I do," replied the conductor.

Civil War veterans at a reunion in Shiloh, Ohio (*courtesy of Shiloh Area Historical Museum*).

The last photo of the ill-fated *Sultana*. A faulty boiler exploded while the steamer carried the last survivors of Andersonville home. Only about 500 of 1,700 men survived (*Library of Congress*).

CHAPTER 2
METAMORPHOSIS

By January 25, 1862, the recently mustered 82nd Ohio was ready to leave the rolling hills and familiar confines of Kenton, Ohio and move south into the mountains, valleys, and internal strife of what is now West Virginia, then northwest Virginia. Several Union victories in the summer of 1861 in this region by General George McClellan secured much of this pro-Union territory for the North. However, many small bands of pro-southern bushwhackers still roamed the countryside and inhabited the villages. In 1863, President Abraham Lincoln set the borders of West Virginia and then declared it a state, the only one created by Presidential decree.

I can feel myself merge or metamorphose into *Hiram*.

I was filled with conflicting emotions. I was excited about seeing new places but was apprehensive about what dangers awaited in the avenues of war. Around me the drilling grounds of Camp Simon Kenton in Ohio took on an air of excitement as soldiers packed canteens, cooking utensils, and other bits and pieces needed for survival and military action. The rattle of pots and pans filled the air about camp as we got ready to go to war. My thoughts turned to home and family. Would they be able to make it without *me*? Should *I* have signed up—oh well, too late now!

Corporal Sam Armstrong of company F parted the flaps and peered into my tent. A cold wind caused me to shiver. I huddled by the stove and anxiously fingered a square of a hard flour biscuit, commonly called hardtack. An anxious feeling gnawed at my stomach. Winter in the mountains of western Virginia would be brutal. I worried about freezing in a sleet or hailstorm with little food. Corporal Armstrong did little to lessen my fears.

"You think this is bad with all of our supplies right next door, Hiram? Wait until we get to Virginia and supplies are miles behind as we march on those God-forsaken muddy roads!" Corporal Armstrong, a shoe cobbler and an older soldier, had given careful thought to the matter of survival for the soldiers in his squad of ten men. Squads were formed into a company and companies formed a regiment under the command of a colonel.

Corporal Armstrong came closer and examined my pack. "You know Hiram, each man needs to think ahead and make provisions for hard days and nights. Our rations will not be enough." His hands fingered the flap of my backpack. "Store up beans, dried fruits, nuts and such when you can get them, and learn to live off the land." He then pointed to my shoes. "And take care of your shoes! Those brogans are the best friends you have!"

Live off the land? I thought of my great grandmother, a Blackfoot Indian. She lived with us on the farm after her husband, my great grandfather Abraham Terman, died. She had found Abraham, a wounded Revolutionary War soldier, on the battlefield, nursed him back to health, and later married him. Though quite old, she had taught us many of her ways; to hunt, trap, and lay up berries, nuts, and edible roots. Maybe food would be less of a problem if I could find a way to store it. I blurted out this idea to my corporal.

"Could I have another backpack for storing food I collect?"

"Oh? Are you going to have your own private pack mule? How are you going to carry your rifle, ammunition, bedroll, and tent plus a pantry? Learn to pack well, soldier, your survival depends on it!" He then left, chuckling and shaking his head.

What to carry and what to leave behind? Could the members of my squad each carry a separate item? Some could bring parts of the tent, some blankets, others cooking utensils, another food, and so forth. Seth Hall, one of my new friends, scratched his head. "What happens if one of us carrying the skillet gets killed? What then? Do we eat our food raw?" Nothing is certain in the uncertainties of war.

The weather turned warm and clear on the last Sunday before the regiment left Camp Simon Kenton. A local preacher came to camp with a load of Bibles and a sermon. He wanted to prepare us for what trials and tribulations lay ahead. The meeting took place in an open area on the edge of camp. About twenty men huddled in the bright winter sun around a rough wooden pulpit.

An older rather heavyset woman, the preacher's wife, approached the podium. "Ahem...my dear soldiers, would you turn to page 106 and let's all sing, *Nearer, My God, to Thee.*"

The morning sun was midway up the eastern sky. The warmth of its rays offset the cool temperatures of the Ohio winter. The reverend's wife raised her arms. She looked like a large pigeon. The accordionist, a plump young girl, probably the preacher's daughter, sounded the familiar refrain. Most soldiers sang it from memory. I did.

I had sung it many, many times on Sunday mornings, Sunday nights, and Wednesday evenings at prayer meetings in the Presbyterian Church in Rome, Ohio, my home town. This church was the center of my family's life and its resources were called on before I left to meet the train at Salem to go to camp.

Reverend Stanley Sams, a square-headed, rotund man with a perpetual smile, approached me as I bowed at the altar. In his hands was a brass pot brimming with clear oil. "Oh Lord Jesus, protect our dear boy Hiram Terman as he goes to the land of secession and slavery. Give him courage to confront the enemy and defend the righteous honor of our beloved country!" He then laid hands on me and anointed my head with oil. As oil ran down my face I turned and saw my father cry. I had never before seen him shed a tear. He was a tough hardscrabble farmer from Pennsylvania who had wrestled a meager living from the fertile but rocky and forested Ohio soil. On the way home, my father spoke as I had never heard him speak.

"Hiram, I know life has been hard on you, losing your mother and sister." He flicked the reins and looked off in the darkness. The sound of the horses and the turning wheels of the wagon made it hard to hear. I leaned forward in the old farm wagon. "You were just a child when the Lord took Catherine. And Sissy, your best friend, was snatched away when she was only ten. Never saw a brother and sister get along like you two." He pulled out a large red handkerchief and blew his nose. "Now you're goin' off to war. Oh my, the ways of the Lord!" He then turned on the wagon seat and hugged his new young wife, Priscilla, who was expecting. I leaned back and looked up at them. My father's aged profile contrasted sharply with the straight back of his young wife. I felt like I was a remnant on the fringes of a new family.

Though like the wanderer, the sun gone down, Darkness be over me, my rest a stone. Yet in my dreams I'd be nearer, my God to Thee. Nearer, my God, to Thee, Nearer to Thee!

The tune tugged at my heart, the hymn made me feel uneasy. I stopped singing and looked off to the far side of the camp. The Sunday sun silhouetted the tents of the camp against the horizon. I thought of the mother that I had feelings for but never knew and an older sister who perished too soon, leaving a younger brother and me alone. The only motherly comfort we knew came from my great grandmother, an elderly Indian woman with a deeply tanned face and wiry, tough constitution.

Life had been too sad, happiness too elusive for me to feel very near to God. I took a deep breath and closed my eyes. Even in this great adventure, I seemed to be wrapped in a vague sense of apprehension with a lot of sorrow from the past. It began to well up in my throat.

The next hymn chosen was *Come, Thou Fount of Every Blessing*. Not feeling prone to count my blessings, the melody and words flew by me as I stood with my eyes closed, my mind sorting through my thoughts. My conscience stirred with these words.

Prone to wander, Lord, I feel it, Prone to leave the God I love; Here's my heart, O take and seal it, Seal it for Thy courts above.

After the last chords, the soldiers sat down, and an older thin, kindly looking man with a gentle demeanor came to the pulpit. He had a round hat, clerical collar, black shirt, and gray pants. He carefully removed his hat and gently placed both hands on the edge of the pulpit, scanned the small congregation of soldiers, smiled and began to speak.

"Young men, thank you for coming out on this winter's day for this call to worship. The Bible Society of Hardin County is giving you a Testament today. Please keep it close and read it. The power of the Holy Spirit and our Lord Jesus Christ will sustain and keep you. I know not what you will face in the coming days. The battles and deprivations of this war to come are unknown at this point. I do not know what battles you will face in the field. However, I do know about the "inside battle". It has plagued us humans since time began. There is a battle raging in you for your humanity—your soul! The choices you make will bear consequences; each action will reap a result. Choose what is good and even though you die, you will live! Follow evil, and you will die not only in body, but your very soul will perish! Read your Bibles, pray, and live for Jesus and the power of God will help you endure the coming days. You are involved in a noble venture to save the Union and set a people free. May you all bring honor to your country, your families, and our Lord. Farewell and may God go with you."

After saying this, he asked all present to bow their heads and he did as he entreated us to do. He prayed a long and heartfelt prayer asking fervently that we hold onto our faith.

I felt a strange cascade of warmth flow through me as I walked out of the meeting area and back to my tent to finish packing. Not many soldiers in the camp attended the church service. On the way out of the meeting, I passed an officer quietly sitting on a barrel whittling away at a piece of wood making what appeared to be a cross. Those who did not attend the service sat around fires fixing coffee, cooking, or conversing. Just before getting to my tent, I passed a group of soldiers gambling, laughing, and raucously swearing as their luck turned sour.

"Oh Harry, damn you, not another game of Chuck-A-Luck. Before you throw those dice again, can you give me a loan till next we get paid?"

"Jim, you know the paymaster is already two weeks late. If you can't pay, don't play for God's sakes!"

"Well, listen to you! Old Jones has a euchre game going and I bet he won't be so uppity!" As I walked by, I instinctively felt my pocket for my wallet. We got paid $13 a month and I was not going to squander it like that poor sap.

Early the next morning the orders arrived to form up and march to the railroad station in Kenton. I checked and double-checked the contents of my pack. Lifting it onto my back, I fell into line with others in my squad. A chill of excitement ran along my spine as I looked over the soldiers ahead of me. We marched the mile or so to the town square of Kenton. It was a grand sight. The muskets pointed to the sky and rocked back and forth as our long blue line tramped over the white, snow-covered Ohio countryside. I felt lightheaded as the cheering crowds urged us along to the town square.

"Give 'em hell, Buckeyes! Bully for the Buckeyes!"

"Hurrah for Ohio!"

"Farewell brave boys! Farewell!"

This last call came from an old soldier, his white beard indenting a faded blue uniform. Some disabled veterans of the Mexican War had formed on the sidewalk in front of the courthouse where they displayed their uniforms and waved flags.

Even the sound of the regimental band playing, the presentation of the regimental flag by a society of ladies, and a stirring speech by our Lieutenant Colonel Durfee did not remove the sting of that last call from the wounded soldier, "Farewell Brave Boys". The lump in my stomach reminded me that I was indeed marching off to war and death would be a constant companion. Leaving the front of Colonel James Cantwell's home (our regimental commander who was reportedly in Columbus), we proceeded once more around the town square of Kenton.

The glance and wave of a pretty girl removed my uneasiness. I smiled back at her but then her glance fell on another soldier, braver than I in such matters, who threw her a kiss. She squealed in delight and pointed her admirer out to some friends who then became excited.

Nearby, I noticed Nancy, the daughter of a Mennonite pastor from Rome. She was standing off to the right of these girls. What was she doing here? It was a long way from Rome to Kenton. Lifting her hand to wave, she smiled and gazed at me as I marched on by toward the waiting railroad cars.

Nancy was an attractive girl with blue eyes, a wide smile, and a gentle, sensible disposition that attracted me—and many others. I could not believe she was here to see me off. Nancy planned to become a pastor or missionary's wife and I did not seem to meet that ambition. I had gotten to know her at a church picnic a few weeks before. How well I remember what she said as we walked around the camp.

"Hiram, I am waiting on God to give me a husband who will save men, not shoot them!" She turned away then faced me. "Must you do this thing? You don't have to join up. There are plenty of men who can't wait to go to war. Can't you stay home with me?" Nancy then grasped my hand.

"I can't stay behind when every man my age is enlisting. How could I walk around Rome and be the only man twenty years old not in the army? No, I have got to go." My hands tightened and I put them in my pockets. "Remember what our teacher Mr. Williams said about the Revolutionary War?" Nancy gave me a quizzical look. "Sometimes war is necessary to settle things, you know, to fight wrong."

Her expression became puzzled. "What do the McMullen's say about that?" The McMullen's were pacifist relatives on my mother's side, leaders in a nearby Brethren in Christ church.

"My cousin James McMullen is heading up an artillery unit. That's what he thinks about it."

She then looked away and sighed deeply. I followed and placed my hand between her reluctant fingers. Nancy smiled and drew my hand to her chest. Her bosom pressed against the back of my hand as she placed her head on my shoulder. Somehow the chemistry still clicked between us as we walked around the picnic grounds. I yearned for a secluded spot and a kiss.

Just as darkness fell, her parents pulled up by us in their buggy. Nancy's arm dropped and she immediately pulled away from me. Her father, an outspoken pacifist, gave me a stern look. He was a tall, slim man with a trimmed beard and no mustache, wearing a clerical collar. "Time to go home Nancy, get in the carriage my daughter!" Nancy quickly climbed into the back seat as her father stared at me. As they pulled away, I heard him ask, "Who's that boy?" Nancy said something about the army. The minister shook his head as he slapped the reins on the rump of his handsome chestnut mare. As the buggy disappeared in the distance, so did my hopes of a relationship.

But here Nancy was in Kenton seeing off our regiment, watching me! What was she doing here? Her father would be angry. A realization then came to me that reduced my excitement. She did mention that she had an uncle who had left the Mennonites to become a chaplain in the army. He was leaving today as well. *I knew it, she wasn't here for me!*

I turned back around to look at her again. She was still following me! *Oh, Lord! She is looking at me.* She even moved to keep me in view, skirting some onlookers as she stepped along through the crowd. After a last wave and smile, she faded off into the crowd. Sam Armstrong, off to my right, barked.

"Eyes forward Hiram, stop that gawking, and try to act like a Union soldier!" Embarrassed, I turned and saw the railroad station in the distance. A warm feeling welled up in me as we approached the steaming locomotive and the long line of cars. *Should I write to her?*

Many a bonnet and handkerchief flew into the air as the regimental band played patriotic tunes. The crowd cheered as the regiment boarded the cars. "Godspeed you brave boys! Show them Rebs the cold steel! Rally round the flag boys!" Cheer after cheer went out. In time, the crowd thinned out as car after car filled with blue-clad soldiers. Just a few family members who lived in Kenton lingered to get in a last goodbye.

When we got to our car it was so dilapidated that we had to wait for it to be removed and a more acceptable one to be hooked up. There were rotten floorboards and rat nests in the seats.

"Get this damned thing out of here!" yelled one of our officers. "These are soldiers going to war! Bring us a car worthy of them, by God!" Revolted, we backed out of the reeking car and sat down on the bank. I looked around for Nancy but she had gone. Finally, the new car arrived and was hitched up. The train hauling the 82nd Ohio was ready to go south.

My closest friends, made during the month's stay at camp, were Isaiah Rinehart, a Baptist minister's son from Lucas, Ohio and Seth Hall, a college student from Ashland. Isaiah sat in the seat beside me and Seth across the aisle. Beside him was Bushey Thomas, a stocky, talkative soldier from Shelby with a quick sense of humor. "Hmmm, I miss that "la fragrance of the rat" we had in the first car, don't you boys? Makes me miss the old barn on the farm." A soldier in the seat behind him flipped Bushey's hat from his head.

"Ah, shut up Bushey, you old hayseed. I bet you'll be seeing plenty of rats in the land of cotton where we're goin'!"

After a long wait, the train lurched forward and the engine's whistle pierced the cold chill of the Ohio winter as the train chugged toward Columbus. The hum of conversations coursed through the cars as the train left town.

"Just wait till the 82nd gets into the fight, we'll show those slavers a thing or two!"

"How dare the Rebs destroy the greatest country on earth? Won't be long and we'll bring the Johnnies back to their senses!" Isaiah, Seth, and I sat quietly listening to the various boasts without comment.

Isaiah was light in complexion and somewhat short and heavyset, but rather handsome. He possessed wide set eyes that revealed a kind spirit and a thoughtful sincerity. At every opportunity, he pulled out a Bible, stroked his chin, and closed his eyes in prayer. He was also concerned about politics and the military and was fiercely loyal to his commanders and the Union. We often heard him exclaim at the end of his prayers, "God bless Abraham Lincoln and the generals. May God lead them and us to the Lord's victory."

Seth was slim, of average height, and dark in complexion. He was good looking but in a tough sort of way. He had deep-set, piercing brown eyes and a ready smile that was most engaging. Highly educated and quick-witted, he was a keen observer of nature. Somewhat sarcastic and often profane, he nevertheless had a spirit that invited conversation. He did not like the religiosity of Isaiah but enjoyed engaging him in philosophical contests just the same. I often found myself in the middle of these debates.

Both Isaiah and Seth stared out the window as the train moved along to Columbus. We were excited but apprehensive about what lay ahead. The rocking back and forth of the train car soon relaxed us. I gazed out the window and wondered what the capital of Ohio, Columbus, would look like. I had never been there even though it was only seventy-five miles from my home.

We stopped at several towns along the way to get out, stretch, and relieve ourselves. At every stop, we were cheered and given coffee, apples, pies, and other delights.

We strained to get better looks at the young women that frequented every station, waving, and throwing kisses. "Hiram, look at that one in the yellow dress over there? I think she likes you."

"Shut up, Seth. She's waving and throwing kisses at everybody." I took a longer look at the girl and sure enough, she was looking at me! I turned red and managed a smile and a wave. What a glorious crusade. I enjoyed it to the hilt in this, the first leg of our journey. My apprehension retreated, for now.

The sinking sun sought out the windows and its afternoon rays danced across the blue woolen uniforms as the train entered the outskirts of Columbus. I saw the biggest building I had ever seen. The buildings in Mansfield, the nearest large town to Rome, did not compare to these rambling structures, in particular the state capitol building.

The train came to a screeching stop at the railroad station. Outside a large crowd gathered. They cheered us as we disembarked from the long line of cars. As we stepped onto the platform, Seth leaned back and whispered. "Look at those ladies, Hiram, they just get more beautiful as we go along." Chills went down my spine as a band played patriotic songs.

We formed into columns and marched to another train heading east to the Ohio River. Cheers and hurrahs filled the air and women who lined the streets gave us large cups of coffee and sacks of biscuits. "Here boys, this should warm your innards," said a smiling round-faced woman with a large coffeepot. I shivered and relaxed as the warm coffee went down my throat.

Isaiah tapped me on the shoulder. "Look over at that platform car. Those are the whipping sticks of the Lord." The cannons on a nearby flat car reminded me that we were headed for war, a serious struggle for the survival of a nation and the freeing of a whole race of people and not a fun adventure.

Once we reached the second train dock, we boarded boxcars with straw spread on the floor. Seth kicked the straw into the air. "What the hell? Are we cattle? What happened to the passenger cars?"

"Settle down Seth," said Isaiah as he bunched up some hay and leaned against the wall. "You didn't expect to go south first class all the way did you?" I took a seat opposite the sliding door with my comrades by my side.

Corporal Sam Armstrong sat at the head of the car. He glanced at us and then tilted his hat over his eyes. The train lurched forward and the cars began to sway in the customary back and forth motion, as we made our way east to the Ohio border and the Ohio River.

Several soldiers near the corporal began to talk loudly, laugh, and enter into jovial conversations. "Whoa there, Charley boy, how many times did she kiss you? A hundred juicy ones?"

"You shut up Henry or I'll kick in your guldernated teeth!"

"Don't get so riled up Charley, she didn't kiss me that many times!"

Corporal Armstrong abruptly told them to "pipe down". This banter did not attract us. We wanted to relax but apprehension gripped us. Finally, Seth, looking out through the cracks in the boards, broke the ice.

"Look! All the bridges have picket guards. We must be getting closer to the fires of secession." Seth's father was a college professor and Seth's vocabulary reflected his father's influence.

"Are the Rebels in Ohio?" asked Isaiah. Isaiah Rinehart was the son of a Hard-Shell Baptist minister in Richland County and a staunch Republican. The presence of a Rebel threat in Ohio was almost incomprehensible to him even though a strong peace movement was afoot and plenty of southern sympathizers called Copperheads were gathering headlines.

"Well, those guards aren't there for the pleasure of it," replied Seth. "You never know what the Copperheads will do. They really stirred things up in Holmes County. Tried to talk men out of signing up. The government had to step in and arrested a bunch of them sons of perdition." I tried to correct Seth.

"Those weren't Copperheads in Holmes County. They were Amish and Mennonites, not the same thing."

"We don't need our own people causing trouble," mumbled Isaiah as he tried to get more comfortable on the hard floor. "You are either for the grand ole Union or against it! Ain't no middle ground." Nancy's father and my Brethren relatives flashed through my mind.

"Things ain't that simple, Isaiah. Not everybody is as cocksure about this war as you." A hush settled around us and everyone looked at me with a quizzical stare. My words surprised Isaiah.

"Well, Hiram, seems that a fellow should be sure before he enlists." Seth came to my aid.

"Oh, hell, Isaiah. How many men do you think are sure about anything in this war? Most of us signed up because we were afraid not to enlist. Some fools thought it would be fun. Don't get on Hiram because he has a doubt or two." Silence. Only the rumble of the wheels on the rails filled the tense air.

From across the car Bushey Thomas cleared his throat. "Ahem! Seems a bit late for philosophy since we're in this here car headed for Rebeldom. I suggest you gentlemen recognize the obvious."

A quiet soldier on my right then spoke." That's what I say, by God. The cards are on the table. We best settle in and play the hand we're dealt." He looked at me sternly, daring a reply.

"I ain't backin' out of nothing!" My sharp reply surprised me. "It's just that some folks don't..." Seth interrupted me.

"Hiram, shut up. We know what you mean. Let's get some sleep."

The train rolled on with occasional stops for refueling. Each town gave us a warm reception but the numbers of people decreased as we approached the eastern edge of the state. Beyond the broad river was the South and the Rebellion.

The hills became steeper as the day waned and we neared the Ohio River and Bellaire. This river town had many paddle-wheeled transport boats to ferry us across the river. From a crack in the boxcar, I saw the crests and ridges of the higher mountains to the east. The glow of the moon made them appear eerie.

I wondered about my knapsack in the freight car ahead of our boxcars. Did I have everything I needed? *Quit worrying, you can't plan for every contingency.* I struggled to shed my doubts and commit to the mission. We left the cars to stretch our legs, eat, and take care of the demands of nature. After this, we gathered in formation in a nearby open area.

The Ohio River, dark and whipped with winter winds, flowed between flanking mountains. The cold wind blew across our faces and flapped our overcoats as Colonel Cantwell addressed us. "Men, prepare to head into western Virginia, the land of the Rebellion." He flipped up the collar on his overcoat, stroked his mustache, and began walking back and forth in front of us. "Up to this point you have been treated pretty well by northern citizens. From now on do not take water or food from people along the roads. There are reports of poison." A murmur came from the ranks. "We will be in the land of the enemy soon so be on your guard. Now, pick up your rifles, packs, and prepare to board the transports."

The first boatloads headed off into the glow of late evening. A golden moon illuminated the river producing a ghostlike scene. Our turn to board the river transport boat soon arrived. I picked up my pack and followed Seth closely as he and Isaiah walked onto the gently rocking paddle wheeler.

Black smoke from the engines stung my eyes. I looked down at the river. Dark swirling currents coursed along the side of the boat as it headed out from the dock. A huge fish broke the cold water and flopped on the surface. Lanterns from the boat revealed ripples that radiated out in a circle. Soon we arrived on the other side, joining the massing numbers of soldiers. Each man's breathing gathered to form a cloud on the riverbank, the collective breath of the regiment.

"Attention! Shoulder arms!" We put on our backpacks, lifted our rifles and marched to the railroad depot of the Baltimore and Ohio Railroad. The Virginia residents showed both friendly and hostile glances. The crowd noise was different from the uniform patriotic cheering we received all through Ohio. The uneasiness of the political climate caused me to be anxious. Even though this was Union controlled territory, violent behavior could erupt at any place, any time.

A nervous dampness formed beneath my hat as we marched to the railroad platform and its encircling guards. There we waited while groups of men glared at us and then sauntered off. "Those bastards will be shooting at us from the woods, mark my words," said a man behind me.

In the darkness we boarded the boxcars for our trip to Grafton, Virginia, our training camp. The boxcar had no source of heat; cold bare boards surrounded us. I wrapped my overcoat around me and huddled between Seth and Isaiah. A soldier with chattering teeth yelled from the other side of the car. "Things just keep getting better and better, don't they boys?"

The cars of the train jostled and shook on our odyssey through the mountains and valleys to Camp Tod. After a few hours, we stopped to take on water for the engine. A perimeter guard was deployed and Seth and I were ordered out.

The captain of our company walked up to us. "Private Terman! You and Private Hall keep an eye on the riverbank. Don't let anyone through your guard line!"

Illuminated by the dim rays of a cloud-covered moon, Seth and I walked to our positions. I peered out into the night as I leaned against my rifle. Seth was standing at attention about twenty yards away, his shape visible through the bare branches of the surrounding trees. He paced back and forth following everything by the book. I chuckled to myself.

"Feel like a soldier yet, Seth?"

"Hiram, you best shut up and shoulder that rifle!"

"All we have to do is watch, we don't have to strut like turkeys out here," was my relaxed reply. In the moonlight, I could see the train, its steaming engine swallowing large gulps of water from a tower.

A cracking in the branches signaled an approaching figure.

"Private! What are you doing leaning on that rifle? Shoulder that damn gun and walk your beat. The rest of us are dependent on you...you dumb ox!"

The stocky Colonel James Cantwell came right up and looked me in the eyes, the bills of our caps almost touching. Cantwell was older, balding and had a stern demeanor. He looked to be almost middle-aged to my young eyes.

"The next time you are on guard duty, son, you'll be doing it right. Now get back to the train, we're heading out."

Seth came up behind and mumbled. "Told you so." A nauseous feeling flowed through me as I walked back to the boxcar and waited for the signal to board. The beating of my heart produced a pulsating in my head as I climbed back into the boxcar and flopped on the floor. The train lurched forward and picked up speed. The chugging of the engine kept saying "you dumb ox, you dumb ox." Yes indeed, I did have a lot to learn.

Our train crept along the Baltimore and Ohio Railroad tracks across northern Virginia to Grafton. These same tracks led to Baltimore, Maryland, a city infamous for mobs attacking Union troops. "Lincoln even had to sneak through Baltimore," said Seth.

Black, glistening coal seams crept out of the mountains and rivulets of mountain streams cascaded down the slopes. The rays of the moon reflected light off them as the train climbed the curves and crept closer to Grafton where we would learn the ways of a soldier.

The screeching of wheels and the release of steam announced the end of our journey. The door of the boxcar opened and from the darkened depths we saw the silhouetted shapes of old buildings, some on stilts, lining the muddy streets. Grafton was a barren looking place and the dank, drizzle magnified its miserable appearance.

"My God, would you look at this place," muttered Seth as he viewed the wet town that reeked of mildew and dreariness.

At the shout of an officer, we left the boxcars and found our assigned quarters in Camp Tod. Here, as at Kenton, we quartered in tents with wooden plank floors and a sheet iron stove. While somewhat rough, it was bearable, even in the cold winds of the Virginia winter. We soon made the tent our home.

Fairgrounds at Kenton, Ohio, site of Camp Simon Kenton.

Recruits in camp (*Library of Congress*).

CHAPTER 3
THE WAYS OF A SOLDIER IN THE 82ND OHIO
"BE JUST AND FEAR NOT"

As we cooked our meals and prepared our beds in the darkness of early morning, we wondered what kind of training was to come. Off to the east was the gathering storm and the reality of its presence now began to test the strength of every soldier's commitment to serve in the Union Army.

Even though some men had deserted at various stops on the way to Camp Tod, the next day found our regiment nearly the same as when we left Ohio. "I am proud of the boys in the 82nd," boasted Isaiah as he stretched, trying to awake. "None of us has left in the face of the danger to come. May the Lord be with this blessed regiment!" Seth stretched and rubbed his neck as he too emerged from the short night's sleep.

"Don't get on your high and mighty horse just yet Isaiah. We don't know what's comin' in this here training camp. Even you might feel like leavin' the party once we get into it!"

"Lord forbid that I should shirk my duty at this hour of my country's need. Seth, I will be there, I will serve honorably!" Sensing an eruption between my two friends, I tried to refocus the conversation.

"Seth, what do you think lies ahead for us at this camp?" At Kenton we had learned to form companies, get into columns and respond to drum cadences and bugle calls for advance and retreat. We knew the basics of how to shoot our Enfield rifles and how to attach a bayonet, but that was about all.

"Oh I expect it will be rougher than at Kenton, that's for sure. Sure as thunder, we're about to meet the Rebs soon and we can't skedaddle like at Bull Run."

The mass panic and fleeing of the Union troops at Bull Run was a deadweight on everyone. After that battle, cowardly soldiers were held up before comrades and branded on the cheek with a letter "C". One of the men in our tent rubbed his cheek. "Good Lord, how could you face your family coming back home labeled a coward, a big scar on your face?"

"And it would eat your guts out to know that most of the others who ran got off with no punishment," added another man.

Our officers made it clear that the training at Camp Tod, near the small town of Fetterman on the western edge of Grafton, would be rough. "Soldiers trained here will be ready! No more will Union troops flee like an unorganized mob. You will be ready!"

That we were beginners in the arts of war and ill-prepared for the nerve-numbing trials of battle was obvious. We knew nothing of the teeth gritting courage it would take to confront an oncoming Rebel soldier eyeball to eyeball and kill him without remorse. The faces of Seth and Isaiah reflected this grim reality, as they lay open-eyed on their beds.

Seth then rose up on one elbow. "Isaiah, you're about the most religious person I know, how in the devil are you going to kill those Rebels once we get into it?"

"Read your old Testament, Seth. God used his people many times to smite the ungodly."

"But how about the New Testament. Don't it say love your enemies?" Once again, a rousing argument was in the works and I had to intervene.

"All right, all right. I ain't exactly wanting to get into a big debate just now. We got a hard day coming tomorrow and we need to get ready!" Seth, sounding disappointed, laughed.

"So be it, Hiram. I'll shut up but it seems damned incongruent to me."

"It ain't …whatever you said…to me," replied Isaiah as he crawled out of the tent and made his way to the sinks.

The next morning we awakened to a cold, uncomfortable rainy day. Would we be expected to get out in this weather? The answer came with the order to gather for roll call. Looking out at the falling rain, Seth exclaimed. "My God, are we going out in this? Do they think we're a bunch of ducks?" Under a sky crowded with dark, rolling purple rain clouds, we marched double-quick to the firing range and lined up in ranks. The rain came down in coughs and spits, blowing in the wintry winds.

Keeping my powder dry was a challenge as we loaded and fired according to the commands of a sergeant. "Take out your cartridge, invert, tear off the paper, pour in the powder, ram the Minnie ball down, return the ramrod, half cock, place the cap on the nipple, full cock, aim and fire!" As rain dripped off the visor of his hat, the sergeant paced in front of us, scanning every man.

"Again! Again! Load and fire that cussed rifle 'til you don't even think about it. It won't be long before your hides will depend on it."

Before long I was able to fire shot after shot, the various moves flowed in sequence without flaw. Major Robinson, who prowled up and down the line looking for the slightest sign of slowness or incompetence, was impressed.

"Good men! Good! A battle-ready soldier should be able to get off three aimed shots a minute in the heat of battle!"

Colonel Cantwell rode his horse up behind us. The leather creaked and his mount snorted as the leader of the 82nd Ohio dismounted. "The heat of battle, Major, now what would that be like?" Cantwell then walked up to us with his revolver cocked. "Resume loading and firing men." We turned and began the firing sequence. Cantwell then fired his revolver right next to the ear of a soldier.

The soldier jerked and lead balls spilled on the ground. As the man groveled on the ground trying to scrape these together, Cantwell calmly addressed us. "Men! We must do better. This is nothing compared to battle." The Colonel then came to my position on the end of the line.

Lord give me calm nerves, I said to myself as the crunch of his heavy boots drew near.

"Load and fire at that target Private."

Cantwell cocked his revolver and placed the gun next to my head. I could hear the cylinder change positions. The side blasts from the pistol parted the hair on the back of my neck but miraculously I was able to bite, tear, pour, tamp, cock and fire— and this three times in a minute!

"Excellent! Excellent!" proclaimed the Colonel as he proceeded to the next man then the next. Leaving the line and remounting his horse, he turned. "Major Robinson, kindly show the men the next step in what the heat of battle will be like!" Major Robinson saluted and smiled wryly as Cantwell rode off.

Thank you Lord, I thought to myself thinking the ordeal over. As we resumed loading and firing, a line of soldiers marched up to our left stopped, turned, and fired live shots over our heads. A volley went over us sounding like a flock of blackbirds. Some of the bullets felt much too close.

"My God! We're going to be killed before we even get to see any Rebs," said the man next to me. The line of soldiers fired again. The bullets thudded into trees in a nearby woodland. All of us flinched and crouched lower. Major Robinson rushed up shouting at the top of his husky voice.

"Get up! Get up! Keep firing! Keep to your task!" He came right up to Isaiah. "Do you think we're doing this for fun?" Isaiah shook his head. "This is what the party will be like in a few weeks. You don't want to miss it, do you?" Isaiah shook his head more emphatically. Robinson smiled and addressed us all. "Tomorrow we will see how you do with shell and canister whizzing over your darling little heads. You better learn to bear it 'cause it's coming sure as blazes in Hades."

The next day found us in a trench with cannons behind us. Boom! Boom! The earth shook with each explosion and heavy clumps of metal whizzed over us, exploding in the distance. "Load and fire, men! Load and fire!" Major Robinson bellowed like a bull moose. Many men trembled, spilling powder on the ground. Some even sobbed, their emotions surfacing despite gut-tightening efforts to prevent it. Even though I felt shocked, I never let the tears rise above my eyelids. We were subjected to this trial under fire repeatedly until our nerves came under, if not control, a type of forced management. Keeping control was not the goal in the next introduction to the arts of war, the use of the bayonet.

Robinson led us to the edge of the drilling grounds to large bags tightly packed with straw and soil and hung from tree limbs. "Fix bayonets, men. I'll show you another use for your Enfield rifles." The clang of metal against metal reverberated up and down the lines of our company. At this point, Robinson, a big husky man, demonstrated the moves designed to impale and disembowel a man.

"En garde! Plunge! Pull up! Retract!" yelled Robinson. A fierce grin spread across his face as he handed the rifle back to the young private who stood at the end of the first line of soldiers. He was a slim boy with a peach complexion and freckles.

"Now, my fine ladies, it's your turn. Remember, that bag is a man who wants to cut your head off so don't be shy."

The freckled private was first to go down the line of bags. With a yell, he plunged his bayonet into the first bag but barely broke the covering.

"You lily-livered, spotted, sissy skunk! Go to the second bag and you bloody well better rip that one apart or I will hang your ass from that tree. Now go to it!"

The peach faced soldier almost put his entire rifle through the straw bag and came up growling like a rabid animal.

"Now you got the idea my boy, now you got the idea," said the full-bearded officer as he rocked back and forth and waved his hand for the next soldier to perform, me.

Somehow saying a short prayer before this exercise seemed inappropriate. With a sharp move forward, I rammed my bayonet into the bag. It swayed and the blade glanced off to the side.

"Private, you are now dead. How in blazes are you going to survive on the battlefield if you can't stab a damned bag of straw?" He put his hand on the back of his neck and gritted his teeth. "The Reb you attacked has his blade up your gizzard!" Robinson spoke as if he knew about this grizzly business. "Now get back in the ranks. You are going to do this again and it better be right next time."

Without looking around, I immediately went back to my place in line thankful that I was not subjected to more ridicule. Finally, it came my turn again.

"Ah, here is my walking dead private. What is your name soldier?"

"Private Hiram Terman, sir!"

"Well Private, you and your other dead comrades will have the pleasure of resurrecting these bags of hay for tomorrow's bayonet drill. Maybe you will learn to kill before you are killed next time."

I spent the rest of the afternoon and evening with other "walking dead" filling bags with straw and soil. I finally got to our tent around midnight. Isaiah rolled over and opened his eyes. "Hiram, ask God to help you. You will make a good soldier." Seth groaned as I stepped on his ankle making my way to my bed.

"Blast it Hiram! Step on me again and God will have to help you!" Isaiah chuckled. Images of burlap bags bleeding rivulets of soil and straw went through my thoughts before I went to sleep.

The next day we repeated the bayoneting exercise. I emitted a growl and a fierce lunge that brought a smirk to Robinson's face as I leaped from bag to bag, fiercely ripping each bag and emptying the soil and straw that I had spent all night digging and packing.

"Now you're getting it. You might just make it as a fighting man of the 82nd Ohio!" He then slapped me on the back. "Be just and fear not!" This last phrase was a favorite of Robinson, we heard it often.

After what seemed hours of this, we next were marched for long treks around the camp alternately running and walking. Officers took turns yelling obscenities into the ears of the slow or hesitant.

Those who were not able to control their anger were pulled out of line and sent to the camp guardhouse, a solitary log building on the edge of camp. Above the heavily barred door a slit admitted a most meager amount of light. Conditions inside the guardhouse were bad and, if possible, avoided. Other forms of punishment for even the slightest infringement included sitting on a narrow beam or rail for hours or carrying a log on your shoulder for even longer periods. Such treatments were the offspring of the "Great Skedaddle" at Bull Run.

I was often thankful for the respect for authority and restraint my family upbringing had instilled in me. I never yelled at my father even though excessive farm work often fell on my shoulders. "Hiram, you'll have to plow one more field today. Now, get that look off your face! You know this has to be done!" My father would then leave me in the field while he walked back home. Many times, I swallowed the bitter dross of anger without saying a word. This self-control kept me out of the guardhouse and off the rail which no doubt kept me healthier.

Order and cleanliness in our quarters also kept away many diseases for our tent. All of us detested the filth around camp. Frequent baths, washing clothes, and thorough cooking of our food kept us from many a contagion.

Measles and typhoid had attacked an adjacent regiment and filled hospital tents in Camp Tod. Two caskets a day came out of the Indiana camp. Many in the 82nd Ohio also filled up the hospital tents. This loss of men to disease worried our commanders.

Colonel Cantwell left camp to attend to some official duties leaving Lieutenant Colonel Bradford Durfee in charge. While standing guard near headquarters, I heard Cantwell address his junior officer. "Durfee, we must get this measles epidemic under control. I want this camp clean as a hospital when I get back." Durfee relished the job, as he was a strict disciplinarian.

This strict oversight worked. It not only decreased the spread of disease but the consumption of "bust head", a type of homemade whiskey. Seth, Isaiah, and I generally supported Durfee although some soldiers in camp did not. They were used to good times, especially with women who frequented the camp.

Clandestine meetings with prostitutes were a constant problem. Local women made destitute by the destruction of war offered themselves and even their young daughters to soldiers for money. Seth, Isaiah, and I witnessed this first hand while on guard duty.

On a warmer than usual winter day, we were stationed at the front gates of the camp near some trees along a dry ravine. We heard some voices coming from nearby. I approached carefully with my rifle at the ready. In the draw under some branches I saw a drunken soldier with red hair gleefully unbuttoning the cloak and dress of a young blue-eyed blond girl. She looked young, just a child.

Her eyes were in a trance-like state as if she had hypnotized herself to endure the ordeal. As he was putting his hand inside her dress I rushed up and stuck my bayonet by his head. "Get off of her before I run you through!" The image of a sand bag flashed through my mind. The soldier turned over snarling, his foul breath erupting between brown tobacco stained teeth.

"Who do you think you are you little piss ant! This here is between her and me. I'm paying this little whore two dollars for this fling. Now get out of here and let us be you damn Puritan!"

Cocking my rifle, I glared at the swaggering soldier who was now unhitching his pants.

"Unless you want to go to the guardhouse, you best get back to camp. What you're doing is rape. She is only a young girl! Now get out of here!"

He pulled up his suspenders and started toward me. I lifted my rifle. Seth and Isaiah came running up. "Hiram, what's going on here?" Seth first noticed the girl, my raised gun, and then the enraged, burly soldier.

"I caught this man trying to rape this girl!"

"Damn your hide, I told you I paid for this whore!" Isaiah rushed up next, his rifle at the ready. He scanned the girl then the man at the end of our Enfields.

"She's just a child!"

All three of us then pointed our rifles at the man. "You best leave now soldier," said Isaiah as he stared angrily at the man and then at the sobbing girl. Swearing and shaking his fists, the man slowly made his way down the ravine and up the hill to camp. At the top of the hill, he turned and glared at me.

"We will meet again you son of a bitch!" He then turned and went back into camp.

I encountered him only twice more, the first about a week later. This occurred as I walked by one of the hospital tents. Looking through the door, I spied the red-haired soldier hunched on a bed in the back. A balding, middle-aged surgeon came out of the tent wiping his hands on a badly stained apron.

"What do you want, son?"

"What's wrong with him—that red haired man on the last cot?" I asked making sure to stay hidden behind the tent's door flap.

"Him? Too much whoring around. He's got a bad case of the clap. Serves him right if you ask me." Looking curiously at me, he asked. "Do you know him?"

"Let's just say we have made each other's acquaintance," I said with disdain as I turned to leave. The old doctor then put his hand on my shoulder, his fatherly eyes meeting mine.

"Best stay clear of his kind, son, he'll only drag you down to perdition." He then turned to attend another soldier complaining of having the screamers, otherwise known as dysentery.

"Can I keep the two dollars?" asked the blue-eyed girl as she snapped out of her self-imposed spell, got up, and then buttoned up her dress.

"Go ahead," said Isaiah, "and here is a dollar more." His sense of Christian duty and empathy rose to the surface as he searched his pockets for the money.

Smiling dryly at Isaiah, she asked "And what do you want for that?"

"Not a thing and you'd better think twice about getting money this way. Nothing's worth taking that kind of abuse!" Isaiah then handed the dollar bill to the girl who wiped her hand on her thin dress before reaching out for the money.

"Anything is better than starvin'," she mumbled watching his hands closely.

Suddenly another woman came up, reached for the dollar, and knocked the bill out of Isaiah's hand. The greenback fluttered to the ground in front of the three of us. The woman, apparently the girl's mother, was strikingly beautiful, although her sad eyes and hard expression hinted at an innocence lost. A difficult life had obviously taken its toll, in particular her face had a dull, tired, and lonely look.

She was, nevertheless, attractive with a slim, angular, but shapely torso covered by a loose fitting dress beneath her coat. As she leaned over to pick up the bill, she paused and went to her knees. She then leaned forward with a sensuous slowness; her loose dress fell forward revealing a large pendulous pair of breasts. Knowing her female attributes were in full view of our downward gaze, she little by little folded the dollar bill and placed it in her cleavage. I had never seen such a sight! Maybe a rare view of an ankle or at most a knee— nothing like this dazzling sight that lay full bloom before me.

As she rose, she drew close to Isaiah, placed her hand on his groin and strategically squeezed. Isaiah was unable to move, he now being the one in a trance. He uttered a low groan. A seductive giggle possessed her; she next looked Isaiah in the eyes with a cold stare.

"That should make us about even, soldier."

With a wry smile, she turned to her daughter, who was paying close attention to the finer points of style and execution in the world's oldest profession, and sauntered away.

The stirring of one of our most powerful instincts produced a breathless, open-mouthed stare from the three of us as we watched the woman and her daughter make their way up the ravine back to the road.

After my breathing returned to a more normal pace, I cleared my throat and turned to my friends. I did not notice the glow of Christian charity in Isaiah's eyes as he righted himself. Neither did a proper righteous indignation reside in the countenance of Seth as he strained his neck to follow the women as they disappeared around the bend. Thin is the line dividing love and lust—and the red-haired soldier and us.

I thought of the "inside battle" in the sermon at Kenton. Such was the nature of the soldiers in our army at Camp Tod, those with honor and those without, those noble and those depraved, those who resisted and those who did not, all of us capable of both.

"What chance does that girl have with a mother like that?" I asked.

"Won't be long till she's in the brothels," said Seth as he returned to logic after his foray into passion. "In a few years she'll be quite a favorite for the boys, I reckon."

Isaiah scowled at Seth, shook his head, and walked away saying, "I'm praying God will rescue her."

Succumbing to the ills of illicit sex was not the only danger to those venturing too far from camp. Soldiers alone were easy prey for wandering bands of bushwhackers and Rebel cavalry. Several pickets had been captured or shot and our officers were determined this should not happen to the 82nd Ohio. "You pickets! Keep your wits about you. Don't get too far out and keep your reports loud!"

A strict system of checking written passes was in effect. I followed procedure to the utmost detail, as did my fellows on picket or guard duty. My earlier dressing down by Colonel Cantwell was painful but a valuable lesson for surviving in this troubled land.

I also kept a watchful eye as to what I ate. Avoiding bad water or spoiled meat, washing things, cooking a little longer; all kept the screamers away. Surgeons and sanitary commission workers reminded us. "If you don't want to see us, mind your table manners!"

I must admit that avoiding disease under the conditions at Camp Tod was nearly impossible. Flies coated shanks of hanging meat and food was often dirty and undercooked. Latrines and animal wastes often ran into the streams. Cooks worked in filthy conditions. Only a strong constitution could withstand these conditions but having access to medicines was important.

My knowledge of medicinal plants learned from my great grandmother benefited us many times. I collected sassafras roots, yarrow leaves, mints and other plants known to cure various ailments. Also, advice from surgeons, hospital attendants, and the sons of physicians helped us avoid many unscrupulous vendors and sutlers at every town or village who tried to sell us useless snake oil.

An ever-present problem was lice, "graybacks" as we called them. Every soldier became an unwilling host to these pernicious parasites. Washing clothes and frequent baths helped. We even boiled our clothes or held them close to the flames of a campfire to force the little buggers out of our woolen uniforms. I checked many sutlers shelves for an effective treatment. The most useful was a powder made from chrysanthemums.

Another temptation was whiskey. I admit to getting near drunk once but the gut-wrenching vomiting and splitting headache that followed cured me of a second exposure to "bust head". Seth imbibed frequently but did not get drunk. Isaiah avoided even the aroma of alcohol.

Gambling was another enticement. Soldiers bet on everything from cards and throws of the dice to cockroach and lice races. I succumbed to this temptation twice at Camp Tod. I won twenty dollars on the roll of the dice where two dollars was the entry fee. I then lost five dollars by choosing the wrong tree to which a crow would fly.

As a rule, I kept the thirteen dollars a month we were paid for soldiering and sent as much as possible home to Ohio, keeping only what I needed for survival needs. I learned to hide money and guard other items such as shoes. Thievery was common and anything left out was soon gone. Friends took turns guarding everything from combs to blankets that we were forced to leave in our quarters while on various duties.

While arduous and taxing, the weeks spent at Camp Tod yielded rewards. A shy, naïve Ohio boy, wide-eyed and afraid of the unknown, had become a confident soldier. I now knew I possessed the requisite skills to serve and more importantly, survive. The same was true of Seth, Isaiah, and the rest of the regiment. As we prepared to leave for war, I scarcely recognized the officers and men of Kenton—they had been transformed.

Officially, we were the 82nd Ohio Volunteer Infantry Regiment, attached to the District of the Cumberland, Maryland, Department of Western Virginia. At the end of our training in March, 1862 we were assigned to the Department of the Mountains.

Before going east into the war, the regiment went on dress parade in front of officers and visiting dignitaries for review and inspection. The day before was spent shining shoes, rifles, and bayonets, washing and cleaning clothes, and tightly packing backpacks and bedrolls. Regimental bands practiced tunes to perfection. Each regiment put on its best performance as we made our way to the drilling grounds of Camp Tod.

As I stood facing the officers in front of us, Captain James Crall, an officer who had carefully watched the training of Company F, stopped in front of me. His eyes scanned me from top to bottom. He then gave a tug on my jacket and patted me on my shoulder.

"Private Terman. I notice your guard duty skills now equal your marksmanship. Evidently Colonel Cantwell got through to you!"

"Yes, sir!" I replied. One never knows the value of a mistake paired with a later victory.

I glanced at Isaiah and Seth on either side of me. Both seemed to be amused at my facial expression. Crall then moved on down the line. I noticed that he stopped quite a number of times. He was a good officer and the men in Company F held him in high regard.

By noon on March 18, 1862, the regiment had packed our equipment, gathered into formation, marched to the station in Grafton and boarded the railroad cars. From what our officers told us, we were headed into the Lost River Region of western Virginia, a narrow valley just to the west of the Shenandoah Mountains near the Shenandoah Valley. The train would take us to the town of New Creek and then we were to march down the valley to Moorefield, there to await the opening of spring and weather suitable for war.

The Baltimore and Ohio Railroad followed the valleys and lowlands along rivers that were on the northern edge of the Allegheny Mountains. The scenery was magnificent. The mountains ran north and south like the folds of a large accordion. The Shenandoah Valley was the keyboard of the accordion. The railroad was an iron thread that coursed through the pleats of the accordion, stopping at the town of New Creek, a button in a fold.

New Creek was at a bend where the tracks sharply turned to the north. Our train stopped here and we disembarked. We somehow knew it would be a long while before we would ride a train again. From here on out, we traveled by foot followed by long lines of supply wagons.

As we stepped out of the boxcar in the late afternoon and placed our feet on the soil of New Creek, Seth leaned over and whispered. "Hiram, we're now on the footstep of the war." I looked at the cannons on nearby hills. "Are you ready? Won't be long before Rebs will be in the sights of your rifle and on the point of your bayonet." I looked at Seth, somewhat startled and put out.

"Well, how about you? Are you ready to be shot at by men wanting to kill you?" Neither of us knew how we would react nor how soon these possibilities would become real.

My anxieties would soon find their resolution. Winter was loosening its grip on western Virginia. Warmer temperatures, melting snow, and thawing streams stirred our army into action as we prepared to march to Moorefield, a valley town on the edge of the war.

During March and April, it rained about twice a week and the incessant moisture made our commanders anxious. We were to join the forces of General John C. Fremont, the "Pathfinder of the Rocky Mountains", and General Robert Schenck as they invaded Virginia to confront the people who would destroy the Union. The 82nd Ohio was assigned to Schenck's brigade, which numbered about three thousand.

The atmosphere of war enshrouded the town of New Creek, a major point of deployment for Union troops coming from the east. Concentrations of tents dotted hills and artillery pieces overlooked major roads.

We bivouacked on some flat areas on the hills as the sun slowly set in the west. The cold chill of the night air enveloped us as we crawled into our blankets. After a short pause, Seth, in his logical style, broke the silence.

"How about this march to Moorefield tomorrow? How do you think it will go? Think our shoes will hold out? Think we will hold out?"

Our corporal Sam Armstrong was a shoe cobbler in Rome. He knew how to take care of this vital part of our equipment. We coated our shoes with beeswax for waterproofing and reinforced the seams with extra threading according to his instructions but it was impossible to know how things would go for our shoes or us. Those answers would come in the days and nights to come as we tramped along mountain roads and through cold streams and rivers.

The next morning was cool, crisp, and overcast, another example of the inclement weather that had plagued us. A persistent sun probed the scattered rain clouds but without success. We rose early, ate our breakfast, and packed our bedrolls and backpacks. Could we really carry all this stuff? The drilling and marching in Camp Tod convinced me we could and I had a good feeling about what I could endure.

"I think we will do just fine, Seth, at least as good as the other fellows." Little did I know of the Herculean task that confronted us.

The first day we marched down a narrow band of flatlands following a creek between two round-topped mountains. The scenery was glorious even with the cloudy weather and the persistent rain. I soon developed a nagging cough that worried me. *Am I already getting sick? Come on, Hiram, we've just got started!*

I took solace in the first buds that dotted the branches of some of the trees. They promised warmer weather. We marched with an unhurried pace, stopped frequently for rest, and eventually camped on a farm.

Our intrusion made the farmer angry and his strong secessionist comments lost him some hay and straw from his barn for our bedding. I felt better after chewing on some mint leaves and getting a good night's rest.

Southern men who were running from conscription stopped by our lines, apparently heading west to get away from forced service by the Confederate general, Stonewall Jackson.

As I stood on guard duty for the night, a man, woman, and young child approached me. The man had a patch over one of his eyes. An affable and open expression was tinged with fear as he approached me.

"We're leaving the Shenandoah Valley and wish to make our way to Kansas—is the way ahead free of Confederate troops?"

Before answering, I looked them over carefully, following the protocol of Union guardsmen in enemy lands. Assuring myself that they were genuine, I opened up to them.

"Hello sir, hello ma'am." The wide eyes of the young boy scanned my uniform. The face of his mother revealed fear as she glanced around at the shadows. She was a plain but beautiful woman. Her hair was rolled into a tight bun but her eyes danced with a vivaciousness that drew my stare. "There are many bushwhackers and Confederate sympathizers ahead of you, sir. They would gladly turn you over to the Confederate army or worse." The man looked at his wife who gripped the arm of her husband. "You and your family should stay near to Union troops and avoid strangers. Why are you going to Kansas?"

"We are Mennonites and fear what you speak of in the Shenandoah." His wife looked up at me, scanning my face for a response. "We are peaceful people and do not involve ourselves in war. We wish to take up farming in Kansas away from the war." He looked at his young son. "I can no longer stay in Virginia with the army grabbing every man off his farm whether he desires it or not." He put his arms around his wife and son and ushered them down the road. "Thank you Private and I wish you God's protection. We will follow your advice."

"Thank you! May our Lord watch over you and your family." The man turned and smiled, somewhat surprised at these words from a secular soldier. His wife gave me a fleeting glance and a subdued smile. She reminded me of Nancy.

This young family faced quite a challenge. The Confederacy was conscripting every available man. Bushwhackers often shot those on the spot who refused to enlist. I hoped this man avoided serving in the Confederate army even though I was caught up in the workings of our own. I wondered how many men in gray were like this fellow, unwilling soldiers commandeered at the point of a bayonet.

Marching on to Moorefield, we saw more stragglers and deserters from the Rebel army. If they took the oath of allegiance to the Union, we let them pass unless we suspected them of being spies. Recognizing the telltale signs of an imposter was a gift many of our officers learned fast. Hanging around, peering into every corner, or asking the wrong questions could get you into the sights of a firing squad or on the end of a noose. Most of these men walked by in silence but I overheard a conversation between two Rebel deserters.

"Gawd, am I glad to be out from under ole Jack," exclaimed one thin Virginian to a shorter, more ragged looking comrade.

"Many a good man lies buried by the road back yonder. That cussed Jackson nearly killed us by marchin' all over tarnation in the dead of winter. Wouldn't treat a dog like he treated us!" Both moved on up the road still cursing Jackson. I wondered what would happen to them if the local home guard rounded them up again.

The next day we were on the march again, with heavy packs, walking on muddy roads and paths. The weight of my pack and rifle tired my body to the point of exhaustion. The short stops to warm up some coffee knitted together body and soul. Sometimes the band would play to keep our minds off our sore feet and aching muscles.

As night approached, we camped on a large farm owned by another vocal loyal secessionist. His defiance lost him some soft hay that enhanced our sleep as well as his wagons and teams that we used to carry our supplies.

The next day we marched about twelve miles further into the mountains. Bushwhackers or roving cavalry were rumored to be in this area. A man belonging to a Connecticut cavalry unit was shot in the leg by a bushwhacker as he relieved himself in the bushes along the road. This angered his comrades greatly who soon found the culprit and shot him out of a tree. The Rebel fell from branch to branch like a rag doll. Seth, Isaiah, and I walked by the corpse. A mass of hair and blood lay atop a beardless face with bright blue eyes.

"My God!" exclaimed Seth. "He is just a young boy! What kind of people are these that get children to shoot at us?" Isaiah closed his eyes in prayer as he walked by the lifeless young form at the base of the tree.

Eventually our long column of troops, supply wagons, and artillery emerged from the mountains onto a broad expanse of flatter countryside. This was the floodplain of the South Branch of the Potomac River.

We marched along this landscape until we came in sight of the town of Moorefield on the other side of the river. Moorefield was a beautiful town, framed by mountains and interlaced with farm fields. It was however, a pro-Confederate settlement and even had two Union soldiers in the town jail. The freed men came out and told their story. "By golly, sergeant, we was snatched while on picket duty, sure enough." The humiliated soldier rubbed his jaw. "The little lizards don't make a sound. You walk your beat and the next thing you know you got a Bowie knife at your gizzard!"

The men of the town were all gone with the exception of some older fellows and some Negroes. Women in the town were openly negative to our presence but for some reason forced themselves to be civil. Perhaps they reflected the confused state of allegiances typical of this part of western Virginia. We were both cursed and praised. Secessionists told us to leave while Unionists freely told us about enemy activity.

At Moorefield, we waited for more regiments to join us and for the weather to warm and the roads to dry. Supplies of corn and wheat were plentiful; we even had access to a mill to grind our flour so our time here was pleasant.

Our camp routine generally was breakfast at seven in the morning followed by sick call and guard mounting. Then we drilled, first in squads, then companies, and then larger groups. Dress parade occurred around four followed by supper, tattoo (light beating of drums), and retiring to tents at nine.

One day Isaiah, Seth, and I were able to secure a pass and go into town to buy supplies and food. I looked for beef jerky and dried fruits and vegetables to supplement my meals. This visit to the general store not only nourished our bodies but our spirits. While we argued with a clerk who wanted only coins for payment, Isaiah approached with a young blond girl with the most piercing blue eyes.

"Hiram, Seth, does this young lady look familiar?" Isaiah turned her in a circle like a ballet dancer. Seth and I examined her closely. Her blond hair was neatly washed and combed and her smiling blue eyes complimented a light yellow dress and white apron.

"You are the, ah, ah, girl at Camp Tod," stuttered Seth as he recalled the scene with the red-haired soldier while we were on guard duty.

"How did you get here?" I asked, marveling at the change in appearance and attitude of the girl we rescued from the rape.

"Momma said I had to go, she couldn't take care of me no more and that I had to make it on my own like she did when she was my age." She looked at Isaiah. "You men were the only ones who ever gave a lick about me so I decided to jump in one of the boxcars as you soldiers left."

"Boxcars! You mean with the soldiers?" inquired Seth skeptically.

"They were real nice to me, didn't do anything nasty. Gave me things to eat and even a blanket to keep warm with. I got a job helping a cook when I got off at New Creek."

"How did you make it to Moorefield? That's pretty rough country between New Creek and here?" Seth asked, still in his skeptical mood.

"I rode the supply wagon down to Moorefield with the cook. He took me to the red brick church in town. The preacher's wife got me this job sweeping the store and I am staying with them. I help clean the church too."

"Well praise the Lord!" exclaimed Isaiah. Even Seth was amazed at the confluence of events in this girl's story amidst the overwhelming presence of the war. In a move of unexpected kindness, the clerk now agreed to take our greenbacks. As we left the store, Seth said she was "damn lucky" not to have gotten in with the wrong regiment at New Creek, and indeed, she was.

Colonel Cantwell was still not in camp, which left the disciplinarian Lieutenant Colonel Durfee still in charge. Cantwell said he would catch up with us later on in our march. At Kenton, Durfee stopped men from individually going for water from the river, building fires on guard duty, collecting wood, and was fastidious about grooming and appearance. He also declared Saturday afternoon as a time for purification and preparation for Sunday services and became angry when his expectations did not meet reality. This caused an air of uneasiness to spread through camp (which was called Camp Durfee).

As I stood on guard duty, a joking, half drunk soldier walked by Colonel Durfee and gave him a perfunctory salute. Durfee was livid.

"Sergeant, write this man up and send him to the guardhouse. I will not tolerate disrespect. An army runs on discipline and I will have it!" Rather than watch this episode any more, I turned quickly on my beat and walked in the other direction.

Not only did discipline roll down on us, the skies opened up with torrents of rain. We all wondered when the roads would dry and we would head south into war and all of its glory. Many soldiers were afraid the war would end before we got a chance to "get into it." Our ignorance of Virginia roads was only exceeded by our desire for the return of Colonel Cantwell, the removal of Lieutenant Colonel Durfee, and our gullibility about the realities of war.

The West Virginia mountains through which the 82nd Ohio marched.

CHAPTER 4
INTO THE WHIRLWIND OF WAR: THE BATTLE
OF MCDOWELL

The rain came down hard and water rose through the floor of our large, circular Sibley tent prodding its occupants to action. We rushed outside and dug drainage ditches. Our wet, woolen uniforms became soaked as we shoveled the heavy Virginia clay. Satisfied that we would not float away in the night, we jumped back into the tent and sat by the stove until the warmth covered us and the chill drained away. The drum of the rain on the tent mesmerized us, but soon Seth, his face glowing red in the glare of the fire, spoke.

"When do you think we will move south down the valley?" We looked quizzically at each other. A man in the back of our Sibley tent spoke up.

"Word has it that as soon as the roads dry out, Fremont wants Schenck's brigade to go all the way to Knoxville."

"I heard we're going to the Shenandoah Valley," interjected another man. Isaiah came over next to me and helped me remove my wet coat.

"Have you heard anything, Hiram?" After hanging my wet shirt closer to the stove in the center of the tent, I turned to Isaiah.

"There's all kind of talk going around. The main thing is that sooner or later we are going to have a battle and we need to be ready." I surprised myself with my bluntness.

Isaiah seemed surprised. "Do you think there will be fightin' soon? Hiram, did you hear this from the officers?"

"No, not from any officers." I could feel the others focus in on me. "You just hear the boys talking from time to time. I don't know any more than anybody else in this army." I hoped this would remove me from the center of attention of the group in our tent.

Isaiah looked over to Seth who was squeezing water out of his socks. "Seth, do you think you'll be ready for real fighting? I mean shooting somebody?"

Seth, straining to pull off his wet sock, replied. "Nobody knows that, Isaiah! We'll just have to wait and find out." Seth discovered a hole in his sock. "Where's my housewife? I need a needle to darn this." He found his small packet and extracted a needle and thread. "I suspect I will be as ready as anybody else in the regiment."

The thread ripped through the rotten sock. "Damn it!" Seth threw the sock into the fire. "Damn government issue."

Isaiah shook his head. "Seth, do you have to swear about everything?"

I decided to intervene. "About time you changed socks anyhow, isn't it? You've been wearing them since Kenton."

Seth searched through his haversack for another pair. "Ah, here they are! Thank goodness, mercy sakes, I put in a second pair." Seth looked over to Isaiah with a slight grin. Both chuckled. To my surprise, this capped the conversation and we slept as the rain alternated its rhythm between heavy downpours and intervals of quiet drizzle.

The next morning was clear and the sun highlighted the beauty of the country enfolding our camp at Moorefield. Rich farmland and clear streams spread out across a valley floor framed by mountains; some large, rounded, and elongated and others small and more pointed. In between the mountains were narrow, steep gorges with streams that disappeared down dark ravines. The roads in the area were narrow trails formed by horses and wagon wheels. We were waiting for these to dry enough to support supply wagons, the wheels of the artillery, and thousands of foot soldiers.

Seth stepped out of the tent and slipped in the mud. "Tarnation, this damned mud is like lard! Will it never stop raining?"

During the long wait in the damp and cold weather, I became sick. My eyes watered and my nose swelled, literally pouring out mucous as I hacked and coughed. I spent four days in the hospital tent recovering from a condition called catarrh. Two older doctors from Moorefield visited our hospital, one rather gruff and short and the other approachable and gentle with a pleasant bedside manner. They reflected the dualism of this region.

"Well, my goodness soldier, you look miserable," said the kindly old southern doctor. "What's your name?"

"Hiram Terman." A hospital attendant by his side wrote my last name with a "u". I was too sick to correct him.

"I can hardly breathe and feel cold with chills and cough up mucous all the time." My red eyes produced tears that ran down my cheek.

"Oh, you will have to tough it out for about a week but once you lick it, it tends to leave you alone for a while." The doctor looked me over for a moment. "You look tough and wiry, young fellow, you'll be all right soon."

"The way we've been getting wet and cold, marching all the time, it's a wonder we all ain't sick," I said after sneezing and blowing my nose.

"I can see you fellows are really putting it on the line down here. You left home and family, do you think it's worth it?" The doctor put his hands on his knees as he sat on a stool beside my bed and peered at me with an intense look, waiting for me to reply.

"I hope so. Can't let the Union split up. And slavery, well, ain't right what's going on. We had some escaped slaves come through my home in Ohio and talked in church." I started to cough and hack. "Terrible things happened to them. We got to put a stop to that. Yes sir, to me it's worth it."

"Well, son, there's a heap of folks here that agree with you but a bunch more that don't. The farther you go into old Virginny, the more of the second kind are going to show up." He then stood up and patted me on the shoulder. "Take care of yourself young man." He then moved on to the next miserable soul.

The old doctor was probably a Unionist but it was hard to tell. Not so with most of Moorefield. They had obvious loyalties to the Confederacy. Most of the men in Moorefield were now fierce fighters in Stonewall Jackson's army, not far away down the mountain slopes to the east.

However, occasionally we picked up stragglers and deserters. Our army paroled most of these men if they took the oath of allegiance and agreed not to take up arms again. I heard one of our officers talking to one of these deserters as I stood on guard duty.

"Now, Joshua Jameson, you took the oath. You realize that this parole means that you do not take up arms again for the Confederacy, don't you?" The thin Confederate deserter held the parole slip upside down and peered at the paper as if it were some queer item.

"I cain't read a lick there Captain but I ain't gonna shoot at ya. I didn't wanna fight in the first place. Had to or they would have shot me. Lordy sakes, I got a woman and ten little ones to feed."

"Well Joshua, if we catch you again with the Rebels, we will shoot you on the spot. Do you understand?"

"Yes siree, I sure do. Shoot me on the spot. You ain't gonna see me no more!" The skinny Rebel then made his way down the road trying to fold the parole slip and put it into a pocket.

The women of the town were not so easily pacified, continually questioning why we were there. A heavy set, matronly looking woman with a parasol addressed our captain, James Crall, within our hearing down town.

"Captain, why is it that you and your men are here in Moorefield pushing this horrible war into our beautiful town. Why can't you leave us alone?"

" Ma'am, you do have a right smart town here, beautiful, but we're here at the call of our national government. States cannot just up and leave, we have a government not a gentleman's league."

"But you people up North are different from us southern folk. You Yankees don't respect the old ways, everything is money, money, money, hustle and bustle. We're different you know."

"Ma'am, every state in the Union has different customs and such. We're here to preserve the government that allows us all to be free, you, me, even the Negroes."

"Why you blasted abolitionist! That's what I mean, upsetting the natural order of people that God set up. I will never live under an abolitionist flag!"

When the star spangled banner was placed above the courthouse, it caused much consternation. Crowds formed in the street and men, women, and children waved fists in protest as a young soldier raised the Union flag into a gentle breeze. As the flag reached its pinnacle, the protest grew louder. "This is Virginia, by Gawd! Take that damned Yankee flag down. We're under Jeff Davis now, not that gorilla Lincoln!" One of our officers fired a pistol into the air.

"If you people take down that flag, we will burn this beautiful town of yours to the ground! Do you want us to do that?" An uneasy rumbling coursed through the crowd. "Do I make myself clear? Disperse this instant and go back to your homes." I felt bad at the severity of this exchange. Soon the angry crowd melted away. Our stay was uneasy at this beautiful oasis but we had plenty of food and hay for our beds.

On April 8, Colonel Cantwell rejoined our regiment much to the joy of the troops. Cheer after cheer arose as he rode his horse through camp. Soon after, Lieutenant Colonel Durfee left camp after resigning over a dispute with the governor about the date of his commission. To me this was a shame. Durfee was a disciplinarian but a good officer. I agreed with his calls for cleanliness and order. His downfall appeared to be his temper.

The order from General Schenck, our commander, spread across the camp like a stirring breeze. "Prepare to move out, men! We're going down the valley to meet the enemy." Men took down tents and packed knapsacks and bedrolls. The supply wagons, packed with box after box of food, ammunition, and the other necessities of life for the army, lined up on the muddy road. Engaged in the interminable battle between beast and master, the braying of mules, whinnying of horses, and the cursing and hollering of teamsters filled the air.

On April 25, the regiments moved down the valley from Moorefield towards Petersburg. As we left Moorefield, we could still see the Union flag waving over the courthouse.

Arriving in Petersburg, we found the constant rains had swollen the river. The deep water and swift current prevented us from crossing and we camped in Petersburg for four days. Once the water level dropped, we loaded farm wagons with huge rocks and placed them into the stream as a base for a footbridge across the river. Our company got a taste of this backbreaking labor as well as the adventure of crossing this improvised bridge.

"Ain't this the reason you joined this glorious army, Hiram?" Seth lugged a huge rock through the cold water over to a sunken wagon. I was so cold from standing in the frigid stream that I could not answer back. I just shook my head. Isaiah came up next and dropped his load.

"Ugh!" The stone splashed into the submerged wagon. "Every rock hauled here counts as much as a bullet fired on the battlefield." Seth looked at me open mouthed.

We finally departed Petersburg on May 3. A scouting party of three companies left early on a rougher northern path to clear away any bushwhackers who might be awaiting us. The rest of the regiment took the southern route. This road rose to the higher elevations from which the South Branch of the Potomac River originated. It was rough, muddy, and difficult marching.

Despite the bad conditions, we were happy to leave the lower lands. The slave owning farmers there did not hide their anger. An older man on a horse rode by our columns and turned down a lane to a farm. Stopping, he yelled, "Why are you down here? We don't need your abolitionist garbage!" Another man followed him, also on horseback. Even more incensed, he got down from his horse and walked along our lines with a pointed finger.

"Wait till you blue bellies meet ole Stonewall!" He spat out a wad of tobacco at our feet. "You'll wish you never left home Yanks, by God you will!" We kept closed ranks during these episodes of bluster. Others yelled at us from further back along the road sitting on their porches. A universal downcast expression told us we were hated without measure. From behind us in the ranks, I heard Bushey Thomas quip.

"Boys, I don't think they give a damn whether we live or die, do you?" He chuckled and poked his partner to his right. "Just bothers the hell out me, don't it you?" It did bother me.

About every hour the column of troops stopped to rest and refresh. Seth, Isaiah, and I made our way to a little rivulet to fill our canteens. The water was clear, cool, and felt like liquid velvet as we gulped it down.

"Do you think that Reb farmer back there was right? Are we going to be facing Jackson?" Isaiah placed his canteen in the stream and stirred up the bottom. Muddy water flowed down stream.

"Would you watch what you're doing Isaiah? You clumsy Jonah! You're getting mud into our canteens!" Our future was as turbid as the water; we did not know where we were going and what awaited us.

The response of the people in the mountains was completely different from the farmers in the lowlands. Everywhere we went, people stepped out of their dwellings and offered encouragement, waving the flag of the Union. They did not own slaves and barely survived on the hardscrabble soil of the mountains. While passing a small cottage by the roadside near a humble mountain hamlet, an old lady stepped from her porch, waved her handkerchief with a bony arm, and with a smile that went from one side of her face to the other, said "God bless you Union boys! God bless you Union boys, I say!"

We stopped and gave her a royal salute. Some soldiers even broke ranks and hugged her, including our tough Corporal Sam Armstrong. A strong hurrah followed. Embarrassed, Armstrong yelled. "Get back into rank!" He then released a grin he could not restrain.

On May 4 our column arrived in Franklin, a small hamlet nestled in a gorge. We established a temporary supply depot there and then went into camp to rest our weary bones.

Seth laid back on his blanket and looked around. "Ever see such a state, Hiram? The people in the lowlands on good soil hate us while the people in the mountains on hardscrabble love us. Why the difference?" Isaiah had a ready answer.

"The lowlanders don't want to lose their slaves. Seems pretty clear to me. Don't you agree, Hiram?"

"Nothing is clear to me about this place."

"You know what I think?" Seth rose up on his elbow. "Most of them just plain don't like us down here. Can't say as I blame them. How would you like it if they came up north into Ohio?"

Isaiah was amazed at the question. "Why would they do that? We don't have any slaves and we're not trying to leave the Union."

"Oh! We're perfect, aren't we now?" replied Seth sarcastically. This conversation went on into the night without resolution.

The scouting party sent out from Petersburg arrived the next evening, bringing our regiment back to full force. The next morning, Wednesday, May 6, a courier from General Robert Milroy arrived. The dispatch asked our commander Schenck to make haste to the town of McDowell. Milroy had stirred up none other than Confederate generals Stonewall Jackson and Edward "Allegheny" Johnson. Now, he needed help, fast!

Milroy had a reputation as an aggressive general. One of our officers described him as a determined patriot with wild white hair who had no fear. From what we heard, Milroy had encountered a large force of Confederates (Jackson and Johnson) headed west. Outnumbered three to one, the 32nd Ohio of Milroy's brigade was first to confront this hornet's nest and had lost most of its supplies. Milroy right away pulled all his troops back to the tiny valley town of McDowell to await reinforcements from us, General Schenck's brigade.

This was the situation awaiting our first combat experience, a baptism of fire from the hottest torch of the Confederacy, Stonewall Jackson. "My God, that Reb farmer was right," said Seth as he packed his supplies.

Colonel James Cantwell of the 82nd Ohio was excited as we assembled to march. He walked in front us, stroking his mustache in a motion peculiar to him. First, he parted the hairs by widening his finger and thumb toward the corners of his mouth. Next, he used his forefinger to separate the hairs beneath his nose. He often did this when agitated. After the last name on the roll was called, Cantwell addressed us.

"Men, ahead of us in the mountains near McDowell awaits the Rebel army. There's going to be a fight and this regiment has work that must be done, the work of war." He looked at me directly. "We're about to have an all day and night march of the roughest kind followed by fighting against one of the South's most honored brigades." He walked down the line staring at each man. "If any of you here is not convinced of our cause, now is the time to let me know. I will find duties for you to suit your situation." He stopped speaking and looked each one of us in the eyes.

Each of us was at a crossroads—a choice confronted us. I seriously considered the consequences of speaking up or remaining silent. *How can you not go?* I glanced at Seth and Isaiah. Seth was wincing but Isaiah stood resolute, his chin and eyes straight ahead.

After a long silence, Cantwell exhaled and spoke proudly. "Well all right then! Men of the 82nd Ohio, form up! There's work ahead boys!"

We left at ten in the morning and marched without stopping to Monterey, arriving at midnight, a day and night march of twenty-three miles. Exhausted, we stopped to rest for four hours. Seth rubbed his legs. "My Lord, Hiram, can you believe this? Did you see all the men who dropped out along the way? In the name of blazes, how can we fight when we get to McDowell if we can't walk?" I was so tired I felt nauseous as I dropped to the ground. Isaiah was on his back next to me. I wandered if he were still alive.

"Isaiah, you all right? Isaiah?" His eyes fluttered and struggled to open.

"Don't worry, Hiram, I'll make it. I just need to renew my strength." His lips quivered. "Oh Lord, please help…." Isaiah entered a deep sleep as did Seth and I.

More than a quarter of us did not answer when the drum for roll call sounded for the final push into the town of McDowell. The Provost Guard prodded the uncooperative into line. Moans, groans, and pleas for mercy came from men who a few days earlier "couldn't wait to get at the Rebs."

Those of us who could then moved out and marched through the mountain trails with only the moon's light to reveal tree, rock, and ditch. The rhythm of trampling feet developed an unconscious pace for the regiment, like a metronome. My legs moved with no thought from me. Seth and Isaiah on my right and left kept up with me. From time to time, a soldier would gasp and fall out, causing the rest of us to leap over him. Terse words followed. "Damn it Robert. Keep running or get out of the way!"

"I can't, Jim, I just can't! I'm done for."

Finally, the column stopped, cut down by complete exhaustion. In the murky darkness, we collapsed, caring not whether on grass or rocky ground.

In what seemed only a moment, the officers roused us up again. We rose like ghosts in the mists and grabbed our rifles. Colonel Cantwell moved among us, urging every man to hurry. "All right men, get up now. I know you are tired but we need to get moving. Time is short. Leave your backpacks here, you can get them later."

In the dim light of the moon, we then marched along a winding eleven-mile path through brush, across small streams, and over ridges. As the morning sun ascended, we descended into the valley town of McDowell. On a field next to a Presbyterian Church, we again fell out to rest.

About mid morning, I awakened and noticed soldiers carving their initials into the red bricks of the church. "How do those boys have the energy to do that?" Seth removed his shoes and rubbed his feet. Isaiah got up and went over to the church. Seth, carrying his shoes, hobbled after him. I remained, resting in a shadow of the church steeple.

Many soldiers from the past had etched their initials into the bricks, even some enemy soldiers. Isaiah waved his hand, beckoning me to the church.

"Hey Hiram, come here. Carve your initials into a brick. Leave your mark."

"No, you go ahead, I can hardly move my legs, they're cramping up." Seth and Isaiah then walked over and pulled me up. My legs felt like they were on fire but my friends persisted.

"Here is a pen knife, scratch something for your descendants to see," said Seth as he admired an "S. H." he had carved. Reluctantly, I put the tip of the knife between my thumb and forefinger and engraved the year "1862" on a brick not far from the doorframe. "Aren't you going to carve your initials, Hiram?" asked Seth.

"No, I see too many "H. T.'s" there already," I replied as I put the finishing stroke on the number 2. I saw no other bricks with dates. I had been unique in my commonness.

As we looked into the distance, we were able to see for the first time the movements of the enemy on the upper slopes and prominences of Bull Pasture Mountain. Seth drew close to me.

"My God, Hiram, there they are! See those Rebs over there on the mountaintop?" I squinted trying to focus in on the distant hump.

"Yeah, Seth, I see 'em. Looks to be a lot of them, too." Isaiah joined us.

"So finally we meet. Lord help us to gain the victory." Isaiah closed his eyes and his lips moved in silence. The drums played and bugles sounded as we gathered our rifles and cartridge packs.

"Look at all of them up there," said a man next to me as he shielded his eyes and craned his neck to look up the mountain. "What are they doing?" A officer next to him was looking through a pair of binoculars.

"They are forming a line of battle. Looks like they are moving brush and digging in along the ridge in front of those open fields." If we were going to attack them, we would have to go up those fields and steep slopes.

I turned to see a battery crew set up cannons on a nearby knoll. "Boom!" A shell roared toward the men in the distance. I could follow it as it traversed in an arc toward the mountain slope. The smoke from the exploding shell drifted away and revealed small figures in the distance scattering like ants.

A stomach-turning numbness swept over me. The audacity and nerve of war shocked me. *"My God, it begins!"* In front of me was something raw, unfeeling, and without compassion of any kind.

I jerked as another shell was sent to the Rebels on the hill. Again, the lines of the enemy parted as another smoke cloud rose above the mountain. The artillerymen were mechanical as the officer in charge shouted commands. Repeatedly, the cannons belched and shell after shell found its mark burrowing into the mountain scrambling the small antlike figures.

The grim thing gripped me. We were down here to kill those who opposed us in the South. It did not matter the peculiar circumstances of those little ants. Slaveholder or not, secessionist radical or moderate, volunteer or conscript, the only fact that mattered was they were there, on the other side, and deserved no mercy.

I struggled with being caught up in something so cold and vicious. *I am not like this. How can I do this?* Nevertheless, I would soon be a part of this lethal business. *What choice did I have now?* Seth walked up next to me. A solemn look was on his face.

"That old abolitionist John Brown was right. The sins of this guilty land must be purged with blood! Now we must draw the sword, Hiram."

Yes, but I am a reluctant warrior. I was in a death struggle now. Hiram Terman's Civil War had begun!

"I don't like our position here," exclaimed Seth as he maneuvered to get a better look. He almost ran into a couple of officers hurrying along to our front. We heard their conversation as they paused close to us.

"Therein lays the dickens in all this," shouted Lieutenant Colonel Robinson. "If they get their guns up there, they can rip us apart down here in the valley. We're in a pit here!" Veins on his forehead emerged and formed a "V" as he looked around. "If ole Jackson gets guns up there he will grind us to a pulp, get us running, and steal our wagons and supplies. Take note, Captain, we're in a hell of a bad spot here!"

A soldier delivered a message to the Captain who opened it with haste and with a pause, replied." Yes sir. Generals Milroy and Schenck want us to attack the Rebels now before they get batteries on the heights. There are also long lines of Johnnies coming from the east up the turnpike from Staunton."

The news of our precarious position spread across the regiments from colonels to captains to corporals to privates. We had to attack now so we could escape to Franklin where Fremont was gathering a larger army. If we waited and did nothing we would be overwhelmed by the superior numbers of the enemy.

"Well, how's this for our first battle?" Seth remarked with a grim look. "We either attack a bigger force or don't attack and get blown to bits!" He rubbed the back of his head and removed his forage cap. "Isaiah, if prayin' helps you best get to it!"

"God will watch over us." Isaiah walked between us and put his hands on our shoulders. "Hiram, what does old Robinson always say to us?"

"Be just and fear not," I replied. "I would sure rest easier if the Dutch would hurry up and get here!"

The predominantly German division of General Blenker was supposed to arrive from Fredericksburg adding many more men to our number. The talk around the regiment was that they got lost but hopes were high for the Germans to make it. Without them, Jackson could overwhelm us even if we did escape to Franklin.

About four in the afternoon, the order came down to form in companies and report to headquarters, a large brick house said to be built with slave labor and owned by a prominent local named Hull. I took my position between Seth and Isaiah and then marched from the Presbyterian church around the bend to the Hull house.

We took our position in tight formation with the rest of 82nd Ohio in the right center of the group of regiments. There were about two thousand of us all together. Our waving muskets looked like the quills on a porcupine. The bands played and the drums rolled. Suddenly, a quiet hush came on the mass of men.

Generals Schenck and Milroy came out on the porch of the headquarters building. Both men had the look of leaders who had come to a grim but sure decision. Schenk stepped forward and addressed us.

"Soldiers! Prepare for battle!" Schenck pointed to the top of Bull Pasture Mountain. "You are to charge up those hills to the enemy and engage him! Do not let him get guns on those hills! We're in a vulnerable position here." He turned and pointed north down the valley behind him. "We need to get to Franklin to join General Fremont." He paused and looked at us. "Can you give us the time, men?" A hearty hurrah came from us. "All right men. Remember your training! Do your duty and Godspeed!"

Milroy then walked to the front of our group. He looked at Colonel Cantwell and then surveyed the 82nd Ohio. "Men, I know this is the first battle for many of you." He walked right by me and our eyes met. He did have a distinctive appearance, reminded me of a sketch of John Brown I had seen in a newspaper. Milroy's deep voice resounded over us. "Remember that you are from Ohio! May you bring honor to your state, your community, and your families! They are all depending on your honor and courage this day!" He raised his sword in the air as he walked along the lines. A wave of emotion grabbed me and I "hurrahed" at the top of my voice.

Like Moses before the Red Sea, General Milroy thrust his sword toward Bull Pasture Mountain. "Forward men, Forward!" His face froze in a stern expression and the muscles of his neck tightened below his wild white hair. "Onward, men, onward!"

Ahead of us was a bridge that crossed a stream and led up to the two mountains. The second mountain was the one crowned with Rebel flags and troops. I heard the distant sound of the enemy drums and bugles. My mind raced. I had to force myself into breathing. My heart leaped against the walls of my chest. *Oh Lord, be with me.*

Colonel Cantwell raised his sword. "Men of Ohio, move out!" The drums rolled and we moved, slow at first and then faster and faster. Corporal Armstrong was beside us.

"Double quick, Boys! Double quick!" We came to the brushy slope of the first small mountain. I looked for a way up through the thick undergrowth, trees, and branches. It was impossible to stay in a group. I plunged into the brush. I struggled on. *Damned branches!* My profanity surprised me. We were not yet in the view of the enemy muskets. As I forced my way along, I heard the sound of our batteries off to the right and behind me. Whoosh! The shells roared overhead.

"*Lord be with us,*" I prayed as I tried to penetrate the trees and bushes on the steep slope. Whack! A branch whipped across my cheek raising a small red welt. *Damn it! Forgive me.* I ducked my head and pushed forward; branches and vines pulled at my rifle and clothes. I resented the presence of my gun. I wished I could throw it down and use both hands to clear my way.

The hill seemed to resist our efforts to scale it. Was it consciously trying to hold us back? Was nature itself saying, *don't go young men, don't you know what awaits you on the other side?* Men to the right and left were stopping to catch their breaths. Many, still weak from the forced march to get here, gave up and fell panting to the ground.

"Get back in formation, keep up with your companies!" Officers hollered on our sides and from behind as we emerged into an open slope.

I reached the top of the first mountain. The sun was behind our backs and the slopes of the second mountain were cloaked in smoke. When the smoky curtains parted, the raw battle expanded naked before me.

What a spectacle! Puffs of smoke rose from rifles on the ridge of the hill. Bullets whizzed around my head like deadly bees. They thudded against trees and burrowed into the ground. I crouched, frozen stiff with fear. *Where can I go in this hail of death?* Colonel Cantwell appeared on the crest of the hill, waving his arms, and compelling us forward.

"Down the hill, quickly! Keep charging men, don't stop!" I thawed and ran forward. Cantwell increased his pace down the hill, his sword above his head. *How could this old man run so fast?*

The vegetation thinned out and I ran freely, almost flying. Bullets buzzed over my head as I entered the open fields at the base of the mountain. One zipped by my ear. *Oh no! Was I hit? They say you can't feel it until minutes later.* I instinctively stopped and crouched to the ground, trying to keep myself as low and as small as possible. Again, I heard Colonel Cantwell.

"Come on boys, keep running. Quickly now, up the hill!" I leaped forward and looked to my right. "Thud!" A Minnie ball found its mark.

"Oh! Oh mother!" The man fell to the ground and grabbed his face. Blood began to squirt out between his fingers. My mouth dropped as I gaped at the blood pumping out like a small red fountain.

"Keep going soldier, don't stop for the wounded. Win the battle first," shouted an officer behind me. I turned to see who this officer was and saw him double over and fall to the ground. *Oh God!* I kept running. The irony of the moment swept over me and I yelled in anguish over the randomness of this dance of death. I wildly darted one way and then another hoping to find a way through the hail of bullets. A voice inside spoke to me. *Do not fear death. As long as you live, go forward.*

A sort of reverential peace suddenly befell me and the voice inside turned quiet. I scaled a steep concave hollow in the mountainside that led to a brow or ridge. I could hear the Rebels on the ridge yelling, "Here they come!" Thunk! A soldier in front of me grabbed his leg, rolled over on his back and began swearing. "Damn! Oh! My kneecap is shot off! Oh my God, help me! Help me!"

Two soldiers ran to his aid, crouched on the ground, dropped their rifles, and picked him up. *I could help.* A third soldier joined them and they started back down the hill.

With reluctance, I passed this group and fell behind some fallen trees with a line of other soldiers. Isaiah and Seth were nowhere to be seen. Where were they? We had been close together. Had they been shot? A ball blew by my ear and I could feel its hot breath. I dived to the ground and burrowed into the branches.

The Rebels had cut and piled the trees below the ridge to keep us from getting at them. Much to my relief, this pile of debris protected us. Sweaty, panting soldiers in blue fanned out on either side of me. I did not recognize anyone. Where was company F?

The enemy soldiers fired down at us from a steep angle and most of the balls went above our heads. The Rebel officers yelled "aim lower, boys, aim lower!"

To do this they had to raise up and lean forward which profiled their heads against the dusky sky. The sharpshooters in our ranks now took a toll on the enemy, shooting them down like so many pumpkins on a fence. Open-mouthed, I gaped at the human forms screaming, throwing up their arms, and falling from view. The fight, thus engaged, continued for what to me seemed like a time without end.

A large group of soldiers to my right charged up the ridge and forced a group of Rebels from their position. The line of men around me shifted to the right and I moved with them through an open area. My spine tingled as I expected a ball to tear my flesh. It did not happen and to my relief, I found a downed tree to get behind. *Thank you Lord*! I crawled behind it and tried to gather my senses.

Up on the ridge just taken by our charging soldiers, I saw a countercharge by the Rebels and a bayonet struggle ensued. One of the blue soldiers near the edge of the ridge doubled over, the blade of an adversary emerging from his back. After a savage yell, the enemy soldier withdrew his blade only to be shot by a Union soldier off to his left. Meanwhile, the bayoneted soldier fell and rolled down the steep bank writhing in pain and came to rest against the log in front of me. Cursing and thrashing, the bloodshot eyes below the thick red hair beheld my startled face. It was him—the man who tried to rape the girl at Camp Tod while I was on guard duty. *Indeed, we meet again!*

" Oh shit, not you Puritan. Ahhh! Damn it all to hell! I'm a goner Puritan. You won't be proddin' me off any more wenches! Oh, damn, damn, damn…" His gaze became hollow and filled with terror. His arms reached out as he struggled for breath, bubbles of blood forming at the edges of his mouth. I grabbed his bloody outstretched hand across the log, mindless of the bullets flying around us. His grip went limp and the air came out of his corpse. On his face was the strained, frozen stare of absolute horror. I released him, let him sink down, and settled behind my side of the log.

A volley from the enemy moving in from the left flanked a group of West Virginians in that area and refocused my attention. The Rebels were firing down their line! These men not only had to fire up the ridge but also to their side and rear. I watched in horror as men fell in great numbers. Responding to a force from their right, the Confederates then returned to the brow of the ridge, relieving the pressure. One of the Yankee Virginians jumped behind the log next to me and exclaimed amid the fury of battle.

"Tarnation, I thought I was a goner! God bless that regiment to our right. There's a heap more of them Rebs up there than I thought!" He then moved back near his fellow Virginians who had regrouped.

"Aim carefully, fire at will, and pick off the Rebs," yelled Colonel Cantwell as he raced along our line. I could see his coat sleeves shiver with the passing of some bullets. He stopped and yelled at the Rebel line.

"Can't you slavers shoot any better than that?" Cantwell then moved out of my sight, disappearing in a veil of smoke. A soldier off to my right exclaimed.

"Good God, how can Cantwell tease the devil like that? The bullets just tickle him!"

Captain Thomson moved along the same line as his colonel but with much more care, jumping from tree to tree. "Fire at will, boys! Pick 'em off as they show their heads!" He looked in my direction. "Some of you men are not firing! Commence firing, boys!"

Crouching behind my log, I heard bullets hit the branches and spin out of control, emitting a distinctive fluttering sound. Others struck the soil on the steep slope and bounced along like sizzling pebbles. I felt paralyzed and guilty.

Finally, a sense of duty overtook me and I rose above the log and took aim at a silhouetted form about seventy yards away. Boom! The rifle recoil pushed me back down behind the log. The smoke from my rifle prevented me from seeing the results of my first aggressive act.

Whack! A bullet struck the front of the log and a powdery puff of wood dust went up my nose. "That party" Robinson promised back at Grafton was here. I reached for another cartridge, heard a twang, and felt a pull on my rifle. A bullet ripped the leather strap attached to the barrel.

A soldier to my left fell to the ground. He rolled over and pulled a splinter from his cheek. A bullet had splintered the stock of his rifle. He crawled over to the body next to him, grabbed the dead man's rifle, and returned to his position.

I pulled out another cartridge, ripped off the paper tail, and tried to pour the powder into the barrel. Most of it fell on my stomach as I was on my back behind the log. I then pushed the Minnie ball down with the ramrod while still lying down. With half a charge in my gun, I took aim at a slouched hat with a yellow plume. I could actually see the ball strike the man in the back. He fell, got up and stumbled to the rear. As I turned to reload, I thought. *"You can thank me for your furlough home today, yellow feather."* It was the only time I knew that I had hit another human.

The enemy soldiers on the ridge were following a sequence. The man in front shot his rifle and then retreated to reload. In a few seconds, the next Rebel became visible as he prepared to shoot. I timed this sequence and it took about fifteen seconds before another Rebel appeared. I raised my rifle and took aim at a rock on the ridge, waiting.

The smoke of battle made it hard to see as I sighted in on the rock. A blurry form moved over the ledge. *God bless your soul!* I slowly squeezed the trigger. Boom! The rifle recoiled and jumped out of my grasp, falling beside me. The sound of the rifle reverberated in my ears and stunned me into silence. *Lord, I cannot hear!* I was now a deaf actor in this deadly play of death, pain, and suffering. To my relief, I rejoined the world of sound in a few seconds.

I quickly retrieved my weapon. It was undamaged, no exploded barrel. Had I put a double charge in my gun? *Terman, keep your mind about you!* I began shooting again and again while the battle raged.

From time to time, I saw the shells from our batteries rip into the ridge. With a wrong turn of the elevation screw, they could land on us. Screams came from the ridge as the exploding shells ravaged the Rebel lines. *The view up here sure is different than from the camp!*

During a lull in the firing, I could hear the enemy in the dim light of dusk.

"Don't our boys fight nobly," remarked a Reb officer standing by a tree up the ridge and off to my left. A single shot rang out and I saw the officer fall to the ground, grabbing the man beside him. A sharp yell came from the Union private firing the shot. "I got him! I got him!"

"Avenge his death! Avenge his death! Avenge his death!" An enemy officer ran up and down the line screaming at his soldiers as he passed over them.

A cascade of firing then erupted and reverberated down the slope and across the hollow, the rim of which glowed in the evening sun. I felt a bullet burrow beneath the log in front of me and sting my left side. I gasped and reached down to my hip. I could feel no hole or see any blood. The ball was still hot as I fished it from my pants and examined its shape. It was flattened a little but otherwise almost spherical. The shot had come from a smoothbore musket and not the rifled Enfield that I held in my hand.

Smoothbore muskets are easier to load with a hot barrel but are inaccurate beyond fifty yards and accuracy was an advantage in this battle. Our soldiers were picking off the enemy with regularity from over one hundred yards away.

Of the sixty cartridges I started with I now had less than five and it was getting dark. As the golden orb faded behind the mountain, so did the firing. I rolled over and closed my eyes as moonlight crept into the battleground still fuming with smoke.

In the eerie haze, I heard the Virginia regiments of the Union yell at the Confederate Virginia regiments. The men came from the same area and knew each other.

"Hey Jimmy Struthers, this is Henry Frye, remember me? I am with the grand ole Union now. Better keep your head down or we'll give ya a har cut!"

"Henry, you Yankee turncoat! Shut your mouth or I'll put a ball between your teeth. You boys are in a helluva spot there. Once we come rollin' down, there'll be hell to pay!"

About this time, a Rebel officer came to the ridge. He stood close to the brow; no doubt sure he was safe from the Union rifles below. From my position, I could see him in full profile. Should I take a shot? *No Hiram, the battle is just about over— let him be.*

He was a big man with large ears. He moved closer to the ridge and began pointing in different directions. As he turned to leave, a shot from our ranks rang out. He bent over, grabbed his leg and shouted shaking his fist. "Goddamn that Yankee!" A man to my right turned to his comrade.

"Did you hear that Reb officer? Better not let old Stonewall hear that, he'd be whipped sure as blazes."

The officer limped off, having received a ball in the foot. We later learned that this was General "Allegheny" Johnson himself.

The shooting again heated up. *Here we go again!* In the darkness, I learned to shoot at the flashes of the rifles up on the ridge. After a short time, the firing died down and we were ordered to retreat down the slope.

The order spread from soldier to soldier along the lines. Men nodded and sighed with relief. I grabbed my rifle and began descending the slope. Twigs and leaves snapped and crackled as hundreds of feet moved down the slope in the murky sinister stillness.

The smoke lay like a shroud on the ground. Each step felt like I might plunge into a bottomless pit. Step by step I moved to my left along the steep slope. I knew the Rebel line was close by somewhere in the darkness.

As I stepped behind a tree, I heard a low groan. "Oh dang, you're steppin' on my dad-burned leg!" The deep southern accent alerted me that I had stepped on a Confederate soldier lying on the ground. I righted myself and put my rifle against his chest.

"If you're going to shoot me Yank, do it right in the heart, I don't want to suffer," said the Rebel with a lot of pluck for his circumstance.

"Are you armed, Reb?"

"You'd be dead if I was. I shot my wad up during the battle. I'm at your mercy, Yank. I caught a ball through my leg. It hurts like hellfire and I'm about bled out."

A flickering beam of moonlight pierced a gap in the tree leaves and revealed the form of the enemy soldier. He lay under a spreading bush. His face was ashen and a thick beard framed his pale features. I put down my rifle and examined the calf of his leg. A large, burley hand grasped his thigh.

"Let me have a look at that," I said carefully watching his other hand. He gave a weak groan as his arm dropped from his bloody leg to the leafy ground. I carefully felt along his beefy leg. The bones were not broken. It was a flesh wound but was bleeding profusely. I pulled the belt from my trousers, wrapped it around his leg as a tourniquet, and applied water from my canteen to keep the wound moist.

"Can I have a swig of that Yank, I'm like to die of dryness." I propped him up against the tree, gave him the canteen, and started to leave. The man then grabbed my arm. Startled, I turned and beheld a large square face grinning through a full wavy beard.

"Sam Parker, that's my name and I wanted to get a good look at y'all. Thank you Yank for givin' me the second mile. What's your name?"

"Hiram Terman. Your surgeons should get to you by morning, Sam. Try to keep that belt tight but not so much you lose feeling." The burley hand released me. We looked at each other as if in a tunnel of time in another place. I nodded and the illusion ceased, the smell of gunpowder, smoke, and screaming wounded returned.

"Much obliged, Hiram."

"Good luck, Sam."

I departed Sam Parker and made my way down the slope, coming to where the ground became more level. Here I found some Union soldiers lying motionless on the ground. Not wanting to leave any wounded behind, I passed from body to body feeling the faces with the back of my smoke blackened hand. All dead. The coldness of the ground had claimed them.

A dead blond soldier with blue eyes leaned against a tree. A German Bible peeked out from his open coat. He had a hole in his forehead and the back of his head was almost gone, his golden hair a bloody mass. I left him staring at the sky through eyes that did not see.

Moving down the slope further, I came to an officer, lying curled on his side. No pulse from his neck, cold. I turned him over and beheld his face. His countenance was calm even though he died a miserable death from a gut wound. Between his fingers next to his disheveled shirt and canteen was a small, hand-carved wooden cross. I left the cross but picked up his canteen and moved on looking for the road at the base of the hill.

In the distance, a number of soldiers groaned as comrades helped them down the slope. I came upon a man helping a soldier of our company with a huge gash on his thigh.

"Hey, can you give me a hand here? He can only hop on one leg and I can't keep him moving."

"You bet." I recognized the wounded soldier as John Powers of our company, who was in our Sibley tent at Camp Tod.

"John, what happened to you?"

Wincing with pain, he talked as we carried him to the road that led into McDowell. "As far as I can figure, a ball plowed down my leg as I was laying flat on that slope. The blamed thing then went into my boot and lodged in my foot. I bled like a stuck pig." We bumped into a tree hidden by the darkness. "Oh, that hurts, Hiram."

"Sorry John, can't see nothin' in this soup of smoke."

"Let's get the hell out of here, Hiram. I have had enough dancing with the Rebs for tonight."

On the edge of town, I noticed a young Union soldier prodding along two Confederates he had captured up on the hill. Each Rebel looked twice the age of the young Union private. This caused quite a commotion as the soldier delivered the captives to his captain. We paused to hear the conversation.

"Private Morey, what have we here?"

"Two Rebs trying to sneak around our flank on the hill, sir. I seen 'em as soon as they started down the hill. After they fired their muskets I ran up on them before they could load again and told them to surrender. You know something Captain, my gun was empty."

The two Confederates turned toward each other and shook their heads as they joined a larger group of prisoners. The story of this capture of two enemy soldiers with an empty gun flew around camp. (Years later I learned that Delano Morey was awarded the Medal of Honor for his deeds on that steep hillside at McDowell.)

As I scanned the group of prisoners, I noted one with a yellow plume extending from his hat. *Could it be?* I walked up to a guard and asked, "Could I talk to that fellow over there?"

"Well, all right, but make it quick. We want to get these people to the rear as soon as possible." I walked over to the slim but wiry Confederate and stopped about two feet in front of him. Each of us took the measure of the other.

"What ya want, Yank? Never seen a true son of the South up close?"

"How did you get caught?"

"I got knocked senseless by a spent ball up on the ridge and wandered right into a bunch of Yankees that took part of our line. Before I knew it, I was being marched down here." He paused and looked carefully at me. "What's your name, regiment Yank?"

"Terman— Hiram Terman, 82nd Ohio."

"German you say?

"Terman—with a T!"

"Sorry Yank, guess my ears are still ringin'! My name is Comfort, Theodore Comfort, 12th Georgia. I knowed a couple of Terman brothers in the 15th Georgia, originally from Pennsylvania I reckon. Could they be kin of yours?"

"Could, but not likely. Did the ball hit you in the middle of the back?"

Turning and showing me a blood stained circular patch on the back of his butternut jacket, he exclaimed, "Blamed if it didn't. It hit me with a thud, knocked the wind out of me, and then just bounced off. How did you know?"

"Cause I was the one that shot you. I had about half a charge in the barrel. I was shakin' so bad I couldn't pour my powder straight." He gave me a short quizzical stare and then grinned.

"Well, ain't this the darndest set of circumstances. Just before I was hit, I poured all my powder on the ground; I was a-shakin' too."

The guard came up waving his bayonet at the prisoners, telling them to form up. I extended my hand to the Rebel. "Nothing personal, just doing my part in this war." He responded in kind.

How can this be? I had met two Rebel soldiers tonight and liked both of them. What does a proclamation of war do to us where people kill each other in one moment and then become friends the next? What happens to our humanity? Why can't words settle disputes rather than bullets?

Such is the curse of our kind. We ignite our anger, it spreads to others, and violence leaps to our armies and guns, exploding, and in the words of President Lincoln, bypasses "The better angels of our nature". We seem powerless to stop this process and I was caught up in the grinding flow of men and machines of death, honor-bound to stay within the ranks. Why couldn't the controls on our hatred be as advanced as our weapons? Lord, help us.

"See you in hell, Billy Yank!"

"See you in hell, Johnny Reb!"

Campfires dotted the moonlit darkness around McDowell as soldiers struck match to tinder, ignited wood, boiled coffee and began to talk. Isaiah and Seth saw me by the glittering fire and came up. I saw them approach and spoke first to Isaiah.

"Where were you two during the battle? I didn't see either of you?" Isaiah looked quizzically at me.

"We were wondering about you. We were next to you by the road and then suddenly you were gone. We thought you caught a bullet or something."

"Well, I ran up the hill and fell out along the downed trees near the top. Where did you wind up shootin' from?"

Isaiah came up closer, he now had a frown on his smoke tinged face. "You got way up there?" He looked over to Seth and then back to me. "We got about half way up the hollow and were pinned near the ground for the whole battle. We pushed up dirt and rocks for cover." He looked at his scratched and bruised hands and rubbed them against his pants. "The lead was so thick we couldn't move."

Seth then examined me closely as if looking for a wound. "We had a hard time shooting over you fellows, by the way. You got all the way up to the ridge?"

"God be praised!" Isaiah was amazed. Seth looked somewhat peeved as he continued questioning me.

"You must have gotten up with the first set of companies that formed the original line of battle. Did you see Captain Crall or Corporal Armstrong?"

"No, but Cantwell was right near me." Seth looked at me with a blank stare. Isaiah scratched his chin and remarked.

"I heard Crall and Armstrong were busy prodding on stragglers down by the road. I'll be switched, Hiram! You were with the leading edge!"

Tales of near escapes and of friends wounded and killed began to surface.

"I'm just thankful to the Good Lord for preserving us," said a thoughtful and reflective Isaiah. Seth looked up from the campfire with a puzzled and questioning look.

"As far as I can see, it's just a matter of luck, pure chance who gets killed and who doesn't. A bullet or shell ain't particular who it hits. Isaiah, how can you think God protected us and not the ones that are dead on that mountain side?"

Isaiah, impacted to the core, stood up, walked to the far side of the fire, turned and looked at both of us. "How can you say such a thing, Seth? I know praying to God makes a difference. I prayed for all three of us and I know His hand was on us today. I've got to believe that."

"Believe what you can, Isaiah. I've seen too much evil today and no hand of God holdin' it back. Many good and decent men got killed up there, some of them prayed like thunder." Seth threw a stick into the fire. "A lot of good it did them!" Seth then got up from the fire and walked to the edge of the darkness. Isaiah came close to me.

"Hiram, what you think, don't you believe that prayer changes things?" I took a deep breath and searched my mind for a response as I looked out on Bull Pasture Mountain sprinkled with the enemy's campfires.

"Well, I've seen bad and good ones die out there. The good die better, I'll tell you that." Isaiah slapped me on the back.

"That's what I mean, that's what I mean! God gives us peace in the midst of the battle." He left and walked in the direction of Seth who paced along the edge of the fire's radiant reach.

As our bacon sizzled, officers circulated among us. "Pack your gear, add wood to the campfires, and form up for moving back along the road to Franklin." We looked around to see what officer was speaking. It was Cantwell himself. "Get up you men! Pack away your food. We're moving out. Fall in behind the ambulances and be quiet about it. We don't want to stir up the Rebs." The wounded were soon loaded on wagons and the whole brigade fell into line as we left the town, our campfires burning bright.

"Why did we add wood to the fires if we're leaving?" whispered Isaiah as we started marching.

"To fool the Rebs into thinking we're still here, you dunce! Can't you figure anything out?" Seth was still recoiling from the previous discussion with Isaiah.

"I didn't know! Hiram, did you know why we were stoking the fires?" I did not know but nodded that I did.

As we reached the heights above McDowell, we saw the campfires we left behind shining like stars in a low sky.

"The only problem with our ruse is that the fires are not flickering as when soldiers walk among them," said Seth as he pondered the situation. "The Rebels might be on to us before long." We marched north up the valley to Franklin and our opinion of Seth climbed. "I never knew that," repeated Isaiah several times.

We marched about nine miles and then rested. Pickets were chosen from the men not engaged in the battle and the rest of us got a chance to sleep for a few hours. On a pile of leaves, sleep flowed over me. Every muscle and nerve relaxed. The Terman insomnia did not show itself and I started to dream. The faces of Sam Parker and Theodore Comfort appeared and then faded from my mind. This rethinking of the battle did not last long. I was glad.

I awakened feeling the hands of Isaiah Rinehart shaking my shoulders. "Get up Hiram, we're off marchin' again." Isaiah looked off into the distance. "No sign of the

Rebels yet. Maybe we fooled them after all. At least they are keepin' a respectful distance."

We marched on through the night guided by the moon and the light of some large fires burning on the mountain slopes. To slow the enemy's pursuit, some of our supplies along our retreat had been set afire. The glowing yellow black sky produced sinister surroundings as we marched up the valley. Our knapsacks and other gear were sent ahead on the wagons to Franklin.

The lighter load and the rhythm of marching soothed my senses and I dozed as I sauntered along. As the sun rose the next morning, Seth, Isaiah, and I were half asleep on our feet and did not wake until we stopped and stacked arms in an open area above the town of Franklin.

A yell came from our pickets. A large Rebel force appeared on the horizon. "Those buggers are still after us. Don't they ever quit?" Seth reached for his rifle and cartridge belt.

We formed battle lines at the entrances to the town. Company F was on a small rise to the right of the main road. As I readied my rifle, my bones ached as if they were raw and stripped of muscle. The forced march, the battle, and the return march had drained me from top to bottom. I looked down the barrel of my gun with tired eyes and wished with every fiber that the Rebels would leave.

Our big guns in town began to fire out into the lines of enemy cavalry and supporting infantry coming down the valley, their flags waving. "Look at all of them Johnnies! We won't be able to hold 'em! Oh mother, what are we going to do?" yelled a man to my left as he vacillated between crouching and running. Panic spread through me as I saw the enemy lines spread out. A series of shouts then came from behind us.

"General Fremont is coming with Blenker's Division! The Dutch are here by God, they made it!" A wave of relief went through me as I looked behind me and saw the lines of blue soldiers pouring into Franklin. Rebel officers saw them too and halted the advance of their troops. Like an angry beast deprived of its meal, the Rebel cavalry probed our lines, charging and then withdrawing.

Our force now approached twenty thousand with the coming of General Blenker's German troops. Like a hunter running from a wounded bear, we welcomed these new arrivals of artillery, cavalry, and infantry. The creature we angered now growled and threatened but kept its distance. It feared the growing numbers of his adversary. Gradually the Confederates pulled back.

That night after the Rebels retreated, fires erupted in the woods lining the hills and our pickets witnessed quite a show. The rest of us tried to locate our backpacks in the many wagons piling up in Franklin. "Hiram, how did you find your pack so derned fast?" Seth started searching another wagon. I had carved my name "H. Terman" on the flap and tied a small yellow ribbon around one of the buckles. I spotted it on the first wagon I searched. Soon Isaiah and Seth found their packs and we set up camp. It was comforting to have my supplies and personal items as we encamped that Sunday night, our pickets still on alert.

On Monday, the 82nd Ohio was sent out on picket duty. The enemy still showed signs of being in the area. In a wooded glen on a slightly elevated hill, I saw a Confederate horseman ride up, stop, get off his horse and fire a round at our lines. Like a wolf on the edge of his territory, he told us to keep our distance. Sometimes I fired back but at the distance of a thousand yards or more, I knew nothing would come of it. This was true except for the literal last moments of my Battle of McDowell.

The sun sat in the west and the slopes below my observation point were cast in a golden glow. A dark bearded, gray-coated soldier rode up on a black horse, leveled his gun in my direction and fired. The bullet thudded in the tree above me, its energy nearly spent. Sitting on his horse as though taking in the scenery, the Rebel gazed in my direction. *All right my friend, if you insist.* I aimed my Enfield up at an angle of about fifteen degrees and allowed about twenty yards for wind effects. I squeezed the trigger, the rifle fired, its sound reverberated over the open ground in front of my perch. A little patch of dust exploded in front of the Rebel and his horse reared. The surprised Confederate righted his steed, looked in my direction, deftly tipped his hat, and then rode off down the slope.

Should have been twenty degrees up. Watching the horseman fade into the distance, I found myself glad for the miscalculation.

After a few more days of demonstrating, Jackson withdrew his troops. "My Lord, that man holds on like a mad dog," said Isaiah as he scanned the empty horizon. "I thought the Rebs were never going to leave!"

"Jackson is a careful general," chimed in Seth as he walked up beside us. "He wants us to know that this land is his." All of us knew that we were not going to leave Jackson alone. The telegraph wires sang with admonitions from Washington to attack, engage, and drive the enemy. Our little force had slapped the great Rebel beast in the face and barely escaped his jaws as he came running after us. Now Fremont's legion was growing and flexing its muscle. Could we now become the hunter and kill the snarling lion that roamed the Shenandoah Valley?

For myself, I discovered the animal of war that resided within me. I had resolved the issue of killing and believed myself to be in a just cause. I saw "the elephant", the blood stained face of battle and survived. I followed all its rituals and had drunk of its violent essence. I was now a Union soldier, worthy of my pay if the paymaster would ever show up.

Bull Pasture Mountain (right) in McDowell, Virginia. The 82nd Ohio was camped on this open ground and charged up the slopes to confront Stonewall Jackson's troops coming from the east.

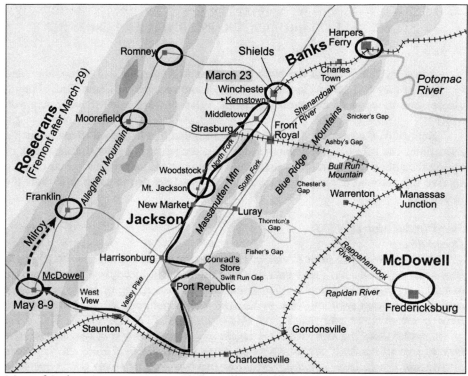

Map of Jackson's movement to McDowell and Milroy's movement to Franklin after the battle at McDowell *(map by Hal Jespersen, www.posix.com/CW).*

Initialed bricks on the Presbyterian Church in the village of McDowell.

CHAPTER 5
COME HELL OR HIGH WATER: THE BATTLE OF CROSS KEYS

I told my family about the battle in a letter to Rome, Ohio. I knew they were worried, as they had said so in the two letters I had received at Camp Tod. "Hiram, please send us news of how you are doing. What has happened to you? Are you well?"

Somehow, the words did not come about all that had happened to me in such a short time. The pain of forced marches, the absolute terror of battle, and the shock of seeing the aftermath shook me to the core. I could not assure my family that I would survive this war and it was just beginning. Even so, I set pen to paper and wrote the following:

Franklin, Va. May 15, 1862
Dear Father:

I write this to you from Franklin, Virginia as I sit around a campfire trying to heat some coffee. We have very little to eat as the supply wagons from New Creek are not arriving due to rain and swollen rivers. We get one ration of bread plus coffee and sugar per day until supplies arrive, which does not seem likely. I am lucky to have a bit of jerky and dried fruit that I purchased in Moorefield. Tell great grandmother that I am using what she taught me. Many a poor soul here has no idea how to live off the land. We may have to move just to get food since this is a very barren and mountainous country. I have just survived my first battle, which occurred at McDowell, a small mountain town to the southeast. I faced death many times in the short four hours that I was engaged in battle on the steep side of a mountain. I do not know how I survived as the bullets filled the air. Many of the men did not. I do not know the exact numbers yet but close to 300 of us were injured, killed, or captured. I thank God that I am alive. I do not know if I killed any soldiers on their side, possibly so. I do not want to know and will try to forget if I do find out that my actions have squelched a life. I am in a deadly business here, Father, and I do not know what lies ahead.

John Powers received a huge gash on his leg from a ball. He seems to be doing all right though. I saw General Fremont when I was at the hospital tent visiting John. He is a tough, raw looking man of moderate size. He had a sorrowful look as he visited the wounded soldiers. It must be a heavy burden. I think Fremont will go east and take us out of the mountains into the Shenandoah Valley to face the Rebels again. After all, that is what we're here for, to confront the enemy and quell the Rebellion. I will write when I can. Pray that I will be able to bear up under whatever the future holds. Give my love to great grandmother, mother, and the young ones and tell my brother I pondered much over his ideas on peace in these last days.
Your son,
Hiram

Food became scarce for us soldiers as we camped in the small mountain hamlet of Franklin. Supply wagons could not reach us fast enough from the supply depots at New Creek on what we called the "Cracker Line". The mountainous country provided almost nothing to eat except what could be foraged off the few hardscrabble farms. The men of our army were like a hoard of locusts and soon exhausted this meager resource, much to the misfortune of the local residents. Eventually some cattle were found and slaughtered providing small bits of beef but not near enough. We were desperate, and serious measures were needed.

Cattail roots from a nearby swamp provided some food, as did captured animals. I noticed tracks, nibbled branches, and droppings near our tent and I made a trap out of twigs, strings, and bits of wire. When an animal entered to get a bit of bait in the back of the trap, it pushed a hanging treadle capturing the critter. Isaiah was amazed at my success.

"How did you catch that rabbit? Hiram, where did you learn to do such things?"

"From my great grandmother," I replied.

"Your great grandmother?" Seth stepped up quickly imagining the meat in our next stew.

"Who cares how he got it! Let's get the thing skinned and onto a stick over the fire! I'm starved!" Seth grabbed the animal, pulled out his knife, and gutted it. "My God, what are we coming to in this army when we have to catch rabbits and rats to stay alive?"

On May 25, we backtracked to Petersburg to get supplies. "Why are we going back to Petersburg? The Rebs are in the Shenandoah," asked Isaiah as we packed.

"Well Isaiah, not everybody has a Hiram to feed them off the land. If we don't get food, this army is going to starve or worse, just up and quit," said Seth as he hoisted his backpack. "General Fremont knows we can't go on without supplies, don't matter what old Abe says." It was rumored that telegraph after telegraph from President Lincoln pleaded for Fremont to march as soon as possible to the Shenandoah Valley and take on Jackson.

A dilemma confronted us. We needed to pursue Jackson but we also needed to eat. The gnawing hurt and growing weakness of our bodies overwhelmed our fear of disappointing our leaders, including "old Abe". Messenger after messenger from the President rode up to Fremont as we trudged damp, cold, blistered and continually hungry back to Petersburg. *General Fremont, why are you going west? Why aren't you going east to attack Jackson?*

We saw Fremont throw a telegraph message down in the mud in frustration. "Why can't the President understand that we cannot go after Jackson with no supplies and a tuckered out army!"

"Jackson really cut us up at Front Royal and Winchester but we can still whip him if we can just get there in time." Colonel Cantwell pounded his fists as he talked to us. "If we combine with our forces coming from the north and east, we might just get that old fox!"

We were given rations and a night's rest when we arrived in Petersburg on May 26. The next morning we commenced a rapid march back to Moorefield, crossing the cold Potomac River. Each man fended off the rapid, waist-deep current by holding on to a rope stretched from bank to bank.

Emerging from the stream wet and cold, we looked like walking corpses. Every man, swallowed up by fatigue, collapsed on the ground upon reaching Moorefield on May 27. We called on deep reserves that we did not know we possessed and somehow set up camp, built a fire, and cooked our food.

"Oh Lord, why did I sign up back in Ohio? I never thought I would be getting into this!" Seth groaned as he tried to find comfort on the rocky ground. Finding a stone in his blanket, he hurled it into the fire. "We march all over this country, get our butts beat by Jackson, almost starve, and now we're right back in Moorefield where they hate our guts! Glory hallelujah!" Seth noticed some cedar branches brought in by Isaiah.

"I thought these might help you sleep a little better Seth." Isaiah pushed a bundle over to Seth who, with a sheepish look, put them under his blanket.

"Well, thank you ole buddy, these will definitely help." A smile crossed Isaiah's face.

"Your welcome Seth but we should thank God. We could have perished back at Franklin." Seth lay back on his new bed of cedar.

"Thank God? What about just us? How about Hiram and his great grandmother? We were the ones who set the traps and killed the damn squirrels and rabbits. You talk as if we just opened our mouths and God filled them with holy manna!" Another argument was raising its contentious head. I tried to stop it before Isaiah could reply.

"Well, Seth, God helps those who help themselves! Haven't you heard that?" Seth smiled and lay back on his blanket.

"Good ole Hiram the peacemaker." He turned over and bunched some clothing into a pillow. "Maybe so, maybe so. We had better get some sleep, could be another rough day tomorrow."

Tattoo sounded through camp and our tent became quiet. Seth mumbled as he rolled around trying to find a comfortable spot. "Great grandmother! God help us." He then chuckled. "Hiram, you keep your head down. If you get shot, the rest of us will die in three days!" He then dropped off to sleep. It was nice to be appreciated.

The next morning, we marched eastward up the slopes of South Branch Mountain on rocky mountain paths and narrow muddy roads. To add to our misery, it rained hard. The cold dampness of the mountain produced an incessant bone-rattling shiver. Still we marched on trying to catch Jackson in the Shenandoah Valley off to our east.

A violent thunderstorm erupted as we hurried on through the night. Loud booms of thunder, brilliant flashes of lightning and a howling wind made us feel like we entered the zone of a cold hell on this mountain slope.

We had no shelter. To lighten up for a faster march we left our tents in wagons, miles behind us, stuck in the mud. Only Seth's planning that morning saved us. "Hiram, Isaiah, be sure to pack your oilcloths. There is a red sky in the east. Bad weather will hit us sure as blazes!"

Only the most fit were able to keep going as many soldiers got sick and fell out. Ambulances filled with shaking, shivering soldiers and many died. Fremont noticed our falling ranks and reluctantly stopped for the night.

Seth, Isaiah, and I built a small fire beneath our shared oilcloths under a bent branch of a tree. We used gunpowder from a cartridge and some dry tinder Seth had carried along.

"Gather in close and hold down the edges, try to keep the wind from blowing out the fire," directed Seth as we tried to keep out the wind and rain. "Isaiah, I hope you appreciate that God told me to bring along dry tinder." Isaiah smiled and nodded as he held down the flapping end of his cloth.

When the tinder started, the wet larger twigs crackled and hissed but grew into a warm fire. Before dozing off, I found a large but wet log and added it to the edge of the fire.

We awoke the next morning a ring of bodies around the warm coals. Legs and arms would not move when we tried to get up. Finally, as the blood coursed through our limbs, we creaked into motion, crawling out from under our flimsy shelter. The weather still threatened a storm.

I looked across the camp and saw the ranks of General Blenker's German troops (who already had been severely tested when they got lost in the march from eastern

Virginia). Almost half of them still lay on the ground after roll call was ordered. Fremont road up to the head of our lines and spoke to the chief surgeon.

"General, as your medical officer, I demand you halt our march. Only about half of our soldiers are able to walk." He pointed to the Germans. "It is barbarism to make these men march in their wretched condition in this weather."

A pained expression settled on Fremont's face. A clap of thunder and a streak of lightning raced across the sky. It then rained without mercy. Fremont in disgust then waved his hand and ordered a halt. It was the morning of May 29 and we were at Little North Mountain. For the rest of the day we huddled under our shelter next to a smoky fire. During the night the rain stopped.

Early the next morning, a long blue snake of troops uncoiled and marched down the mountain path toward the Shenandoah and Jackson's army. Seth had somehow come across a diagram of the troop positions. The head of our long snake of blue soldiers (advance guard) consisted of Ohio, Virginia (Western), and New York troops under Lieutenant Colonel Gustave Cluseret. The end of the advance guard consisted of General Stahel's New York, Pennsylvania, and Virginia forces. Following these (the main column) were Colonel Zagonyi's cavalry, General Robert Milroy's Ohio and Virginia troops followed by General Robert Schenck's Ohio and Connecticut forces (in which we were located). Behind us (the rear guard) was General George Bayard's brigade consisting of Pennsylvania, Maine, and New Jersey soldiers. Forming the tail of the snake were ambulances and ammunition trains followed by New York and Pennsylvania men.

Thus formed, the blue snake slithered through the mountains. Such was it's length that the head rested while the tail kept moving. When the coils tightened, the whole animal then expanded and again squeezed forward. The 82nd Ohio was two-thirds down the column where the movement was crowded and difficult. Those at the head of the snake had the easiest marching.

On June 1, the long blue snake descended the slope of Little North Mountain into the Shenandoah Valley at the town of Strasburg. The sound of cannons belching in the distance hurried our steps. The fear of being in another battle surrounded me like the storm on the horizon. Fear marked the faces of Isaiah and Seth. Between breaths, we glanced at each other as we moved toward the roar of the cannonade.

Large dark storm clouds brooded over the valley and thunder mixed with the sound of cannons in the distance. As if aggravated by the human tempest, the sky contracted into a dark black slate etched with brilliant bolts of lightning. Under this foreboding sky, we formed a line of battle and peered ahead where explosions erupted from a vague line of advancing Union cavalry.

Torrents of rain then poured down squelching the skirmishing and the roar of the cannons. We sat down with our muskets without becoming engaged, the rain pelting down on us, soaking us from head to shoe. Thunder and lightning roared over us as night fell around the troops.

As we huddled in the darkness, a rider came thundering by. "We have met Jackson, by God, we got here in time! We got here in time!" Word filtered down the lines that we had encountered the rear guard of Jackson's retreating army and had engaged him in a fierce running nighttime skirmish. We saw flashes of artillery in the darkness as we waited through the night.

The next morning we descended the slopes near Strasburg and then turned up the Shenandoah Valley in pursuit of Jackson. Soon a battalion of Pennsylvania infantry that wore deer tails or bucktails on their hats ran past us.

As we came down from the heights, hail the size of hen's eggs pelted us, chasing us into the trees. "Dammit Isaiah, I thought you said God was on our side!" Seth grimaced as he put his arm over his head to dodge the ice balls. This thought played with our minds as Jackson moved farther down the valley keeping just out of our reach.

We were now in a grand footrace with Jackson's army going south down the valley. His rear guard skirmished with our cavalry but seldom with our advance infantry units who could barely keep up with their mounted brethren. This occurred over June 2nd and 3rd.

As I marched forward, a small dot in the long line of Union soldiers, I noticed a scattering of blankets, muskets, clothing, broken ambulances, wagons, and other articles left behind by the retreating Rebels. Hundreds of Confederate stragglers and prisoners fell into our hands. They were a haggard looking bunch, some shoeless with horrible gashes on their feet. Seeing them made me feel better about my own estate, bad as I felt. As the line of prisoners passed us, I tried to look at each man but most walked with their head down, eyes sunken into hollow sockets. Even so, these men had a nobility or valor about them—a look of those who knew they had given everything, holding nothing back, the famous foot cavalry of Stonewall Jackson.

Occasionally, I saw blue coats wandering back along our lines. These were released Union prisoners captured by Jackson at either Front Royal or Winchester. These men cheered us on as we pursued the ones who had overrun and defeated them. For some reason, seeing them produced a cold chill, almost a sense of foreboding.

Pursue we did until June 4 when we reached Mount Jackson and a wide, flooded river valley. Jackson's army had burned the bridge so we were on one side and the disappearing rear elements of Jackson on the other. As we watched the Confederates fade into the distance, another heavy rain came and added to our misery. It rained so hard that the river rose about ten feet! Sitting in the downpour, Seth exclaimed. "My God, Isaiah, maybe Jackson does have God on his side!"

We were without food having eaten every hardtack cracker, bit of meat, and other morsels in our haversacks. Since the supply trains were bogged down far to our rear on the muddy roads and overflowing streams, the troops began to wander and forage over the countryside while the engineers began constructing means of fording the river with a pontoon bridge. The whole countryside was being scoured by Union troops, bringing in all sorts of food items.

The local residents were terribly distressed by this foraging activity, much of it done by undisciplined stragglers. In the custom of European wars where the spoils of the countryside go to the victors, the German troops not only took food but every kind of household item they could carry. This infuriated the locals and did not sit well with our officers who ordered the activity to stop. This did little to stem the tide as we discovered while checking traps that I had set.

We found a small shack occupied by what appeared to be an old woman with two young children who had been raided by the "Dutch". She was sobbing on the front porch, the young ones pulling on her dress, crying, and asking for food.

Seth, Isaiah, and I were so distraught by this that we gave her some greenbacks and some rabbit meat to feed the hungry children. After initially withdrawing from us, she responded to our chorus of apologies and outstretched a young looking hand to receive the money. We could see that this was a young woman disguised as an old grandmother. She had taken out her false teeth (even young women lost teeth early), dirtied her face with soot, and put on an old shawl over her blond hair.

"Thank you, Yanks. I guess I'll buy some chickens with this after you'uns leave." After brushing the hair away from her face and trying to quiet her children who pawed at her dress, a scowl appeared. "Why do you tolerate those Dutch doing such things to innocent folk?"

"We're all so terrible hungry, ma'am," said Isaiah.

"Still, ain't no excuse!" She drew an old shawl over her firm bosom. "If I hadn't looked so old those beasts would have raped me for sure!"

With this, she gathered her children and went inside the house to cook the rabbit. What a terrible thing it is for an area to be descended on by an invading army, especially a starving one.

Isaiah, Seth, and I were able to supplement our diet with rabbits, squirrels, and even some fish we hooked with fishhooks that Seth had packed back in Moorefield. As we filleted a large bluegill, I recalled his comment. "You know there are fish in all those streams we're crossing."

After two days, we were able to cross the flooded Shenandoah at Mount Jackson. Walking across a pontoon bridge with hundreds ahead of and behind you was quite an experience. It feels like the bridge is a living organism, swaying and heaving as it obeys the forces of the moving men. We were almost seasick when I got to the other side of the river.

On June 5, we reached New Market and on June 6, we headed toward Harrisonburg. As we marched, a long line of horses galloped by us toward the front, throwing dirt and mud in their wake. Later we heard that a battle was occurring at Harrisonburg between Union and Confederate cavalry units.

A flamboyant horseman riding a black stallion, General Turner Ashby, led the rear guard of Jackson's army. Locals referred to him as the Black Knight of the Valley.

A black Stallion? Did I see this man following the battle of McDowell? As the day went on reports came back that not only were cavalry now fighting but also infantry, including the famed Pennsylvania Bucktails under Lieutenant. Colonel. Kane.

As we hurried on rumors passed down the lines. "The Rebels are retreating! The Black Knight has been killed! He was shot by his own troops! No, the Bucktails got him!"

A soldier returning from the fight approached us at a rest break. "I tell you boys, that old Ashby was something. When we caught 'em, the Black Knight dismounted and charged ahead of his men yelling 'Charge men, for God's sakes, Charge!' After this, a bullet caught him in the chest killing him on the spot. Worst thing is, it probably came from his own men." The man shook his head, becoming almost solemn.

We also heard that Lieutenant Colonel Kane of the Bucktails had been wounded and captured along with Sir Percy Windham, an English officer leading the First New Jersey Cavalry.

After we passed through Harrisonburg on June 7, we walked over the site where the fight occurred. As we marched, we observed soldiers loading the wounded on ambulances to be taken to hospitals. Some soldiers came by and were speculating on the place where the Black Knight was killed.

"I heard he was up there on that rise ahead of his men who were back here," theorized one corporal to his squad.

"No, he would have been directly in front of his infantry if that was the place," replied another soldier.

"Well, some say he was shot from behind so that makes sense to me," replied the corporal.

"How about his horse, the black stallion, what happened to it?"

"The horse was shot too, probably over there, and I heard the Bucktails shot Ashby," chimed in another soldier heretofore quiet. An officer rode up.

"Well, more than Ashby got shot here, men." Pointing to the ambulances, he continued. "Let's get back to trying to save those still alive." That was the last of the conversation I could hear as we marched on by the battle scene.

After a few miles, we camped for the night. What would the next day hold? We were certain that a battle of major proportions was in the offing if we caught up with Jackson. We were biting him in his rear quarters. When would the beast turn, stand its ground, and fight?

Images of dead and wounded soldiers proceeded through my mind as I rested under my oilcloth listening to the rain drip through the leaves of the trees. Would I be among their number in the days ahead? Would people wonder, "Where did Private Terman bite the dust"? Unlike Ashby, who would ever care?

I had already seen many men die and be left behind. Who would ever know what happened to the soldier buried by the enemy in a mass grave only a foot below the surface? An overwhelming sense of being insignificant came over me. Some deaths, like Ashby, would be remembered and revered for time immemorial. Generations of people would stop at his monument and wonder at his bravery. Who would remember us common soldiers, the small cogs in the machinery of war? I dozed off as this question dissolved in my mind and drifted off into a vague sense that I had been here before—or would be again.

Before sunrise on June 8, the drum and trumpet roused us from our sleep. Some of the supply wagons had come in and I hurried to eat a small piece of hardtack, a bit of salt pork, and some dried fruit followed by a swig from my canteen. I grabbed my rifle from the stack of arms, tightened up my belts, double tied my shoes and fell in for roll call. Colonel Cantwell informed us that more than likely we would be seeing some action today and to get prepared. I quickly closed my eyes and took a swallow, girding myself for what the day had in store.

We followed a good road with a solid surface for about two hours and then turned onto a muddy clay road that had been trampled and rutted by Jackson's army ahead of us. The marching became difficult, each step contested by the suction of the wet clay against our shoe bottoms. The reinforcements we made on our shoes proved their worth as many soldiers had the soles sucked right away from the uppers and were forced to march barefooted.

We were now in the foothills of Massanutten Mountain, a prominent hump in the middle of the valley. Up on its slopes, we saw Confederate signal flags waving. Jackson knew we were coming.

Two branches of the Shenandoah River lay ahead of us. Where would Jackson stop and fight? We knew that another Union army was coming from the north, hoping to catch Jackson in a trap. Would it happen? We all had the feeling that soon we were about to find out.

Early in the morning, we heard that our advance guard had encountered the enemy near a small tavern at the hamlet of Cross Keys. Even though we were miles away, we heard muffled thunder in the distance, the sounds of battle.

We hurried our march up the slopes and around the hills. The sound increased to a steady rumble that heaved and roared as we drew nearer to the battle. Smoke filled the horizon. The dots of blue ahead of me flowed into this cauldron like a thin blue river, their rifles dipping from side to side as they marched along.

We arrived on the field of battle about one in the afternoon. The Rebel position on a wooded ridge was visible from our position on a long slope descending into a valley. The enemy was in a good defensive position facing rolling open hayfields. A small creek ran in front of the wooded ridge. Off to the sides we saw Confederate cannons placed so they could rake the open areas. Seth's mouth dropped at the sight.

"That old Jackson has done it again. He has drawn us into a spot where he can shoot down on us while we have to cross open fields and claw up to him across creeks and ridges!" Seth rubbed the back of his neck nervously. "Just like at McDowell!"

Isaiah looked at Seth and then at me. My mouth became dry as I envisioned an exploding shell blowing apart a group of human beings. Isaiah noticed the fear on my face. "Don't worry Hiram, God will be with us and General Fremont and Schenk will do the right thing." Seth shook his head and mumbled something I couldn't hear.

We kept marching. Soon the mile long battleground came into view. Our front troops, mainly the German regiments, were engaging the middle and right sides of the Confederate lines. The battle was on and roaring.

The column that I was in turned to the right, heading for a cemetery in front of a small church. General Schenk began shouting orders for us to follow the brigade of Milroy who was in front of us advancing toward the Rebel lines on the ridge. The artillery of our brigade raced out in front of us, stopped, set up, and fired shells into the ridge. The boom of the guns soon became constant drowning out any attempt to talk.

The constant firing of the guns from both armies filled the sky with missiles and smoke enveloped the field. Occasionally a breeze lifted the veil and exposed the naked battle. Most of the enemy's shells were falling to my left in the open fields on our advance guard. Sometimes a shell fell among us, dug a pit two feet deep and threw soil in all directions. One of these shots struck a horse, taking off its head and shoulders, throwing blood and guts all over the nearby soldiers. Our shells were falling on the ridge in front of us and to our right.

As the battle progressed, more shells came our way. Every incoming shell causes a curling numbness that starts in the middle of the lower back, flows up to the neck and settles in the chest. First, the blast of the cannons is heard in the distance, then the shell screaming through the air. In seconds, the shell hits. A ball of smoke about the size of a haystack erupts and metal fragments of all sizes then come whirling all around. The small ones make a high-pitched sound and the large pieces a lower buzz. Those with jagged edges sound like a combination of whirs and whizzes.

There is no use in jumping or moving around as a shell comes. We learned to press into the ground and try to get as small as possible. After a burst, if still alive, we looked to see who was thrashing around or laying still with no head or bowels hanging out. It is singularly awful and terrible. A soldier's relationship with God and man is evaluated in those seconds as in no other time and all of a man's shortcomings become clear.

After a shelling, a clearness of thought and a keenness of perception not available in safer conditions takes hold. A man can see and think with insight he never possessed out of harm's way.

When the shells stopped coming, Seth, Isaiah, and I marched forward to a wooded area. Here we encountered a line of enemy soldiers who fired at us. The air filled with smoke and bullets whizzed by us as we returned fire into the woods. I was not nervous or afraid as we moved forward through trees toward a higher ridge about half a mile to the right. Rebel soldiers could be seen peeling off and retreating up the ridge.

As at McDowell, I was amazed at my calmness in the battle. I fired my rifle about five times but could not see what I hit in the smoky fog. Gray forms appeared and disappeared about one hundred yards in front of me. The Rebels tried to flank us to my right but our batteries convinced them to go back to their position to our left. Finally, we reached the ridge and stopped. The regiments in front of us now assumed the brunt of the fighting and I could see soldiers in blue falling as they encountered the enemy. Meanwhile to our far left where Milroy advanced, the battle seemed even more ferocious.

Colonel Cantwell came into view to our front as a gust of wind cleared the smoke. He was talking to Lieutenant Colonel Robinson who then turned and told us to stay put and take cover.

Seth and Isaiah were close by as was our squad leader Corporal Armstrong. Armstrong ran up in front of us and returned a short while later. "Boys, the Johnnies are retreating. Seems our cannons are really getting at them."

"Form up here," said Captain Crall as he moved along the line of men. Seth, Isaiah, and I immediately moved into position following our corporal.

Lieutenant Colonel Robinson then appeared in front of us. "We are on their flank, men. When I give the command, charge like the devil and we can roll them up!"

Images of a bayonet encounter appeared in my consciousness. Calmness left me and I began to tremble. The image of the bayonet through the red-haired soldier at McDowell flashed in my mind.

"Retreat slowly to the left, men." What? Did this command come from Robinson? What was going on? Why were we retreating? Were we losing the battle in the open fields in the middle of the battlefield? I slowly began to retreat looking left to see if a flanking rush of Rebels was coming. Nothing. Suddenly Schenck's artillery behind us opened up with rapid firing.

The exploding shells danced along the ridge. After withdrawing a short distance, we stopped and formed a new line. The firing in the center of the battleground dropped off. We could see masses of our soldiers to our left withdrawing. Isaiah looked shocked and Seth angry.

"Our men are running! God forbid, they're running!" Isaiah shouted as if he were the general. Seth hunched up closer.

"I told you the Rebel line was too strong up there, didn't I? My God, Jackson will be coming down at us! We had better dig in!"

Seth, Isaiah, and I looked for and soon found trees to protect us and waited. The sun sat above the ridge throwing out a yellow glow. No attack from Jackson—just some sporadic shelling and skirmishing out in the darkness by some of our pickets. Later in the evening, all grew quiet with the rising of the moon. Seth told us to stay ready. "I don't put it past Jackson to mount a night attack."

Off in the distance we could hear the movements of the enemy.

"What are they doing out there?" Isaiah asked as he peered out into the darkness.

"Probably moving in more cannons to blow us up as we gloriously run up that ridge in the morning," quipped Seth as he leaned against a tree.

"Don't you think Fremont will hammer the Rebs with cannons tomorrow rather than charge, Seth?" Charging up another ridge bothered me and I wanted to explore this further. "He really used the batteries today and we did not charge."

"Well, somebody charged over on our left and got their butts kicked. Probably ole Milroy and maybe the Dutch." Isaiah and I remained worried as a low rumble continued to roll out of the enemy lines.

Most of our supplies were now in the rear of the battlefield. With the descent of darkness, campfires flared and men prepared the meager morsels that filtered down to us. Everywhere conversations examined what had happened in the day's engagement.

"What did you hear about the fight to our left? Why did we retreat when we were going to charge?" Such was the mystery of our actions that Isaiah was almost beside himself, going from man to man along our lines.

A young corporal from another Ohio regiment stopped by and related his version. "Well, I heard that the advance guard, the Germans, got really chewed up and was running about the time we got in sight of the Rebs on that far ridge." He took a swig of coffee. "Lordy, that's good! Well, old Fremont got worried that the Rebels would flank us from the middle and all of us retreated together to hold our line here, that's what I hear."

"I wonder what would have happened if we would have charged from our position? The Reb line looked weak from what I could tell." I asked this knowing that we had considerable forces in our position. The Ohio corporal scratched his chin.

"I guess that is what Milroy wanted to do. His soldiers were hopping mad when the retreat order came. That could have been something. Them rolling us up from their middle and we flanking them from their left."

Seth made some quick lines with a stick on the ground.

"We might have been able to do it!" Seth made some sweeping marks barely visible in the light of the fire. "If the Union army coming down the other side of the valley is over on ole Jack's right, my God, we would have had them sons of a bitches trapped!"

"Seth, how can you swear at a time like this? We may be meeting our maker tomorrow." Seth was so focused that he did not respond.

"Damn! What if we would have kept going? Guess we will never know. Maybe we would have all been torn up like the Germans."

"Yep, we only know what did happen," I quipped.

Seth poked his stick on the far edge of his dirt map. "I have a hunch we will attack in force tomorrow once the Generals get their heads around this. Maybe the other army is not over there yet."

Seth further analyzed his rough map. "We were the reserve force today." His mouth dropped open as he looked up. "My God, Isaiah, we in Schenck's brigade will be in the lead tomorrow morning!" Seth threw the stick into the fire. "Better say your prayers tonight, Hiram!"

A little ruffled, I quickly replied. "We all better get ready, Seth, you included."

"You and Isaiah pray enough for all of us. Let's get some damned sleep."

The rumble from the enemy up on the ridge continued, punctuated with an occasional shell and some skirmishing.

Sleep did not come easy for me, especially with the night shelling and skirmishing episodes. Would it be us cut to pieces and chewed up like the German regiments come morning? Was the enemy preparing for a final push against us? Would the artillery shells be tearing at our ranks? Would Hiram's honor be on display or his cowardice? *Oh Lord, be with us! Help me to be ready.*

At sunrise, I awoke stiff, sore, and tired from a night of tossing and turning. I did not want to get up. We hastily ate some breakfast, examined our rifles, and checked our supply of cartridges, replenishing what we needed.

Just as Seth predicted, Schenck's brigade and the 82nd Ohio were in front this time, ordered to lead that day's battle. As the drum beat, my heart raced in my chest as we walked by the blue masses. "Bully for the Buckeyes! Give 'em hell, 82nd!"

Soon after formation, the command to advance was given. We moved at a slow but steady pace looking for the enemy pickets in the thick woods at the edge of the field over which we were walking. I watched for any sign of movement or the telltale smoke from a musket. When would those terrible artillery shells come screeching down on us? *Oh Lord, be with us.*

In a short time, we entered the woods. *Where is the enemy?* Next, we came upon the scene of the previous day's conflict and to our great surprise, no enemy pickets, muskets, artillery, nothing.

Still at alert, we walked through the terrible scenes of battle. At the skirmish line, I saw two soldiers, one in butternut and the other in blue, with bayonets through each other's body. What kind of death struggle ensued there? How could they have stabbed each other? Seth paused a moment over the two corpses. "I'll be damned; can you figure that one out?"

Further on the Confederate dead became more numerous. Our massive artillery barrage produced a gruesome stew of human legs, arms, and headless torsos. In some spots, only a bloody mush greeted our nauseous stares. The sounds of vomiting occasionally pierced the rustling noise of our steps through the woods. Veteran soldiers mocked the weak stomachs of our fresh troops.

"Come on, Billy, you haven't seen nothin' yet. This was just a skirmish. Wait until we get into a real battle."

"My Lord, how can I take more of this?" I then passed by a young Rebel soldier with a large hole in his forehead. When I peered closely, I could see that he actually had a smile on his face as though dying was a welcome event. Further, on I saw a headless corpse standing upright on its knees with arms outstretched in a pleading posture. That was enough! I stopped examining the carnage and fixedt my gaze forward; trying to hold down what little food I had in my stomach and keep a keen eye for the enemy.

Soon we came to a house now used as a hospital and I was forced to witness the fruits of war again. The dead lay around the building like a silent choir. At the door to the building was a young Confederate officer, evidently placed there as he was covered with a blanket. He was one of the most handsome fellows I had ever seen with a very symmetrical face, large eyes, and thin features below wavy auburn hair. One of the soldiers removed the blanket and we could see that he died of a bullet to the stomach. Somewhere I suspect a very pretty woman and perhaps some beautiful children would be in mourning when the news of the day reached this officer's home.

We continued our advance over the battleground eventually coming to the Mill Creek Church, the house of worship for a local pacifist group called the Brethren. Again, many dead soldiers gave evidence that this was a hospital. I immediately thought of our pacifist friends, the McMullen's, back in Ohio and their influence on my brother. Tears welled up in my eyes. Isaiah came up to my side. I immediately composed myself, cleared my throat, and spoke.

"Isaiah, have you ever seen anything like this? Maybe these pacifist folks here at this church are right. We should all throw down our guns and stop this business." I could hardly get the last words out. Isaiah pointed to a man by the church.

"A man named Yoder over there said that there are men from the congregation fighting out west in some Iowa regiments."

"Men from this church? In the army, fighting?" I could not believe this. Isaiah looked off and then at me.

"Maybe sometimes the evil is so great that even peaceful folks like these get into it." The thought of my pacifist relative James McMullen and his Ohio artillery unit flashed through my mind. Would they have signed up after seeing this? Would I?

From here, we moved on toward the Shenandoah River and the town of Port Republic, a small hamlet nestled at a fork on the river. Far ahead, a column of dense black smoke rose from where the main bridge crossed the river.

What was going on? We rushed forward to find the bridge engulfed in flames. Jackson's army with all his wagons and supplies filed off in the distance on the other side of the river. We immediately set up our batteries and began shelling the last parts of Jackson's train, hitting a few wagons and killing some horses. It was a futile attempt.

Seth was angry. "What the hell are we doing? Those are ambulances over there! Stop the damn firing!" He yelled repeatedly but the ranting of a private is nothing.

Unable to cross the river, we encamped on its banks for the night. Later in the evening reports filtered to us that Jackson had escaped us only to muster all his forces and engage the second Union force coming south down the valley under General James Shields. The battle was hard fought with Jackson being victorious, even though he himself narrowly escaped capture by some advance elements of Shields" army.

Evidently, the swollen rivers had impeded Shields arrival in force (just as had happened to us) and Jackson was able to overwhelm small groups of Federals strung out along the river. When all of Shield's troops did arrive, Jackson attacked en masse and drove the Union troops back up the river.

What was Jackson doing now? He seemed to be leaving but we could still see Rebel cavalry probing our lines.

The next day we awoke in a drenching rain to sounds of men building a bridge across the river. This activity then stopped with orders to retreat to Harrisonburg. Why were we stopping? Had all the pain, misery, and death been in vain?

Sustained by the hope of capturing Jackson and making history, all of us had drawn on stores of energy from the deepest reserves of our souls. Seeing the Rebel general slip away brought a wave of disappointment that crept over our camp like a fog. Men wept as misery and pain reclaimed their bodies. Hundreds now fell sick from the extraordinary exposure, fatigue, and nervous strain of our long marches and the battle. Ambulances were filled with only the most grievous cases of the sick and wounded. Thousands, although sick, were nevertheless required to walk or remain behind to be captured by the probing Rebel cavalry. As we marched away, the mob of stragglers equaled the number of regulars marching with the colors.

This spread out mass of humanity now passed where the German troops had fought and been decimated the day before. The Confederate dead were piled in heaps and dead horses lay everywhere. Again, the lethal results of our shelling were evident. I could barely take in the scene, which unbelievably was worse than our earlier exposure to the horrors of war.

The veterans were right. We had not seen anything yet. Our senses dulled, we trudged along, aching to get to Harrisonburg. We wanted to stop and rest but Jackson's cavalry attacked us all along our route. Fremont was now convinced the Rebel army had reversed course and was now pursuing us!

We kept going past Harrisonburg, down the turnpike to New Market, finally resting at Mount Jackson where Fremont felt he could fend off the Rebels. Still fearing Jackson, Fremont then marched us to Strasburg, and then to Middletown. On

24 June in Middletown, we joined forces with Generals Banks and Sigel. Weary in body and soul, we then awaited further adventure.

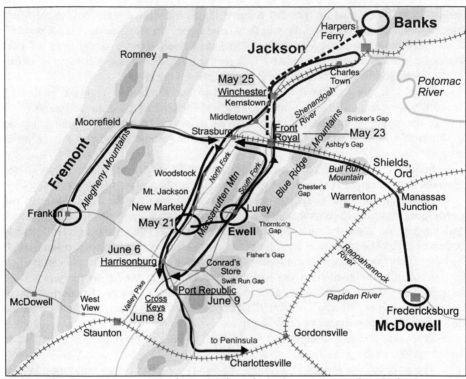

Fremont's movements east in pursuit of Jackson *(map by Hal Jespersen, www.posix.com/CW).*

Cross Keys cemetery at the Cross Keys, Port Republic battlefield sites.

CHAPTER 6
MILROY'S BOYS, CEDAR MOUNTAIN, AND FORDS OF THE
RAPPAHANNOCK

We in the ranks were not the only people growing weary of the progress of the war. President Lincoln, hoping to reinvigorate the troops and try a new approach, decided to reorganize the various parts of the army. He put the Army of Virginia under one commander, Major General John Pope.

General Fremont could not abide serving under a man he considered his subordinate and asked to be relieved. President Lincoln granted his request. Last, we heard, Fremont had gone to New York.

We were now in the Army of Virginia, First Corps under General Franz Sigel, a favorite with the German or Dutch troops who were a large part of our corps. Our brigade commander was now the impatient and impetuous General Robert Milroy and we became "Milroy's boys". All of this filtered down to us at Middletown as we recovered from the deprivations of our Valley campaign. Seth seemed sad to hear the news of Fremont's departure.

"In a way I hate to see old Fremont go. He was careful and slow to attack but I felt he tried to protect us soldiers." Isaiah joined the conversation.

"Fremont worried about supply lines and getting good positions for artillery instead of attacking." Seth groaned as if it was painful to hear Isaiah's opinion. "Careful commanders don't win battles. You have to attack and hold nothing back. You then depend on God to bless your efforts. That's what the Rebel Jackson does and look how he defeated us with half the men." For some reason this praising of Stonewall did not sit well with Seth.

"Isaiah, Jackson is a fanatic and he is in his own land and is helped by his own people."

I chimed in. "Isaiah, you must admit that he's got a big advantage over us."

"He's still a God-fearing general and we would be better off if we had more Christians leading us." For some reason, this brought no response, for a while.

I tried to get a fire going. Seth brought up our new leader. "From all the talk, John Pope is one of these attack, attack types. Christian or not, those types scare the hell out of me." Seth poked a stick around the fire and a flame erupted. Seth continued. "And now the 82nd is under Ole Milroy! You remember how he ran up that hill at McDowell? Tried to charge that ridge single handed."

Seth shook his head as he put the coffee pot over my growing fire. "We would have been shot to hell if we followed him." Flames now licked at the pot and water sizzled. "At Cross Keys, he galloped in front of his troops and had his horse shot from under him. My God, the man has no fear." We watched the pot heat until water boiled out the spout. " I think we are in for it now. No more being in the rear or held in reserve."

"I guess we will find out soon enough," I replied vividly picturing the events Seth mentioned at McDowell and Cross Keys. Milroy was nothing if not aggressive. He was also inspiring.

On July 4, following a stirring reading of the Declaration of Independence by a chaplain, General Milroy stepped into the bright sunlight of a clear sky and proceeded to give a fiery, patriotic speech. He began by denouncing the Confederacy and calling for men to step up and lay down everything for the cause of liberty.

"Every man must die sometime. Men, why not give your life for something that counts? There is no greater love than those who lay down their very lives for each other and the blessed flag." Waves of applause rose up from the troops who were genuinely stirred to a high pitch of enthusiasm, especially Isaiah.

As I listened to Milroy, I grew uneasy and so did Seth. After Milroy's speech, we milled around our tent, looking out at the activities of the camp, wondering what was coming.

On July 6, orders came to leave Middletown and go east out of the Shenandoah Valley through Luray and Thornton's Gap to Sperryville, there to join forces with other regiments. Our officers told us that Pope wanted to concentrate the troops that were spread out from Winchester to Fredericksburg and mass them together. If this happened, Pope said the enemy would have to come north to defend the Orange and Alexandria railroad, a major supply line to Richmond from the fertile Shenandoah. Seth figured it out. "This means facing Stonewall Jackson again, somewhere, and sometime soon."

As we suspected, Milroy's Brigade was in front of the column of troops as we marched out of Middletown. No more were we back in the middle of the column eating dust, but we were the long blue snake's head, the advance guard.

This meant less dust and more comfortable marching but it also put us in the vanguard, the first to see action, a fact that invigorated our General Milroy but caused me to be nervous.

True to form and heedless of the oppressive heat, Milroy rushed us along. He rode in the front and often came back along the lines. "Hurry along boys. Soon we will be the first to meet and smite the enemy! Glory and honor await us at the front!"

Even though many dropped out from heat exhaustion and sunstroke, the Milroy brigade reached Front Royal. We camped near a house where it was rumored the famous female Confederate spy Belle Boyd was residing after her parole from Federal authorities. She supposedly seduced many a Union general and extracted information using her feminine charms. All of us wanted to get a look at her. None of us got this privilege but reports from those near headquarters said she was nothing special in appearance and looked fatigued and careworn. I doubt if she was there.

After leaving Front Royal on July 7, we reached the Shenandoah River, crossed it using pontoon bridges, and camped at Luray. Luray was a very pretty village almost untouched by the depredations of war. The Union troops there earlier had respected the landowners and their possessions. The fences were still up and lined the farm fields. Miraculously, farmers tilled the fields and tended to crops amidst our army. This peacefulness and orderliness was about to change, as was the orderliness of Milroy's command over his troops.

The next morning, the coils of the blue snake of troops bent back on itself. The head—Milroy's brigade—refused to move. Incredibly, most of Milroy's men, not the 82nd Ohio, refused to move until they were able to draw rations.

Milroy tried to convince them that rations would be brought up with the wagons. This was not believed by the hungry and worn out men who stood by their demands. Exasperated, Milroy told them "to go to the devil and come when they wanted to." He then left with the only regiment that would go with him—us, the 82nd Ohio. With this, the blue snake at last extended. Three days later in Sperryville, Milroy's brigade finally resumed its full composition as the rest of his command came into camp. Such was the state of discipline in our army and the challenge to General Sigel to restore morale in the troops.

That Milroy very much appreciated the 82nd Ohio was shown by his treatment of us later that day as we marched ahead of the men who stayed behind. Upon finding a cherry orchard filled with fruit, he turned us loose to eat our fill. He even joined us in climbing trees to get to the largest cherries. It was a good thing that we were not attacked. We had no pickets out and a band of Rebels could have easily captured the lot of us.

Having eaten our fill, we marched on to Sperryville and then later to Woodville where we arrived on July 9. Here we stayed for a long rest to allow our sick and fatigued soldiers to heal and return to health.

The pretty countryside around Woodville was gently rolling with magnificent views of the mountains and intervening hills and valleys. The unplowed fields were loaded with blackberries and the soldiers named our camp "Camp Dewberry" after this delicious fruit. Many deep discussions occurred between us in this relaxed atmosphere. Some became intense, starting from the humblest of observations.

"Did you know the botanical name for the blackberry is *Rubus canadensis?*" Seth asked as he reclined beneath a large tree eating berries he had gathered and put in his cap.

"No, Seth, that thought never occurred me," I replied licking my fingers which stung from the scratches of the thorny bushes. "I only wish ole Rubus whatever did not have those crazy thorns. I have scratches all over my hands and arms. Why does something so good have to have so many thorns?"

" 'Cause of the fall," interjected Isaiah who was listening to our conversation. He came up and sat down with Seth and me. "When man sinned, God said we would have to work and there would be thorns and such because Adam disobeyed God by eating the apple."

"I never heard such simple-minded foolishness. Haven't you heard of the theory of natural selection by Mr. Charles Darwin? His book was all the rage around the college when I left. Father had gotten his book *Origin of the Species*, one of the first copies out from England."

"What's natural selection?" I asked.

"Well, those blackberry bushes with thorns survived better than those without thorns. The bushes without thorns all died off, they are not around anymore. Those with thorns survived and that's why you are being scratched now. Natural selection, don't you see Hiram?" At this moment, an observation from our farm came into my mind.

"I do remember noticing that the rats in our corn crib and barn were tough and mean after the winter. The tamer and weaker seemed to die off, probably killed by the stronger ones. Sounds like a reasonable theory to me. " Isaiah became incredulous.

"Not to me it doesn't! God made all the plants and critters the way they are on the day of Creation. I don't see this natural selection going on!"

"Isaiah, you wouldn't see the backside of a horse's butt unless it farted in your face! Look around you! Darwin's theory explains everything; you don't have to bring God into it."

Isaiah got up shaking his finger. "Seth, you are on dangerous ground removing God from the world. Why, we're fightin' this war because God wants us to save the Union and put down the Rebellion."

"Well, Stonewall Jackson says the same thing! Who's right, you or him? Natural selection is even operating in these battles we're fightin'." Seth looked around at the masses of blue soldiers. "Those that win and survive are the ones that will be around in the future. If we win, the Union carries on. If Stonewall wins, the Union dies and the Confederacy reigns. That's the way the world works."

"Whoa you two," I said realizing how violent things could become. "Couldn't God use this selection thing in his creatin'?" I put my hand on Isaiah's shoulder. "God can still control things, Isaiah and it may be more complicated than your sayin', Seth."

Isaiah, looking wounded, walked to the other side of the tree. The sun was well below the horizon and men were walking back to their quarters. Guards and pickets were being placed. Soon the drum rolled for tattoo and we went back to our tents where the debate continued into the early hours of the morning, mercifully ceasing when Corporal Armstrong poked his head into the tent and said "pipe down"!

Whether from natural selection, God, or the devil, the famous orders from General Pope came down to us. The first showed up on July 14. The last of his orders was delivered on July 23. His address to the officers and men of our army was pompous in the extreme.

He insulted many of our former commanders by saying that we no longer would look for "strong positions" and protected "bases of supplies". We would attack as he did in the western theatre where they saw "the backs of their enemies". Subdued cheers and mild rounds of applause accompanied these remarks as men and officers tried to digest what the portly and loud general was proclaiming.

His next sequence of orders instructed the armies to "subsist upon the country in which their operations are carried on" and to punish with possible death disloyal citizens harboring bushwhackers and guerillas. Furthermore, all local males refusing to take the oath of allegiance to the Union were to be arrested and removed.

These orders angered the local residents and our enemies. It also released on the land the most brutal, undisciplined elements of the Union army. Sigel's Corps was considered one of the worst in this regard, mainly because of the German troops. In Europe, occupying armies pillaged an area as a natural consequence of war and some of the German troops followed this maxim. The non-German regiments like the 82nd Ohio, who restrained from pillaging, were all painted with the same ill-fated brush. Many of our officers openly criticized this order and the way our men were treating the local citizens.

An encounter we witnessed at a small farm near Woodville illustrated this unrest. Immediately after Pope's orders were posted, some German troops raided the granaries and stole chickens and horses. From the road, we could see the woman of the house and some of her slave servants chasing and screaming after the men. Upon reaching one of them, she exclaimed,

"My husband voted against secession and for the Union for God sakes! Last month a Union deserter shot him and now you are stealing from us? What kind of people are you? My children and I will starve if you take the things we need to farm. Please, I beg of you!"

"Ve do not understand! Ve do not understand!" This was all the reply she got as her house, barn, and outbuildings were picked clean.

One of our officers then rode up to her and offered her a voucher that she could use for reimbursement after the war if she and her family took the oath of allegiance. I saw the woman throw the papers on the ground. She screamed and stamped the ground as she hit the side of the officer's horse with her fists. It was all we could do to keep marching down the road and leave this terrible scene behind.

Forced gatherings of people for administering them the oath of allegiance raised the level of hatred in heretofore tolerant if not peaceful residents. Before Pope's orders, we were able to stop and talk to local citizens, sometimes pleasant conversations even sprang up between soldiers and local women.

On one occasion while we were in Woodville filling our canteens from a watering trough at the town pump, I wandered behind a building and discovered an older woman hiding hams and other supplies in a small hidden cellar. Startled, she quickly turned trying to hide her stash.

"Don't worry ma'am, I won't tell anybody about your cellar." Relief flowed over her face as she shut the brush-covered door to the cellar.

"Thank you soldier. This food is precious to my family." I turned to walk away when she came up to me.

"I can tell a boy with a good heart just by watching how he moves, shows manners, and such."

"I ain't no saint but I do try to remember who I am and I try to not dishonor my family by my actions."

"Family is everything isn't it?" She smiled and then led me behind the store to a bubbling stream of water coming out of a rocky bank. The woman then watched me closely as I filled my canteen, took a drink, and refilled the canteen. After looking around, she approached me, put her hand over her mouth and spoke in a hushed tone.

"Not everybody in the South is a secessionist. My grandfather fought in the Revolutionary War right along with Washington, gave his blood and suffered mightily for the Union. While I have to be careful about showin' it, my people are with the government and not Jeff Davis." After again scanning the surroundings, she asked, "What's your name soldier and where are you from?"

"Hiram Terman, I'm from Mansfield, Ohio just north of Columbus."

"Ohio? Some of my family is up there near Columbus. I am Carlotta Ross Jenkins."

"Carlotta? What an unusual name, sounds Spanish."

"My father wanted a boy named Carl but what he got was me and I got Carlotta!"

A troubled look came on the face of Carlotta as she looked at me. It was if she saw something hidden. Drawing yet closer, she put her hand on my arm and spoke in a more solemn tone.

"Hiram, if you get captured I have a nephew who is a clerk for the Confederates in the prison in Richmond. He puts on a front of being a Yankee hater but he'll do everything he can to help the prisoners. If you get into a scrape, just remember the name Ross, like in Betsy Ross, who made the grand ole flag you boys are fighting to preserve. God bless and protect you, son. I will be praying for you. "

I regrettably had to leave her after this because we were forming to march out of town. After a long look and wave backward at this gracious southern but yet Unionist woman, I joined our column.

This exchange took place before Pope's orders were posted. All such conversations between Union troops and residents withered after Pope's edicts and reports of the legalized raiding would soon inflame the Confederate army heading our way.

The thought of being captured by the Rebel army, while always in my consciousness, seemed remote but the name Ross came to mind many times when viewing the flag. The name Carlotta also stuck for some reason. I did not mention this encounter to Seth or Isaiah.

On July 19 a detachment of cavalry and some infantry regiments were sent out to scout for the Rebel army some miles to the south. It was not long before reports came back. A major movement of enemy troops was heading toward us. In preparation for this, we had a brigade drill followed by another stirring speech from Milroy.

"Men, when you get into battle, go forward, have no fear. To die in the cause of liberty is to be desired. God has a time set for all of us. You will not fall unless it is His will. Be brave my soldiers!"

A division level drill on July 29 and a sham battle directed by General Sigel followed on August 5. Pope himself reviewed our Corps on August 7 and reveled in the cheering of the men. Seth, Isaiah, and I were in Milroy's Brigade next to a stately oak tree as the General looked down on us from a ridge.

All of us sensed that it would not be long before we were to have another battle. Confederate troops were detected crossing the Rapidan River. Where would they strike? Where should we maneuver to meet them? These questions filled the agendas of the generals and the talk around the campfire.

On August 6, soon after ex-President Martin Van Buren died, we could see a long column of Union troops, the flag at half-mast, going by our camp at Woodville. These were the troops of General Nathaniel Banks. Jackson at Winchester routed these same men and you could see a determination in their manner that this time would be different. We watched them pass and wondered when we would move out. Milroy was almost beside himself, pacing like a caged animal. He could smell the coming battle.

On the evening of August 8, General Sigel, after asking Pope repeatedly, finally figured out where he should go, or so he thought. We headed south toward the town of Culpeper. When the orders came, Milroy literally leaped on his horse and led the column south from our peaceful camp at Woodville into the grips of the next engagement. Seth, Isaiah, and I marched in the same rank. Isaiah seemed deep in thought as we marched along, fifes playing, and pots rattling.

"Don't think about the Germans at Cross Keys," quipped a sarcastic Seth to the thoughtful Isaiah as we walked along with the advance guard. "They had to go into the battle first and you know old Milroy, he'll have us right in there."

"Be quiet Seth. I'm ready to do my duty and, if my time comes, to meet my maker. If we have to go in first, so be it!" I was surprised at the intensity of Isaiah's response. Seth did not have his usual ready reply. Isaiah's words wounded his wit.

We marched through the dark countryside and reached the Hazel River north of Culpeper about an hour before midnight. The troops stopped according to the orders of Pope to rest and encamp, with the exception of Milroy. Impatient to not miss the action ahead, he ordered us to keep marching on to Culpeper.

Such was Milroy's insistence that a reluctant Sigel allowed him to keep going which was highly unusual. We did not mind this, however, because night marching, though sultry, was much preferred to the intense sun and heat of the day. My fear was that we would run into the enemy and be forced to fight without any reinforcement.

We marched on through the darkness without event and arrived in Culpeper just as the sun was making its appearance above the horizon, declaring the day of August 9, 1862. After filling our canteens at the town well located near the courthouse in Culpeper, Milroy led us to a wooded area just east of town and told us to get some rest.

Weary, thirsty, and dusty we needed no further encouragement. We dropped beneath the shade of the trees and scornfully watched the sun creep up the blue sky, its morning rays growing intense, promising misery to all who were unfortunate enough to be exposed to the burning rays. The lone peak of Cedar Mountain loomed in the distance. Seth, Isaiah, and I lay on the leaves and closed our eyes, enjoying the creeping stupor of sleep as it claimed our weary bodies.

About mid-morning our sleep was interrupted by the sounds of battle in the distance toward Cedar Mountain. Because of an inability to sleep soundly like the snoring Seth and Isaiah, I was the first to hear the artillery and musketry in the distance.

"Seth, Isaiah! Wake up! There is a battle going on by Cedar Mountain! Hear the cannons?"

"I'll be damned if there ain't," replied Seth raising himself up and peering off into the distance. Any word of marching orders?"

"That's just it. Not a word going around yet." I looked around for some movement among the men, most looked confused and were just peering off in the direction of the booming cannons.

"What's going on?" Isaiah asked stretching himself awake and walking up to Seth and me.

"Oh, nothing but the biggest battle yet," replied Seth sarcastically. "Still ready to be the first to sacrifice yourself for the cause?"

"I'm ready," replied Isaiah confidently as he looked around for his knapsack and rifle. Seth seemed surprised that Isaiah did not come back at him. I tried to calm the now busy Isaiah.

"Relax, Isaiah. Milroy would have us up and out of here if we had orders to move." I sat back down under a tall oak and wondered how long my rest would last. I still ached from the all-night march. I also had a huge blister that was oozing and needed to have its cloth bandage replaced.

Unexplainably, we stayed in the woods all day and observed two more divisions come into Culpeper from Hazel River. We could see them from our woodlot. The bands were playing and troops were cheering. The Germans were especially loud as their bands played native songs and the troops competed with each other for the most demonstrative cheers. The excitement drew us to the cheering troops. At 5 p.m., orders from Pope came down to move to the front and the cheers became even louder.

With the cannons booming in the distance and cheering behind us, Milroy's brigade led the way at the front of the column. The late afternoon August sun beat down on us as we marched toward the ever-louder battle at our front. Along the way, some of the locals taunted us with comments like "Ole Jackson will bury you boys!" "You scum will now pay for what you've done to us!" "The soil of Virginia will drink your blood!"

It was especially heartrending to see children shaking their fists at us. What kind of hatred had we engendered for generations to come? Occasionally we saw some Negroes gently waving, holding their hands low, and concealing their farewells from their masters.

It was dusk by the time we reached the scene of action. The night sky revealed a vista I will never forget. Brilliant flashes of light trailed across the sky in the distance. At intervals along the way, campfires burned and framed signal officers transmitting messages. Long lines of soldiers on the hillsides were revealed by flashes of light from volleys from hundreds of muskets and rifles. Missiles from cannons lit up the sky. It looked like a huge Fourth of July fireworks display except hot ripping fragments of metal accompanied each beautiful exhibit of lights.

As we approached the front, hundreds of blue soldiers could be seen making their way toward us. Were they retreating? Was the battle lost? What were we heading into?

As we neared the battlefield, we encountered wounded soldiers and stragglers along with ambulances full of wounded, moaning with every bump in the road. Stories of what was going on emerged from the soldiers who called to us as we marched along.

Evidently, General Banks had arrived with a small force and charged a larger number of Confederates. Initially the Union troops had broken through the Confederate line of battle but then Stonewall Jackson himself came up and rallied the Rebs who then got reinforced and turned the tide of battle, chasing these poor fellows about two miles back toward us along the Culpeper Road.

"Our regiment was cut to pieces," yelled one fellow with a bandage around his head.

"It's a meat grinder up there boys!" yelled another as he ran toward the rear.

"We first got a real twist on 'em but then fifty thousand more Johnnies came at us!" chimed another as he hurriedly limped along.

In contrast, a private came by holding up a hand with three fingers shot off. "I could keep shootin' with two gone but not three. Can't somebody load my gun for me? I'll get back into it if somebody can just load my gun!" A correspondent from *Harper's Weekly* helped him load his gun and he got into line with us. Amazing!

Next, a group of four men came along with a captain. "This is all that is left of my company, just four of us! We got into a real hell spot I tell you. Oh, and I don't know what happened to the General," exclaimed the officer.

"General Banks is wounded, perhaps killed," said another soldier helping a limping man along. We later learned that Banks was not injured.

"My God, what are we walking into?" Seth exclaimed as we began to encounter smoke and could see shells exploding to the front, still lighting up the darkening sky.

Bullets whizzed all around us but most were spent. The thin whirling sound of the Minnie balls was different from the humming sounds of musket balls. The whirs and wangs made for a deadly chorus against the booming of the cannons whose missiles were now directly over our heads, the fragments falling all around us.

"My God is with me, Seth," replied Isaiah as he sternly looked forward.

"Well, He had better be!" Seth retorted as he crouched his head lower. "That battery up there, it's going to tear us apart unless we can knock it out!"

The shells exploded all along the road, mostly in front of us, each projectile flashing a brilliant orange. As the shelling grew more intense, the line of retreating troops broke into a panic. Mayhem ensued. Wagons left the road and went in all directions, some overturning. Horses broke loose and galloped wildly through the lines of the wounded, teamsters ran after them, swearing and yelling. The road became jammed with a mass of humanity and materials. Groups of retreating soldiers now began to run, some dropping wounded comrades as their panic spread.

Sigel and Milroy rode up in this pandemonium and issued orders to set up cannons to fire on the battery causing so much panic. At that same time, Milroy ordered us to deploy to the front. We had to go right through the wild running men going the other direction. Soon our guns off to the left began firing and the shelling from the other side diminished.

"Stop those men and turn them around!" An officer yelled riding his horse from the battle. Our men started blocking the fleeing soldiers with our rifles. The yelling and swearing became prodigious. I stuck my rifle out to stop a fleeing soldier.

"Get the hell out of my way! I'm not dying for the damned generals who sent us into this meat grinder!" He ran against my rifle butt and stopped, looked into my face, almost foaming around the mouth. He flinched with every shot from our cannons that were firing in rapid order into the woods in the distance.

"Hey soldier, we're going up there in force now and we could sure use your help." He looked at me, shuddered, and eventually his demeanor changed.

"Well, I was a firing away and suddenly all around me was Rebs and everybody else was running. A fella can't hold 'em off by himself. I'm no coward but I can't do it by myself! All right, all right, I reckon I can pick up a gun somewhere, I still got cartridges."

With this, I left him and followed my company forward, lying down on the ground in the forming line of battle. The artillery continued firing round after round into the Rebel line.

At this time, General Pope joined Sigel and gave orders to stop our batteries from firing, claiming we were hitting our own men still forward in the woods. Soon the missiles from our side stopped. Sigel did not agree with this and told Milroy to be on his guard. A general quietness then descended on the battlefield as we looked into the darkness at the woods in the distance.

I asked Seth who was to my left, "Getting pretty dark, think they still want to fight?"

"I think they intend to drive us from the field so, yeah, they will be coming shortly. Got a full charge in that Enfield?"

"Ready as I will ever be. Remember to aim low, Isaiah."

Isaiah yelled. "They're coming with cavalry!"

Colonel Cantwell shouted coolly as he moved along the line. "Pour it into them boys, don't let them horses get too close!"

I picked out a horse in the dim night about one hundred yards distant and fired at the legs. I heard a pitiful shriek. I hated to shoot a horse as much as a human but the battle subsumed all such thoughts. I turned and reloaded. By the time I was ready to fire again, the charging cavalry had turned back. Many in our regiment were still firing and the sound reverberated along the open fields. I later learned that Generals Pope and Sigel were nearly captured by the Rebel cavalry but were saved by the volleys of the infantry.

I turned to our rear and could hear columns of men coming up behind us. Soon we were at full force in front of the Rebels and the noise of battle suddenly fell quiet. The night sky was now radiant with the piercing light of stars. Amazingly, whippoorwills soon began singing their constant warbles across the fields, mingling with the cries of the wounded. We remained in line of battle and slept with our arms, awaiting the oncoming fight in the morning, Sunday, August 10. Seth, looking out into the darkness in front of us, began talking.

"I heard Stonewall does not like to fight on Sunday. I hope to hell its true." He looked to Isaiah for a response but none was forthcoming.

With the rising sun, the Rebel cavalry again mounted a charge. Seth shook his head and looked at Isaiah and me.

"Well so much for keeping the Sabbath holy," he said as he licked his finger and shined up his rifle sight. He did not have to fire a shot. The enemy immediately retreated when they saw the masses of blue-clad troops.

Milroy then jumped up and began firing his pistol at the retreating Rebel cavalry, yelling, moving after them. He then turned to us and said, "Charge the Rebels, men! Up soldiers, let's give them a taste of Union lead!"

"Here we go," said Seth seemingly resigning his fate to our wild-eyed leader. We rose to our feet and started across the field, following Colonel Cantwell who looked valiant on his horse. Milroy, also mounted, led the way, sword drawn. Any minute I expected to see a line of Rebel soldiers rise, the smoke of their muskets belch, and hot bullets pierce my chest. I felt utterly exposed and wondered what would become of my body.

"Lord forgive me. I am ready to meet you anytime," I prayed as I watched the clumps of brush and trees growing ever close to us.

"Forward men, double quick!" Cantwell shouted as we stormed into the mysteriously silent woods.

We found the woods empty of enemy soldiers. I felt faint and almost fell with the dizziness of relief. Jackson had retreated to the slopes of Cedar Mountain off to our left.

Some skirmishing broke out to our far left but Pope, seeing the strong defensive position that Jackson had on the elevated slopes, called off the advance.

An afternoon thunderstorm burst as we began to pick up the wounded in the area of the battlefield we controlled. We could hear a few cries of the wounded up closer to the Confederate lines but were not able to get to them. The exposure to the sun and excessive heat had finished off many a wounded man but some still survived being now drenched by the rain.

Mercifully, a flag of truce was arranged the next day, August 11, for burying the dead and caring for the wounded. Many had been exposed to the weather on the disputed ground ahead of us for over forty-eight hours. We were assigned to fatigue parties to do this task. Many dead were already black and bloated from exposure. The shells had blown others apart but many wounded still lived!

One private called to us and pointed to his leg. "You've got to get the surgeon to take off this leg, its already turning purple! I will die in a matter of hours, please hurry!" We loaded him into an ambulance with others in his same condition. I wondered how many would die as the poison of gangrene crept through their bodies.

I came across another soldier who had crawled into a corn shock to escape the sun. He had been shot five times but still lived! We pulled him out of the shock and gradually gave him some water that he fanatically tried to gulp. He had wounds in the head, neck, arm, side, and leg. His will to live was amazing to us all.

While we buried the dead and removed the wounded, the Confederates picked up rifles and stacked them for removal. One of our officers protested this stealing of our arms but the collecting persisted, the Rebels claimed that the guns were the spoils of victory. This irked us to no limit but we could do nothing in these circumstances. Occasionally we entered into a conversation with the enemy soldiers.

"Where you from, Yank?"

"From Ohio, you?"

"Georgia, I'm with the 12th Georgia Infantry."

"Do you know Sam Parker? Did he survive McDowell?"

"I don't reckon I know."

"Tell him Hiram Terman of the 82nd Ohio sends his compliments!"

As quick as these conversations started, they ended with orders and reprimands from the officers.

Seth, Isaiah, and I returned to picking up bodies and hauling them to open pits.

"Well, Isaiah, Providence sure protected this fellow today," quipped Seth as he and Isaiah carried a corpse without a head to the burial pit.

"It was his time to go and not yours Seth," retorted Isaiah. You could tell Isaiah and Seth were headed for a battle themselves.

"His time to go? Why don't you just admit it. A fellow has to watch out for himself. This poor bloke got in with one of those glory hound generals, attack and the devil take all! Mark my words, Hiram, Milroy will do the same thing to us! "

"Hey, leave me out of this fight," I scolded as I looked into the face of another dead soldier, an officer, his features swollen and black. He had his socks and shoes removed by the Rebs but he somehow retained a daguerreotype of a woman, maybe his wife, in his hand. There was no name on the picture or anywhere else on his person. How would this woman know his fate? I placed the picture into his shirt and dragged him to the burial pit. From that time on, I had identification on me at all times.

Before the truce expired, more of our troops began coming up. Jackson noticed this and decided to withdraw during the night, leaving his campfires burning on the slope of the mountain. As the clear night sky enveloped us, we watched the fires in the distance on the slope of Cedar Mountain, again wondering if a full-fledged battle was coming or if the wooded slopes would be empty in the morning.

"Hiram, do those fires seem to flicker to you or are they constant in their glow?"

"I can't see any flickering, seem pretty constant to me," I replied.

"Good, I think the fighting is over for this battle." Seth exhaled as if he had a deep relief come over him.

" I tell ya, Hiram, I am worried about what's coming with Milroy. We're going to be the first ones into the fire next time and we will be getting mowed down like those poor bastards we buried today."

"I felt that way yesterday when we charged the woods," I said reflectively. "Do you and Isaiah have identification on you? I would hate to be one of the dead just thrown in a pit and forgotten, an unknown."

"Nobody is unknown to God, Hiram," interjected Isaiah who was lying on his back, his head on his knapsack. "Our names are written in the Lamb's Book of Life which is most important." Isaiah then took out his Testament and started to read by the light of the fire. *"Yea, though I walk through the valley of the shadow of death, I will fear no evil."*

Seth muttered something unintelligible as he surveyed the distant campfires and unpacked his blanket and oilcloth. Following Seth's example, I reached for my oilcloth, laid it and my blanket on the ground. The smoke and smells of the battle cloaked each of us as we lay back to sleep, staring at the sky, enveloped by the thoughts of the day. As the night progressed, the campfires in the distance faded like so many extinguished candles as Stonewall moved his weary troops across the Rapidan River.

The next day we probed the battlefield and, sure enough, the Rebels had departed leaving us the ground so fiercely fought over. We pushed south to near the banks of the Rapidan River, halted, and encamped awaiting further orders from Pope.

As always, food was in short supply. Various groups of soldiers came in with chickens, pigs, and whatever else could be scavenged from the countryside. This left a bad taste in my mouth as we caused much anger among the farmers and local citizens. Why can't our own supplies be brought up? Do we lack the basic organization necessary to feed ourselves?

I decided to go hunting for a deer down by the river. I scared up a big buck and dropped it on the run at about one hundred yards. This both amazed and delighted my friends who shared in the venison with much gusto. Hungry men came to our fire in droves and the venison was soon gone.

Straggling and desertion increased, reflecting the hunger, low morale, and lack of discipline growing in our ranks after the beating we took at Cedar Mountain. In moments of weakness, I even entertained thoughts of just leaving and making my way back to Ohio.

However, deserters were now being shot. Court martial committees, consisting of only a few officers who happened to be around when a deserter was apprehended, were generally harsh and unforgiving. A quick decision was made and the poor soul could be up before a firing squad. Officers who wanted out, however, were usually let off, being able to just resign and leave. This did little to restore our respect for our leaders.

Finally, orders came down for us to move back across the Cedar Mountain battleground in another deployment. We heard about a raid across the Rapidan that captured a Rebel cavalryman with some of General Lee's orders. Jeb Stuart, a famous Rebel cavalryman, narrowly escaped capture in the same raid.

Knowing Lee's intentions, Pope decided our location between the Rapidan and Rappahannock Rivers was a poor position for defending ourselves. Consequently, Pope's army rapidly moved north of the Rappahannock. This time we in Milroy's brigade were the rear guard, following the wagons.

On August 17, this movement of men and materials bogged down. We watched the mass of humanity struggle to get going all day. Time after time, we broke camp, marched up to the last wagon, and went nowhere.

The long columns were stalled by a stuck wagon here and a stubborn mule there, creating a sluggish caravan that refused to move. Word filtered down that General Pope was in Culpeper swearing like a lunatic trying to get the trains moving. General McDowell himself went to the various choke points and with a long whip, encouraged both mules and teamsters to "move it along"!

General Milroy was beside himself with the slowness of things, again anxious to hit the glory road. Finally, by the next morning, the column got into motion and we broke camp for the final time. The hot sun bore down on us as we marched to the north, our noses covered with handkerchiefs to filter the clouds of dust.

Around noon on August 19, we went by the Cedar Mountain battleground. Fresh graves littered the landscape. As we looked at the mounds of soil, we could see in our minds the faces of friends known recently but now gone forever. A quiet hush surrounded the scene; only the sound of the rhythmic marching of feet interrupted the silence. The ground still smelled of death and vultures could be seen circling the sky.

This was the second time I had crossed the field of a battle in which I had participated, the first being Cross Keys. As we left the scene, I curiously wondered if there were enemy soldiers that were hit by my bullets in those mounds of soil. I know one of those horses swelling out there was shot by my Enfield.

At sundown, we went through the town of Culpeper and were again subject to the jeering of the citizens. News of the battle had filtered back to the town.

"Well boys, how did it go with ole Jack? Aren't as many of you now as before, are they?"

Several soldiers lost their temper and broke ranks to chase some tormenters but were quickly reprimanded and put back in column by the corporals and sergeants. I was too tired to even look at our tormentors. We went through Culpeper and marched far into the night, finally encamping along the road in a field when we could stand no more marching. All three of us immediately removed our shoes and began treating blisters, wiping blood and ooze, applying a poultice of moss recommended by my great grandmother for healing wounds.

On August 20, the trek began anew as the summer sun crept up the skyline preparing to scorch the long line of blue heading toward Warrenton and Sulphur Springs. That evening, we crossed the Rappahannock River on a bridge near Sulphur Springs where the river comes down from its source in the Blue Ridge Mountains. We encamped on the other side of the river.

How we wished we could go to the spa at Sulphur Springs and relax in the waters! However, we could almost feel the jaws of the enemy who we knew were moving somewhere behind us. On the morning of August 21, we moved south toward Rappahannock Station until we joined other troops moving from the east that had crossed the day before at Kelly's Ford.

This backtracking movement was confusing until we realized that we were trying to increase our numbers for a fight that our officers warned was imminent. We rested near General Pope's headquarters until two in the afternoon. Our cavalry circled around us, constantly moving like guard wolves on the outside of the pack. The river was smaller here, being no barrier to either army.

Soon, the armies began to get at each other. Skirmishing and artillery duels broke out as we marched toward the river. We stopped by the edge of a wood and waited for orders to advance that did not come. Milroy, frustrated, then withdrew us back away from the woods where we encamped. We were full of trepidation but with empty stomachs.

Where were the troops from McClellan's army in the east that were supposed to leave the Peninsula and join us to fight the growing mass of Rebels? We could tell that Rebel armies had grown in numbers by the long rows of troops we observed across the river. It was obvious that they wanted to attack us in force but from where? Was it going to be at Warrenton?

Long lines of butternut-clad soldiers were moving to our north, which confused us. Where were they headed? Our generals seemed baffled. I doubted if the officers knew anymore than we did. They had their hands full just trying to keep our lines together, gathering up stragglers who began wandering into the countryside in search of food.

The pangs of hunger increased as rations became scant and infrequent. Our supply trains and quartermasters could not keep up with our movements. In addition, the skirmishing and artillery shelling across the river became more numerous, preventing us from ever relaxing. We were constantly taking shelter behind our artillery batteries as they fired at the hills on the other side of the river, trying to stop the cannons of the enemy.

On August 22, we met the enemy head-on near Freeman's Ford where the Confederates had finally crossed the river and engaged some of our infantry and cavalry. As soon as Milroy heard this, he rode ahead to a nearby hilltop where Rebel cannons began firing at him. He immediately brought up his own guns and engaged in an artillery duel until about three that afternoon. Meanwhile, we sheltered ourselves in woods behind our cannons. I will never forget one incident that occurred as the shells from the Rebel cannons fell around us.

"Hurry, men, form up in this low area behind the battery. Keep low. One place is good as another. Our guns will silence the Rebs soon." With this, Colonel Cantwell quickly crouched down at the foot of the mound in front of us. Suddenly a shell came screeching through the trees and struck a soldier on the right. The missile severed his head which then landed in front of us, the eyes, mouth, and face still intact! The body shuddered and twitched about twenty yards away. The man's head lay still, gazing at the stunned soldiers. "Good Gawd!" Seth shouted as he beheld the ghastly scene. Isaiah and I looked on stunned, developing a bad case of shell fever.

Soon, however, such carnage failed to stir us as such incidents became more commonplace. A kind of numbness takes hold and protects a soldier from emotional collapse in scenes like this one. I had felt its presence growing in me through the battles I had been in so far. If this lack of sensation did not come to the soldier, he would break from shear nervous exhaustion. Indeed, many did in the constant shelling that marked our trek along the Rappahannock.

Before long, our guns chased the Rebel battery from its perch on the far hill. The shelling stopped for the time being, and we formed up to march again. We observed some of the spent shells stuck in a bank of earth. They looked like sections of iron rails. Were the Rebs this hard up for shells? Later we learned that they were using European style shells that were long and rifled for greater accuracy. Friends of the separated man were reuniting his body and covering it with a blanket as we left.

The river was about two hundred yards wide here and about waist deep. A heavy rain commenced and the river began to rise. Nevertheless, some of our troops under General Henry Bohlen went across the river and attacked the marching line of Confederates. Milroy sent some of his cavalry and infantry across also. Like a swarm of bees, the enemy gathered and eventually chased the thin lines of Union troops back across the river, killing many in the water. General Bohlen was shot off his horse and killed on the Rebel side of the river.

Immediately we of Milroy's brigade began providing covering fire from the woods on our side of the river for the retreating troops. The rain was coming down heavily now. I got behind a tree and spied a man on the other side taking aim at our troops who were desperately trying to cross the stream back to our side.

I leveled my rifle. The rain made it difficult to see. The Enfield fired; the smoke quickly disappeared squelched by the falling rain. The enemy soldier in my sights fell back, threw up his rifle, and rolled down the far bank into the river. He did not move. As far as I know, this was the first man I had killed. Who was he? Probably a common man just like me.

I reloaded and looked for another target. A bullet then hit the tree I was standing behind and splinters of bark fell down on my head, the rain-washing them off. The smoke of the battle settled down on the stream making it difficult to see targets distinctly. I pulled the trigger again but my gun did not fire. The powder was wet and I would have to use a screw tool to pull out the wet charge.

After the short affair was over, a truce was declared and Bohlen's body was recovered along with other soldiers who were floating dead in the river. Some of the dead had no wounds, apparently having drowned. The rain continued heavy throughout the night raising the river even more.

The deluge did not stop Jeb Stuart and his Rebel cavalry of fifteen hundred horsemen from raiding Pope's headquarters at Catlett's station, far up the road toward Washington D. C. and in our rear. We later learned that McClellan's army moving from the east was to protect our supply lines from Washington but this was not done. Stuart easily routed the surprised small Union force guarding the depot and helped himself to the supplies, even taking some of Pope's uniforms which Stuart offered to trade for his own hat captured earlier in the Union cavalry's raid across the Rapidan.

As difficult as it was in the rain, I was able to get some sleep beneath my oilcloth next to a board fence amidst some bushes. The little niche provided good cover against the wind and driving rain. The next day, August 23, we marched toward Sulphur Springs with orders from Pope to destroy the Waterloo Bridge, a major crossing point on the Rappahannock. Pope wanted to prevent the enemy from coming across again. On our way, we again got into it with the Rebs.

First, we met them at Great Run Creek and again entered into an artillery and shooting duel. The Rebels were in a line of trees on one side and we were in woods on the other side. We fired back and forth at each other until darkness took our targets away. I had no clear shots and generally shot my rifle in the direction of smoke puffs. The fight died out and we encamped in the woods. During the night, the enemy retreated, leaving a half-burned bridge behind so we could not follow them.

The next morning, August 24, our engineers quickly repaired the bridge. Milroy, wanting a fight, led us across the river again. He saw some Rebel cannons without supporting infantry and thought he could take the guns.

As soon as he and some cavalry and infantry got close to the cannons, the enemy opened up on him, driving him back across the river. Just as we were forming up to make another charge for the bridge, a courier rode up and delivered orders from Sigel to "leave the bridge alone" and push toward Waterloo Bridge as Pope had instructed. Milroy angrily stuffed the orders into his pocket, shook his fist at the enemy, and turned us back toward the road to the Waterloo Bridge. We arrived at this bridge about five that evening.

Confederate sharpshooters were up in the hills on the other side of the river shooting at any soldiers approaching the bridge. To stop this, Milroy immediately placed some cannons on a nearby ridge. When artillery firing commenced, some groups of our soldiers tried to move forward to burn the bridge but could not because of the heavy return fire.

The back and forth shooting continued well into the night. I rested behind a good-sized rock flanked by two trees. Bullets ricocheted off the rock and kept me awake all night.

In the morning, the artillery dueling resumed at full pace, the shells falling among the trees but not dislodging the Rebels defending the bridge. About three in the afternoon, a frustrated Milroy rode up to Colonel Cantwell of the 82nd Ohio and addressed our balding leader.

"Colonel, could we have the honor of hearing from the 82nd Ohio concerning this blasted bridge? I hear that you have many excellent riflemen in your regiment, used to shooting deer on the run. If well placed, could they dispose of those gray fellows over in those trees that are now vexing us?" Cantwell stepped forward proudly.

"Not only will we shoot those fellows over there, but we will rush groups ahead and burn the bridge. Just leave it to the 82nd Ohio sir! The Rebs won't be using that bridge to get at us!"

"Very well, Colonel, you can commence." Milroy rode off to place more artillery units to support the action. Cantwell proceeded to go along the lines of the 82nd selecting some to be sharpshooters and others to charge and fire the bridge. Group after group in front of me began to run off to their assignments. Cantwell finally came to Company F and his glance caught mine.

"Think you can shoot under fire now Private, when it counts for more than deer meat?"

"Yes sir!" I responded wondering how in the world he heard about the deer.

"Conceal yourself on that ridge over there and provide covering fire for the men firing the bridge."

With an inward sigh of relief, I followed my squad and Corporal Armstrong to a line of trees. I did not want to be in the group charging the bridge. I crawled along the ground and looked for where I could see the puffs of smoke coming out of the trees on the other side of the river. Finding a place behind a large root, I poured a charge of powder into my Enfield and took aim at a blurry form in some bushes about midway up the far bank.

I performed some mental calculations. Aim about three degrees up for distance and left a bit to account for wind. I fired and then closely watched the bushes on the other side. Nothing moved. I watched for some more smoke puffs at other places. There were numerous eruptions of enemy fire but none from the bush in the middle of the bank. Had I killed another man?

Occasionally a bullet from them would whiz by my head or strike the root in front of me. It was all I could do to raise my head to look for another target. I was in danger but not like those soldiers below me on the riverbank trying to charge and burn the bridge. Man after man was shot down trying to bring up combustible material to start the bridge on fire. Eventually a few got through the gauntlet and were able to set it aflame. I only hoped that I helped those brave men who were the real heroes of Waterloo Bridge.

As the bridge burst into flames and the area filled with black smoke, a huge cheer arose from our boys. The structure burned all afternoon and into the night. The huge fire continued to light the growing darkness as we left and returned to the road to Warrenton.

Would the enemy just move up the river and attack us again? We constantly scanned the far bank for likely places but had no engagements. Our columns arrived near Warrenton just as the sun was rising the next morning, August 25. There we encamped along the turnpike and waited for further orders.

As always, we were hungry and exhausted from fighting and marching, all the while waiting for that one shell with our name on it to find us and blow our bodies asunder. I felt the urgency to write another letter home. I had received several letters since my last one but the constant marching, fighting, taking cover from shells, and searching for food kept us so busy that I could not find the energy to write. Now finally, the pace slackened and I was able to find some paper and pen and write down my thoughts, maybe my last words to my family back in Ohio.

Northern Virginia
August 26, 1862
Dear Father,

I have a rare break in our marching and fighting. We are camped near Warrenton after an almost continuous shelling duel with the Rebels as we both made our way up the Rappahannock River. From your last letter, I know you are concerned about my safety. I am still alive but quite drawn out and exhausted. We have not been fed too well by our own supply wagons that constantly fall behind us and we have had to forage off the countryside to keep alive. If it were not for the lessons taught me by great grandmother, I might have starved by now.

Even so, I have come to appreciate how strong one can be if pressed by hard circumstances. Since my last letter, we fought battles at Cross Keys and Cedar Mountain and have been in constant skirmishes and artillery duels along the Rappahannock River. I have many times escaped the hot metal and explosions only by being in the right place. Many of my friends have not been so lucky. I feel that we are going to have a major battle soon as both armies are gathering in great numbers and we soon must face each other. I do not know when or where but feel I must write lest I perish in this coming battle without revealing my thoughts. I am not afraid to die. I

have seen my own death many times and the prospect does not cause me to be as afraid as it used to before I experienced battle first hand. Death is after all just death. As General Milroy keeps telling us, we all are going to die sometime. Will it be an honorable death that counts for something? I feel strongly about saving the Union and setting the slaves free but the killing and fighting bothers me. Is this really what we are supposed to be doing? I do not see how I can avoid doing my duty. Pray that God will be with me in the days ahead. Give my love to all.
Your son,
Hiram

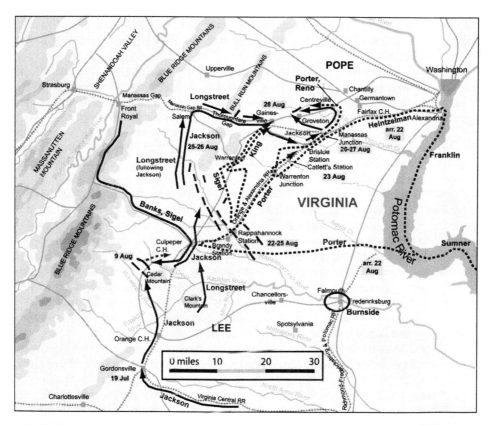

Movements leading to Second Bull Run and author at the Waterloo Bridge *(map by Hal Jespersen, www.posix.com/CW)*. Hiram was in Sigel's command.

CHAPTER 7
THE MISERY OF SECOND BULL RUN

After mending body and soul at our camp about a mile east of Warrenton, we were ordered to march to where our generals thought we might find the army of Stonewall Jackson. First, rumor had it that Stonewall was near Gainesville and then word came that he was at Manassas Junction. In truth, nobody knew and our armies probed the area like hunting dogs looking for a very elusive and sly raccoon.

We marched one way and then countermarched back. Orders from General Pope to General Sigel seemed to change with the hour. Seth, who had his ways of finding out such things, said Pope, was convinced that the Rebels were retreating to the Shenandoah Valley.

We all knew that Pope's plan was to corner the Confederates and attack with superior numbers. He was afraid of Stonewall Jackson and for good reason. We knew first hand that the crafty Southern general was not only cunning but also vicious. No general in his right mind should face Stonewall without being totally prepared.

Many of our officers speculated openly that Jackson was not going anywhere but was in truth waiting to be reinforced by none other than General Robert E. Lee and his trusted old warrior, General James Longstreet. If this was the case, the coming battle would be cruel indeed.

While the 82nd Ohio awaited orders, the late morning sun reached its zenith and revealed a vast army that spread like a living blue blanket over the rolling and wooded hills of northern Virginia. Seth, after leaving us for a while, approached Isaiah and me as we were packing cartridge belts for the coming confrontation.

"Thanks for packing my ammunition. I just saw the generals up ahead and Sigel seemed to be nervous. He was on his horse pointing his finger and yelling at Milroy to follow his orders, not go off on his own. I guess Pope is really on Sigel's back and Sigel passes it on to ole Milroy. I don't think any of them cares much for the others."

Isaiah looked up and commented. "I don't like Pope. I've never heard anybody swear at us like he did there in Culpeper. No call for that at all, I say."

I tried to support Isaiah by adding my observations on our beloved generals. "McDowell can lose his temper too. Did you see him whip those mules at the crossing in Culpeper?"

"Well, I will be damned! You boys getting your prissy little ears lowered, are you?" Seth boasted relishing his worldliness. Isaiah, looking frustrated, started to speak but stopped. He really seemed to be in pain. This exchange revealed a fundamental difference in worldviews among friends close on the battlefield but distant in the world of the mind and spirit.

Trying to relieve the tension, I brought up the historical aspects of the hour. "Believe you me, boys, something big is brewing. Have you ever seen anything like all this? How does it feel to be making history?" Seth, still tense, replied.

"You can just feel it. All these men, Stonewall Jackson, Lee, and Longstreet." Seth looked out into the distance. "McDowell, Cross Keys, and our dance along the Rappahannock with the Rebels were just little skirmishes compared to what's coming. Mark my words, Hiram, you ain't seen nothing yet." Seth then inspected a long line of troops passing by us. "Yes sir, everybody's coming to this party."

Somewhat irked by Seth's comments, I commented on my feelings about our previous battles. "Cross Keys and Cedar Mountain, even McDowell, were more than skirmishes to me. I've never been in crowds like that in my life. Thousands of soldiers. You move to this place and that place never knowing what happened until the whole business is over and then you find out that you got whipped. It's nothing like I expected."

Seth took a minute to consider the analogy. "Yeah, and who knows when you will get squashed like a bug? All those bullets, exploding shells and canister—God! What really gets me mad is lining up and walking into a line of muskets. The poor bastards who go in first really get crapped on and I know Milroy will lead us there, just wait and see."

Isaiah, still quiet, hesitated but eventually spoke out. "Well, isn't that why we are soldiers? That's what we do. We follow orders and offer our lives for the cause. It's an honor to be the first in—as Pope says—honor and glory are in the attack."

"That's just bull, Isaiah, its one thing to follow a general who knows something but these jackasses don't know nothing. There ain't no honor in dying for an idiot."

"Ah, come on Seth, give our leaders a chance."

I rolled my eyes. The discussion flamed out of control again. Isaiah and Seth were about to push the argument further when drums called us into formation for another march, this time toward Gainesville.

As we got near the river (Broad Run) at Buckland Mills, we surprised a detachment of Confederates guarding a bridge. Soldiers to our front fired at the Rebels who formed a line of battle as we prepared to advance. The enemy retreated when our cannons were brought up and our front lines charged. Soon, the all clear sounded and we marched across the bridge toward Gainesville.

We arrived at Gainesville about mid-evening on August 27 and surprised some of Jackson's stragglers, taking about one hundred and fifty prisoners. They were a haggard looking bunch and had been marched hard. Most had rags wrapped around their worn out shoes.

Where had they come from and where were they going? Had Jackson got ahead of us somewhere? We encamped off the Warrenton turnpike near Gainesville, again sleeping under arms, ready to spring into action.

The answer to these questions came to us the next day, August 28. Pope now ordered us to Manassas Junction, a Union supply depot that was intended to provide us with our next set of rations. However, something had happened to the lightly guarded depot. Huge billows of smoke were rising in the distance. Some of our teamsters had just come from the burning depot. One of these men was off to the side of the road telling a small group about what he saw.

The teamster had climbed down from his wagon and was waving his hands and swinging his hat around like a flag. As we drew near, I could hear him speaking.

"Lordy, I have never seen such a sight." He drew his arm across his mouth and paused, searching for the words.

"Locomotives were derailed and burning, shot with cannon shells. Boxcars were strung out over a mile long, loaded with food, munitions, and everything from oysters to nuts was burning." He waved his hat in a broad circle.

"In every direction boxes, barrels, cans, hard bread, sabers, muskets, blankets, tents, and ammunition was scattered over the ground. Great piles of bacon and cured beef were burning and Jackson's Rebs had crapped all over any edible food. My Gawd, what a mess!"

He now paused and looked at the lean, wide-eyed troops.

"The sorry part is that there ain't enough supplies there now to feed a church mouse."

A big groan went up and swearing men stamped their feet and walked in small circles, pounding their fists into their hands. The man continued his grizzly tale as I walked on dejected. What a waste!

We soon realized that Pope had it wrong again and Jackson was not around Manassas Junction but had moved on to near the old Bull Run battlefield. Siegel now turned north and Milroy's brigade was to lead the way. So, we marched away from Manassas Junction ahead of the other troops toward New Market.

Reports of the enemy being here, there, and everywhere passed down our lines. All these stories did was to make us nervous. We expected to bump into the Rebs around every bend as we marched through the countryside. That was what happened a mile outside of Manassas.

In the twilight, we observed some Rebel cavalry in the woods. Milroy ordered an attack on the shadowy forms. Forming a line of battle, we crept forward while our cannons behind us threw shells into the woods. We were in the lead group. A curling feeling crept up my spine. Boom! Boom! Boom! The Reb cavalry opened up just as we entered the woods. We dropped to the ground and the bullets whizzed by us. We then fired a volley. Soon other troops were brought up and this increase in numbers plus the growing darkness caused the Rebels to fall back. Milroy, ever looking for battle, rode back and forth searching the front of the woods like a hound dog for any signs of the enemy who by this time had vanished into the distance.

Sounds of a bigger battle now came to us from the west. Milroy, not wanting to miss out, took some scouting companies and moved towards the battle leaving most of us behind. After he left we heard distant high-pitched yelling that indicated somebody, most likely the enemy, was charging. "That's the Rebel yell," said a man behind us. "Sure gives me the heeby jeebies," said his friend. Excited and at attention, we waited further orders.

However, no order to advance came and we eventually set up camp. Later in the evening, Milroy returned. Jackson, hidden in some woods along the road, attacked some of our trailing regiments starting an intense battle. After fierce fighting, Jackson withdrew and moved on to who knows where.

We moved on to set up camp on the old Bull Run battleground near Buck Hill, looking down on a landmark of the battle, the Stone House. A sense that tomorrow a huge battle would engulf us permeated camp. Milroy, frustrated that he did not get a chance to attack Jackson that night, relished the thought.

The old battleground, so infamous for its Union losses and dishonor the year before, provoked many conversations around our campfire. All around us lay the graves of the soldiers who had died in that conflict. Some graves were shallow and the corpses were emerging. We could see bony arms, feet, and sometimes skulls protruding as if their owners were slowly trying to extricate themselves from the soil, leaving their flesh behind. Adding to this ghoulish scene, the large old Stone House cast a ghostly image against the night sky, like a huge tombstone. An eerie uneasiness, announcing a second macabre act to this dance of death, emanated from this old theatre of war.

As we sat around the fire, a captain from another company in our brigade joined us. An officer stopping at a gathering of enlisted men was unusual to say the least. What was on his mind? He was a tall man with a thin mustache, large eyes, and a slender nose. He had a solemn look about his person. He sat down and began talking as if he knew us intimately.

"Hello boys. Could I join you at your fire? My soul is heavy and I need to talk to someone. You know that tomorrow this great cataclysm will commence. I know that I will not survive it and I cannot bring myself to tell those in my company." He looked out into the darkness. "Yet my insides are twisting and I must tell someone and your campfire beckons." The officer surveyed the profiles of the great house off to our left. "I will die in the first charge..." Isaiah immediately went to his side before he could finish.

"Sir, many men are going to meet their maker in the coming battle. However, nobody knows who will live and who will die, only God."

"Private, I know you mean well but there are some things that just sink into your soul and you know that they are true—this is one of them. I know tomorrow is my time."

Seth got up from his seat on the ground and brazenly approached the officer. "Well, what do you want from us? What do you want us to do, agree with this strange feeling?"

"I'm sorry boys, didn't want to get you upset, just had to tell someone. I had better get back to my company now. Just saying it out loud helps calm my soul." Isaiah again came to his side.

"Sir, are you a Christian, do you know the Lord?"

"Oh for the love of God, Isaiah, let the man go," scolded Seth who then strangely gasped, as if he realized something profound. Ignoring this, Isaiah walked off with the captain into the darkness.

"Hiram, have you ever seen anybody like Isaiah? Everything is solved by God and praying for this and that, makes me sick sometimes. That captain just needs to watch where he goes, take cover, do what we all do to avoid a bullet." Seth then became quiet and looked into the fire, poking it with a stick, watching the sparks ignite and then go dark as they drifted into the night.

After a long silence, Seth continued as if he could not bear to leave his thoughts unfinished. "Tarnation, doesn't he know we all fear getting a bullet or shell?" Seth passed his hand over his head and closed his eyes. "Why did I get into this damn war? Just another pile of crap heaped on me in this life. If there is a God, I sure don't see him."

Bewildered, I was not able to say anything to my troubled comrade. I had my own problems. Every time I dozed off, the face of my father's young second wife briefly appeared. She then drifted through a gate to meet the form of my mother. When my mother turned, she had the face of my young sister, who cried and looked like she was sitting in a cage starving. What was it about this place that evoked such nightmares?

Later, Isaiah came back and we all settled down for the night. For August, the night was cool. The chill seeped into our very souls. Throughout the night, I looked over at my comrades. Both Isaiah and Seth rolled and turned. On their backs, they studied the heavens with eyes that sleep would not close. To avoid dreaming I stayed awake most of the night.

The morning sun rose in the east and threw its rays through the trees, casting shadows over the stirring forms on the ground. Suddenly the cannons of both sides began to boom followed by the beating of drums calling us to attention. The form of General Milroy mounted on his horse appeared before us.

"Get up boys. We're going to go at the enemy now. Get up! We're going to lick them before breakfast. Come on, men. Lick 'em before breakfast."

Turning his new war horse (his previous one was shot at Cross Keys), he rode down the hill and inspected the long line of blue soldiers now forming in front of Matthews Hill along a two-mile stretch. Rising like a Greek god, he stood erect in his saddle and motioned to the 82nd Ohio to step forward. We gathered our rifles and marched up to the right center of this mass of soldiers, in front of the Stone House along the Warrenton Pike.

We were now the closest regiment to the enemy that was hunkered down behind an unfinished railroad embankment not quite visible in the distance. The scene was charged with anticipation.

Milroy panted with eagerness and before the battle line was even complete, he ordered us to advance. Fear welled up in me and my tongue felt enormous, as if it would swell out of my mouth. *Settle down Terman*! I took some deep breaths and moved with the command "Forward March!"

We walked about five hundred yards through a field before we encountered the advance skirmishers of the Confederates who were located in a wood to our front and right.

Milroy was about to order a charge when General Sigel ordered us to halt and wait for the rest of the regiments to catch up. Milroy grimaced and grabbed his saddle horn in frustration. He looked back and forth at our troops and the enemy lines to our front.

The field extended to an old railroad embankment with a gap (afterwards to be known as "the Dump"). Off to the right was the stretch of woods harboring the Confederate skirmishers. A small schoolhouse was on the edge of the woods just across a small road. Behind the old railroad cut were the stalwart troops of Jackson.

Isaiah began to pray. "Dear Jesus, be with Hiram, Seth, and me today. Protect us from the shell, bullet, and sword and give us victory over our enemies." Seth looked at me but did not say a word. He swallowed hard, looked at the distant embankment with fear, and actually trembled. I was shaking too. A quick drink from my canteen seemed to help my tongue deflate.

When the rest of the blue line came up, Milroy and General Schenck rode up to the top of a rise to get a better look at what lay in front of us. When they reached the top, the enemy in the woods fired on the two generals. A shower of bullets whizzed over us as the generals with haste rode their horses back down the hill and to our line.

Colonel Cantwell galloped up to the front of the 82nd Ohio. He raised his sword and looked across the open field to the now visible railroad embankment. He turned toward Milroy and waited. An uneasy silence ensued. Seth leaned toward me.

"Hiram, I told you Milroy would get us into the first charge and damned if he hasn't done it. We're going to charge over that open ground to the railroad cut. The Rebs will blow us apart!" Seth closed his eyes. "Oh, God be with us!" Both Isaiah and I threw a curious glance at Seth.

Milroy's eyes blazed as his sword dropped and he spurred his horse forward, yelling "Charge!". Cantwell yelled "Men of Ohio! Forward!" Musket shots rang out in the distance from the woods to our right. Bullets hummed by us. They were the introduction to the coming fury.

Off to my right in one of the Federal Virginia regiments, a loan officer leading a company of soldiers fell to the ground. What misfortune! The battle was just beginning.

Milroy ordered up his artillery. The caissons rushed into action following a well-practiced and familiar routine. Soon the projectiles flew from the belching cannons and I could feel the ground shake with each firing. The smoke thickened and drifted down the long slope. The shelling stopped the rifle fire coming from the Rebels. Next, our batteries fired on enemy soldiers forming to our front on the edge of the woods. These men also retreated after which we started forward.

The "tramp, tramp" of thousands of feet filled the smoky air. Soon we passed the woods. One of the Rebel batteries fired shells into our lines. A big iron ball bounced along and struck a man on my left removing his shoulders and head. I gasped at the sight! His torso remained standing and gushed blood like a waterfall.

A collective scream arose from the men around me. Another shell exploded overhead. Hot metal fragments pierced the air, sizzling like water striking a hot skillet. Men off to my right fell down and screamed. Others just fell and remained quiet. I jumped into a shallow depression and covered my head with my arms. Seth and Isaiah were beside me. "*Please, God!*"

Two of our cannons came forward, fired, and quieted the Rebel guns. Seth, Isaiah, and I slowly rose. A volley of muskets from the embankment followed, the bullets whizzing by us, striking men, creating a chorus of thumps, thuds, groans, and screams. A small ravine appeared in front of me. I jumped in next to Isaiah and Seth. We looked at each other, our expressions asking. *Are we going to help each other or is it every man for himself?* Isaiah put his hand on my shoulder. "Let's stay together—keep an eye out for one another."

The deluge of lead momentarily stopped. Milroy rushed forward his sword pointed to the woods to our right. Colonel Cantwell followed, beckoning us to follow, waving his sword in semicircles. For a moment, I thought I could see two of him. Shaking my head chased this image from my view.

We immediately ran to a wooded area that was low, marshy, and thickly vegetated. In this wooded entanglement, we suddenly realized that we were directly in front of the railroad cut, a ten-foot tall embankment harboring the enemy.

Moving through the trees, we came to "the Dump", a gap in the bank. Hundreds of enemy troops rose and with a loud yell poured a volley full in our faces. Upon seeing the troops rise, I immediately dropped to the ground and rolled behind a log. Seth and Isaiah crawled over beside me. Bullets thudding into the log and whizzing over us made our spines tingle and our stomachs nauseous. All around us men were dropping.

"Come on boys, charge through the gap! Give them the bayonet!" hollered a man with sergeant's stripes. Yelling wildly, we rose and ran toward the enemy. I could not believe what I was doing! Completely exposing myself, screaming violently, I hit the side of the embankment and plunged into the gap.

An enemy soldier rose in front of me. He was an older man, thin with hollow, sunken eyes and a large mole on his forehead. His rifle discharged right in front of my face, the ball zipped by my temple and the powder burned my ear. I put my bayonet to his chest like I did with the straw bags back at Camp Tod. This bag however, yelled back.

"Oh, for God sakes don't!" His eyes literally begged me to stop. I recoiled, hesitated and said, "Get out of here, Gramps!" The man gazed briefly at me and then melted from my sight, disappearing into the trees to the right. *Some soldier you are Terman!* Isaiah grabbed my arm and pulled me back out of the gap to the slope of the embankment.

"Cantwell is dead. Everybody is going to the rear."

"Where's Seth?" I looked around and I saw him lying on the embankment with his rifle above his head firing down at the Rebs on the other side. Running up to him, I grabbed his leg and pulled. "Come on—we're pulling back!" He looked at me as if to refuse but leaped down when the bugle sounded retreat. Like a receding tide, the blue troops flowed back to the rear.

We passed by the body of Colonel Cantwell. He had been shot off his horse that was faithfully standing nearby, blood running out of its chest and neck.

We stopped over him. "My God!" said Seth. Cantwell's head had a huge hole that exposed his brain. Blood flowed profusely out of his mouth and nose over a neatly separated moustache. Even though any one of the deadly missiles flying by us could have rendered us like him, we paused to realize the moment.

Our beloved and respected leader was gone. In a second's time, I both mourned and reminisced about Cantwell's extraordinary esteem in the 82nd Ohio. Brief as it was, I felt again my personal relationship with him. Even in the din of battle, I felt both a tender moment and the nausea of deep grief.

I then looked up and saw the enemy coming at us. "Here they come! Run! Run!" Rushing over the fields Seth, Isaiah, and I found a small stand of trees where the survivors of our charge were gathering in a line of battle. We flopped to the ground in a small depression. I looked at my friends who were covered in smoke and dirt, eyes wide with fear and anger. It was now about ten in the morning. We had been fighting about four hours.

Seth could hardly talk. "How did we… ever make it… out of that hellhole?" He eventually gathered his breath. "I am beginning to believe you two are right …!"

Just then, a ball struck above his head, splintering a branch and dropping chips on his head. Seth ducked and left his sentence unfinished. Enemy soldiers were now advancing in front of us and we fired a volley into them. A thickly bearded man came into my view. I fired and he doubled over and fell; with the next shot, another, then another. After an hour of this, my gun barrel was too hot to hold. Still they kept charging! *What am I to do?*

Our cannons then fired into the butternut lines and they finally fell back, many of their soldiers blown apart by the canister and grapeshot. A warm stench begotten of blood and torn bowels drifted over the field. As the morning passed to afternoon, the enemy tried to break through twice more but fire from our reinforced positions stopped them. The bloody fields collected more corpses, increasing the foulness of the field.

We had been in the fight since 6:30 a.m. and now it was late afternoon. The screams of the wounded were coming from everywhere, desperately calling for water and care. No longer able to ignore the pleas, Milroy sent out a band of skirmishers to keep the enemy at bay so we could collect the wounded and dead. The firing slacked off a bit and we went forward and brought back those who were shot or killed.

Even after several attempts, we were not able to retrieve the body of Colonel Cantwell who was too far forward on the field of battle. Later, Cantwell's brother, Sergeant Jacob Cantwell, found the body but it was so decayed that it was buried on the spot. His sword was found and removed.

What a great loss! With his personal talents, Cantwell could have done even greater things. As it was, his bravery will never be forgotten.

Finally, about four o'clock, the 82nd Ohio made its way back to the rear of the battle toward the turnpike. As I walked over this ground where we started our attack, I saw a lone officer lying on the ground, no other wounded or dead near him. He had a narrow mustache with a bullet lodged between his closed eyes above his thin angular nose. The bullet protruded from his head like a dart. The long distance shot lost most of its power, but still had enough force to crack his skull and kill him. This man had visited our campfire last night. I stared at him in disbelief. He did know he was going to die today.

Toward late afternoon and evening, we saw wave after wave of New England regiments charge the unfinished railroad only to be repulsed when reserve Rebel troops came forward. They penetrated deep into the enemy line and had engaged in deadly hand-to-hand combat, losing many men before being driven back. Down trodden, hollow eyed men walked by us as they went to the rear. We stared at them in silence as they went by us. Seth leaned close to me and whispered.

"Hiram, all those charges, all those deaths, and what did they accomplish? Hell, what did we accomplish?" I had no reply.

Even with this fierce resistance, our officers told us that Pope somehow still believed the enemy was retreating. Given the numbers in front of us, the idea seemed crazy. In the late afternoon, we moved across the Warrenton Turnpike to the base of a large, sparsely vegetated hill (Bald Hill). Here we readied for more attacks but these did not materialize.

At dusk, we marched back to just below the Stone House. Exhausted, bruised, and aching from every joint, we rested and tried to recover from the harrowing experiences of the day.

The sun sat orange and angry on the horizon, its dying rays tinged black and gray by the smoke of the battlefield. As darkness set in, we started a fire. The night was cold and we had no rations. I discovered a few dried apple slices in the bottom of my knapsack and quickly chewed them down. I felt guilty as hungry eyes watched me chew and swallow.

The ghostly profile of the Stone House was even more ominous now. It screamed. Surgeons performed their grizzly tasks of removing arms and legs shattered by Minnie balls, shrapnel, and bayonets. Seth had found some coffee and heated water from a nearby stream. The coffee warmed our insides as we sat in silence thinking about the battle.

"I saw the captain's body that was at our campfire last night. His body was by itself right where we first began to move." Seth and Isaiah drew closer to me, their mouths agape. "A sharpshooter must have hit him from the far woods. The ball had lost most of its steam, barely penetrated his skull." The words took a while to have their effect. Seth spoke next.

"That must be a shot from over a thousand yards! What are the chances? Damnation that's a weird thing!"

"When your time is up, it's up, you will die," said Isaiah pensively.

"Why does a man get a vision of his own death when he can't do anything about it? What good does it do him?" I asked.

"If I had a vision that strong I would have found a way not to be in the charge. Hell, I would have gotten the biggest gut ache in the army. No way would I have charged!" Seth said this with a little chuckle.

"You would have just died in the next fight," continued Isaiah. Silence.

The complexity of the subject numbed our minds. We watched the fire as the muffled sounds of a growing night battle reverberated in the distance.

My thoughts began to run wild within me. *When, Oh Lord, is going to be my time? Will I know it? Lord, please do not do this to me. Bring my death on suddenly, quickly and clean! No, your will be done.*

Cannon flashes in the distance interrupted my thoughts. They exploded like fireworks and their light revealed soldiers retreating down the road. The bedraggled men began yelling at us.

"Retreating, like hell, the Rebs are not retreating. There's thousands of them down that road," bellowed a large, bearded corporal who stopped by the road and directed his men into our lines. A group of Union cavalry galloped down the road toward the flashing lights of battle.

"You fools! You don't know what's up there! You'll get cut to pieces!" yelled the burley corporal at the mounted men. His words were prophetic. Later we heard that enemy soldiers engulfed the cavalrymen and only a few were able to make it back, the rest being shot out of their saddles from hundreds of muskets hidden in the night.

After the firing ceased and calmness settled in, we heard the enemy pickets talking. While we could not understand the banter, we knew they were numerous and close.

Peering into the night, I made an observation. "Doesn't sound like they're retreating to me!"

Even Isaiah was now having problems with the Union leadership. "Regiments charging well fortified positions again and again. Generals arguing. Reports of enemy positions being ignored. Is there no plan at all? What kind of generalship do we have?"

As we peered up the hill beyond the Stone House, the forms of General Pope and his staff could barely be discerned against a moonlit sky. They were considering the day's work and what the next day would bring. Occasionally some officers would point to the left and then others, mostly Pope, would extend an arm to the center of the battlefield, toward the railroad embankment where the 82nd Ohio and other units had lost so many men.

"Do you think Pope is going to attack the center again?" I asked Seth who was still staring at our leaders.

"Who knows? Lord knows I don't want anything to do with that damned railroad cut!"

"I can't believe he would order another charge there," replied Isaiah, looking out across the darkness.

We turned our eyes away from the leaders of our army and lay down. The cold ground drew us close and we huddled up against each other. The tiredness of our bodies brought on sleep borne of complete physical and mental exhaustion. I did not have my dream.

The rising sun of August 30 revealed a stark and injured landscape. We groaned and struggled to drive the cold from our joints and muscles and the dread of the dawning day rested on our faces. Singing birds and a gentle breeze contrasted sharply with the acid smell of gunpowder and the decomposing bodies of men and animals. As awareness reluctantly came upon us, so did the disconcerting questions of being in an unfinished battle.

What were the Rebels going to do? What would Pope do? What would happen to us? Thank God, I had no feelings of impending doom—or did I? As I slowly rose from the ground on knees and legs that ached and refused to straighten, I noticed lines of Union prisoners captured yesterday marching by our encampment.

"Why are the Johnnies releasing our men so soon?" Seth rubbed his jaw, captured a large louse, examined and crushed it. "Blasted grayback!"

"The Rebs are retreating. We heard their officers talking it over last night," shouted a young soldier on the edge of the line of released prisoners.

"That can't be," grumbled Seth. "A retreating army does not act the way the Rebs did yesterday. How about all that night fightin' to our left? Lord, how can those prisoners believe the Rebs are retreating?"

"That's what the Rebs told them," replied Isaiah. Seth gasped and walked away mumbling.

We stayed in formation near the Stone House the rest of the morning, nervously awaiting orders.

About two in the afternoon, General Sigel sent out scouts to our left to explore the disposition of the enemy down the turnpike. They reported that the enemy was not only in force in that area but was advancing. Sigel immediately informed the Union commander. Pope, however, continued moving troops to the center toward the railroad embankment where we had attacked yesterday.

On the hill, we could see Sigel wave his hands in disgusted frustration. Pope thrust his arm angrily at the railroad embankment. Sigel rode back to our troops.

"He still thinks he can turn de Rebs left flank over there! By Gott, dey are dere! On our left flank! The fool will get us all kilt," said the frustrated German general to his aides.

"Ve must puts de men on a line here to stop dem Rebs coming from over dere," said Sigel as he ran his arm along the turnpike to his left. He rode off to again confer with Pope who continued to point to the center of the battlefield. Shaking my head, I walked up to Isaiah.

"Why the hell are we going to attack that embankment again? We couldn't knock the Rebs back yesterday with charge after charge? Sigel is right! We better get ready for those blasted Rebs to attack at us here on the left!"

Isaiah came up to me and placed his hand on my shoulder. "Hiram, don't swear. Who knows why General's do what they do? We just have to obey orders. God will help us like he done yesterday." Seth, focused in on the generals, did not hear this.

Isaiah's passive acceptance bothered me as I surveyed the hills and woods in front of me. *How can he have such simple blind faith?* Cannon shots exploded off to my right as masses of blue moved across the fields toward the embankment, the same area we were in yesterday. Clouds of smoke rose into the air. "Looks like lines of blue coal being fed into a furnace," remarked Seth solemnly.

It was now early afternoon and the hot sun bore down on the pulsating battle. Blue clad troopers began falling back to our lines, some wild-eyed and dirty with the grime of battle.

One man came by me shaking his head. He briefly looked at me and I asked, "What's going on up there?"

"We got through that blasted embankment. I got into it—choked a Reb with my bare hands—then bunches of them—shells started flyin'—we had to get out of there!" He gritted his teeth as he wandered on behind me where an officer grabbed him by the arm and told him to stop. In frustration, the soldier hit the officer in the face, knocking him down, and then ran off into the smoke.

"Oh my Lord, what's happening to this army?" said Isaiah, his mouth open with disbelief.

The enemy now advanced on a broad front in the distance, massing in front of us in the woods down the hill. It was now late afternoon. David Thomson, our new regimental commander, rode up and shouted orders to the captains and sergeants. Expecting to see our beloved Cantwell, I paused, and again felt the reality of Cantwell's death. The words of Thomson brought me back to the present.

"Form up here, boys, and move up to that sunken road and deploy in line of battle! The Rebs will soon be coming up that hill. Hurry now!" We soon were in a defensive position that faced the enemy now gathering in the woods below us. The banks of the road afforded good protection from the bullets now zipping around us.

"Thank you Lord for this sunken road," said Isaiah.

"Amen," replied Seth.

Seth, Isaiah, and I lay prone against the bank, our Enfields aimed at the lines of figures now coming at us. The landscape undulated and writhed with humanity. A gray wave was breaking in front of us by the woods and blue soldiers washed back against us, their faces white with fear as they rolled through our lines.

I cocked my rifle, looked to my side and saw Seth slap Isaiah on the back as they took their positions. Again, an unspoken understanding emerged among us three friends. We would do everything in our power to protect each other. A squad of Union soldiers passed us, crouching, firing their rifles but retreating with haste.

"The Johnnies are comin' thick and heavy right out of those woods! We got to get out of here, boys!" The soldier looked at a comrade in front of him who was kneeling on the ground, trying to load his rifle. "Come on Wilson, get out of there, come on!" Wilson immediately threw down his gun, turned and ran through our lines, jumping down to the road beside his friend. They turned and looked at us in disbelief, like we were sacrificial lambs being left behind.

Enemy soldiers now yelled and charged out of the woods. The yell raised the hairs on my neck and sent a contraction down my back. Between them and us was an open field of grass that grew narrower by the second.

"Here they come," yelled Isaiah as he leveled his rifle and took aim at a Rebel soldier making his way up the grassy slope.

"Damnation, there are hundreds of 'em," exclaimed Seth as he looked up and down the battle line. His eyes met mine.

"We can handle it, Seth—we have so far." He grimaced and then got to the business of shooting and reloading.

I aimed at a Confederate officer slightly in front of some enemy soldiers forming a line. Before I could fire, this man fell backward, dropping his sword. I moved my sites to the right and located a man with a red bandanna. He rose up, yelled and pushed his rifle forward. I squeezed the trigger and the man and his rifle lurched backward.

The enemy line belched smoke and bullets plowed into the bank in front of me. Some plunked into the soil and others ricocheted off rocks. I fired again and dropped down to reload—all without thinking about what I was doing. A vision of Colonel Cantwell holding his pistol near my ear passed through my mind.

I took a deep breath. The smoke stung my lungs and I coughed violently. A shell exploded about twenty yards behind me and dirt and gravel flew over us. The cannon that fired this projectile was off to our left, enfilading our line. Fear gripped me as I knew this battery would rip us apart.

Suddenly a row of our cannons behind us fired grapeshot and canister at the enemy, right over our heads. The noise and shock waves of the huge guns compressed my body into the bank of the road. Hot powder and fiery pieces of paper rained down on us.

Pulling myself up from my flattened position, I again peered through the smoke to see if the enemy battery was there. The gun was gone, its wheels off and the soldiers operating it were lying on the ground. One of our cannons had taken it out.

I next looked down the hill where the enemy was reforming. A black fog lifted and I saw heaps on the ground, some of them moving, some screaming in pain, some still and others waving their arms in jerky movements. They were about one hundred yards away down the hill with the woods at their back.

Suddenly, a new line of men emerged from the woods yelling, running at us. I aimed at a tall, thin man waving a pistol. The smoke from my gun obscured my view. I strained to see if I hit the man. I didn't, he was still coming. Boom! Another round of cannon fire rolled from behind us. I pressed against the bank—my ears ringing and I could not hear anything.

The battle raged around me in silence, my brain stunned. Soon the ringing left and the battle with all its explosions and yelling reemerged into my consciousness. I looked to my left where some Rebel soldiers jumped into us and swung their bayonets and rifle butts at our soldiers. They were shot and fell to the bottom of the ditch. One of these men was still alive. I saw his eyes move as he surveyed the blue forms above him.

I shook myself away from this scene and again took aim at the running forms darting in and out of the smoke in the distance. Picking out no one form in particular, I fired, dropped to the base of the ditch and began reloading. The thought occurred to me I was now behind a protective embankment and the enemy was charging in the open. I understood what the running forms in the distance were going through. I could almost feel what they felt as our bullets and shells zipped and burst around them.

An enemy soldier leaped at me from the top of the ditch. I moved my bayonet to catch his charge and the blade sank deeply into his chest. He yelled and my rifle discharged. The blast blew him off my blade and he fell beside me. A large bloody wound gaped in his chest. I went into shock, staring at the human being I had just eviscerated.

Isaiah put his hand on my shoulder. Startled, I turned ready to kill another soldier.

"Hiram, it's ok, you did what you had to—we all are!" I looked into his sincere eyes and they quieted me. The next thing I knew, I had already loaded my rifle and was firing at the butternut figures forming again at the bottom of the hill.

"When will it stop?" A tired Isaiah gasped and wiped his stinging eyes.

Wave after wave of Confederates tried to break through our line. When gaps occurred among us, other regiments filled the holes. Each new arrival in our battered ranks rejuvenated us and frustrated the enemy.

The constant charging and repelling continued into the early evening when it stopped and we were finally given orders to pull back. A soldier behind me, a member of a regular U.S. Army regiment that had reinforced our lines, calmly remarked.

"We sure put a twist on General Longstreet, didn't we?"

I nodded my head. The order to pull back passed from soldier to soldier and exhausted men left the sunken road. I took one more look at the man I had bayoneted. A blackening reddish hole in his chest glared at me. His lifeless eyes scanned me. The sight made me gag with dry heaves.

We left the sunken road and moved backward, keeping low, dodging bullets. Their sound informed me of the position of the enemy. The hummers, more numerous, were from a long distance and the zippers, more scarce, were from nearby. I exhaled to relieve the tension. *Oh Lord, how did I survive this? Don't count your chickens too soon—you still need to get to the rear!*

The enemy commenced shelling despite the descending darkness. Orange flashes exploded randomly around me. *Just a few more minutes, Lord!* I kept moving, feeling my way along, looking for the common voices of Seth and Isaiah. "Hiram, over here," yelled Seth. Isaiah stood close by him. Eventually we reached the hilly ground near a stone bridge that crossed Bull Run. This was on the road that led to Centerville, back toward Washington.

Thousands of men in blue massed in the area of the bridge. Some units were intact and orderly but others straggled, wandering aimlessly, confused, looking like scarecrows, dragging themselves along looking for their regiments. Some cursed our generals; others were just despondent.

About 2 a.m., the 82nd Ohio in the dark of night, walked over Bull Run creek. After we crossed, the bridge was destroyed. We were among the first on the field and the last to leave it. Lightning now rolled across the sky, revealing growing and dark storm clouds. Seth stopped and looked at the gathering tempest. "Must every battle end with a blasted storm? What else could happen to us? We get our asses whipped and now even God vents his wrath on our poor troops?"

"Keep the faith, Seth. God is still with us," yelled Isaiah, his face lit up by a flash of lightning and washed by the falling rain.

Our next line of defense was the earthwork at Centreville seven miles away. We heard sounds of enemy infantry and sporadic explosions to our rear and flanks. "The blasted Rebels are still chasing us," yelled Seth through the thunder and noise. Regiments ran by us going north.

"Where are those men going?" yelled an officer to our side.

"Ox Hill!" screamed a mounted cavalryman. "Kearny is the man leading us."

We reached Centreville in the early morning. Holding onto our rifles and shivering to the bone, we took up defensive positions in muddy trenches not knowing if the Rebels were coming or not. It was miserable. To add insult, Federal forces of McClellan's coming out from Washington to reinforce our lines jeered us, saying "Hey boys, you heading for Richmond? You look a mite tired!"

A man to my right yelled. "Where were you when it counted, you damned laggards?"

The morning of August 31 came in with another rain. Seth, Isaiah, and I surveyed the pitiful aftermath of the battle piling up around us. Wounded came in from all directions on ambulances or hobbling along as best they could. Stacks of amputated limbs piled up at makeshift hospitals, mere shacks and cabins where surgeons had set up shop.

Rumors of a possible attack filled the air and soldiers hurried around trying to find their regiments and leaders. Pope had set up soldiers with signs that helped immensely in finding our units. After finding the 82nd Ohio, Seth exclaimed, "Well at least Pope did something right!"

The next day confirmed news of Rebel movements on the north. Troops immediately moved out to meet the threat. We moved in behind these advanced regiments and took up a position in reserve. After a few hours, we marched east to Fairfax Court House.

Another violent thunderstorm broke and illuminated the sky as we had never seen before. The thunder rolled over us vibrating our teeth and curling our spines. Even Isaiah was moved to superlatives. "Lord Almighty! My Lord, what are you telling us?" Through the thunderstorm and its lightning, we heard the muffled sounds of a large battle to the north.

We learned that we had met the Rebels near Ox Hill or Chantilly in a fierce engagement amidst the violent storm. Two of our generals (Stevens and Kearney) were killed. Confused by the darkness and storm, Kearney actually rode up to the Confederates and asked them to what unit they belonged. He received a bullet for an answer.

A grizzly soldier staggered by us. Tobacco juice stained his uniform and whiskey was on his breath. Another soldier asked him what had happened to General Kearney. "Well old Kearny bent over close to the saddle as he rode away from the Rebs…and wouldn't you know it…the ball entered one orifice and exited the another, leaving no trace". The raucous soldier then laughed wildly. Isaiah was livid at such disrespect and yelled as he turned away in disgust.

"Oh, please shut up! You are a disgrace." The soldier lumbered on in his stupor giving Isaiah no heed.

The storm eventually brought peace to the battleground. The torrents of rain soaked gunpowder and exhausted the troops on both sides. The Confederates mercifully withdrew around 3 a. m. and the battle was over. Isaiah was right, God had been compassionate to us after all.

We marched on to Fairfax Court House and into the Defenses of Washington, a series of forts surrounding the city. We headed for Fort DeKalb near the bridge crossing the Potomac River.

As we drew closer to the center of the city, we came across General McDowell yelling at a Colonel of a regiment slowly walking by a courthouse. McDowell ordered the regiment to halt and let other troops pass. "Go to hell," was the Colonel's reply. When McDowell reprimanded the officer the regiment leveled its guns at him! We stood opened mouthed in front of this spectacle; just a sample of what Pope and McDowell had to endure after the battle.

When General McClellan, the newly appointed commander of the Army of the Potomac, rode up and greeted Pope, the troops gave Little Mac three cheers. General Pope acknowledged McClellan with a wave and rode off. We later learned that Pope was sent to Minnesota to help put down an uprising of the Sioux tribes and that McDowell and other generals had been relieved of their duties. After getting to Washington D. C., I decided to write my family a letter, long overdue.

Washington D. C.
Fort DeKalb, September 19,1862
Dear Family:

Getting right to the point—I am alive after some of the most horrendous fighting of the war. The second battle of Manassas ended with the Rebels in control of the field and us retreating to Washington. I feel like my unit fought well but we had bad generalship leading to our defeat. I was in the thick of the fight both days, both being shot at and shooting at the enemy. I have done my duty and killed other men which leaves me sad yet proud I was able to persevere. I have never been so worn out and used up in my life. We marched in terrible weather with little or no food for days. We slept in the rain, shivered in the cold, and then rose up to fight the enemy in the worst of situations. I do not know how I survived. Even our beloved Cantwell is gone.

September 4 finds us at Fairfax Court House near the Chain Bridge at General Sigel's headquarters. We are now in the 11th Corps with a new reorganization of the army. Our officers tell us that out of nine hundred men in the 82nd Ohio who came out of Camp Tod, we now have only two hundred seventy five fit for duty! I am amazed that Seth, Isaiah, and I have survived. The 82nd Ohio evidently is well thought of as we have been made Provost Guards for General Sigel. This means that we will get some well-deserved rest but must put up with drunken soldiers, deserters, prostitutes, and other malcontents of which there are plenty. The Army of the Potomac is at a low point. Lincoln's appointment of General McClellan to replace Pope has lifted many spirits and order is slowly returning to the camps. We are at Fort DeKalb, close to the city. My health along with Seth and Isaiah's is responding to more food and less exposure. We can buy additional food although the prices are too high for me. I will continue sending what money I can home. We occasionally get to go into the city and visit buildings such as the Capitol, Treasury, and Post Office. You need not worry about me partaking of the sins of this city. I am so indebted to God for his protection that I dare not risk it. Pray for me that I may remain faithful.

Your son,

Hiram

P.S. I heard that Salem has been renamed to Shiloh. Is that true?

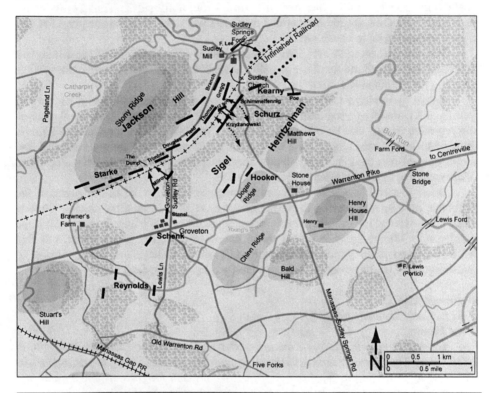

The precarious position of Milroy's brigade at The Dump early on August 29, 1862 and a post-battle sketch of the area *(map by Hal Jespersen, www.posix.com/CW and sketch from the Library of Congress).*

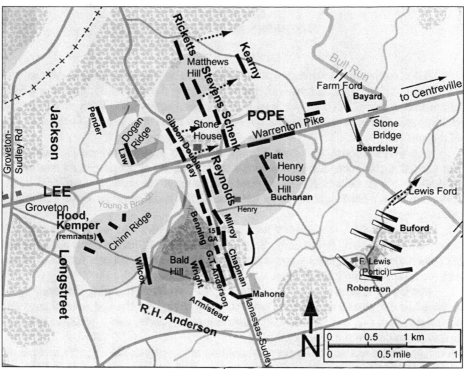

Positions of Milroy's brigade and the 82nd Ohio late on August 30, 1862 *(map by Hal Jespersen, www.posix.com/CW)*.

The Stone House at the Manassas battlefield. Milroy's brigade set up in this sunken road (now the highway) when they fought off the attacks of Longstreet.

CHAPTER 8
THE DEFENSES OF WASHINGTON

After resting in Washington from the misery at Manassas, we were loath to march again. Our leaders, however, wanted to know the whereabouts of the Rebels and ordered the 82nd Ohio out into the Virginia countryside. With what we had endured and winter at the gates, these forays tested us to the extreme. Such is the fate of the soldier.

Our first excursion was back towards Manassas Junction where Jackson's raid had caused such havoc. As we neared the battlefield, we again passed the multitudes of shallow graves, some with grisly skeletons coming to the surface, uncovered by the rains. This was a hard sight for all of us in the 82nd as those poor souls were comrades not long ago.

As we marched, the weather turned cold and began to snow. The weather was literally killing us off. Fortunately, Seth, Isaiah, and I had blankets and oilcloths and together found ways to keep warm and survive. There is no substitute for good friends and the mutual caring among them.

Having scouted out the country to the west without engaging the enemy, we returned to the village of Fairfax Court House. It rained for the last several days and the mud sullied this war torn land. The courthouse, however, was a beautiful building. It was like a diamond in a sea of misery.

The view from our camp revealed nothing but hopeless, skinny, scraggly people scratching out an existence in a war-torn and ravaged landscape. The war had scoured the countryside and it depressed the soul and mind.

Things became somewhat better for us soldiers. We had tents and stoves, beds on fence rails, and food to cook. Still, we longed to settle into more permanent winter quarters with warmer wood huts and better stoves. However, our officers continued to hold us ready for battle and on the move. The latest rumor held that General Ambrose Burnside, Lincoln's replacement of the reluctant-to-attack General George McClellan, was in a major operation near Fredericksburg.

December found us near Fredericksburg, the scene of a terrible battle where thousands of Union troops were slaughtered before a stonewall at the top of a hill beyond the town. Thank God, the 82nd Ohio did not get into this battle. I had never seen the enemy with better ground from which to fight. It seemed that this was always the case but here the advantage to the Confederates was insurmountable. Seth, Isaiah, and I walked to a place where we could see the battlefield from the other side of the river.

"Why do we keep throwing our troops at the Rebs when they have such well defended positions?" Isaiah looked across the river to the stonewall at the top of the hill in the distance.

"By God, Isaiah, you answer that question and you'll save a lot of our skins," exclaimed Seth shaking his head. "Hiram, what do you think about the state of our generalship?"

"At least the 82nd Ohio did not have to charge up those slopes—makes Provost Guard duty almost a Godsend."

I said this recalling the police duties we had to carry out in our first days at our camp in the defenses of Washington. Particularly memorable was the night we patrolled a bordello near General Sigel's headquarters at Fort DeKalb near Georgetown and the Chain Bridge.

Seth, Isaiah, and I were in a squad of Provost Guard troops assigned to round up deserters and soldiers absent without leave and rumored to be in the bordellos. We were headed toward a seedy row of one-story wooden buildings and a house of ill repute called the Haystack. Seth actually seemed to be excited about this duty. Isaiah and I were hesitant to say the least.

"Well boys, you are going to see what it looks like down on the line. Don't let all the horizontal maneuvers get you all upset!" Seth chuckled as we marched across the Chain Bridge into the city and headed for its lowlands. As we neared the area, women left the street side and darted into the shadows. "Those gals can recognize a Provost Guard at one hundred yards," said Seth as he strained to see a red dressed woman peering out a window. Her large breasts briefly showed as she drew the curtains. The woman at Camp Tod came into my mind and stirred some thoughts I did not want to entertain.

As we moved deeper into the line of whorehouses, a musky stench pervaded the air. Soldiers ran from house to house as we approached, some tugging up trousers, others running in their underwear. We stopped as many as we could catch, looked for passes, and even arrested a few officers.

Soon we were guarding a group of twenty angry, swearing men. Many others avoided our capture or were able to persuade our commander to leave them alone. As we went by one of the houses I saw a man urinating on a staircase, swaying and laughing, obviously drunk. "Arrest that man!" Our sergeant ordered three men into the filthy building.

In another grimy house with torn pink curtains, a man and woman coupled on the floor near the door, moaning and groaning as we approached, oblivious to our presence. "Private Rinehart, use your bayonet to poke that bastard and arrest him!" Isaiah was embarrassed as he prodded the half naked man off the woman, revealing more than he wanted to see.

"Whoa, let me get my damn pants on!" His partner quickly pulled down her dress and followed him.

"Gimme my money! Gimme my money!" She was still yelling as Isaiah marched the man out of the house into the growing group of arrested men.

"Sodom and Gomorrah! God of righteousness, deal with these sinners!" An angry Isaiah shook his head as we walked deeper into this pit of human depravity.

Isaiah's demeanor changed as he stared at the pitiful seductive gestures of a sickly, thin woman standing in the doorway of a tin shack. Two skinny children peered at us from inside the hut on the other side of a sagging bed. The pathetic condition of the woman upset me. "Good Lord, what a sorry state of affairs." Seth came up beside me.

"My God! What a place for two children!"

The wages of sin! The words of Preacher Sams resounded in my head as we marched out of the area passing more shacks with groups of soldiers lusting after scantily clad women lounging in the garish glow of red lanterns.

A potent look into the human condition, this type of duty depressed our officers and it was not long before Colonel Robinson requested field duty for the 82nd Ohio. We soon left for Fredericksburg.

"No doubt about it Hiram, we were not supposed to be in this battle," stated Isaiah matter-of-factly as he looked across the river at the long slope leading up to the stone wall where thousands had died in the cold of winter.

"Ah, if we only had your faith, Isaiah, all of this would be so simple!" Seth grinned at Isaiah and slapped him on the back. "Let's get out of this rain." Seth pulled his kepi over his shoulders and we wandered back to our tent.

As the Union army gathered itself the next month after Fredericksburg, the 82nd Ohio, as Provost Guard, was ordered to march at the end of a huge movement of men and wagons. We learned later that this was a secret flanking movement up the river to catch the enemy by surprise, this time from the north of Fredericksburg.

Unfortunately, the weather did not cooperate. The skies opened up and the roads became impassable quagmires. The whole army bogged down in a pitiful morass of men, mules, and machines, wallowing in the mud in a cold blowing wind and rainstorm. If that was not enough embarrassment, the Rebels taunted us from the far banks of the Potomac, raising signs that said "this way to Richmond".

We followed this pitiful expedition collecting stragglers and guarding the wagon trains from attacks from behind. As we moved through the muck and mire, we came across broken wagons, hundreds of dead horses and mules, and ammunition and equipment strewn by the roadside.

This "Mud March" rivaled the waste and damage wrought by Stonewall Jackson on Manassas Junction. As bad as the campaign under Fremont was, it was rivaled by this cold, slogging, misery in the mud. This second disaster at Fredericksburg led to the resignation of General Ambrose Burnside and to the installation of General Joseph Hooker, as our new leader.

We heard about this change of leadership at our winter quarters at Stafford Court House. Finally, we were able to build good shelters and stop marching all over Virginia in the cold wet winter.

"Ah, Hiram, I forgot how good a full stomach, clean clothes, and a warm fire feels, didn't you?" said Seth as he leaned back on his bunk with his feet near the stove.

"Sure beats sleeping in the rain on the cold ground," I replied.

Isaiah pulled his blanket over his head and muttered a faint "Amen".

The new year of 1863 found us still hunkered down in our huts. Our main concern beside staying warm was keeping our mind occupied. I secured a copy of Victor Hugo's *Les Miserables* and read it through twice. I relished how the kindness of a priest lifted a thief from the depths of criminality to become a benefactor to a town and the child of a prostitute.

"What are you reading about, Hiram?" Seth also enjoyed reading, especially novels.

"The triumph of the human spirit, the power of love," I replied. Seth stared out across the camp and its many tents.

"Must not be a true story."

Our time of inaction was interrupted by a historic announcement, the Emancipation Proclamation of President Abraham Lincoln. The retreat of Lee at Antietam, the only "victory" Union troops claimed in this area, was the stepping off point for the announcement. The historic proclamation blew across our camp like a snowstorm.

A soldier passing our hut yelled to his comrades. "I ain't fighting this war for no nigras! What in the hell is the President doing?"

A voice from a nearby hut answered him. "Freeing the slaves is the reason for this war! It's about time Old Abe made it official!" Arguments in camp sprung up like mushrooms on a swamp.

Word also came that General Sigel was leaving. We did not know why, only that the German troops were in an uproar. General Oliver Otis Howard now commanded the 11th Corps and the 82nd Ohio was now an unattached battalion of sharpshooters under the direct command of Major General Carl Schurz.

"Well, Hiram, your reputation as a squirrel hunter has finally brought fruit," mused Seth as we hovered around a fire in our hut on a cold January night. "We're now a bunch of eagle-eyed riflemen under Schurz, and unattached at that, a special battalion."

Seth pondered further. "The Dutch in this army are going to be furious over the firing of Sigel, you can bet on that." Seth took a drink of coffee and closed his eyes, relishing the warmth going down his gullet. "I don't envy this new General Howard. I've never seen so many men in an uproar in my life!" Seth drew a long draft from his pipe and gently exhaled, blowing the smoke toward Isaiah.

Isaiah waved away the smoke. "I expect better leadership under General Howard. He is an upstanding Christian officer. I do wonder about Schurz. I hear he is an intellectual."

Seth leaned forward toward the short iron stove in the middle of the hut, his eyes illuminated by the flickering flames. "Well Isaiah, why do you wonder? Don't you know our fate is already determined, hammered into history? We are the bloody 82nd Ohio, and you know we will be in the thick of things! God wills it and now he has one of his prophets leading the 11th Corps!"

Hoping to avoid the inevitable clash of philosophies between these two, I interjected an observation. "This war is going to be more hateful too since old Abe's proclamation freeing the slaves. I've heard stories that the Rebs are shooting officers commanding colored troops on sight—no inquiry, no nothing. What do you think of slaves becoming soldiers?"

Seth, noticeably dislodged from his verbal duel with Isaiah, looked at me quizzically. "Well, they can take a bullet as well as anybody. Why not have 'em fight, I say. What say you, Isaiah?"

"They want their freedom. I expect the Negroes would make good soldiers." More emboldened, Isaiah continued. "Haven't you seen the way the contrabands in camp responded to the Proclamation? To a man, they began singing praises to God and President Lincoln. Saving the Union is good but freeing a whole people makes me even more proud to be a soldier."

Seth rolled his eyes. "So now we have a Divine mission." He looked at me and smiled. "It would be nice, though, to have a general who would not slaughter us chargin' up against stone walls. I just want to get my sorry ass out of this war in one piece."

" Well, we've had Pope, McClellan, Burnsides, and now Joe Hooker is going to lead us," I said matter-of-factly. Seth took a deep breath and exhaled slowly.

"Would to God we had somebody like Grant. I hear he is beating the Rebs in every engagement out west." Recalling some news from home, I added a tidbit of information about Grant.

"The town where I enlisted even changed its name in honor of Grant's victory at Shiloh."

"Where did you enlist?" Isaiah asked, somewhat intrigued.

"A small whistle stop called Salem. Its Shiloh now." Seth jumped back into the conversation.

"Well, Grant has got to be better than ole Burnside. I ain't ever seen the likes of that charge up to that old stone wall at Fredericksburg. How could a general do that? And that damned mud march…!"

Seth's voice became melancholic as he peered blankly at the flickering light dancing across the floor of our hut. "God, such an army as we have now. Hiram, how much longer can you stand this?" Somewhat shocked, I paused and then replied.

"I know a lot of men are thinking of deserting. One man in the company down by the horse corral got some civilian clothes sent to him by his wife and tried to walk out of camp, claiming he was a reporter from *Harper's Weekly*. He would have made it too except one of his men called him by name just as he walked by the guard at the gate. They nabbed him and now he's in the guardhouse."

Isaiah drew closer to us, held his hands up close to the warm stove, and spoke solemnly.

"Such men should be shot! How can they leave the army and the government now when we need them the most? I'm glad only a few do such things." As could be expected, Seth erupted.

"Only a few? Hell, Isaiah, we even got men that are going across the river, joining up with the Rebels, coming back into camp and acting as spies." Isaiah looked shocked.

"They should pay with their lives."

"They are," said Seth as he glared at Isaiah. "One of the boys from the 25th Ohio told me he saw one of these slimy snakes being executed. They marched him into camp around a double file of the regiment, stood him up by a coffin, shot him, and dropped him right into the box while he was still kickin' and coughing up blood. What a sight that was! Still we got men leavin' every day. I tell ya, things are bad."

Isaiah turned to Seth, looked him right in the eyes. "I tell you we have a new order coming now Seth, General Hooker is different. Already you can see things are improving. Look at the food. We're getting vegetables and clothes. They're even starting to issue furloughs! While I know you don't like it, we're drilling and training better. We're going to win this war and General Hooker will lead us!"

Somewhat bewildered, Seth turned away and walked to his bunk, laid down, and groaned. "We'll see, I have heard that every time a new general takes charge. I'll believe it when I get one of those furloughs."

The winter progressed and we settled into camp life, the Confederates on one side of the river and us on the other. We spent the time performing the various duties of soldiering like cleaning the camp (fatigue duty) and guard duty while we waited on spring and warmer weather. No furloughs were granted to us.

With the coming of March, winter loosened its grip on the Virginia landscape and the Army of the Potomac, like a slumbering bear, began to stir. General Joseph Hooker's influence showed up all across the various regiments and divisions. Each newly organized division adopted a symbol. Ours for the 11th Corps was a crescent moon. The discontent and deserting lessened; even Seth seemed to have a new attitude.

Our cavalry made excursions across the river and the report of a horse and saber battle along Kelly's Ford spread through our camp. While walking around camp, I heard two officers conversing.

"Can you believe it? Our cavalry gave the Rebs everything they wanted. By God, you know things are changing when our cavalry keeps up with the Rebs!" Things were heating up and an air of expectation about the prosecution of the war emerged with the buds of spring.

President Abraham Lincoln himself came to our camps and reviewed Howard's 11th Corps on April 9. I heard that he was especially impressed with us, mentioning Schurz's command by name in the earshot of one of our officers. This news spread among us like a welcome warm breeze, lifting our spirits.

I saw Lincoln up close in a Division review. He sat on his horse with General Hooker by his side. The lanky president's legs dangled below the horse's belly. Even though there were many hundreds of soldiers passing by, I felt he looked right at me. His deep-set eyes, humble bearing, and genuine compassion profoundly impressed me and I was moved by the occasion. Later in camp in our hut, my feelings came to the surface.

"Seth, Isaiah, what did you think of ole Abe at the review?"

Isaiah replied first. "He struck me as having the cares of the world on his shoulders. I don't think I have seen a more sad looking man in this whole war, and that's saying something!"

Seth, looking thoughtful, added. "Well who can blame the ole cuss for looking sad? He has had bad luck from the start from McDowell to McClellan to Pope to Burnside. The whole bunch has let him and us down. Now he has Hooker. Lord knows we've got the Rebs outnumbered and out supplied in every way and still we can't whip 'em. I am getting frustrated and I know Lincoln must be at the end of his rope."

"I don't know, after seeing President Lincoln today, I actually feel better about what we're doing. Having a leader like that makes all this somehow worth it." My words surprised both them and me.

Isaiah came up and slapped me on the back. "Hiram, that's the first time I can remember you really stepping out about this war."

"Isaiah, what do you think we have been doing up to this time, play acting? Hiram has put his life on the line many times…you have too." Seth leaned back on his knapsack and shook his head in mild disgust.

Isaiah immediately responded "I know Seth but this is the first time he has really said anything about how he feels. Sometimes it's easier just to follow along, doing what's expected but not really speaking up for something. We've reached a point in this war where we need men to step up and speak out, not just be silent."

Seth glanced at Isaiah and then at me. His face had a confused expression.

I decided to explain myself more. "Well, seeing Abraham Lincoln today really affected me. I mean he is not handsome, forceful, or anything like that, maybe just the opposite, but he strikes you as being a good and righteous man. Makes me feel like I am on the right side of things. Putting down the Rebellion, saving the Union, freeing the slaves, all of them came together for me today when I marched in front of President Lincoln."

This last statement settled on us like a warm blanket as tattoo rolled across the camp. I am sure many conversations like this bantered about the tents and huts of our encampment at Stafford as the cold winds of winter gave way to the warming breezes and rains of spring.

Some of these rains were intense. On a stormy night, some water came through a seam in the roof of our tent and found my bed, wetting my blankets. I spent a terrible night trying to keep warm, feeding damp wood to a sputtering fire. The next day I had an intermittent fever and chills and spent the night in the regimental hospital. I did not get better even though I returned to duty, fighting a terrible cough. When my chills came back, I returned to the hospital on April 17 and spent another night close to a warming fire.

Feeling better the next day, I again returned to duty. The toughness of my body and its ability to return to health surprised me. Long marches, days without food, and sleeping in the cold had strengthened my constitution. Many other men in our regiment succumbed to these hardships and had either died or been discharged and sent home. At this point in the war, in the words of Mr. Darwin, only the "fittest" remained.

Rumors about how and when General Hooker planned to attack the enemy drifted through the ranks. We knew that when the roads began to dry and firm up, we would move. After much analysis, Seth thought he knew Hooker's plan. "If I was him, I would cross the river and then try to come around back of the Rebel army." He began to draw his plan in the dirt floor of our hut. "Hmmm, let's see. Part of the army should stay here around Fredericksburg to keep the Rebs busy." He then drew a sweeping arc, stopped, clapped his hands, and smiled.

"If Hooker does this …!" Seth then paused and scratched his chin, contemplating his drawing. "My God…! We have the men to do it too!" I drew closer, looking over his shoulder at his diagram in the dirt.

"Seth, that's your plan. How do you know Hooker will do the same thing?"

"Well, we will see. This is just a flanking move, standard military procedure, but it's a hell of a long march."

Monday morning, April 27, found us preparing to move out. We loaded up more than usual as our officers told us that it might be eight days before we could get new supplies.

"Eight days? Hooker is planning on a long march." An air of confidence enveloped Seth. "He is going to do it! My God! He is going to do it!" Seth was more animated than we had ever seen him.

Soldiers did not know what to make of him. "We're just going out on another march, what's he so excited about?"

With bent backs holding near sixty pounds of supplies and ammunition, we marched down to Falmouth and General Schurz's headquarters to await orders directly from him since we were an independent regiment of sharpshooters under his command. That night we bivouacked near the Rappahannock, the river we would have to cross.

The country across and up the river was aptly called "the Wilderness". Thick brush, trees, briars and vines made for a nearly impenetrable landscape. Scattered farms, churches, and buildings appeared occasionally but most of the country was an unending eerie matrix of tangled vegetation penetrated only by narrow roads and two rivers.

The Rappahannock and Rapidan Rivers coursed through this wilderness, coming together and forming a "V" northwest of Fredericksburg. If Seth was right, we would flank the Rebel army coming from this same area. As dusk fell, Seth was still questioning the details of his forecast of Hooker's plan. I had to get ready for my turn at picket duty.

"Terman—front and center!" The words came from an officer outside our tent. I immediately gathered up my rifle, wrapped up in my overcoat and exited into the cold night air. The officer was a thin young man with a handlebar mustache and serious demeanor.

"Keep an especially close eye on the Rebs across the river tonight. We need to know of anything suspicious. Nothing is too minor to report, do you understand me?" I nodded. "Again, private, report any suspicious activity to me. I will be at headquarters tent when you are relieved in four hours."

With this, the officer walked off and I made my way through the deepening darkness to my post on the bank of the Rappahannock. I gave the previous picket guard the password and took up my lonely post walking between two huge oak trees. I could faintly hear the voices of the enemy across the river and could see the glowing lights of their campfires glittering in the night.

Guard or picket duty is dangerous when you are so near the enemy. You are out on a limb so to speak and subject to being picked off by sniper fire or captured by groups of the enemy feeling the boundaries. In winter quarters, however, a convention of war emerged discouraging the shooting of pickets. By this time in the war, needless violence was avoided if possible.

Even though I felt relatively safe, every unsuspected noise emanating from the darkness raised the hairs on my neck and focused my attention. Tonight the weather was cold and uncomfortable, requiring that I keep moving. I envied the enemy soldiers across the river sitting beside warm campfires. I yearned to be relieved by the next soldier who could then endure the rest of the night.

As I walked along the crispy, leaf-covered forest floor, I heard the musical sounds of a hymn coming from the enemy camp. I stopped, looked down at the ground, cupped my hand around my ear and strained to pick up the notes.

How firm a foundation, ye saints of the Lord, Is laid for your faith in His excellent word! What more can He say than to you He hath said—To you who for refuge to Jesus have fled?

I knew this hymn. We sang it many times in my church back in Rome. It was a favorite of my father's. "This hymn clears the air, binds us together," he always said after singing it.

Now here I stood in the midst of a terrible war and both sides sang the same hymns. No doubt in other times I could have walked up to the group of young men in gray over there and joined them in chorus, blending right in. I stepped out into the moonlight to see if I could pick up the other verses of the hymn.

"Hey Yank, better step back into the shadows. I got a good bead on ya! Hate to end your enjoyment of the boys singing." Instinctively, I crouched and backed up into the darkness and took up a position behind a tree.

"That's more like it Yank. You're going to live another day, not that I won't shoot you next we meet in the light." I scanned the dark riverbank trying to locate the voice that was so concerned for my safety. I noticed a flash of moonlight off a bayonet by a large spreading tree near a ravine. A shadow moved around the trunk of the tree.

" Hey Reb, you better keep yourself behind that ole hickory in that ditch or you're likely to taste some lead too!" I yelled this although we were directed not to engage in communication with the Confederates by our officers. This rule was often disobeyed, even to the point of trading tobacco and coffee by floating little boats across the river.

"Thank you kindly, Yank. I thought I was hid pretty good. You got a keen eye!" Keeping in the shadows I continued to walk the path along my post. A long silence ensued. My friend across the river then broke the quietness of the night again.

"Yank, you ready for this war to end?" He had changed positions so that he was directly across the river from me although I could not see him. I remained quiet and scanned the trees and brush that lined the other side of the river.

"Yank, cat got your tongue? Had enough of all this fightin' and killin'? Why don't you boys just go back home and leave us to our business?" Before I could answer, a shot rang out from down the river and a slug slammed into the tree by my head. I immediately dropped to the ground and crawled to safety.

"Jake! Jake! You damned idiot. Stop shootin', don't you know we don't shoot at pickets now!" A beam of moonlight illuminated the slouch hat of the man as he cupped his hands to yell at his comrade down the river. Instinctively I put him in my sights and pulled back on the hammer of my Enfield but released the tension as the unwritten rules of war came back to my consciousness.

"Yank, are you all right? Hey, are you all right over there?"

"Yeah, Reb, I am still here. Good thing your boy over there is a bad shot."

"Sorry about that. New recruit. Jake is just a boy. We're down to robbin' the cradle over here and everybody is hungry and damn touchy."

About this time, one of our officers hailed me and asked about the shot.

"What's the situation there Private?"

"Just a young Reb with a touchy trigger finger, sir. Nothing is going to come from it. His superiors are after him."

"Very well, Private, keep your head down. The enemy is still on their high horse after Second Bull Run but old Hooker is going to change that. Damn Rebs! Shooting at our pickets in winter quarters. It won't be long before we teach them a lesson. Carry on Private."

Lincoln reviews the troops *(Library of Congress)*.

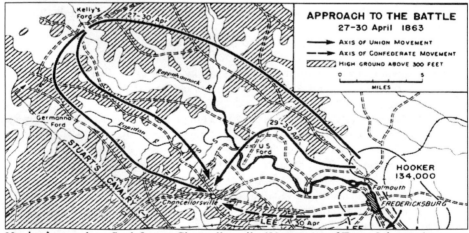

Hooker's march to flank Lee at Chancellorsvile *(University of Texas Libraries)*.

CHAPTER 9
THE CONFUSING EMBARRASSMENT OF CHANCELLORSVILLE

The morning of April 28 found the 82nd Ohio marching down a long narrow road along the river. Scrubby pines and brushy small deciduous trees lined the sides, shadows and bright sunspots alternated along the path. I felt refreshed by the mild weather and a short but good night's sleep. Through gaps in the trees I glimpsed the opposite bank of the river and wondered about the enemy soldier I talked to last night. Who was he? Would I meet him or his young friend Jake in the days to come? Would I shoot at them or they me? Seth, panting heavily to my side jolted me out of my daydream.

"Hiram, slow down, take a breather. We're stopping here for a short spell." He groaned and grimaced as he twisted and lowered his heavy pack to the ground. "I am going to shed some of this. With all our rations plus the blasted ammunition, this pack is too heavy. It's rubbing my shoulders raw."

We soon realized that we could not carry such heavy packs on this long march. Something had to go. If Seth was correct, we would be marching a long way in order to flank the Rebs. In addition, these heavy packs would never do if we had to get down into the water to ford the river. I dreaded the tough decision on what to leave or keep as Seth, Isaiah, and I threw our packs on the ground.

"I guess I will keep my overcoat and shed this blanket. Can you keep your blanket, Seth? We have to keep our oilcloths though, don't you think?"

Seth looked up at a distant dark cloud bank. "Yeah, we are bound to get rain." Seth reached for some cartridges. "I'll keep my blanket. Could you carry some of this ammunition?" I nodded and recalled the past.

"Remember with Fremont when all this was carried on the wagons? Now we've got those blasted mules!"

Isaiah came up looking at the mule train up ahead. "Sometimes I feel like one of those brutes. What doesn't fit on those critters, we have to carry." Seth grimaced as Isaiah and I spread our blankets on the ground and filled them with cards, pipes, tobacco, cups, and other desired but now discarded items. Seth looked at the pile with pain on his face.

"I hope no cussed Rebs get these."

Off in the distance in a clearing we heard some singing, like a melodious moan sung in pleasing harmony. Through the thick trees, we saw the forms of several slaves, gathering wood.

"Let's give our cast offs to those Negroes," exclaimed Isaiah. We piled our discarded items in two blankets, which Isaiah carried off toward the singing. At first, the dark forms retreated but stopped as Isaiah extended his hand and the blankets.

Through the brush, we saw a black man bow as he accepted the gifts. When Isaiah patted him on the back, the man's head rose and a broad smile became visible. We faintly heard, "God bless you, Mr. Yankee."

"That sure beats throwing the stuff on the roadside," Isaiah declared as he returned. The song emanating from the clearing increased in cadence.

Our columns gathered and we marched into the afternoon and early evening when rain began to fall. We pulled out our oilcloths.

"Glad we hung on to these," I said as we pulled them over our heads. The rain increased and soon we began to slip and slide, the mud clinging to our shoes. On we went through the fading day and into the falling night.

We reached Kelly's Ford at dusk, went into the woods, dropped our loads, and ate a cold supper. The rain was now a sporadic drizzle. We sat in the dark on the ground forbidden to make fires. "Pipe down you men and no fires, no smoking tonight! The Johnnies don't know we're coming and we want to keep it that way," said Sam Armstrong as he checked on his squad.

At around eight in the evening, we walked across a pontoon bridge to the other side of the river. "Route foot! Route foot!" The officers by the bridge urged each man to be careful. "Don't get into a rhythm where you rock the bridge!"

The rain-swollen river roared beneath us tugging at the pontoons. "Hope those moorings hold," said Isaiah as he grabbed a taut rope.

"Hope the Rebs don't see us out here on this bridge," said Seth as we came to the middle of the stream. "We're like pigeons on a fence."

What an eerie feeling—walking in a line of men in pitch darkness on a flimsy pulsating bridge in the middle of a rushing river. At any moment, I feared the eruption of flashes of muskets and whistling bullets. The hair on my neck stood up and my spine tingled. Finally, finally, we reached the other bank and no enemy soldiers were there. Thousands of us crossed under a midnight moon that peeked in and out through the dark rain clouds.

We then plunged into an eerie damp forest of scrubby pines. In the quick flick of a moonbeam, I saw Seth's face. His eyes danced as he surveyed the dense forest on both sides of the road. "Damned scary place, ain't it Hiram?"

"I can think of other places I'd rather be," I replied.

"How about the Haystack back in Washington?" Seth snickered in the darkness. Getting no reply but a grunt from me, Seth looked for Isaiah. "Isaiah, you over there? Can't see a foot in front of my face in this darkness."

"Yeah, Seth I'm here."

"You best get to praying that we don't have to fight in this brushy hell. You can't see where to shoot and bullets and shells could come from everywhere and nowhere!"

We walked on silently through the thicket, thorny branches grabbed our clothes and twigs snapped under our feet. A branch whipped back from the man in front and slapped Seth in the cheek. "Ouch! God almighty that hurts! I could have lost an eye!"

Isaiah, walking methodically on my right side, replied without hesitation. "Almighty God will watch over us Seth. All of this is His creation. We will be ok."

Seth grunted but actually seemed relieved. The gruesome sounds of the eerie forest increased as our columns of blue plunged deeper into the tangled abyss. I was unable to see the man in front of me, only hearing the snapping twigs, crumpling leaves, and his fearful breathing. At three in the morning, we halted in the dark void for some much needed rest. We fell into the unconsciousness of sleep having no idea what kind of place surrounded us.

A ray of morning sun pierced the thick foliage of an overhanging tree and awakened me. Around us was a thicket of vines, brush, and pine dissected by the road. Where we lay was a thick mat of moss, dead leaves, and pine needles. Isaiah tamped the spot with his foot and quipped. "The good Lord provided a nice spot for us last night, didn't he?"

It was Wednesday, April 29. We rose from our stupor and marched all day until we reached the banks of the Rapidan River. Here our advance pickets surprised a small band of enemy soldiers working intently on building a bridge. With no shooting, we captured the lot of them. Our engineers then laid down pontoons. As I passed the prisoners I heard one of the captured Confederates question a guard. "Where did you Yanks come from? What are you doing all the way over har?"

Later in the night, a rainstorm erupted and we camped on the other side of the Rapidan. Isaiah, Seth, and I crawled under some low hanging branches of a pine tree and made a nice shelter using our oilcloths for a roof. As the rain pelted down on the oilcloths, Seth lit a candle. We talked about what might be awaiting us the next day, Thursday, April 30.

"Sooner or later we have to come up on the Rebs," said Seth as he held his hand over the sputtering candle. "I hope we can surprise them slavers and roll 'em up and end this war. I tell ya, boys, I am ready for it to be over." Isaiah and I, scrunched together in the darkness in our little cavity, responded together.

"So are we."

Seth chuckled at our short symphony and replied, "Amen."

We broke camp about noon, found a larger corridor through the thick trees, the Plank Road, and marched east toward the small hamlet of Chancellorsville. The farms here were in much better shape than on those on the other side of the river. The fences were up, fields intact, and the roads were solid. A man off to our front remarked. "The lustful god of war has not raped this fair land yet."

Seth, impressed by the man's words, quickly added his own eloquence. "But alas, his musky stench, pawing hands, and panting fiery breath are not far away."

We marched along in good spirits, enjoying the relative peace of the day. With the arrival of night, we went into camp along the Plank Road about two miles from Chancellorsville. The sounds of some skirmishing to the south and artillery booming toward the east arrested our attention.

"That must be our boys over near Fredericksburg," said Seth. Every man became quiet and listened, staring out into the distance, our vision frustrated by the impenetrable forest. Suddenly a shell passed overhead and hit some trees. We crouched awaiting another. Several hours passed with no further action and we relaxed for the night.

Remembering Seth's prediction of Hooker' plan, Isaiah asked. "Seth, are we going to attack in the morning?"

"Could be, Isaiah, why else would we march all this way—we're not going to sit here and just twiddle our thumbs." Seth pulled together some more pine needles for a bed.

Had our flanking movement been successful? The officers we saw riding by at the crack of dawn appeared quite satisfied, smiling and slapping each other on the back, pointing out toward the east.

The word came down to form up and we gathered near the lone building that defined Chancellorsville. "Here we go boys," said Seth as we marched up near the lonely building. I checked my cartridge pack and gripped my rifle. We did nothing.

Without explanation, our officers ordered us to retrench and take up defensive positions. Seth was confused. "If we're not going to attack, why did we march all the way over here in such a hurry? I don't understand this. We are here on the enemy's flank. Why are we not attacking?"

I was also perplexed. "I thought Hooker was our fighting general, Fighting Joe!"

Seth kicked at his heavy knapsack on the ground. "I can't figure it out, Hiram. I must have it all wrong. I have never understood these cussed idiots and should quit trying." Isaiah tried to console us.

"We just have to be patient. We don't know what they know." Orders then came detailing where the various regiments should take up positions. The 11th Corps and the 82nd Ohio were placed on the far western edge of the army farthest from the most likely action. From what I could see, the 11th Corps was strung out along the Plank Road with some German regiments stationed to the west of us. Our guns and rifle embankments pointed to the south, the most likely place for an enemy attack.

As the afternoon wore on, we relaxed, eating and resting up. Bands played mainly German tunes and a herd of beef cattle grazed in a nearby opening. Wagons of all sorts were parked everywhere. Cooking kettles boiled with meat and vegetables. The fragrant smell of food wafted over the army. Pipes were smoked, card games appeared, and laughter laced the conversations.

Seth, Isaiah, and I had found a place under a large oak tree. To our rear stood a small church and off to our right and front was a farm, its fields bordered by the thick woods. We made a fire and thoroughly enjoyed our first good meal in many days. "Oh thank you Lord for this bounteous meal," said Isaiah, his mouth full, as even he ate before completely giving thanks.

After a leisurely afternoon and evening, we turned in. The woods were alive with singing insects and birds. The underbrush rattled with squirrels, rabbits, and critters busy in their nighttime activities. None of this prevented us from dropping off into a contented deep sleep.

Chirping birds awoke us the next morning, May 2. A stiff figure with a brimmed hat on a white horse rode along our lines. Seth rolled out of bed and quickly jumped to his feet.

"Blamed if that ain't Hooker down there in the clearing," Seth yelled as he peered into the scattered light of early morning. Immediately Isaiah and I leaped to our feet and followed him.

"I heard Hooker rode a white horse and there it is beaming like a lamp against the darkness of the woods!" How Isaiah could be so eloquent so early surprised me.

"I wonder what he is doing way out here?" I asked squinting and trying to shade my eyes from the morning sun.

Hooker was meeting with Generals Howard and Schurz. Howard was on his horse and was easily identified by the lack of one arm that he had lost in a previous battle. The bespectacled Schurz was standing on the ground holding the reins of his horse. His tussled hair wafted in the early morning breeze. This meeting was only about two hundred yards away from us.

Hooker pointed to the west to the edge of our flank. Schurz nodded his head and became more animated pointing in various directions. Howard remained still, even yawning. A rider then came up and delivered a message to Hooker. After reading it, Hooker rode off with Howard toward Chancellorsville. Schurz then mounted his horse and moved to his nearby headquarters, close to the farm.

We looked at each other and after a short silence I asked, "What do you think they were talking about, Seth?"

"Well, we're on the far western flank and I bet Hooker didn't like what he saw here."

Isaiah had a questioning look on his face. "Why, what's wrong with the way we're deployed?"

"Well, what's out there with the Germans? Embankments? Batteries? Hell, no, just groups of men in an open field in front of that woods. We should be digging in! That is our flank and its up in the air!" I was confused.

"Why, dig in out there? Aren't the Rebs off to our east and south?" I asked the question knowing I had set myself up for a verbal lashing.

"Hiram, don't you remember what happened back in Manassas? The Rebs, and especially Jackson, hardly ever come right at you. You got to watch for them devils on the flanks." Isaiah immediately saw the point.

"Seth, we have to tell our officers about this!"

A blank stare came upon our faces. We all knew the impossibility.

General Schurz, responding to reports of enemy movements to our west, did take action to defend our flank. The 82nd Ohio moved away from the Plank Road to a defensive position on a road coming in from the west. The small church was to our left and behind us. A farm and Schurz's headquarters was to our right. With the exception of Schurz, most of the 11th Corps still faced south.

Even though Seth still fidgeted about the lack of embankments and cannons on our flank, we relaxed and felt easy about things. The battle sounds were far to our east and the woods to the west were almost impenetrable. Still, we cast a wary eye in that direction from time to time.

After coming off guard duty in the late afternoon, we settled in for a quiet evening. Isaiah, Seth, and I relaxed on a slight ridge near a tall tree. The quiet around us was disconcerting. Always a keen observer of his surroundings, Seth stood up and looked around. "Why are those woods so quiet? The birds are usually singing loud now."

We then heard artillery and skirmishing off to our south and saw some regiments in our division move off in that direction. Not much later, an officer rode by us to Schurz's headquarters, quickly dismounted, and rushed into the farmhouse. After a few minutes, he came out exclaiming. "The fools won't listen! I know what I saw! The Rebels are to the west, lots of 'em!" Schurz later came out and moved our regiment to a fork in the road, facing more west. About five in the afternoon we saw some deer and rabbits run through our camp.

This struck me as strange. "I have never seen that before! Why are those animals running out of the woods?"

Without hesitation, Seth jumped to his feet. "Hiram, Isaiah! Something is behind those varmints! The Rebs are coming at us on our flank!"

We picked up our packs and grabbed our rifles. A loud crash of musketry sounded and smoke rolled in from the west. An officer rode by us yelling. "To arms! To arms, men!" My heart pounded in my chest. Memories of the horrible fighting at Second Bull Run flashed through my mind. We formed into a double-ranked line of battle and nervously scanned the dense woods and the fork of the road. I stood between Seth and Isaiah in the second rank of soldiers.

Cannons boomed and bullets whistled, the roar of battle increased and suddenly seemed to be all around us. To my left along the Plank Road hundreds of men, wagons, cattle, and mules ran through regiments of soldiers desperately trying to form up for battle. "My Lord, look at that!" Seth yelled, his face was white with fear.

To our front, a disorganized mob of terrified men and animals approached us. They cursed in German and hollered at us, waving. "De Rebs are coming! Run! Run!".

General Schurz rode up behind us. "Stand your ground! Stand your ground! Fire one volley when the enemy comes out of de woods, and then charge on my command!"

Seth erupted, slapped my shoulder. "A bayonet charge? What in blazes? They are over there in force! Thousands of 'em! We will be lucky just to slow them down while we retreat. My God, what idiots!"

Isaiah attached his bayonet, turned, and calmly addressed the flustered soldier. "Seth, we will do what we have to do." My blood ran cold as I fumbled for my bayonet. Seth shook his head as he slammed his bayonet on the end of his rifle.

Colonel James Robinson and Major David Thomson then moved along our columns. "Hurry men! Fix bayonets and be ready to fire on our commands!"

A fleeing straggler ran by us, his face full of fear. I looked at the edge of trees now clouded by gathering banks of smoke. A whir of grapeshot whistled into us thudding into flesh, producing screams of pain. All the memories of combat exploded into my consciousness, paralyzing me for a moment, and then, strangely, peace.

The shadowy forms of enemy soldiers now appeared on the edge of the woods. Each man emerged as if from a tar pit, pulled himself from the brambles, and joined an advancing line. This line now gathered and charged yelling like banshees. Men in blue in front of us threw down their rifles and ran by us to the rear. "Steady men, stay here, no running in the 82nd," said a calm Colonel Robinson as he walked behind us. "Be just and fear not."

Resoluteness settled on me. *Come on, come on.* My mouth became dry and I licked dry lips.

"Ready, aim, fire! Fire at will men! Let them have it boys!" Our captain ran along back of me and slapped me on the back. "Fire, soldier, fire!" I aimed my rifle at a man running full speed at us, waving his arms and rifle like a windmill. My bullet stopped him dead in his tracks and he fell to the ground about one hundred and fifty yards to our front.

"Good shot Hiram," yelled Isaiah. I glanced at him and began the loading process. The bayonet on my rifle made this a more difficult task.

Bayonet? Are we really going to charge? I looked around at our lines and everyone was busy firing and loading. No command to charge. General Schurz then yelled. "Move to da rear men! Keep order now! Center on da flag!"

Amidst whizzing bullets and bursting shells, we moved in mass about a quarter mile to the rear. The enemy lines slowed as they gathered and organized. Some Rebel lines to our left started to move south. While making our way to some shallow rifle pits, we saw General Howard sitting on a horse in an ocean of stragglers near the church. With a flag held under the stump of his amputated arm, we heard him yell. "Stop men, stop! Form up, here! Don't you love your country? Stop, I order you!" Only a few gathered around him.

Before long, we reached a line of hastily dug rifle pits. Seth, Isaiah, and I jumped into one these thin depressions. "These pits are too shallow," exclaimed Seth as he tried to push more soil up in front of him. Isaiah and I did the same thing. The wet clay squished between my fingers and the rocks cut my hands. Here we awaited the enemy whose numbers seemed to grow with every minute. As they came into view, we started firing. Soon we heard them whooping and yelling not only in front of us but off to our sides, and God forbid, in our rear!

Behind us some guns of our artillery opened up on the advancing Rebs slowing down their pace, scattering them. *Relief! Take a breath!* The respite was short. A broad blast of enemy musketry suddenly silenced our cannons and the Rebels again formed around a red flag on our front.

"Shoot the flag bearer!" Seth yelled pointing straight ahead. I took aim at the enemy color bearer whose flag was plowing through the smoke. I could not see the soldier but fired a round below the waving banner. Suddenly the flag went down but in a few seconds was again advancing. Another man had picked it up and again it was a rallying point, focusing the advancing Confederates right at us.

Bullets now came at us in mass and I buried myself in the soil as balls plowed into the rifle pit from the front and sides. Men in butternut were now among us. A man without a gun darted in and out of the smoke in front of me. He stopped by a dead soldier, went through his pockets, and then disappeared into the smoke. I did not fire at him but dropped an armed soldier to his right.

To my left, two soldiers were in a death struggle, each pushing his bayonet into the chest and throat of the other. I shot the enemy soldier who fell onto his blue-clad adversary. Seth slapped me on the back, pointing to the side of the rifle pits. Rebel soldiers were all around us.

"Hiram, we're surrounded! We have to get to those woods back there." A ball struck the dirt he had piled up in front of him throwing dirt into his face. Spitting and coughing Seth got up on his knees, a bullet zipped by his head. " Isaiah, you take the left, Hiram you in middle, and I'll take the right." As we formed our triangle, the bugle sounded for general retreat.

The cover of the woods was about one hundred and fifty yards to our rear. Treading backwards, our trinity of privates made its way through the haze and smoke.

Off to the side a shell struck a man tearing off his arm and shoulder revealing a beating heart. No screams, just masses of blood spurting from his open side like a fountain. A large gray-clad enemy soldier appeared to our front. Isaiah shot him and he fell into the rifle pit we just vacated.

Seth and I were ready to fire as we ambled backwards like a huge crab. Isaiah looked at us. A nod conveyed "go ahead and load" and he took his eyes off the turmoil and reached for his cartridge belt.

Now a shadowy gray form comes in from my right and I level him with a shot to his chest. He fell back as if kicked by a horse. Seth is now ready as I start reloading. Soon we reached the dense woods to our rear and disappeared into a mass of brush and vines. The thick vegetation pulled at us and literally sang like a harp as shells and bullets plucked the branches and leaves.

As we moved through the smoky woods, it was impossible to tell our men from the enemy. Soldiers of both sides intermingled in the dense brush. Off in the haze we heard a man with a southern accent. "Surrender you cussed Yank! Drop that gun now!" It was a matter of chance whether you bumped into friend or foe.

We continued to move as a group of three depending on each other for protection. Two of us watched the front and flanks while the third kept us going east towards headquarters at the Chancellor House.

Around eight p.m. as darkness settled, we came to the formidable entrenchments surrounding a clearing around the large house where General Hooker had his headquarters. Troops on the perimeter had formed lines of battle to confront the oncoming enemy. In the moonlight, I could see thousands of men milling around. Officers rode through this menagerie of confusion calling, trying to organize their regiments.

"82nd Ohio! 82nd Ohio! Form up here!" Colonel Robinson stood beside our flag yelling, his voice boomed over the turmoil. The sparkle of bursting shells profiled his bearded form against the night sky.

Soon we organized again as a company. Many of us were missing. We later learned that about eighty of our regiment had been killed, wounded, or captured.

From our position in the rear, we saw a spectacle of war that even eclipsed Manassas as the Rebels attacked the 2nd and 3rd Corps in our front. Wave after wave of Confederates assaulted the formidable entrenchments but the battle lines held around the Chancellor House. The noise and sound of the nighttime battle was horrendous, producing an almost supernatural rendering of brilliant red flashes and billowing pulses of smoke. Seth wondered aloud as we watched from our position in the rear. "My God, how can anybody come out alive from that?"

After a while the storms of battle ceased for the night leaving a terrible residue of dead and wounded men everywhere, screaming, pleading for help. Fires burned in the dense woods. With every breeze, the inferno roared through the brush burning many wounded alive. Their screams echoed through the night. It was grandly, awfully terrible.

Early the next morning (Sunday May 3), the 11th Corps moved to the extreme left and posted behind thickset entrenchments. "This is what we should have built on our flank," muttered Seth. The battle again commenced but we did not see any further combat.

The horrible forest fires continued to do their grisly tasks. As darkness settled, the battle lulled into sporadic skirmishing. We stayed at the ready, sleeping on our arms until Tuesday, May 5.

On Tuesday evening, a chilling rain fell and we spent another uncomfortable night, cold and wet, shivering and unable to sleep. We were not allowed to make fires as our Generals wanted to conceal our positions and movements.

The next morning we moved toward the Rappahannock River, formed up in Corps, and prepared to cross the river to the north side at United States Ford. Masses of men in blue blanketed the landscape, waiting for their turn to cross, praying that Rebel shells would not rain down on our concentrated ranks. It took all day and night for the Army of the Potomac to cross.

After crossing the river at night, we bivouacked in a thunderstorm about half way back towards our winter quarters near Washington. "Second Bull Run all over again. What is it about this army that we always retreat in a damn thunderstorm," complained Seth as we shivered under our oilcloths held up by rifles stuck in the muddy ground.

"Hiram, what did we accomplish? Seems to me we flanked Lee, got ready to attack, stopped, retrenched, and got flanked ourselves. By God, we got outgeneraled again!" Seth's anger was evident even through his misery. Isaiah, after a minute, cleared the cold rain from his face and replied.

"I don't know Seth, it seemed like we killed off more of them than they did of us. I think Hooker got them to attack us when we were entrenched, like they did to us at Fredericksburg."

"Killed more of them?" Seth started to cough, his lungs congested from exposure to the elements. "We were crucified in that flank attack. Jackson almost rolled up our entire army." He coughed violently. "And he would have done it if the son of a bitch had started earlier." Isaiah shook his head.

"Seth, please stop swearing."

Seth looked at Isaiah, shivered with a fever, and almost broke down. "How we got through it alive, I will never know." I put my hand on his shoulder. The rain ran off his hat and down my sleeve.

"Seth, you are the reason we made it. If we had not retreated the way you told us all three of us would have been killed, or worse, captured and sent to Richmond to a hellhole of a prison camp." A loud bolt of thunder and a bright flash of lightning pierced the black sky.

"Lord God, Almighty!" proclaimed Seth.

Isaiah, also feverish, smiled and replied. "Amen!" The rain formed rivulets around us as we huddled together, trying to keep warm and sleep in the mud.

We rose the next morning from our miserable slumber in a light drizzle, formed up, and eventually slogged into our old camp near Stafford Court House. Finding our hut, we quickly built a fire, dried off, warmed up some stew, and settled around the stove. After eating, we dropped off to sleep, the first restful night in eleven days of battles and storms.

Little did we know that another tempest was coming after our short rest period. It was born on the newspaper accounts of the battle.

Isaiah was the first to awake and respond to the turmoil outside of our hut. A soldier from another unit was waving a copy of a newspaper, taunting the men of the 11th Corps. He quoted from an article by Horace Greeley blaming the 11th Corps for "the unaccountable and inexcusable collapse at Chancellorsville". Joining his comrades, he turned and yelled at us. "You fights mit Sigel but runs mit Schurz, you tam cowards! Howard's cowards, the running half-moons!"

"Cowards? Cowards? They're calling us cowards?" Isaiah could hardly speak as he came back into the hut.

" For God's sakes, Isaiah, spit it out. Who is calling us cowards?" Seth implored with a concerned look.

"All the newspapers are blaming the 11th Corps for what happened at Chancellorsville. They're lumping us all together with the Dutch saying that we all threw down our guns and ran like deer at the first sign of the enemy."

"We were the last regiment to leave the rifle pits!" I exclaimed. "And we certainly did not leave our guns on the field! Somebody has to tell the newspapers that we all did not run! What are the people of Ohio going to say when they read this?"

Seth walked to the door of the hut and turned to us. "Damned Dutch. I knew they would drag us down with them. Did you hear them cussing at us for staying and fighting as they ran through us at the rifle pits?"

Isaiah rose from his bunk. "Seth, not all the Germans ran. The Wisconsin regiment off to our right held their ground on the first attack and fought like tigers. Almost all their officers were shot. I don't think it is right to lump all the Dutch into one group."

"Well, get used to it Isaiah. Sure as blazes, we will all be branded as cowards in this manure pile of a battle. Even our generals will blame us. What do you bet Hooker and that religious nut Howard will excuse all their blunders by blaming the cowards of the 11th Corps. Dammit... I mean... blast it! Why didn't Hooker attack? I can't believe it!"

In the coming days, we implored General Schurz to explain what happened to the newspapers. This he tried to do but his reports to Hooker and to the papers did little good. We were constantly derided and became the butt of jokes as we marched by other groups.

The German regiments had a rougher time of it. They not only received abuse from other Corps but hateful comments from non-German regiments within the 11th Corps. Thus was the state of our regiment as we awaited the next campaign.

Even though Stonewall Jackson had been killed (we later heard by his own men) at Chancellorsville, we knew we would meet General Robert E. Lee of the Rebel army somewhere soon. The question was where and would we of the despised 11th Corps redeem ourselves when this event happened.

It was time for another letter to my family in Rome, Ohio. When the news about the battle hit the papers, I knew they would be worried.

Brooke's Station Virginia
May 10, 1863
Dear Family:

As you no doubt have heard, the 82ⁿᵈ Ohio was in another terrible battle across the river from here at a place called Chancellorsville. Not to worry. I made it without getting wounded or killed but I honestly do not know how. Our regiment was completely surrounded and overrun by Jackson's Rebs. We had to retreat going from rifle pits to trees in this tangled wilderness. Our regiment then joined up with the rest of the army and crossed the river. We then marched in a terrible rainstorm back to camp, almost like at Second Bull Run. Jackson was killed by accident by his own men.

You probably heard that the 11ᵗʰ Corps ran and are a bunch of cowards but our regiment stood firm and only retreated when ordered. We should not be disgraced like those who did break and run. We should have never been caught off guard like we were if the generals would have done their job.

Isaiah and Seth made it all right too. We are now being supplied in camp. I even have a spare pair of shoes and things are better while we wait on the next big campaign, which should start anytime now. Please pray that God continues to protect us as this is a terrible war. I cannot describe the horrors. Give my love to everyone.
Your son,
Hiram

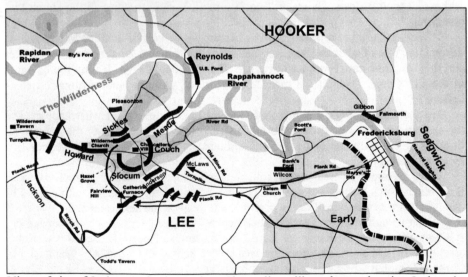

View of site of Jackson's flank attack at Chancellorsville and map showing Jackson's march and attack on Howard *(map by Hal Jespersen, www.posix.com/CW).*

CHAPTER 10
THE LONG MARCH NORTH

The injustice of the blanketed blame for Chancellorsville weighed heavily on the 82nd Ohio. New shirts, trousers, socks, shoes, and coats delivered by railroad brought corporal relief to our army but did little to raise morale lost in the humiliating rush to retreat from Chancellorsville. Our spirits in the 11th Corps languished in anger, self-doubt, and shame.

The thousands of abandoned rifles, cartridge belts, knapsacks, blankets, and coats left on the other side of the Rappahannock now aided the enemy. Never more proud or haughty, the Rebels demonstrated daily on the far banks of the river and Confederate pickets threw taunts about our poor generals across the river every night.

Worse, Hooker barely hid his contempt for the 11th Corps and our own troops ridiculed us. We yearned for a chance to redeem ourselves as we waited for the next campaign.

Isaiah came into our hut reading one of the many Christian tracts that General Howard spread through camp. Howard, a devout Christian, hoped to save souls, revive spirits, and bring on the power of Christian warfare to the dispirited 11th Corps. Howard hoped to "save" the freethinking, beer-drinking Germans who said "give us sauerkraut not tracts". Most of us blamed Howard for not preparing for Jackson's attack and gave him a cool reception. The bitterness spewed out in our tent.

"Isaiah, what are you doing with one of Howard's tracts? Put them out by the sinks where they can be used for a good purpose!" Isaiah, his sense of religious propriety slighted, responded.

"Seth, how can you be so blasphemous about the things of God. Don't you know that any day now you will have to stand before the Judgment and give account of how you lived your life and the things you say? Lord forgive you. I know that Howard made mistakes at Chancellorsville but I believe he is a good Christian man who wants to do the right thing." Isaiah paused. "At least he doesn't swear like Hooker."

"Well, I would rather be me at Judgment Day than him. I didn't cause the deaths of good men by going to bed and ignoring warnings about the enemy massing on our flank. Doesn't God care about that more than me or Hooker swearing? Cursing doesn't hurt a damn thing, ignoring warnings and sending men into a hail of bullets, now that's profane!"

Isaiah sat down on his bunk and thought for a while, being silent almost to the point where I became uncomfortable. Finally, he answered.

"The Bible tells me to love God and follow his commandments, to live for others and not myself. I cannot do this on my own without being changed by the power of Christ. This doesn't mean that I am perfect but I can depend on God for help even if I make mistakes. If Howard made an honest mistake, that's one thing. If he put his own comfort ahead of the army's welfare, that's another. Of course, he will be judged for that. But you will be judged just as harshly for taking God's name in vain, getting drunk, lusting, or other things that offend God."

Seth rose to his feet. "I don't get it. Swearing is just as bad as killing? Strange set of rules you follow Isaiah." Seth walked to the door and then turned. "How about all the killing you're doing in this war? You nearly blew that Rebel in half as we were retreating at Chancellorsville. Doesn't that offend God?"

"War is different, especially this war. We're trying to save our country and set a people free. God does not want wars but he will use them to His purposes!"

Seth chuckled and patted Isaiah on the back as he returned to his bunk. "Well, it sure would help if he gave us a good general or two!" Seth laid down in his bed as if to end the conversation but then sat up.

"You know what I think. Things just happen. Like me being in this damn war. I thought it would be fun and would help my status with the women to put on a soldier suit and come down and whip the Rebs. What did I get? A filthy, stinking mess of a war where good men die on marches or are getting shot and blown to hell by people who think they are doing God's will. I am sick of the whole thing and I don't see God doing a damn thing to stop it." Isaiah gasped audibly. The expression on Seth's face turned to one of full anger and deep contemplation.

Taking a deep breath, I entered the conversation. "Seth, I don't know why life is so mean. I lost my mother when I was three and my sister when she was ten. I can't believe God caused this to happen." This was almost too much for me, a lump formed in my throat.

"Like you and Isaiah, I have seen things in this war that shock me to the core. I don't blame God. Most of our problems are our fault and it's up to us to do God's will to stop them." The lump dissolved. "I do know that we're locked in a death grip with the Rebs and somebody is gonna win. I happen to side with old Abe. Saving the Union and freeing the slaves is right even if this war is the price we have to pay. I hope and pray that God helps us stay alive but if he doesn't, ..."

"Well Hiram, where do you see any hint of God in this hellhole of a world? Things just happen! It's a crap shoot. Sometimes you make it, sometimes you don't. When you die, you're gone like a dead dog or those poor dead soldiers whose bones scatter the fields of war we have come through."

Isaiah put his hand on Seth's arm. "Seth, I pray that you will see God." As the bugler sounded the new song "Taps" that had spread across the camps, Seth patted Isaiah on his hand.

"Get what you can, when you can, believe what you can." Isaiah turned and replied with steel-cold words.

"What profiteth a man to gain the world but lose his soul?"

As I lay on my bunk, the conversation just finished played over in my mind, intermingling with painful visions of battles from McDowell to Chancellorsville. I then wondered about the men I had killed and who they were; their faces were featureless, nameless. I jerked awake and saw Seth and Isaiah tossing about on their bunks.

In the morning, we rose for roll call and learned that the 82nd Ohio, now numbering 350 battle-hardened veterans, had a new brigade commander. Colonel Wladimir Krzyzanowski now commanded us, the 11th Corps, 3rd Division, Second Brigade. Seth left the muster line nodding his head and waved us over.

"Old Kriz is a good one, leads by example, gets up front rather than just giving orders and staying in the rear. Hiram, things may be looking up!" Slapping me on the back, he left for the sinks with a smile on his face. Isaiah and I watched in amazement as Seth sauntered off. Dumbfounded, I exclaimed.

"I don't believe it, what's happened to him?" Isaiah had a ready answer.

"Seth knows that even if we have doubts, we have to go on. How else can we handle what comes at us in this war?"

Isaiah had doubts?

"That's what faith is all about, Hiram, go on through the doubts, do what you have to do and ask God to help you."

The next night I was on picket duty overlooking the river. The campfires of the Confederates flickered amidst the darkness. A golden moon peaked out from hazy clouds, backlighting the landscape. In the distance, bands played and columns of men moved off behind the hills. *What's going on? Are the Rebs up to something?* I reported the movements to my commanding officer after picket duty.

"Yes, we have been getting reports of some fidgeting over there." He scratched a match on the bottom of his chair and lit a cigar. "Might be the first signs of the enemy starting a campaign. Hooker has been kept up to date, don't be surprised if we start to move soon," replied the sandy-haired, moon faced officer as he put his cigar in an ash tray and entered my report and its date into a logbook.

The moon barely revealed the interior of our hut. I tried to step between Seth and Isaiah who were asleep but stepped on Seth's foot.

"Ow! Hiram you big Jonah! Watch where you step!"

"Sorry, Seth, its dark in here." Seth groaned.

"See anything going on across the river?"

"Rebs seem to be moving but who knows where."

"I bet we will find out before long. What do you think, Isaiah?"

"God knows. God knows..." murmured Isaiah, half asleep.

I found my bunk and wondered what lay ahead. Sleep crept on me slowly releasing scenes of McDowell, Cross Keys, Second Bull Run, and Chancellorsville, each succeeding battle more horrible. *How, oh Lord, did we survive those horrendous fights? Is the next battle going to be worse? Probably so. God knows. Go to sleep.*

In the morning, I heard our officers arguing about where we should go. They fussed about details and wavered back and forth about what to tell us soldiers. Finally, they told us to pack three days rations and march north to Dumfries to guard this old former business hub of the South.

On the way, Seth, Isaiah, and I talked, our words coming between breaths, arrhythmic to the marching of our feet.

"If the Johnnies are going north, why don't we just move on Richmond?" Isaiah asked as he shifted his rifle and adjusted his knapsack.

Seth responded in his calculated manner. "Well, I figure we are now after Lee's army, and old Lee, why he is after us, the Union army. It's a matter of fighting and numbers now, not about land and territory."

"Where do you think we will be fightin' next Seth?" I asked looking across to Isaiah who was in the middle of our rank. The dust settled on Seth's face and he coughed.

"I expect Lee will have to move into better country, everything here is shot to ...", he looked at Isaiah, "I mean... used up. Lee can't support his army here no more, maybe Maryland again."

"You mean a battle like Antietam is coming?" Isaiah asked, his voice cracking.

"Hard to say. Lee is a wily fox and he strikes where you don't expect him." This comment numbed us and we tramped in silence through the countryside toward war-torn and desolate Dumfries.

When we arrived, we learned that the Confederates were moving north up the Shenandoah Valley. After a short rest, we were to follow them on the eastern side of the mountains, keeping between them and Washington. We packed our knapsacks, bid our camp at Dumfries adieu, and moved into line. At the bugle, we marched across the wet but drying and firming Virginia roads, heading north.

On June 14, we reached Centreville and rested two days. Damp and cool nights did not keep us from sleeping well right on the ground. Our toughness surprised me.

What used to cause pure misery was now ignored, put out of the mind, suffered with a stoic indifference. We learned how to turn off pain.

We resumed the march and again crossed the bleak and scarred fields at Bull Run. Stretching out across the battlefield were the now familiar rows of shallow graves. The sight of the skulls and bony arms unearthed by recent rains sickened us again. Reaching for the sky, they beckoned to us the living, "you too may become like us."

We came close to a grave by the road. A rib cage with fragments of cloth and dried flesh revealed itself. Seth broke our silent stare.

"What a reward for this poor soldier! Half buried with your innards and bones coming out of the dirt for all to see and nobody knows your name, or even cares."

We realized the difference; the bullets found him and missed us. "Ain't that glorious!" Seth shifted the heavy load on his back, looking to Isaiah for a comment.

"The government won't leave them like that. Someone will be back to give the fallen a proper burial. Just can't do it now." Isaiah strained to adjust the straps of his heavy pack. I reached over and lifted it allowing him to loosen the straps.

"You've got more faith in the army than I do, Isaiah. I don't see how each of those fellows will get a proper burial. There's just too many." I felt for my identification tag hanging down from my neck. "Still got that metal name tag, Isaiah? At least they should know your name should you die somewhere." I don't know why, but the fate of the nameless bothered me.

"Right here," replied Isaiah touching his fingers to a dangling necklace under his coat. Seth peered at the metal tag on Isaiah's chest and noticed a metal cross next to it.

"There are no guarantees your family will ever know what happened even if you do have identification." Seth looked back at the old Bull Run battleground. "Did you die running or charging? A coward or a hero?" Shading his eyes, Seth looked up in the sky at some circling vultures. "Nobody will know but those cussed ugly birds."

The next several days were miserable. Long marches, few rests, sporadic supplies. Scouts reported the enemy was now unmistakably headed for Pennsylvania, invading the north, our homeland. Our commanders, riding on their horses, demanded almost thirty miles a day, almost twice the normal distance.

The hot dry weather beat on us and hundreds of men fell out from heat exhaustion. Clouds of dust from the columns of men and wagons ahead of us permeated every orifice, causing our teeth to grind on the grit.

Angry Virginia citizens, especially women, hurled insults from dilapidated houses and war-scarred farms. Palpable as the dust, their anger cut deep. Yet we endured, did not fall out or faint. The honor of the 11th Corps and the 82nd Ohio was at stake. We must redeem ourselves in the coming battle, especially if it was going to occur on our own soil.

When we looked our worst, ragged, torn, and dirty, we came across new recruits from Washington. The new soldiers, fresh and in new uniforms, stood in perfect formation beside the road. They looked at us with both shock and intense interest. We portrayed their future and waves of doubt were visible on each face. With our dilapidated clothes, dirty faces, and war scarred dispositions, we were apparitions of what was to come. I heard a young voice from the back row declare as we passed. "What did we get ourselves into?"

On June 18, we reached Goose Creek, a little stream south of Leesburg, Virginia. Here we mercifully stopped and were able to rest, wash up, and feed ourselves. For six days we recuperated and got ourselves ready for the next fight with the enemy, wherever that may take place.

We knew the enemy was getting near because the cavalry of Confederate General Mosby almost captured our General Howard. An alert picket and a quick dart behind our lines saved him from the "gray ghost".

It was at Goose Creek after a bath that I threw away my old worn shoes and put on my new ones issued at Brooke's Station. As I did this, Seth asked, "Well was it worth carrying that second pair all this way? You know, if you were more patriotic, you could have carried a few more rounds of ammunition instead," he added smiling wryly.

These shoes, so carefully massaged with oil according to Sam Armstrong's instructions, added new life to my step as we trudged further north toward the Potomac River.

Late in the day on June 19, an order to stop and form companies made its way down the lines. Major Crall and now Sergeant Armstrong called a short meeting of our company. Crall, an officer with a light complexion, fine features, and serious disposition, then addressed us.

"Men, I want to remind you that things are getting serious as we come into this next fight. We need every man to do his duty. If you are thinking of dropping out since we're near home, think again." His expression became solemn as he walked back and forth. "Three deserters were executed by the leaders of the 12th Corps today. I know this seems harsh but we cannot lose this next battle, the fate of the whole nation rides on how well we do. I know most of the skulkers and cowards are long gone but still there are rumors of discontent in the 11th Corps. Be forewarned."

The young officer scanned us for a few seconds but stared longer at a German company before he rode his horse off to the front of the column.

On June 25, we marched down the riverbank onto a pontoon bridge and crossed the Potomac River into Maryland at Edward's Ferry. We entered a new world. Isaiah was ecstatic. "Look at those fields and farms and the crops! The fences are up and the barns and houses have shutters! Lord, crossing that river is like going from darkness to light, hell to heaven."

Instead of cursing, people now cheered and waved, beckoning us to stop for loaves of bread, pots of butter, and glasses of milk. We gawked at the willowy figures of young women as we marched by a school picnic. They waved handkerchiefs and threw kisses as they rushed up to the road. "Oh, I like this! Ain't they something Hiram?" Seth stretched his hand out to a pretty, petite, thin but shapely brunette girl with long hair, tan complexion, and dark eyes. Her white teeth sparkled as she giggled, took Seth's hand, shook her hips, and swung Seth around in a circle.

Sam Armstrong yelled rushing up. "Back in line! Back in line!" Someone soft and sweet smelling pulled on my arm.

Turning, I beheld a beautiful curvaceous blond girl in a yellow dress and bonnet. Her flowing hair, blue eyes, large red lips, and a wide smile engulfed me. I stood in a trance and gawked.

"Hello, there. Where are you boys going?" Speechless, I just grinned and turned red as I beheld her flashing eyes. "Cat got your tongue soldier boy?" She then smiled, squeezed my arm, and faded back into the crowd as officers tried to maintain order up and down our column.

"Oooh, wee, Hiram!" yelled Seth. "That one is a keeper!" Isaiah smiled like a Cheshire cat as a plump red haired girl smiled at him.

"Enough of that! We're not at a dance here! Get back in line there soldier!" Sam Armstrong's hard shoulder brought me back to reality as we marched on. We later stopped in a clearing and ate the best food we'd had in months. Seth and I searched the landscape for those two girls but without success. Their absence left a hollow feeling but oh, how good it was to be back on home soil!

As we marched further into Maryland, I don't know why but I contrasted the girls at the school with what we saw in Washington at the brothel. One was a fresh uplifting breeze and the other a stagnant waft of a swamp. *Lordy, what a difference!*

Further, into Maryland we came upon some people offering food but at high prices and with sour attitudes. A farmer with loaves of bread and a hard-faced disposition approached us at one of our stops.

"Why are you charging Union soldiers such high prices?" Isaiah asked as he held a loaf of bread. "This bread was given to us at the last town."

A scowl descended on the farmer's face. "Well you bastards weren't very generous to Virginia, now were you sonny boy?" He jerked the loaf of bread out of Isaiah's hands. "The bread costs what it costs, if you don't want to buy it, git!" Although our officers warned us that there would be punishments for those offending the local citizenry, these bitter secessionists lost not only their food but chickens, geese, and other livestock.

June 26 found us in Middletown, a strong Union town. There we saw many carriages said to be from Hagerstown. These people claimed that from eighty thousand to over one hundred thousand Rebels with artillery passed through that city. Strong complaints met the ears of our officers about the Rebels foraging off the countryside and then paying in worthless Confederate script.

Along the main street of Middletown, a woman came up and walked beside us as we marched along.

"God bless you young man. God bless you. Where are you from?"

"Ohio, ma'am, Mansfield, Ohio," I tried not to walk too fast for her but I had to keep up with the rest of the column.

"Oh my, oh my!" She stopped and raised a gloved hand to her mouth. "So there will be Buckeye blood in Pennsylvania along with all the rest. Oh my!" Puzzled, I looked back at her as we marched on.

"Did she say Pennsylvania? Are we going to Pennsylvania?" Isaiah asked tugging on my arm. "Seth, that woman said we're going to Pennsylvania." Seth scratched his jaw as he thought through this piece of information.

"Pennsylvania? Pennsylvania? Hmmm. Makes sense once you think about it. Lee can provision up there." Seth's eyes opened wide. "Sweet Jesus, that old fox is taking the war way up north!" I thought about my relatives from Pennsylvania and added.

"The land up there is some of the best for fighting you ever saw. Get up on those rocky ridges and you can hold off twice your number. I hope we get to the high ground first."

"Well, after seeing Fredericksburg Hooker should know that," added Isaiah as we passed out of Middletown and viewed the low, edgy mountains to the north.

When we arrived in Frederick, Maryland we heard that we had a new commander, General George Gordon Meade. "What happened to old Hooker?" Seth asked Sam Armstrong as he passed near.

"I heard he had a run in with Abe. Hooker said if he couldn't send troops where he wanted, he'd quit. Lincoln trimmed his ears back and let him go. Gave the command to Meade."

After we set up camp on the outskirts of Frederick, I asked Seth, "Do you know anything about Meade? "

"Well, the old goggle-eyed turtle is from Pennsylvania. Should know the land." Seth then rolled his eyes and slapped his knee as he got up from the rock he was sitting on. "Oh shucks, Hiram, what does it matter who is leading this army? You know we'll get out-generaled by Lee. Let's just hope that the 82nd won't have to pay the price!"

"You mean like we did at Chancellorsville," I murmured remembering the flanking attack of Jackson. I kicked at a burning log, causing sparks to fly. "Maybe we will escape this time," I said, casting an eye toward Isaiah. "Seems to me that the 82nd has anted up enough."

A stick Isaiah had in the fire ignited. The burning branch spit and crackled as he lifted it.

"This next battle may be even more terrible than Chancellorsville. Those people at Hagerstown said they saw one hundred thousand enemy soldiers go by there. Nobody is going to escape the inferno of this battle. Pray God that we do him honor." The flame sputtered and Isaiah blew it out. The smoke stung my eyes, a tear ran down my cheek.

"Good Lord, Hiram, are you crying? After all we have been through?" Seth laughed.

"No, the smoke..." Seth, oblivious to my explanation, continued.

"I don't think I can cry anymore. This war has drained and dried me like an old piece of leather." Isaiah and I looked at each other and then to Seth who reclined against his knapsack, eyes closed.

"Seth, that is where God comes in. He keeps us human in all this carnage," said Isaiah, a peaceful expression on his face. Seth opened his eyes and took a deep breath.

"Hard to be human in this war. Maybe this battle coming up will finish it off." Silence fell around us as we all leaned back and invited sleep. Real tears formed as I searched the stars blinking overhead.

The next evening, June 29, found us near Emmitsburg, Maryland at a Catholic seminary, St. Joseph's College. We arrived just as the sun was setting and immediately made camp on the grounds of the beautifully manicured campus. We were told to be ready to march early the next morning but later the orders were countermanded. We would be able to sleep a few extra hours. It was a balm for our weary souls.

Late the next morning we answered roll call for the bimonthly muster. The promise of rain was written across the sky, hazy clouds rolled on each other building into thick billowy embankments. Soon, periods of rain alternated with drizzle.

Dressed in our raingear, we explored the beautifully manicured campus. Walkways, flower gardens, and white statues laced the grounds. We entered a beautiful cemetery with ornate gravestones and heard one of the German bands playing marches and polkas for the priests and nuns. We walked toward it and joined a group of soldiers seated in a circle.

A group of Germans soldiers sang "Morgenrot", a Dutch song about a young cavalryman contemplating his own death in an upcoming battle. As we listened, a German soldier to our right translated for us.

"*Morning glow, are you calling me to an early death? Soon the trumpets will blow and then I must give up my life, mine and many comrades! Suddenly, all joy came to an end. Yesterday, still proudly on horseback, today shot through my breast, tomorrow in a cold grave. Oh too soon, the beauty and vision of clouds, proudly displayed like milk and blood, fade away. Alas, even a rose wilts. Therefore, humbly I obey God's will. And if death should come to me, I will have died a brave cavalryman."*

After a period of silence, Seth shook his head and exclaimed. "What a time to sing a song like that, just before we're going into a big fight. What we need is "Rally round the flag boys" or something like that. Not a song about a dead cavalryman!"

Isaiah responded. "I don't know Seth, maybe the timing is right. We need to think about God's will, ask for His protection. You may meet your maker tomorrow." Seth got up from his seat on the ground, looked at the hazy sky, and stretched.

"Maybe so, Isaiah, maybe so."

As we walked back to our tent, it began to drizzle and the air became almost liquid. The moon, however, shone brightly through the haze. Sleep eluded me, tomorrow promised to be one of the hardest days yet in a sequence of terrible days. What did lie ahead?

Trying not to wake Seth and Isaiah, I got up and walked a short distance to an opening in the trees. Heavy breathing and snoring filled the thick and humid air. The pickets announced their positions. "Station ten and all's well!"

As I contemplated my life and the events that brought me here, I said a prayer for courage and guidance, probably like thousands of other soldiers this night, both Union and Confederate. A colorful rainbow appeared, apparently due to the strong moonlight shining through the watery mist. A feeling of peace came over me as I surveyed the colors of this nocturnal miracle. I heard footsteps behind me and turned to see Seth and Isaiah, gazing with open mouths, at the spectacle.

"Well I'll be, have you ever seen anything like that?" A stunned Seth scanned the rainbow from the red to the green to the violet, the arch dipping to the north.

Isaiah suddenly exclaimed. "This is a sign from God! I've never seen a rainbow at night!"

"What does it mean?" I asked Isaiah. "Is it a sign of God's protection in the upcoming battle?" Silence.

As we continued to gaze in wonderment, dark clouds came in from the west and flashes of lightning pierced the sky. The rainbow vanished. We stood there quiet, each of us wondering about what had happened. Did it mean anything or was it a random event of nature?

"A rainbow at night followed by dark clouds and lightning? I don't know if I like the drift of that," said an analytical Seth. Both wonderment and confusion attended us on our way through the misty rain back to our tent.

"There must be a meaning to such a rare event," mused Isaiah.

The drizzle continued through the night. The sound of the rain, coughing, and snoring kept me on the edge of sleep. *Terman, get to sleep! You're going into battle tomorrow!* Sometime after midnight, the sound of hoofs beating against the wet ground awoke me. A messenger pulled up at headquarters and soon after an officer ordered us to get ready for an early morning march. The enemy had been sighted near the town of Gettysburg and was concentrating in numbers.

Seth, Isaiah, and I peered at the brightening sky, yellow, red, and orange. "Red sky in the morning, sailor take warning,' murmured Seth. The clouds hung over us but clearer skies were off to the west. No rainbow. Columns of troops slithered over the grounds of the seminary forming to march. In fifteen minutes, we were gone and the campus was again a place of rest and contemplation.

"His eye is on the sparrow," pronounced Isaiah as we marched north behind the First Division. Intermittent showers fell as we marched to Pennsylvania. The mud coated my newly oiled shoes but my feet stayed dry.

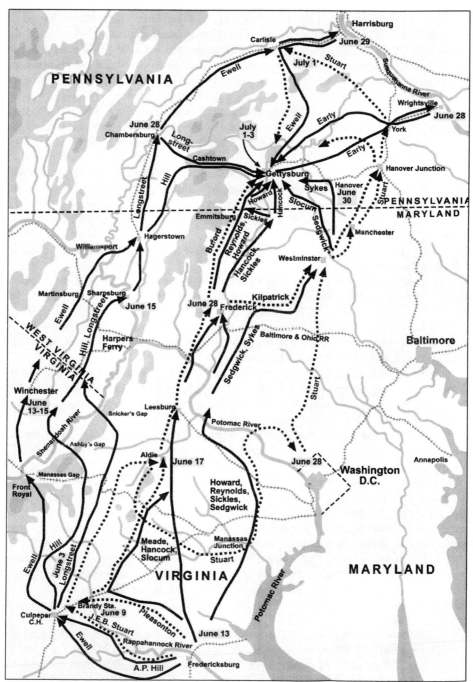

The march north in the Gettysburg campaign. Hiram was in Howard's Corps *(map by Hal Jespersen, www.posix.com/CW)*.

CHAPTER 11
THE GREAT BATTLE AT GETTYSBURG

As we followed the First Division troops, it became clear that we would be slowed down by the wagons and artillery. Our officers then directed us onto the Taneytown Road to Gettysburg, a town about thirteen miles away. This route was two miles longer but was unimpeded by slow wagons. Amidst on and off showers we hurried on slipping and sliding on the muddy road and slugging through swollen streams and marshy lowlands.

When we crossed into Pennsylvania our bands started to play and cheering citizens gathered along the road. The Pennsylvania regiments dipped their flags and cheered loudly for their home state. The scene sent chills down my spine and my heart raced within me.

About 11 a. m. we heard the first faint sounds of artillery up at Gettysburg. The battle was under way. Where would we come in? What would we be asked to do? The clouds rumbled and rain came down hard. The ammunition in my cartridge box, was it staying dry? Should be all right, I had wrapped it in an oilcloth when I packed this morning.

"On the double, men, hurry. The battle is on and you are needed!" yelled an officer on horseback.

Our officers constantly urged us on, to close up ranks, and increase our pace to a run. Men fell out but were quickly met by members of the Provost Guard and herded back in line.

A man who had fallen started to swear and resist the guards, claiming to be "all used up and couldn't go on". An officer approached him, pulled out his pistol, placed it at full cock, and ordered the soldier back in line.

"Get up or I will shoot you!" yelled the officer. I raced by and was soon too far away to hear what happened but I did not hear any pistol shots. My legs ached, my head was dizzy, and my sides felt like they had been stabbed but I continued to run, and run, and run. *Oh dear God, give me strength.*

I watched the feet of the soldier in front and mechanically placed one foot in front of the next, not thinking, just going forward, the sounds of canon growing louder as we raced toward Gettysburg.

About a mile from Gettysburg we mercifully stopped. Beside us was a grove of ripe cherry trees. Some men dropped their knapsacks and gawked at the trees, licking their lips between gasps. Instantly a mounted officer came up and shouted, "Halt, no time men, no time for that. Get back in your ranks!" Grumbling and swearing the men stayed in line, frequently looking back at the trees bent over with their red fruit.

Around noon another cloudburst opened up on us. I tried to catch the water running down my face with my tongue but the small amount garnered was just a frustration. As we came up the Taneytown Road, I could see the town of Gettysburg in the distance, a long blue line of soldiers flowing down its streets. The sounds of battle became louder.

Suddenly the sun emerged like a spotlight, piercing the clouds, highlighting the landscape. From our ridge, we surveyed the town and the rim of hills to the north of Gettysburg. White puffs of smoke dotted the hills as cannons fired from the wooded slopes. We ran by a gathering of officers where men and horses scurried about carrying messages. We then descended the slope into the town.

Citizens lined the streets, some with buckets of water, others with loaves of bread and cakes. We kept running, our officers shouting, "For God's sake, men, hurry, the enemy is coming down on us from those hills!"

I spied a man with a bucket of water and a cup. He was an older man with a round face framed by a white beard. "Here young man, take this!" I grabbed the cup, gulped down the water and threw the cup back to him. Coughing, I kept running. The knapsack on my back sunk into my numb shoulders.

A young woman with a loaf of bread came into my view, about twenty yards ahead. Her eyes met mine and I reached for the bread. My hands went right through her arms and I knocked her backward. "Sorry!" I yelled and looked back as I bit into the bread and continued jogging. She waved and yelled, "God go with you soldier!"

As we went through the town, wagons and artillery were everywhere. The First Corps was on the hills and ridges to the west of town. The smoke and roar of battle rolled in from that direction, engulfing us.

As we ran on, some cavalry officers yelled, "General Reynolds is killed! General Reynolds is killed!" Reynolds commanded the First Corps and was highly regarded, one of the best generals we have—or had. Stunned officers surrounded the horsemen.

We headed for the north of town, came to a slight rise and then ran down to an orchard where the blue lines of our brigade were gathering. We were off to the left of the major road that went north out of Gettysburg.

To our front and left were a group of our cannons unlimbering and preparing to fire on the Rebel batteries positioned on a rise called Oak Hill, about a mile away. To our far left, the storms of battle raged, the sounds rolled over us in smoky, pulsating waves. Our officers told us to stop and rest. "Drop your packs here boys, pick 'em up later." The officer was Captain Costin of our company. Dropping my load felt good and relief flowed through my aching muscles.

Seth dropped his knapsack and began to hunt through its contents. "Better hang onto your oilcloth, Hiram—we may not make it back here." I immediately pulled out my rubber blanket, rolled it, and slung it around my shoulder, tying it off at my waist. I checked my neck to see if my metal identity tag was with me. It was. I felt it anxiously with my fingertips as I checked the chaos around me.

Our band began playing a spunky tune called *The Yankees are coming.* Cheers emerged from the mass of blue troops now tightly packed in this orchard of fruit trees. The roll was called. Band members went to the rear to help the ambulance corps. "Now I wish I would have listened to my mother when she wanted me to play the trumpet," murmured Seth as the band members left.

"Terman?" yelled Captain Costin.

"Here!" I proclaimed, relieved that I was able to speak in the excitement. All around me, men were kneeling and praying.

My view here was much more expanded and panoramic, even more than on Henry Hill at Second Bull Run. In front of me in clear definition were farms, roads, fences, and open plains. I saw the encircling ridge around the west, north, and eastern boundary of Gettysburg.

Looking to my right in the open fields, I noticed lines of blue troops forming columns and deploying in lines of battle. A small creek snaked its way along the far right horizon.

In the distance, I saw lines of gray soldiers appear on the horizon and march down the slopes toward us. The Confederate batteries on Oak Hill began firing. I saw the distant belches of smoke, heard the muffled explosions, and cringed as shells screamed through the air and fell among us. "Oh God, it begins!" exclaimed Isaiah.

A cannon ball bounced along the ground and hit a soldier to my right. His leg with the shoe attached spun through the air like a boomerang, landing against a cannon wheel. The mass of blue gasped. Isaiah, Seth, and I dropped to our hands and knees, rising again when we saw others standing unflinching near us.

The severely wounded man twisted round and round on the ground, emitting but one short scream before succumbing. Another four men off to my right fell in sequence as another cannon ball bounced through our ranks.

"O God, be with us," whispered Isaiah as he watched the horrid scene. Officers walked among us calling, "Stay calm, boys, there is no safe place—one spot is as good as another!"

"The hell it is," muttered Seth as he looked around. "God help us here in this spot!" I looked at Isaiah, surprised at Seth's reverent reference to God.

Our battery in front of us fired back at the Confederate cannons. The sound deafened our ears, causing them to ring. I saw the shell explode in the distance near the Rebel guns on Oak Hill. We all began to breathe a little easier.

Our respite ended as Rebel guns to our right now began firing. Again, the shells exploded and plowed through our ranks. The screaming of the wounded produced a wave of absolute fear and I could barely breathe. I dropped to the ground and clawed at the mulch around an apple tree. Seth and Isaiah were lying close beside me, our faces frozen in fear.

"Get up you men, orders to move are forthcoming!" Ashamed, all three of us stood, adjusted our hats, and tightly gripped our rifles.

Ahead of us to our front and left we could see enemy troops approaching in a line, then retreat back to their former positions. Cheers erupted. "By God, the Johnnies are retreating!" yelled a man off to my right. Groups of men lurched forward, spurred on by the retreating line of Confederates. Seth grabbed my arm and leaned close. "That does not look right. Why would the Rebs be backing off already? We're not even going at them."

Krzyzanowski, our brigade commander rode by and yelled. "Stay here men! The enemy is trying to lure us out from our supporting lines and destroy us by pieces! Stay put, don't move until ordered!"

To our right in the open fields in front of a building used for the poor and destitute of Gettysburg (Alms House), hundreds of soldiers were now fully engaged with the advancing Rebel troops coming from the north and east.

Horses pulling cannons rushed up and groups of Union soldiers ran this way and that. Suddenly bullets flew among us and men fell randomly. I was inexplicably calm as I waited the turn of the 82nd Ohio to move forward.

A brief thought passed my mind. I was a witness to history. The scene before me was horrible and awesome at the same time. Thousands struggled with each other, the battle lines surged back and forth, and the sound was deafening. The god of war raged and strutted in front of me.

To my far right, a brigade left the main battle line and isolated itself just as we had been warned against. Kriz, our brigade commander, started yelling. "What is going on up there? Why is that brigade advancing? That is just what the Rebs want, to get us out from our supports? Who is that?"

An officer to his side reported. "Those are Barlow's men, sir, they must be trying to take the rise ahead of them." Astonished, Kriz rode off no doubt looking for a superior officer. We were still packed in columns in the orchard, ready to advance.

Soon our Colonel Robinson appeared in front of us and began shouting. "The 82nd Ohio will move up to that open field to the right and form the left flank." He rode his horse in front of us oblivious to the whistling Minnie balls that now filled the air. Our brigade advanced in tightly packed columns. I felt the elbows of Seth to my left and Isaiah to my right. We reached a fence that the men in front of us had torn down. Next we crossed the road and out into the open plain.

Enemy cannons on our left and right fired at our advancing blue lines. The exploding shells spread us out like a spilled bottle of ink. The scream of a shell passed over my head curling my spine. Soon, as before in battle, a quietness enveloped my being. I left the present and was now behind a mule plowing the field north of the barn back in Rome, Ohio. My feet continued to carry me through the enveloping curtain of smoke, my eyes burned, but still I saw the plow blade break through the rich Ohio sod. I was there and here at the same time.

Another shell came over my head and exploded beyond me. The force flattened me against the Pennsylvania soil. *Rocky, not as much topsoil as in the Buckeye state.* The roar of battle rolled over me. I was here not there. Through a cloud of smoke, I saw the feet and legs of hundreds of advancing men in butternut.

"Deploy to the right company F," yelled one of our officers, pulling at his horse, which refused to move. We ran behind another line of soldiers firing directly into the lines of the enemy. Through the gaps, I saw the faces of individual enemy soldiers and heard their shouts.

"Let them have it boys!" An officer to my right shouted as he raced along waving his sword. A volley left the line in front of us and the gray columns disappeared in a rolling wave of pulsating black and gray smoke. White flashes erupted that then turned black as they unfolded against the azure sky.

The line in front of us dropped to the ground. I awaited a clear shot. Isaiah was on my right and Seth to the left, both of their faces black and their eyes were red, blood shot from the acrid fumes. We all looked like blackened demons from the fires of hell.

Now for some reason I dropped to the ground—Isaiah and Seth followed my lead. The enemy fired a volley and the pulse of lead whizzed over us like an invisible train. I briefly saw the mule in front of me back in Ohio along with scenes of the house, barn, and my father's face.

No time for that now. Must get off a shot. I rose to one knee and peered through the haze. As the smoke rolled away, I saw the enemy line. They were only about seventy-five yards away. I saw their battle flags, could even read the words. I took aim at a soldier off to the left of the battle flag and fired. The smoke from my gun obscured the result. A bullet went through my right sleeve and passed in front of me to the left.

We were flanked on the right! *Oh God, no!* A red stain appeared on my sleeve and I wondered if I was hit. The arm still moved and I reloaded. Seth and Isaiah now took aim. Seth fired to the front and Isaiah faced to the right. In front of me an officer, one of the few still mounted, rode with his head bent down close to the horse's neck. He was yelling at one of the German regiments. All around us men began to leave individually, then in groups.

The order to retreat came to our brigade. "Retreat boys, we're flanked. Retreat!" Seth started yelling "Like Chancellorsville! Like Chancellorsville! Let's start backing up—now!"

Forming a triangle, we retreated, me firing first, then Isaiah, then Seth. We came to some fence rails and a slight depression in the ground where the three of us gathered close together. The touch of elbows brought comfort.

My gun loaded, I awaited the appearance of a target. A Rebel soldier, thin and barefoot came into view. I fired and he fell back, his bare feet in the air. Another enemy soldier stopped, picked him up, and retreated through the smoke. Seth yelled, "Let's go, head for the town!" We alternated between running backward, and jogging sideward.

Eventually we reached the orchard where we first formed up. I looked for my knapsack and saw Seth spitting out paper from a cartridge. "No time for that Hiram, keep loading and firing! Leave the pack, we need to get through the town and up the hills to the south!"

From here, we ran down the street to where an Ohio battery was preparing to fire canister into the onrushing Rebels. The officer in charge of the battery of four cannons yelled, waving his arms. "Hurry up boys, get behind us!"

After we passed, the cannons fired. Amid screaming and unearthly yelling, enemy soldiers literally disintegrated in front us. The air now reeked of the acrid smell of blood, burnt flesh, and exploded bowels. The cannons now retreated in leapfrog fashion, like us, loading and firing in sequence. This slowed the advance of the enemy troops but they were all around us. Their piercing high-pitched yells and southern drawls mixed with the shouts of northern soldiers to create a Babel of noises.

Soon Seth, Isaiah, and I were running down the main street that we came in on as a brigade. Troops from the retreating First Division and our own corps were now all around us. It was hard to move through the mass of men. I saw a few of the 82nd Ohio but not many.

A private from company F came by us and ripped the crescent moon from his uniform. "First Chancellorsville and now this, I don't want to be with the 11th anymore." As he turned from us, he fell forward; a ball exited his chest splattering blood. A Confederate sharpshooter on one of the rooftops shot him. I dropped to the ground.

Isaiah darted to the left and yelled, "Let's get to one of the side streets." Seth and I followed him to an alley behind a large brick building. Dead and injured horses and mules were everywhere, some squealing and crying in agony. The alley was filled with smoke and it was difficult to see.

We cautiously walked down the alley until we saw a tall fence beside a white house. "We need to get to that hill that we passed coming into town. I bet that is where we will rally again," said Seth as he searched for an opening.

However, there was none. We had come to a dead end blocked by the house and its fences. Seth looked around like an animal in a cage, trying to guess our next move.

"We have got to go through the house! Head for that porch and lets go through the door!" Isaiah and I leapt upon the wooden porch; our steps upon the worn boards sounded like a muffled drum. The door was locked. We pounded on the door shouting, "Union soldiers! Open up! Union soldiers! Open up!" Seth kicked at the door. We could hear rustling in the house and the sound of feet descending stairs into the basement.

Suddenly a squad of ten Rebel soldiers appeared, coming around from the other side of the house, their rifles pointed at us. We were trapped. The bore of a musket barrel was huge as I looked down the gun of a Rebel soldier with a floppy hat, scraggly beard, large nose and growling sneer.

"Throw down your guns and surrender you damned Yankee sonsabitches!" yelled the Rebel officer at the head of the group. As I dropped my rifle, it thudded to the porch floor in front of one of the Rebel soldiers. *Good thing the hammer was forward or it would have gone off.*

A chill now descended from my head to my stomach, causing a sick feeling, almost nauseous in its effects. The thought of leaping off the porch and running crossed my mind but my legs refused to obey. I was in a state of paralysis until Isaiah touched me with his elbow. His lips were moving in a silent prayer. Seth glared at our adversaries, turned to me, and exhaled, "O God help us!"

Soon, another group of about fifty Union prisoners joined us. Enemy soldiers with bayonets prodded them along. A Confederate officer on a big spotted and gray horse rode up, stopped, and slowly looked us over.

With a reserved and calm voice he asked, "You'uns all enlisted men? No officers?" We shook our heads yes and I started to calm down a little. "Well boys, I am afraid you are out of the war for the time being. We're going to take you to the west of town to a field and put you with the other prisoners from the day's action. You'll have a lot of company, we gathered up quite a bunch of you blue bellies."

With this, he rode off and we were moved to the side of the house. The Rebel soldiers formed a circle around us, each holding his rifle at the ready. They studied us intently, especially our shoes. Seth, Isaiah, and I were at the back of the group by the house, near a cellar window.

I looked down through the window. I saw a young woman with some children hiding in the cellar. She looked at me with fearful eyes. I urged her to come closer up to the window. She cautiously came up until I was looking straight down at her. She silently opened the window a crack. She looked familiar. Was this the same woman I nearly knocked over as we came into Gettysburg? What were the chances?

"Ma'am, could you take our addresses and let our folks know that we have been captured?" She nodded her head as she instructed one of the children to fetch a pencil and paper. Soon, a toe-headed young boy arrived with a tablet.

One of the enemy soldiers came up and surveyed the situation. He looked at me and then at the young woman in the cellar. Haltingly I addressed the rather stocky soldier with a thick reddish beard.

"We'd like to give her our addresses, let our folks know." Looking again at me and then at the cellar window, he mumbled, "Go ahead, shouldn't hurt nothin'." He then walked to an officer who also nodded his head.

"My name is Hiram Terman I am from Rome, Ohio." Isaiah gave his name and hometown next, then Seth. Ten other soldiers were able to give her addresses before the Rebel soldiers ordered us to move out. A look of disappointment came over the faces of those not able to get the young woman their names and addresses.

As we walked through the west parts of Gettysburg, we passed houses with people looking out the windows. Many of the buildings were damaged and some were burning. Isaiah, searching for hope, waved to some of the frightened citizens. They looked back at us pitifully, half waving. Seth erupted angrily, breaking a long silence.

"Isaiah, stop that waving at folks. We aren't exactly conquering heroes here. Tarnation, what are you thinking?"

"Seth, this ain't the end of things, just a new chapter. Have faith; we will make it out of here. Bet we will be exchanged before noon tomorrow." Seth looked at me incredulously.

"Good Lord, Isaiah, don't you know that Lincoln's Proclamation put a sour note on all that? The Rebs and us are starting to hold back prisoners. You got a good chance of rotting in a Rebel prison!" Isaiah looked at me in disbelief. I swallowed and turned to Seth.

"Aren't they still giving prisoners paroles, Seth? They did at Chancellorsville, didn't they?" Seth placed his hand on the back of his head and grimaced.

"Hell, I don't know, I sure didn't plan on getting captured so I ain't exactly up on the latest on this." A soldier to our back spoke up. Turning to him, I could see the tower of the Lutheran Seminary off to our right.

" They are sending men to Richmond and holding them there is what I hear." A guard then came by and told us to stop talking, to "hush". We trudged along, hunger and thirst now cramped our stomachs and swelled our tongues.

As the sun went down, we crossed over Seminary Ridge into a lower plain. The night air settled low and strong with the smells of the day's battle. The pungent odor of gunpowder mixed with the putrid smell of rotting bodies from hundreds of dead men and animals.

As we walked through the fields, darkness descended. We came upon rows of dead bodies lined up by burial crews. Their torches and lamps moved across the landscape like huge fireflies in the developing night. Many of the torchbearers were slaves.

One of the nearby guards spoke to a comrade. "Lee's headquarters are right over thar, up towards the Chambersburg pike. I wonder what the old man is planning for tomorrow. Think we will attack or move off toward Washington? The Yanks got a mighty strong position up on that hill south of town."

His friend shook his head and replied. "General Lee ain't goin' to retreat, you know that! No, we'uns are going to be right here tomorrow!" After saying this, the Rebel soldier turned and looked to the rear. Rifle shots pierced the night air and the long column suddenly halted.

"Down on the ground you blue bellies!" hollered a guard. Immediately we crouched low, unable to see in the growing darkness. After a while, the column resumed its methodical pace. Soon the whispered rumor came down the line that some men tried to bolt into the night and were shot by the guards. I turned to the man behind me.

"Anybody make it?" The man stoically shook his head. Seth and Isaiah leaned in to hear. "He says that they were all killed." I had thought of trying to escape but now the risks became more real.

Isaiah wondered aloud. "If we might be paroled, doesn't make sense to risk it, does it?"

We descended to an open field with hundreds of Union prisoners lying on the ground, surrounded by burning torches and Rebel guards with bayonets. Off in the distance near Lee's headquarters a Confederate band played the hymn "Rock of Ages", its well-known pure notes tumbled down on the field of prisoners. A guard with a grimy face addressed us. "Now don't you boys move or get up or you will be shot".

"Can't we even get up to relieve ourselves?" yelled an irate Union soldier.

"It will be the last crap you take if you do Yank!" replied another gruff-looking guard, laughing. Isaiah, Seth, and I found a spot near a rock and laid down to rest. A wedge of clouds approached from the west, penetrating the black slate of twinkling stars.

Periodically, shots sounded in the night. I hoped that soldiers were not relieving themselves for the last time.

Fear mixed with shame. Once again, the 11th Corps had retreated before the onslaught of the Rebels. We had fought bravely, holding on until the very end, especially the 82nd Ohio. Again, we fell prey to the bold moves of the enemy and the poor decisions of our generals.

We figured we were west of Gettysburg beyond Seminary Ridge. What would happen to us? What would happen to the Union Army? Would we be paroled? Sent south? We spent an uneasy night as prisoners of war.

A bright sun introduced the morning of July 2, its golden rays illuminated the farmer's field filled with men forced to lay on the ground without moving. Seth, Isaiah, and I were some of the lucky ones. We had kept our oilcloths as we went into battle. We also had canteens and were able to sip on water from time to time. Others had not eaten or had a drink since going into battle. Their pleas for help for the most part fell on deaf ears, the guards merely repeating "Stay down you damn Yankee".

The presence of a stream nearby and the smell of slaves cooking corncakes for the Rebels almost drove us mad. Unable to resist the pleas of those nearby, Seth, Isaiah, and I shared what little water we had until it was gone. Soon we too began to feel the heat of the rising sun. We used our oilcloths to provide shade, allowing all who could fit to shelter with us.

As the sun reached its zenith, so did our miserable pleas. Off to my left I saw a canteen stretched toward a guard. "Please, in the name of God, get us some water from that stream over there!"

One of the guards moved forward, collected the canteens and went to the stream. When he handed them out to the thirsty prisoners amid the low uttering of "God bless you", his comrades also began gathering and filling canteens.

The guard who brought us water was older and had a large mole on his forehead. He looked familiar. *Second Bull Run, the Dump.* I looked at him for a long time, even stared. "Sonny boy, what you lookin' so hard at me for?" *You're alive because of me gramps.* I doubt if he recognized me. At least he was now bringing us water.

About mid-afternoon the sounds of battle intensified around the rocky hills south and north of town. "I bet they are hitting us on our flanks," said Seth. Clouds of dust gathered and blew over us gradually moving off to the north. Our guards were relieved that they did not have to enter the coming battle. "Jediah, I sure am glad we're here with these Yanks. I got no hankerin' to charge up those rocky hills. Them bluebellies have got to be dug in like coons up thar."

About mid-afternoon the sounds of battle intensified around the rocky hills south of town. Soon lines of wounded Confederates came into tent hospitals set up close to us.

Many new Union prisoners were brought into the yard that gradually widened its borders to accommodate the expanding numbers. I estimated that over three thousand prisoners were in the field now.

We tried to get news from the new men about what was happening but the guards kept us on the ground, prohibiting movement. "I have got to find out what's going on!" said Seth, looking around at the growing numbers of prisoners.

The battle raged long into the late hours of the afternoon and then died down. The artillery and musketry ceased with the increasing darkness. As the crowd of prisoners grew, we found ourselves in the middle of a growing mass.

Seth crawled all over the yard, trying to edge closer to every prisoner that came into our area, moving like a lizard to hide his movements. Eventually he slithered back to us. He looked up at me surprised to see me standing.

"Seth, the Rebels are letting us stand up now." Undaunted he stood up and gave us the news of his wormlike travels.

"The damned Rebs tried to turn our flanks but the boys held! The boys held! Meade is still up there and Lee's boys had a real twist put on them! They lost a lot of men mainly because we was dug in on good ground!" Forgetting he was a prisoner,

Seth looked ecstatic. "Our generals got the high ground, like the Rebs at Fredericksburg. We held!"

Isaiah closed his eyes after hearing the news. "Praise the Lord, thanks be to God." Seth slapped him on the leg "Amen, brother, amen!"

The evening of July 2 was punctuated by the smells of increasing decay of the dead from the first day of battle and the cries of the newly wounded, both in the hospitals near us and out on the fields of battle. Although our own miseries were overshadowed by what we saw around us, we wanted to know who was winning and what that would mean for us prisoners. Isaiah considered what he had heard.

"I think the Rebs really took a loss today. I bet Lee will get back south to save what's left of his army." Seth shook his head.

"Isaiah, do you really think that Lee will leave Meade on the field and retreat while he has any army left? He's won every battle they been in, beat us mostly in case you don't recall!" Isaiah's comment about Lee moving south caused me to think.

"When the Rebs do leave, what becomes of us? We are prisoners here and I don't want to go some hellhole of a prison in Richmond." Seth came closer to me.

"One of the boys from Coster's brigade said the Rebs were giving paroles right on the battlefield. All you had to do was say you won't take up arms against them anymore and you can walk off with a signed parole paper and go home." Isaiah and I savored that thought for a moment before I responded.

"But that doesn't jive with what our generals tell us about prisoner exchanges. The Rebs won't release Negro soldiers and now we won't exchange the Johnnies. I'm afraid we may have to go south with these Rebs."

A breeze blew by us and brought in a horrible stench that caused us to lower our faces close to the ground in an effort to breathe. Seth rose after the disgusting odor passed.

"If that's the case, we need to escape. There has to be some chances with all these men. The Rebs can't watch us all the time."

Before lying down, we looked around at the fires burning bright around us. A strong guard was posted and I saw no easy avenue for escaping. The clouds coming in from the west were now thicker, billowier, like balls of cotton among the stars. I tried to sleep but awakened with every move among the guards. *Oh Lord, how are we going to get out of here?*

The humid air of the morning of July 3 found the Confederate army still at Gettysburg. The guards were still around us, thick as ever. In the distance, I could see soldiers gathering and moving toward the woods to our south, directly across from Cemetery Ridge.

While we were watching these troops, some Confederate officers came into the confines of the prison yard and began recording names and regimental rolls. Rumors spread that the Rebels were going to give us paroles. I fell in line in front of an officer at a desk and slowly moved forward. Finally, I faced a distinguished looking man with a close-cropped beard and wavy gray hair. He looked up at me and then at his paper on the desk.

"Name and regiment please?"

"Hiram Terman, 82nd Ohio, Company F," I replied.

"Very well, please step forward, we will call you with your regiment for the act of parole." *Thank you Lord, I will be going home soon.* I stepped away and waited for Seth and Isaiah.

The process of taking names took all morning. Soon after, the prisoners gathered in groups, each addressed by a captured Union officer. The man addressing our group was tall and thin and spoke with a distinguished manner.

"Men of the 11th Corps, I am here to tell you not to accept the enemy's offer of parole." A murmur ran through us. "Under current conditions, the Union Army will not accept the validity of the parole document and you will be immediately returned to duty. If the enemy captures you again, they can execute you. Please wait on a proper exchange agreement to be worked out. I repeat, do not take the enemy's offer of a parole."

A wave of confusion moved over us. "Seth, what should we do?" Seth scratched his chin and rubbed the back of his head. Off to my right, a man from another regiment quickly made up his mind.

"By God, I am going to take the parole. I'm too thirsty, hungry, and tired to walk all the way down to Virginny to some damn Rebel prison!"

"Well, Dan, if the Rebs catch you again, they'll shoot you. By thunder, I don't know what to do, I tell ya."

Other men immediately gathered around and said, "Hell, let's take our chances!"

An officer of the 82nd Ohio began waving his hand and called us over to him.

"Men, we have been an honored regiment all through the war. We have often been the last regiment to leave the field and have been appointed Provost guard because we could be trusted and followed orders. I urge all of you to wait on a proper exchange agreement." After saying this, he left us and addressed another group of men. Seth, Isaiah, and I immediately got together. Seth spoke first.

"I think we should take the parole. Who knows what will happen if we stay with the Rebs and wait. Most likely we will be taken south to Richmond." Isaiah, visibly troubled, rubbed his neck, looked off, and turned back to us.

"I don't agree, Seth. We have always followed orders and done our duty. Honor is more important than anything else. I'm staying. What about you, Hiram?"

I looked around me at the camp, smelled the disgusting odor, and saw Rebel guards leading groups of prisoners out of the camp. "You Yanks on the parole, over here. Hurry up now!" I was not able to speak as I had mixed feelings with the choice.

A Rebel officer approached and asked, "Will you men take the parole? Quickly now, we're taking prisoners down the road to the north to meet your officials."

Isaiah stepped forward proudly and proclaimed. "No sir, I for one will wait on the proper agreements to be made."

"Very well, you men can return to your places." With this, the officer moved on and a guard marched us away to the interior of the yard.

"Wait just a damn min...." Seth tried to approach the Confederate officer but was unable to get around the men moving back into the prison yard. Struggling against the tide, he tried to yell but was unable to form the words, " Ah, Ah, Ah" was all that came out of his mouth. I, too, felt that a great opportunity for freedom had just passed me by.

A vision of my getting on the train at Salem and leaving my father flashed through my mind. A great sadness settled on my shoulders and churned in my stomach as I moved further into the yard. Seth and I watched the column of men who had taken the parole march out of sight. "Look at all of them!" proclaimed Seth pounding his fist. "There must be over a thousand of them. Oh my, what did we not do"?

Seth's anger grew and festered. "Isaiah, what in God's name did you do back there? That was our ticket home and out of this hell! Why didn't you ask us before you made your grand proclamation?"

"I was speaking for myself, not you Seth."

"Well, the Reb officer didn't take it that way."

"Why didn't you speak up, Seth?" I asked.

"Why didn't you, Hiram? Everybody pushed...."

Just then, one of the loudest continuing explosions that I have ever experienced reverberated across the landscape. For more than two hours, the Rebel batteries fired shells at the Union position up on Cemetery Ridge. The smoke rolled up over the ridge in front of us and settled over the landscape like a huge gray blanket. Our eyes watered from the acid air as we sat in dumb wonderment, unable to converse above the constant roar of hundreds of cannons.

When the Confederate cannons ceased a huge roar from thousands of men in the woods to our south filled the air. Bugles blew, drums beat, and bands played. We heard the noise but could not see what was happening over the ridge.

Our guards cheered and shouted. "The attack is on! The attack is on!" They then growled at us, some even spitting as they poked their bayonets at us. The old soldier I spared at Manassas yelled, "Now you Yanks will feel the cold steel!" Remembering how I let this fellow live at Second Bull Run, I thought— *friend, you should not even be here!*

The noise of battle rattled on through the afternoon. Musketry crackled and artillery shells exploded, now mostly from the Federal lines. Rebel yells met Union huzzahs. Gradually the sounds of battle waned as the sun lowered in the western sky.

Smoke and haze smothered the trampled field where we were lying. Ambulances and wagons carrying wounded and dying men rolled into hospitals to our south and north. Columns of slouching, moaning men passed us. Some shook a bloody arm and cursed. "Wait till you bluebellies get to Dixie, you'll pay, by God, you'll pay!"

The night of July 3 was filled with misery for both the Rebels and us. We had not eaten since coming to Gettysburg. My insides ached. The night dragged on accentuated by the cries of the wounded all around us.

Just when my misery seemed unbearable, a Union band across the hills played "Home Sweet Home". Every aching body and mind temporarily ceased its devotion to agony and absorbed the sweet tones drifting through the night air. Oh, what a day it had been and this sweet sound of a civilized humanity helped assuage the bitter reality of a more savage one

The dead at Gettysburg *(Library of Congress)*.

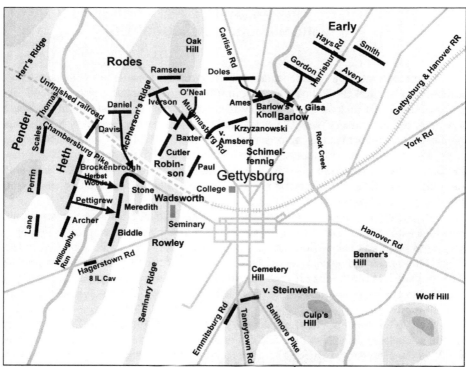

Gettysburg at mid-afternoon on July 1, 1863. The 82nd Ohio was in the Krzyzanowski brigade. *(map by Hal Jespersen, www.posix.com/CW).*

The 82nd Ohio monument and the view north of the town of Gettysburg.

CHAPTER 12
THE MISERABLE MARCH SOUTH

The next day, July 4, Independence Day, the skies were laden with rain. Short, intense showers fell throughout the morning. I thought of nothing else but food. We complained to the guards who said they too were hungry and had nothing to share. Topping off our misery was the news that our new leader, General Meade, had declined Lee's offer to exchange prisoners. Depression joined starvation to torment us.

About noon, the rain began to fall in torrents and the trampled filthy field became a quagmire. Seth, Isaiah, and I used our oilcloths for shelter but most prisoners just endured the downpour. I collected water in the folds of my rubber blanket and filled my canteen.

As night fell, the rain continued and lightning flashed. I feared being struck and flinched with every nearby strike. As the rain fell, the guards ordered us to line up to receive a small amount of flour and a tiny piece of beef. Seth found a tin can for our flour. Others made due with hands, hats, or whatever they could find or improvise. The rain and wet conditions prevented us from cooking so we just mixed the flour into a liquid and drank it down. We held onto the beef in hopes of being able to cook it the next day.

Late in the evening, the Confederate General Pickett came by with men captured on the second and third days. We first day prisoners joined these men and were herded north to the Hagerstown Road. There we stood in the pouring rain by the side of the road and waited until morning.

The next day dawned clear and sunny. We cooked the beef, the first meat we had eaten in four days. Roots, plants, and even insects had gone down my gullet to keep body and soul together. Gradually my senses came back to me as I chewed the meat in small bites.

With the increasing daylight came some shelling from advancing Union cavalry off to our east. The shells flew over our head and burst in the fields to our rear. Rebel troops formed defensive lines behind us.

We prisoners formed a long line marching to the west down the Hagerstown Road. The road was thick with mud from the rains. We trudged in the middle between enemy troops on either side of us. We passed tents stuffed with wounded soldiers off to the side of the road. All the houses, barns, and buildings were also filled with injured men. The shells continued to fly over us and would occasionally strike one of the buildings, causing screams of pain from those hit and still able to cry out. The misery of it was hard to take.

One of the Rebel soldiers beside me in the march noticed my pained expression. "Why are y'all fightin' we'uns for? Cain't you see what's happening?" I merely shook my head but others around me began to mimic the accents causing the Rebs to get angry. Isaiah, trudging through the mud, yelled at the mockers.

"Why don't you just shut up—no need to antagonize them." Seth turned to the man behind us who was still mocking the Rebels and blurted out "Shut your mouth you crazy fool!" The surly prisoner tripped as he tried to take a swing at Seth.

"Whoa, enough of that you foul mouthed Yank," yelled the mocked Reb soldier as he pushed the loud prisoner back in line.

Occasionally we got off the road to let lines of Confederate wagons and troops pass. Long lines of cattle, horses, and hogs went by us. After a herd of cows passed, Seth exclaimed. "My God, the Johnnies must have stripped Pennsylvania bare!"

We slogged on through the mud steadily throughout the rest of the day and gradually approached the inclining slopes of some mountains past the village of Fairfield. The rain again began to fall.

Union cavalry came into sight and we entertained hopes of rescue until the blue horsemen were beaten off by infantry firing down the slopes. Isaiah was dejected. "Why did they stop attacking? There are five thousand Union prisoners to be saved."

Continuing our climb throughout the night, we eventually reached the summit of the mountains where we stopped. I was famished and along with other prisoners asked the guards for food. They told us they had none and that we would have to wait until morning. My stomach and innards growled until mercifully I grew numb and fell unconscious on the muddy ground in the drizzling rain.

The morning of July 6 opened in a dense fog that covered the ground and wetted us down. "What else is going to befall us?" Seth moaned. Eventually it turned into a drizzle. The guards roused us from our fitful rest and gave us a small amount of flour and meat that we gulped down raw. I heard some enemy officers close by conversing.

"We need to get shed of these prisoners, they're slowin' us down a heap."

We were close to a large house. A Reb officer then announced that they were again going to issue paroles. Seth and I quickly joined hundreds of other prisoners who hurried into line. Isaiah hung behind. Seth waved at him to follow.

"Get in line back of us, Isaiah! By God, this time we're going to get out of this hellish mess! Now come on!" Isaiah shrugged his shoulders and came up to us.

"Only if it is approved by our officers."

Seth writhed with anxiety. "Come on, come on—move it up there—let's get this over with and get out of here!" His concern was well placed.

The Confederate General Longstreet rode up and addressed the officer giving paroles. "On orders from General Lee—no more paroles will be given. Even the Federal wounded are to be marched to Richmond. Get these prisoners back on the march!" With this, he rode off.

My heart fell and gloom descended on all around me.

A man just in front of me fell to the ground and cried. "Oh God, why have you forsaken us?" Others started cursing as the guards herded them back onto the muddy road.

The mist still hung low and some of the men around us bolted into the nearby trees. The guards could not see where to shoot and were ordered to hold their fire for fear of hitting their own men. They then ran after the escapees.

Isaiah grabbed my arm and urged Seth and me to run. "Now is the time, let's go!" My heart leaped within me and my eyes widened.

As we stood to run, a guard thrust his bayonet in front of us. "Now you don't want to leave just yet, do you boys? You've got some southern hospitality waitin' on y'all." His grin turned to a scowl. "Now git your asses back to the road!"

Seth was furious and depressed at the same time. "Those boys made it, why not us? God, why not us—just a second too slow! That was our chance—oh, why not us?"

"We will get another chance," whispered Isaiah. "God will not desert us." The guards around us were doubled. The cold reality of our situation descended on me like the cold rain. We trudged on through the day. Periods of sun chased the fog but did not lift the weariness that inhabited our souls.

We marched on as darkness fell, finally halting at the base of a mountain. In the distance, the sounds of battle erupted from a town in front of us. Artillery shells laced the dark skies, producing brilliant displays of light. As we skirted the town, the scene reminded me of Cedar Mountain, a battle that seemed an awfully long time ago. At two in the morning, we stopped to rest south of Leitersburg. Seth, Isaiah, and I collapsed in a pile. I slept with my head on Isaiah's side.

The next day we plodded on toward Hagerstown. Along the way, we passed General Robert E. Lee sitting by the side of the road on a wooden stool. His staff surrounded the great leader of the rebellion as he looked over some papers. A band to the side played discordantly, some notes hurt our ears. Seth, straining to hear, asked. "Isn't that the Bonnie Blue Flag?"

As we passed, the band struck up a more recognizable "Yankee Doodle" in hopes of causing us to move along a little faster. As we got closer the band scratchily played "Dixie's Land". The Rebel entourage around Lee burst into laughter. Lee had nothing of it. The white haired general scowled at his men and continued over his documents.

"There's Lee, the grand Rebel leader himself!" exclaimed Seth as we passed not fifty feet from our famous nemesis. "Now you can say you saw the man who has caused us all our misery!" Isaiah and I marched by in stunned silence. I did hear Lee speak when the rain started, wetting his papers.

"Kind sirs, does the rain never cease in this land?"

About ten in the morning, we entered Hagerstown, Maryland. The citizens of this mostly Unionist town came right up to the edge of our marching lines and shouted, "Cheer up Union men! You have won a great victory in Gettysburg. Your sacrifice was not in vain!"

Isaiah, Seth, and I shortly forgot our pain. "Did you hear that?" said Isaiah, his eyes wide. "We won the battle at Gettysburg! O, praise the Lord!"

"By thunder, the boys did it! The boys did it!" exclaimed Seth.

"Seth, I think we had something to do with it. We did it!" I said, looking over at the guards. Our guards kept right on marching, urging us along, slowly moving through the town.

At every slowing or sign of disorganization, we looked to jump and run. We lost our courage when a prisoner in front of us was shot trying to run down an alley. A gaping bloody hole showed on his back as citizens carried off his body. "Lord, look what a .51 caliber does to a human back," proclaimed a prisoner behind me.

We left Hagerstown in another rainstorm. "Oh my, I have never seen so much rain in my life," complained Seth as we headed for Williamsport, a town on the Potomac River. About midnight, the rain slowed to a drizzle and we stopped north of town in a grassy field where we were given some more flour and some scraps of beef which we again ate raw.

The next morning it was again raining. Isaiah clasped his hands. "Oh Lord, please remove your rain from us for a little bit, please!" In a downpour, we marched into the crowded and dirty town of Williamsport. Thousands of soldiers, wounded men, and prisoners jammed the streets. The incessant rain had swollen the Potomac and its muddy waters roared as we stood on its banks. Seth wondered aloud. "How in God's name are we going to cross that?"

The Rebels stretched ropes across the raging river and these were used to pull boats across. As we approached the dock to cross, bloated bodies of cows, horses, and hogs floated around, swirling and bobbing against the riverbank. These had failed to make previous crossings. "Lord Almighty, what a mess," said a prisoner to my right.

The stench of the town and the putrid mess in the river almost overwhelmed our senses. Still, the guards forced us forward. Just as we got to the dock, the ropes across the river broke and the whole crossing operation was suspended. We then marched back north through the filthy town to our previous camp where we spent another rainy night.

We crossed the river the next day and came upon the Shenandoah Valley pike to Martinsburg. The hard surface made for easier walking. Behind us at Williamsport, we saw Rebel troops swarm to the edge of town. Later, we heard sounds of a battle. "We just missed being rescued again," murmured Seth.

In Martinsburg, the Unionist citizens again welcomed us. Brave women of the town reached through lines of Confederates guards trying to give us food. The sight of food drove us crazy. In the melee, many women fell to the ground causing even further commotion. A mass of Rebel troops converged to stop a general fight.

I saw some prisoners jump from the fray and run down a side street. I started to follow them but I could not find Isaiah and Seth and hesitated. Two guards grabbed me after firing at and missing the blue coats now long gone. One of the guards slapped me on the back. "You missed your chance there Yank!"

After order was restored, the Confederate officers collected the food from the women and gave it to us after we passed through the town. Although I enjoyed the food, I regretted not running when I had the chance. *Seconds, Lord, just seconds!*

The tenth of July found us north of the battered town of Winchester, a place ransacked by the constant back and forth of conquering armies. Recently under Union control, the town was now under Confederate management. Rebel soldiers and all kinds of wagons, ambulances, and materials of war filled the streets.

The water supply was polluted and undrinkable and the whole town reminded me of a huge livery stable, fouled by the excretions of man and beast. On the southern side of town we passed huge fields filled with cattle, horses, hogs, and foraged materials the Rebels had brought down out of Pennsylvania.

From Winchester, we marched to Strasburg, again in the rain, arriving on July 13. Walking was difficult through this rough and rolling country. From Strasburg we plodded on to Mount Jackson. The cold premonition I experienced on our previous visit here with General Fremont now mocked my mind. Instead of being the pursuer, this time I was the lowly prisoner and even more miserable than the ones that passed me back then.

From Mount Jackson, we trudged on to Harrisonburg arriving on July 16. Isaiah lifted his heavy head and murmured. "Remember Ashby? Wasn't he shot over there?" Seth and I were too tired to answer.

Two days later, we came to Staunton arriving in the morning. Here we were led to a rail yard to be put on a train to Richmond.

In Staunton, I found opportunity to pull out some Federal dollars I had stowed in the seams of my underwear. I used them to get some biscuits and sour milk from an old Shenandoah Valley farmer. Isaiah, Seth, and I ate like the ravenous beings we were, literally inhaling the food. The old farmer stared at us, and then at the guards who were busy flirting with some young girls. The old man cautiously came closer and entered into conversation.

"I'm right sorry to see you boys in such a fix. I never was for this war. Our people are peaceful—just want to be left alone." This caught my attention. "I got a boy who had to run from the conscription, took his wife and child and headed east up into western Virginny—hopes to get to Kansas." This pricked my memory and I leaned closer to him, watching the guards closely.

"You folks Mennonites?" The old man smiled revealing a mouth missing many teeth.

"Why, yes—how did you know?"

"I spoke to a man, his wife, and child in Moorefield. They said they were Mennonites heading for Kansas. I don't know how they fared, but they seemed well when I spoke to them."

"What did the man look like?" He removed his hat and drew closer, warily watching the guards.

"He had a patch over one eye." The old man gasped and drew back.

" A patch! Thomas fell on a stick and lost his eye when just a young boy! Oh, Lordy, they made it to Moorefield! Oh thank God! Thank you son!" While the old man cried, Seth was dumfounded.

"You saw those people in Moorefield, really Hiram?" I nodded my head as he shook his head in disbelief. This rare event stunned us. The old man stopped sobbing and again approached us.

"Here, take these Confederate bills. Some of our men who refused to join the army were taken to Castle Thunder in Richmond. The only way they survived was by trading with the guards using money we smuggled to them." A glance from the old fellow revealed concern if not dread for us.

After placing the Confederate money into my hand, he spied an approaching Rebel guard and abruptly left. The guard was followed by one of the young girls he was trying to impress.

"Hey, Sally—ever see a dirty Yank up close? Watch 'em flinch!" With this, he pushed his bayonet past Seth's ear and yelled "Get back thar Yank and keep your thievin' eyes off the ladies!"

Raising his arm for protection, Seth backed up into the crowd. Isaiah and I followed him back into the mass of blue soldiers. There we surveyed our surroundings with fear-laden eyes as the Virginia sun entered its afternoon descent.

At Emmitsburg, we had been paid about sixty dollars each in back pay. Up to this point, the Rebels had been too busy to systematically search us even though quite a few of the boys had been robbed by being at the wrong place with the wrong guard or officer.

How were we going to keep this money? If the Mennonite farmer was right, we were going to need it to survive. Seth had been thinking about this ever since our capture and the farmer's news made things urgent. He now called Isaiah and me together and whispered to us.

"You can bet that the Rebs will strip search us in Richmond and they will find our money, Hiram, even in your stinking shorts. We have to find a way to hide it but how?" Seth turned his questioning eyes to Isaiah and me, both of us deep in thought.

"Well, some soldiers are taking apart the buttons on their coats and hiding their bills in them," suggested Isaiah. I had seen the guards steal the buttons off coats and nixed that idea.

"The Rebs really go for those buttons. Besides, I don't think we can do that sort of thing out here in the open. There's got to be a better way."

Left with this challenge, each of us anxiously fingered the currency in our pockets as if they were certificates of life and death, which they probably were.

Prisoners of war at a railroad station *(Library of Congress)*.

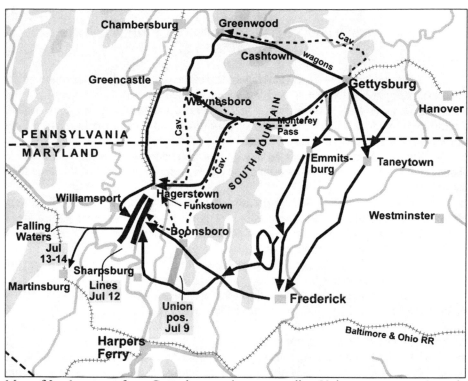

Map of Lee's retreat from Gettysburg and corresponding Union movements *(map by Hal Jespersen, www.posix.com/CW).*

Sketch of Lee's retreat from Gettysburg (*Battles and Leaders of the Civil War*).

CHAPTER 13
BELLE ISLAND: THE BEGINNING OF TRIBULATION

As the golden glow of the sinking sun blanketed the buildings surrounding the Staunton rail yard, a terrible screeching sound pierced the air. The rickety train that would take us to Richmond arrived. On Lee's retreat from Gettysburg, we walked almost two hundred miles in the worst of conditions and were done in, blisters burst forth on our feet and spasms cramped out legs.

"Why do those cars screech so much?" I asked dabbing the ooze from a blister. The sound became painful as the train came closer, stopping in front of the large mass of prisoners.

"The Rebels do not have any grease but lard and it don't do the job," hollered Seth as we covered our ears. Mercifully, the noise stopped and great jets of steam exited from the locomotive. Throngs of soldiers exited from the cars. Some stopped and talked to the guards in front of us.

"That damned Grant got Vicksburg," said one of the officers as he and the guards turned away from us.

Waves of conversation pulsed through the blue crowd. "Vicksburg has fallen! Vicksburg has fallen! By God, we got both Gettysburg and Vicksburg on July 4! Ain't it grand!"

The news permeated through the citizens, guards, and prisoners erupting in group after group. The reports caused consternation among our captors but filled our miserable, aching bodies with a new dose of optimism. The Union was now winning the war!

However, what would become of us? Every face showed unease as the doors of the boxcars opened and guards assumed positions. Through gaps in the crowd, I saw the Rebel officers point to us prisoners and then hurry off. Soon the Rebels divided us into groups of about sixty, having us count off. Seth became agitated.

"By God, we've got to watch this. If we get caught at the tail end of the count, we will be separated and who knows what will happen to us. Isaiah, you and Hiram follow me, we have got to get into the middle of these counts to make sure we stay together." With this, he grabbed my arm and pulled me to the right, Isaiah dutifully followed occasionally grabbing my arm and pulling me through prisoners. Some gave us scornful looks followed by cursing. "What the hell you boys doing, why are you moving so?"

Eventually Seth stopped right in front of the Reb officer counting off groups. The man next to us hollered out " 30", Seth yelled " 31" followed by my "32" and Isaiah's "33". We had gotten near the first set of boxcars.

"Always pays to be first," muttered Seth as the guards came up to our group and moved us toward the boxcars behind the wheezing engine. Next, we marched up a gang plank into a car that still had cattle manure on the floor. The dung soon permeated our shoes, pants, shirts, and coats.

"Always pays to be first," muttered Isaiah as he looked at cleaner cars down the line.

"Shut up and grab a spot by the door and don't let anybody shove you out," replied Seth as he spread his legs and folded his arms and glared at the men following us into the car. Soon a thin, tall guard with long, scraggly blond hair and clear blue eyes took his position next to us in the doorway of the stinking boxcar.

Noting the disdain on all our faces, he waited for a quiet moment and spoke, "We did not have time to clean this car out. If you Yanks have a mind to do it, you can push the shit up to the door here and we can kick it out after we clear town." After saying this, he swallowed hard and exclaimed "but don't try anything or you'll be shot, if not by me, by the other boys riding on the roofs of the cars."

Soon the buildings on the edge of Staunton flashed by and empty blackness filled our view as the doors opened. The feet of sixty prisoners of war, members of the "fountain of Gettysburg", began the coordinated movement of cow manure to the doorway. Once clear of any houses or buildings, Seth, Isaiah, and I and a couple of other Ohioans pushed out the mess into the darkness. *Should I jump and run? No the train is moving too fast.* Soon, we breathed easier. The young Rebel guard smiled at us and commented "right smart, right smart".

Isaiah, who stood closest to the guard, asked, "Do you think we will be exchanged once we get to Richmond?" The guard looked around and then replied. "We ain't supposed to talk to you'uns but I know that a whole passle of Yanks was sent out to City Point from Belle before we left to come here. Now don't ask me anymore questions."

Calmed by this bit of news, we leaned back and tried to sleep in the squalid darkness of the boxcar as it rocked back and forth on our slow, screeching journey through the night. After a couple of hours the train stopped and we sat silently in the dark, peering out through the cracks, listening to unknown voices and the hissing of the locomotive. "Oh mercy, sweet Jesus be with us," murmured a man beside me as he closed his eyes and listened to the commotion outside the boxcar.

Suddenly, with a jerk, the train lurched forward. Men fell against each other, some screamed. "Get off my foot, Harold!"

"Ooh, my aching back."

"Watch where you're leaning Jediah!"

The number one topic was exchange. Would it happen once we got to Richmond?

A sense of foreboding hovered over me. If we were going to be exchanged, it should have happened already. No, we were in the mouth of the beast going down the gullet. I pictured the scowl on Longstreet's face as he rode up and cancelled the paroles just a few nights ago. My head fell into my hands. I closed my eyes hoping to awake from a nightmare. A jolt from the train on the old, uneven rails, the stench from the manure, and the moaning of my comrades convinced me— this was no dream.

As the train rattled into Richmond, I looked out through a crack. The faint rays of the early morning sun revealed the outlines of some breastworks and redoubts without guns. Passing these, we encountered the streets of the Rebel capitol and, even at this early hour, the streets were busy.

Soon the profile of the handsome marble Virginia State Capitol building with its statue of George Washington came into view. The blooming sun now silhouetted the Grecian columns of the building. "We're in the center of Richmond," said the man next to me. "I got a cousin who lives down by the river, saw him two years ago." The man started to sob and choked on his words. "Didn't think I would be comin' back this way!"

Isaiah stared at the statue of Washington until it faded from view. He was obviously distressed by the sight.

"Why are we prisoners of war in a city that has a statue of George Washington at its heart? What kind of evil is going on here? The Father of our country in the capitol of our enemy, presiding over Federal prisoners!"

"Wait until you see what's coming at Libby prison, there you will see evil, " said the sobbing man. He said he had heard all kinds of stories about Libby from his relative, none of them good. His serious tone froze the sinews of my heart.

A quick glance at the somber face of our Rebel guard further unsettled me. The train slowed down and the guards prepared to march us off the car. "Lord help us," murmured the now sober sobbing man.

The door of the boxcar slid open and the Richmond rail yard unfolded before us. Crowds of men in blue, the fountain of Gettysburg, spread out and flowed to and fro, guided by yelling guards. The face of a stout Rebel sergeant refocused my attention. The day was clear and sunny but not the disposition of this Rebel.

"My Gawd y'all stink!" He looked us over as he rubbed a wooden stick with leather straps dangling from a rusty metal tip. "All right you Yanks, march down out of this yar car and line up along that street! No tricks or my boys will run you through, got it now, huh, do you?" Silence. "I said do you understand me you filthy heathens!" Heads nodded.

We walked down the plank and joined a long line of prisoners. From there, we went down a hill to a street that ran parallel to the James River. Out on the river I saw a flat barge filled with emaciated men in rags. I paused to take in the sight. The stock of a musket slammed into my back. "Ow!" I turned to see a short stocky guard with a floppy hat pointing his gun at me.

"Move along there Yank. Those prisoners are being exchanged at City Point. Ain't goin' to happen to you heathen nigra lovers though. You cussed northerners are going to rot here. No hope for you bastards, no hope!" He laughed raucously. Isaiah put his arm around me and towed me along.

"Makes the Rebs at Gettysburg look like gentlemen, don't he?" Soon we came to a row of large warehouses. Some men next to us muttered the names Castle Thunder and Castle Lightning—places where spies, traitors, deserters, and other prisoners of the Rebel government were kept.

I saw shady forms moving like stooped over phantoms in the recesses of these dark buildings. Some guards were stationed across the street with their muskets trained on the windows. "Stick you head out of those windows and the Johnnies will shoot it off," commented a soldier in front of me.

Soon we came to the infamous Libby Prison. I heard rumors around camp there was a sign at Libby's entrance that said "Abandon all hope ye who enter here". I looked for it but did not see any signs above the doors.

We stopped outside of the entrance and were kept under heavy guard. Prisoners already confined yelled "Fresh Fish" out the windows. Seth and I gaped at each other. Were those men or animals? Guards then forced smaller groups of men into the building while the rest of us stayed outside in the July sun, its rays burning and drying us out more by the moment. We drank some water from a barrel on the train but now all of us were desperately thirsty. "Ok, you men, line up by the door over thar," said an older guard. His civilized tone was comforting and unexpected.

Now our group of sixty men walked through the doors of the huge four story prison set into the Richmond hillside.

The stench of the place hit us like a vaporous cloud even though we had just spent a day in a cattle car. Coughing we walked into a large room where a Major Turner addressed us. He reminded me of the irate plantation owners we encountered. Large, boisterous, and overbearing, he addressed us.

"Yanks, I am Majah Tunnah and this is my chief clerk, Sergeant Ross." A thought flashed across my consciousness, the Unionist woman in Woodville. *What was her name? Carlotta!* Ross was a short fellow with a homespun gray jacket that was too large for him.

Ross glared at us with a snarl as he prepared to record our names. He looked anything but friendly as he barked, "Get in line you damned Yanks!" *Should I make my acquaintance with Carlotta known to him?*

Turner continued. "We are going to search you for money and anything that the Confederacy considers contraband of war. You are now prisoners and we have that right." Some angry remarks were muttered. "Silence! If you give us your money now, you will get it back when you are exchanged—which could be any day now.' He looked over at Ross busily writing. "As you can see, we are carefully recording your name and possessions. If you try to conceal anything, it will be confiscated and you will be severely punished. Now step up to the desk, give the clerk your name, rank, and regiment and dutifully declare your possessions." Seth and Isaiah gave me a quick glance as I stepped behind the first prisoner to be interrogated, a Pennsylvania private shaking with trepidation.

He stepped up to the desk and Ross looked him over. "Soldier, you're nervous. You must have something to tell me." The quaking prisoner cried as he handed Ross over two hundred dollars. Ross recorded the amount in a ledger and put the money in a large box that became the focus of Major Turner. "Next!"

The soldier, minus his cash, then stepped into the next room. As he entered, a prisoner with ragged and tattered clothing exited the door. The Rebels were trading our good clothes for their rags!

"What is your name, rank, and regiment?" Ross looked at me with disgust. I could not believe that this man could be a friend to us prisoners.

"Private Hiram Terman, 82nd Ohio Infantry."

"Do you have any money or contraband to declare?" My heart throbbed in my chest.

"I have five dollars Confederate in my pocket. Carlotta in Woodville gave it to me."

Ross stopped his writing and looked up at me and then at Turner who was focused on the moneybox. "Is that all?"

"Yes sir!"

"Give it to me and step into the next room!" I laid the bills on the desk. Ross took the money and recorded the amount. He then glanced at me and then at my name he had written in the ledger. "Next."

I saw Isaiah step up to his desk as I entered the next room. A big man with a gray coat and Union blue pants grabbed my shoulder, looked me over, and told me to strip.

"Take everything off, and by God, you had better not be holdin' back!" I took off my clothing and laid it on the floor, standing nude in front of this brute. He looked me over closely and told me to open my mouth, which he inspected. He then went through my pants, shirt, coat, and shoes closely feeling even the seams of my underwear, something I myself would be loath to do. He wiped his hands on a damp rag. The cow manure from our long night in the cattle car had ripened even further.

"You cussed Yankee filthy pig!" The odor permeated the room like a foul wind. Some large rips in the back of my shirt and coat did not increase his opinion of my wardrobe. My ripped, floppy shoes caused him to shove me back against the wall. The jolt temporarily stunned me.

"You did this on purpose, didn't you?"

"My clothes and shoes were cut up in a bayonet fight at Gettysburg and we had to stand in shit all the way here from Staunton!"

"Take your filthy rags and git out of here!" I hurriedly dressed and joined a long line of prisoners moving out of the building. I hoped Seth and Isaiah would fare as well as I did. There were no guarantees and many a prisoner had his money and clothing taken.

Outside the building, we were lined up along the street and heavily guarded. In what seemed like an eternity, first Seth and then Isaiah joined me in line. Seth came up close and whispered.

"Hell of a bayonet fight, twarnt it and God bless that cow manure! That big Reb told me to leave as soon as I walked through the door!" Turning to Isaiah, he winked and said "be careful not to blow your money!" Isaiah, already very uncomfortable with our plan, barely cracked a smile.

We had rolled our money up into tight cylinders and inserted them into our colons. We were far from feeling safe. Turner beat several men who tried to conceal money. There was talk of us being searched again but there were too many men to process. One man wearing torn rags came up to us.

"How did you fellars keep your duds?" Smelling us and then seeing the rips, he mumbled, "Oh!"

We then marched across the river on a long railroad bridge to a small town called Manchester. From there we walked a shorter bridge to an island in the middle of the James River, Belle Island. Looking back, I saw several cannons in the hillside trained on the Island.

I judged the island to be about a mile and a half long and half a mile wide. The prison camp of small tents was three to four acres in size and stood on five to seven acres of flat ground near the lower end of the island. The rest of the island was more elevated and wooded.

Some buildings, maybe a factory of some sort, were near the prison yard.

A large ditch and soil bank delineated the boundaries of the prison camp. Two gates provided entrance, one on the northeast and the other on the southeast side. Headquarters, a cookhouse, and hospital were off the northeast gate and the southeast gate led to a boarded up path down to the river.

We were among the earliest arrivals from Staunton and were among the first to enter the camp on the afternoon of July 21. I judged about four hundred prisoners were on the island. The Rebel guards funneled us into the northeast gate as we walked off the bridge and onto the island.

"We just fumigated this camp last month, got rid of most of the Yankee stink," said a guard walking beside us.

They offered many taunts and curses at us. "If you'uns hadn't come down here, you wouldn't be in this fix!" Upon entering the prison camp, calls of "fresh fish" erupted and the inhabitants swarmed around us.

Where were you captured? What's going on with Meade? Are we whippin' the Rebs? Any of you gents with Pennsylvania regiments? The talk was incessant and questions came from everywhere. There was no way to address any of the hundred points of banter coming at us.

We were counted and assigned to groups of one hundred. We stayed together by moving in front of the Rebel officer conducting the count. Our group was sent off to the southeast corner of the camp. A guard there said it was up to us to find someone that "might take us in."

Every tent soon filled with prisoners. About five to ten men could shelter under the dilapidated tents salvaged from the scrap heaps of the Rebel army. I wondered how in the world we would find a home in the midst of this wild scramble. Groups of prisoners probed us for information as we looked for a home. "We can't talk now, we got to find a tent," yelled Seth as we moved along. We finally came to the corner of the camp.

Seven soldiers stood around a tent at the end of the line. Their thin and gaunt appearance said these men were older prisoners, not new to Belle Island. The tent was a good one and could shelter us all if we squeezed together and slept in "spoon formation", lying on our sides right next to each other. We did this many times in our winter marches on cold nights. However, you wanted men with clean habits to be part of this fellowship.

The men by the tent believed this as well. They looked at us closely as we walked up.

"Got any room in there for three Ohio boys?" asked Seth.

A corporal stepped forward to greet us and then stepped back, holding his nose. He and his six comrades recoiled from our ripped and manure stained clothes.

"Ohio boys are ye? What were ye, shepherds or stable cleaners or some such? You smell worse than the sinks over there."

Seth quickly answered. "We had to ride all the way to Richmond in a cattle car fresh with manure. We can't wait to clean up but this shit saved our clothes from the Rebs." The men smiled and chuckled. "I am Seth Hall of the 82nd Ohio and these two friends of mine are Isaiah Rinehart and Hiram Terman. We were captured at Gettysburg on the first day as the Rebs came rolling down on us. We held out to the end—the 82nd was the last to leave. The Johnnies then swamped our regiment and pushed us into town where we were captured." He stopped to get a breath. "Forgive us our smell and such; once we get cleaned up, we will be downright pleasant to have around. How did you boys get here?"

"Your right about being clean. If you aren't, you'll die right quick. Ain't nobody going to stay with us that don't clean up regular." After saying this, the Corporal continued.

"We were with Milroy at Winchester. That Rebel Ewell rolled us up on his way north to get you. My name is Bates, Elmer Bates of the 123rd Ohio."

Elmer then introduced his colleagues, all Ohioans and members of the Winchester garrison under General Robert Milroy that was splintered to the wind by General Richard Ewell's Confederates as the Rebels advanced toward Gettysburg. Those fleeing from Winchester to other units were known in the ranks as "the debris of Winchester".

Recognizing the name of our former leader, I spoke up. "We know Milroy very well—served under him at Second Bull Run—a regular bulldog—always attacking."

Isaiah moved in front of me and interjected. "If you ask me, Milroy was a cruel man and not a very good general, did not treat civilians in a Christian way!" Seth cringed but Bates grinned and then nodded to the others in his group, smiling.

"Second Bull Run —82nd Ohio? Volunteers?" Bates looked at us intently. "You boys held off Longstreet on Henry Hill, let the rest of the army get across Bull Run. Some say you boys were the saviors of the army at Manassas!"

"We were the first on and the last off the field, the last regiment to cross Bull Run," echoed Isaiah. I prayed that Isaiah would not go on and talk about Chancellorsville. I could almost hear Seth's teeth grinding.

Bates then looked closely at us, first Seth, then Isaiah, and then me. He stared at each of us for what seemed an uncomfortable length of time, somehow trying to take the measure of our character. We did not glance away. Isaiah broke into a smile that released one in Bates.

"At Winchester we also held on to the last, that's why we was caught. The rest of our garrison ran at the first shots. We did not put out enough scouts or pickets and the Rebs overran us. I don't mind telling you that we are a bunch of loyal Union men here—no shirkers among us. We got beat up but not because we are cowards." Bates focused in on Isaiah. "You fellows seem to be church men, that's good, what we're lookin' for." Bates approached but backed off as the breeze blew from us to him. "Stay with us and you'll never have better friends! Welcome to our mess, we call it the Buckeye Manor. Ye gads, though, you have got to get cleaned up as soon as we get you clued into this place." After this, we shared stories about what it was like to serve under Milroy.

Our friends, captured in June, had come into an empty prison yard after a large exchange of prisoners. They claimed one of the best locations and tents and had supplied themselves rather well compared to prisoners coming in later. These men had quickly learned the stark realities of life in a Rebel prison where prisoner exchanges were being suspended.

"Everybody always talks about exchange, exchange, exchange—but there ain't none anymore so don't count on it," exclaimed a quiet Ohio private in the Winchester captives. His despair was evident.

"Now Ortho, you know we can't let ourselves get down. See if you can locate that wood I brought in for cooking supper tonight." Turning to us, Bates continued.

"One of the worst things you can do is let this place kill your soul. Whenever you feel 'the evil', get up and do something, anything, to help your situation. I have only been here a month and I have seen the blues kill off more men than the Rebel guards."

Other realities of survival included how to read the moods of the prison commandant, a Lieutenant Bassieux, and his two Rebel sergeants. According to Bates, these men were vicious if crossed and it was best to avoid them. We also learned about the deadline, a boundary marked by the ditch where you could be shot by a guard if you walked too near or over it.

The Winchester men also pointed out the guards with whom you could safely conduct a trade and those you should avoid. Talking to the guards and trading with them was forbidden but occurred commonly, usually after dark.

A sort of market or bartering area had developed among the prisoners in the center of camp. Here you could trade for almost anything. Bates pointed out barbers, shoemakers, laundries, and food vendors. Almost anything that you wanted could be had if you had money, especially greenbacks. "You can't survive in here without trading," said Bates solemnly. "Now, let's get you smelly hogs down to the river to clean up."

We walked to the southeast gate and then down a short lane with board walls on each side to the river where we could bathe.

The Winchester men watched over our belongings as we waded out into the river. A guard yelled at us to not go too far or he would shoot. Evidently, some prisoners tried to escape at night by swimming the river and the guards were ordered to shoot any prisoner going out too far in the river.

The gate to the river was also closed at night, which led to the fouling of the prison yard by prisoners plagued by diarrhea who could not endure until morning.

In the deeper water of a swirling pool among some rocks, Seth, Isaiah, and I sat down and washed, stirring up some mud. Pretending to wash our privates, we extracted our cylinders of greenbacks and put them into the folds of our clothing. I was amazed how smoothly Seth and Isaiah pulled this off. I hoped no one saw our maneuvers. It seemed that hundreds of eyes were watching from many unknown positions.

"Don't walk around without letting somebody in the mess know where you are and always leave somebody to watch the tent," warned Bates. All this vigilance convinced us that the Rebels were not the only enemies on Belle Island.

After we returned to the tent, we spread our clothes out to dry and sat down. Two rather coarse looking men stopped at about thirty yards away, eyed our clothes, and us and then moved away. Bates came up with a serious look on his face.

"Those two are raiders, part of a bunch of roughs, mainly deserters and bounty jumpers who will steal your clothes, your food, and slit your throat for a dollar. There is a bunch of them in here now." Isaiah was shocked.

"Where do they come from?"

"Mostly from New York and eastern regiments." Bates shook his head. "You can tell most of them by the way they look and act—mean, profane, quarrelsome sorts, always walking around in groups looking for somebody to bully, attack, and mug. They also hang around the Rebel guards trying to make a deal for spying on their own men. But watch out—some of them look and talk like the parson next door but they are godless brutes who have sold their souls to the devil!" Isaiah shook his head.

"How did the army ever get such as those?" Bates answered almost before Isaiah finished the question.

"They aren't volunteers like you or us. Lincoln has put on the draft now and this is what is coming into the army. Most are conscripts, substitutes, or bounty jumpers— just in it for the money. By the way, don't ever show any money or you'll be a target." I felt a cold chill run down my spine.

About four in the afternoon, the Rebels brought a wagon into the camp containing food rations for the prisoners. For each prisoner, this amounted to about a cup full of coarsely ground corn meal (including the cob), some thin bean soup, and a small piece of raw bacon. To distribute these meager rations, the sergeant in charge of our hundred prisoners collected the food and divided it into equal portions for each group of twenty men. The sergeant of the twenty then divided it into portions for each mess of ten men. The leader of the ten then divided the food given to him equally to each man.

A man with his back turned to the food called out which twenty, mess, or prisoner should have any particular pile. This was done to give some impartiality to what prisoner got which pile of food. Still, many a man griped, sure he got the smallest pile or the one with bones instead of meat.

Each mess was supposed to get a supply of wood to cook rations and build a fire to keep warm. Bates told us that this happened only occasionally and that one of the prime jobs for all of us was to gather, trade for, or get wood in any way that we could.

The Winchester men had built a small earthen stove in the back of the tent. A slanted chimney exited from the back of the tent through a clay extension. The stove was used for both cooking and keeping warm. We pooled our rations and cooked a stew of corn meal, beans, and bacon in a pan. This was then divided among us using old oyster cans, clay bowls, and spoons carved from pieces of wood. Each Winchester man bowed his head before eating. So did we, even Seth.

The hunger I felt here was extreme due to the meager amounts we had eaten since our capture and its various exertions. I literally inhaled the thin stew, as did Seth and Isaiah. The rough texture of the meal made it hard to swallow and we all felt nauseated afterward. Seth made a comment about saying grace for such as this.

"Seth, you have to learn how to eat prison food," replied Bates. They ate the food in small portions, carefully chewing and swallowing each gritty morsel. One of the men rolled the meal into little balls and then carefully chewed and swallowed each one. They also drank only boiled water.

"Eating and drinking carefully prevents diarrhea and dysentery. Keep eating like hogs and you fellows will soon be all cramped up," said Bates in a matter-of-fact tone. Bates then pulled out a sweet potato from under his blanket and cut it into ten pieces with a small knife.

"I traded with the guard just off by our tent here, the quiet one with the short-brimmed hat. For a greenback, he gave me two sweet potatoes. In here, vegetables are more valuable then gold because they fight off the scurvy. Next week somebody else has to get some vegetables either from the guard or from the market."

One of the Winchester men named Walt volunteered. "I traded for a pair of scissors last week and I know a Wisconsin man that will give us some peas for a hair cut." Seth, Isaiah, and I looked at each other knowing that someday we would have to do our part.

Do we trust our friends enough to reveal our cash? Seth shook his head and we agreed for now to keep quiet. A thought about what might happen with Ross, the clerk in Libby, flashed across my mind.

"Do the Rebs search us in here?" I asked.

"Oh, every once in a while the Rebels will roust us out of the pen. Be sure to grab your valuables. They beat the drums, tell everybody to get out beyond the gates. They then go around the tents looking for stuff they want. If you are caught inside, they will club and beat you. They then search for money and count us off as we move back into the pen. Don't delay getting back and come in as a group—somebody always tries to take over the tent." We looked at each other, shook our heads, and collectively groaned.

As the sun sat over the prison pen on Belle Island, the night dismissed the heat of the day and we were slowly covered with a cool, river-chilled dampness. The ten men of the Buckeye Manor arranged themselves like cordwood in the tent.

"You boys smell a lot better now," said Bates.

"It sure does cool down here at night," observed Isaiah as he scratched his head and noticed a louse crawling on the back of his hand. "Oh no, lice!" he exclaimed.

"They're everywhere Isaiah. Graybacks are the wildlife of Belle Island," said Bates as he reclined and closed his eyes. "Be sure to kill every louse you see. You can also hold your clothes over the fire—they pop like corn when the heat gets to them."

"There's a kind of ant that lives in the sand here that attacks lice," said one of the Winchester men in the back of the tent. "The ant comes out of the ground and pulls the louse down after him. It's real interesting to watch sometimes, helps me pass the time."

As darkness crept over the camp, the varied noises of the prisoners merged into an indistinct rumble punctuated by loud laughing. Occasionally the moaning of an individual prisoner, suffering alone, terrified, could be heard.

Being alone on Belle Island was the first step to a death sentence. Who was that poor soul outside our tent, moaning in the wasteland of human depravity, alone with no friends? Could we take him in? The cold reality of the jammed tent cruelly answered "No"!

The Winchester men and we had six blankets among us in our tent. They were closely guarded day and night. "These blankets and that stove are what separates the living and the dead," said Bates.

The small fire in the stove showed its last embers. Eight of us slept while two men with stout poles kept a four-hour watch at the ends of the tent. This was almost like picket duty for our regiment. My turn would come tomorrow night.

Many menacing forms moved about in the darkness, probing, trying to steal blankets, cups, wood—anything that would aid a man's survival. As these forms passed, their faces were illuminated by the burning torches along the deadline of the prison just twenty feet away from our tent. The vigilant nature of our mess discouraged most thieves.

A shadow flickered on the wall of the tent. It was the guard walking his beat along the deadline. As he hollered "eight o'clock and all's well" he and his musket produced the look of a moving tree. As I relaxed, sleep crept over my consciousness. *Oh Lord, thank you for leading us to this tent.*

Morning came with the sound of men's voices hollering and cursing. Someone had something stolen during the night. New men from Richmond were replacing the Rebel sentries from last night. I rose up from the ground with a stiffness and cough that had been my constant companion since joining the army. In the distance, some men stood outside their tents urinating. The smell of ammonia and excrement wafted through the air. "One of the worst things they did was close off the sinks at night," said Bates as he stood in the door of the tent.

The filthy condition of the grounds and the penetrating reality of the stench jolted my senses. Bates, noticed my disgust, and walked up to me.

"Hiram, we will have none of that around our tent or near the messes that are next to us. The boys around us are from Michigan, Indiana, and Illinois. We have a pact to keep our area clean. Disease will kill you quicker than the Rebel guards. Always do your business down at the sinks. Plan ahead. The Buckeye Manor is to remain clean!" Nodding my head, I exclaimed with enthusiasm.

"Amen, Elmer, I agree totally!"

Isaiah, Seth, and I made our way down to the sinks by the river. We passed some men pulling water up from some hand-dug wells. The water had a green scum on it but still the men dipped it out with tin cans. The sinks were crowded and men pushed and shoved as they stood in line.

"Hurry up Francis, blow it out and move on!" yelled a big and burly man with a red bandanna around his head. "Old Jack is ready to take his shit this morning!" With this, he slung the man in front of him out of the way, dropped his pants, did his business, grinned and laughed loudly. "Now there goes a good meal well eaten and duly processed." As this brute walked by us, men gave way and allowed him to pass.

"Who does he think he is?" Isaiah exclaimed to Seth. Seth turned to the man standing behind us in line.

"Who the hell is that?"

"That's Jack Oliver. He's a professional fighter, regular ruffian, and one of the worst bullies on the island. I saw him beat and club a man for just walking away when Oliver wanted his food ration."

Another prisoner, lean, brown, and with a scar on his face spoke up next. "There's more of those brutes comin' in every day since the draft was put on by Lincoln. I heard the city of New York was burned real bad because of riots by these no-goods, right after Gettysburg. The boys that fought there had to go and put the fuss down." He turned and looked around at Oliver who was laughing and joking with some other rough looking men. "There's nothing but bounty jumpers and slaggards coming into the army now. All of us volunteers are dead, shot up, or in this pit of a prison pen. As if the Rebs were not bad enough! My God, what has become of this war?" The man then walked off in disgust.

I fought a feeling of apprehension as I walked back to our tent. I realized the value of the coalition of good men we had just joined—it was our best means of survival in this hellish place.

To be alone, a single man trying to survive, was almost hopeless. Safety and support and thus continued existence were found in community. I resolved to get to know the men in the Buckeye Manor as well as I could because it was obvious I needed them.

I sat down at one end of the tent and watched two men whittle away at pieces of wood, making spoons. One of them raised his eyes and spoke.

"So what do you think of Belle Island so far, Hiram?" This man's name was Fred McAlly and he was from southern Ohio. He had joined the 123rd Ohio just before his company was captured at Winchester.

"Seems like a rough place to me where the strong pick on the weak." By this time, Seth had joined us.

"Kind of like Charles Darwin says, survival of the fittest." Fred looked at Seth with a puzzled expression.

" I don't know about that but there are good men in here, too. Not everybody is a brute. I have seen men share their food with others who are starving. Some give up their coats, shirts, and shoes for their comrades. You can see examples of Christian love if you look for it. Of course, brutality and just plain meanness are way too common."

James Conner, a 123rd private sitting next to Fred, spoke up next. "That's why we chose you fellows, Seth. You, Hiram there, and Isaiah seem to be our type of people." I glanced at Seth who looked away. I then looked at the two men who had stopped their whittling.

"Well, you are our kind of folks. I thanked God last night that I was able to sleep while you two watched out for us." Seth changed his position and I thought I heard him mutter a low 'Amen'.

As the day progressed, the heat of the sun chased us beneath the flaps of the tent. As the time dragged by, we read books or old newspapers, played cards, made tools, conversed or had debates, sang songs, anything to pass the monotonous hours.

I watched the little soil ants do battle with a louse that I threw on the ground. At first, just one ant attacked the grayback but as the struggle went on, more ants came in and soon overwhelmed the louse, pulling it under the sand. Even beneath the polluted sands of Belle Island, the benefits of community were evident.

The thought of food constantly plagued us and the distribution of rations was a major event. Today my stomach growled and I became dizzy. The pain developed into a gripping, internal wrenching that prioritized every movement. Food! Food! Food!

Finally, the Rebels sounded the drum and brought in the ration wagons with their pots of thin pea soup and pieces of meat. The whole camp squirmed to get in line as each man found his spot at the appointed place with his hundred. The getting of food was serious business.

After eating our stew, a drizzly rain commenced. The wetness of the low island in the river made days like this very depressing. Tonight was my turn to stand watch along with Isaiah. Bates gave us instructions.

"Use these poles to fend off anybody you don't know who attempts to approach the tent. If you get more than one or a group coming, sound the alarm with a yell. We will all get up and join you in defense of the area. Above all, don't fall asleep during your watch of four hours. It's just like on picket duty in the regular army, consequences are severe!"

As night settled on Belle Island, the others lay down and began to rest. Isaiah looked at me from the other end of the tent and then adjusted his gaze out into the night. Forms in the darkness appeared and dissolved from sight, hundreds of shadows moving from here to there, that spot to another, no real destination, just collective probing by hungry men and others with more sinister motives.

The rain picked up and rumbles of thunder and flashes of lightning punctuated the evening sky. Drips of water began falling through holes in the tent, splashing on the faces of the sleeping men. The Winchester men did not even stir. Seth awoke and tried to move to a drier spot. There was none. He looked at me and shook his head as he again tried to sleep, tolerating the dampness and drips. The hours passed and eventually the rain subsided as the chirping of crickets pierced the darkness.

In the distance I saw some forms moving closer and heard some muffled voices. Isaiah also heard them and whispered. "Hiram, hear that? There is somebody over there!" He whistled and the sleepers suddenly awoke summoned by an instantly recognized signal. The unknown forms took shape and appeared as a group of about seven large men with clubs. They stood about twenty feet away, their eyes flashing.

"Get the sons of bitches boys, take everything they got!" With this, a large man came running at me and I thrust my pole hard into his midsection. He stopped and glared at me.

"You bloody bastard! You're dead now!" Just before he came at me again, a bunch of men from the other messes descended on him and his fellow thugs and pushed them to the ground. Poles thudded against skulls and howls of pain pierced the evening stillness. Soon the raiders clawed their way back into the darkness, cursing and threatening as they left.

The Rebel guards also sounded an alarm and soon thirty of them lined up along the deadline, pointing their muskets in our direction. A red-headed sergeant walked the line hollering.

"What's goin' on out there? You damn bluebellies settle down now or we will blast your miserable hides!"

Bates hollered back. "Sergeant! Sergeant! We're all right now, some raiders tried to attack us. We swamped them and they left!"

"Well, all right then. Just everybody keep away from this yar deadline!"

My heart was pounding. Bates came near, patted me and Isaiah on the back. "Boys, you did it just right. You can't hold back, those animals will kill you. I doubt if they will bother us again, but keep watch just in case."

Soon, everything settled down, Isaiah and I resumed our watch and the others went to sleep. Seth gave me the thumbs up. Isaiah saw this and grinned.

I looked out into the night and rolled the events over in my mind, feeling proud. In an hour, another member of the Buckeye Manor took my place on watch for the rest of the night and I lay down in his vacated spot. Sleep came quickly to my spent nerves. I barely noticed Isaiah patting me on the back as he too succumbed to sleep.

The long summer days passed and the month of August arrived at Belle Island bringing hot days but cool nights. My growling stomach and dizziness subsided but never left. A numb pain was my constant companion. I had lost considerable weight but my health remained good despite an occasional bout with diarrhea and cramping.

The key to our survival was our ability to buy vegetables and other staples from the guards and the market. As a group, the Buckeye Manor became an economic engine, buying, selling, and trading. In short, we had adjusted to the reality of prison life at Belle Island.

I had not seen or heard anything from Ross, our mysterious clerk and supposed friend at Libby. One evening as Seth, Isaiah, and I were exercising; I decided to reveal my encounter with Carlotta in Woodville and the comment to Ross at Libby.

Seth, after hearing the story, erupted. "Hiram, you can't trust these Rebels, especially the women. You actually told that Rebel clerk you got money from Carlotta in Woodville? I'm surprised you weren't pulled out and beat up. He probably thought you were crazy—at least I hope so!" Isaiah was kinder.

"I think things like that happen for a reason. I bet something good comes of it. Maybe that clerk will help us out sometime." Seth rolled his eyes and moaned.

"Help us out!. He almost hit me when I told him I did not have any money. You can't trust any of these Rebs, mark my words! Hiram, you had better hope that he doesn't come over looking for you if they need some poor soul to blame something on." With this, the subject ended but my mind stayed active all night, keeping me awake, weighing whether I had acted like an idiot or a sly fox.

The long monotonous days that followed brought no irate Confederate officers looking for a Hiram Terman. I was often hungry, miserable, and bored but thankful. All around us was starvation, disease, robbery and murder— if not by the Rebels, then by our own men. We, however, continued to survive because we had joined a group of decent, dependable men who we now counted as our best friends and even brothers.

This mixture of the 123rd and 82nd Ohio, the men of Milroy and Schurz, Winchester and Gettysburg, was confident. We could make it, no matter how long it took, as long as we had each other. The second week of August changed this situation.

Belle Island from Richmond shore near Libby prison (*Library of Congress*).

The now grassy Belle Island prison yard.

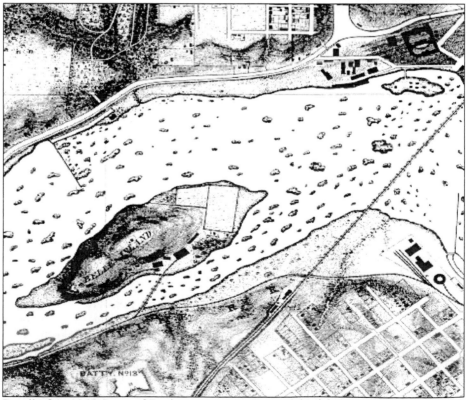

Detail of an 1867 Corps of Engineers Map by Nathaniel Micheler showing Belle Island (*National Archives*).

CHAPTER 14
SURVIVAL ON BELLE ISLAND

The voice of Lieutenant Bassieux was distinctive. A young Confederate officer, his language was a mixture of French and a slow Southern drawl and it was hard for us to understand. It possessed a dawdling and old vintage much like that of his commanding officer, Major Turner. They were both on Belle Island organizing a prisoner exchange during an afternoon in mid-August.

We understood Bassieux perfectly when he called for prisoners to line up for the long awaited prisoner exchange. "Oh thank the Lord, our deliverance is here!" exclaimed Isaiah as we picked up our most valuable possessions and walked to the northeast gate.

First, the walking sick were called. Every prisoner pressed forward, some limping, moaning loudly. Bassieux erupted. "Now damn your hides, get back! We'll decide who's going or stayin'. If you're play actin', you'll wish you never stepped up to this gate!" A long process of choosing and rejecting began with some prisoners being kicked and clubbed by the guards and Bassieux and Turner.

Bassieux then called for the oldest prisoners to step forward, the ones who had been here the longest, and form a line by the north gate. This of course excited our comrades in the 123rd Ohio who had been at Belle Island since June. They moved forward pressing through the swarming mass and joined a group of others captured early on in the summer or spring.

Elmer Bates and the other members of the 123rd looked back at us with a mixture of excitement and concern. Seth, Isaiah, and I were happy for them but utterly unhinged about our own future. If we had to stay here, how could we carry on without the leadership and guidance of our friends? How could we protect ourselves from the raiders? Who would join us as messmates? Could we maintain the discipline and organization that it would take to survive in this hideous, vile place?

Our anxiety was palpable; it flowed from our stomachs up to our faces, contorting our appearance as we tried to smile at the fortunate turn of events for our friends. Bassieux's next words sent all these emotions fleeing.

"All right prisoners, next we want those captured at Gettysburg. As your name is called out, come up here to the gate." Immediately a roar emerged from a large throng of prisoners captured with us. We were caught in a mass of men that surged forward like a huge flock of chickens. Bassieux fired his pistol into the air and the mass congealed.

"Now I warn you—no flanking out here. Don't try to get through this gate unless your name is called. If you try to pull a fast one on us, you will regret it." The rumble of noise quieted to a hum, each man straining to hear the voice of Bassieux's sergeants as they called out the names.

Members of the 2nd Wisconsin, captured at Gettysburg on July 1, were called. These men, like birds kept in a dark hole, flew forward to freedom. Tears ran down our eyes as we saw these men go through the gate. Isaiah pranced up and down.

"Oh Lord, please call the 82nd Ohio. We have been here since mid-July—it's got to be our turn!" Seth and I moved forward next to Isaiah, bumping some other men. One of the men looked familiar but he was very thin and ragged, difficult to recognize. Still, he kept close to us.

Seth, his controls gone, erupted like a volcano, waved his fist in the air, and yelled "Call the 82nd Ohio! Why not the 82nd Ohio!" There was a commotion and

Bassieux looked meanly in our direction. Meanwhile, his sergeants continued the roll call of the redeemed calling off thirty more names. Then silence.

We stood with eyes stretched open, necks bent forward, straining to hear more names but no more came. The gate closed. We prisoners left behind began to pulsate and boil, we lifted our fists high and yelled. The mass of blue seethed and churned in agony.

A Pennsylvania soldier in front of us wandered forward, very close to the deadline. "Is that all? Why aren't more being exchanged? What about us?" Bassieux fired his pistol into the air and the bubbling mass receded, like a pot of stew removed from the fire.

"This is all we can take on the transports today. The rest of you will have to wait!"

"No, no, we want to go now!" Crying prisoners pressed forward. Another pistol shot. Bassieux and Turner yelled with red faces. "Get back to your tents. Any prisoner near the ditch and gate after five minutes will be shot. Now get the hell back to the center of the pen!" A line of guards then came up and leveled their muskets at us.

The Pennsylvania soldier, almost in a trance, sat down near the ditch, the dreaded deadline.

A guard came up and pointed his musket at the melancholy man, then shouted. "Get up you Yank and go back to the pen!" Isaiah, Seth, and I stopped and looked at the unfolding drama.

"Where shall I go?" replied the soldier. "I have no tent, no place to go." The guard fired, the ball removed about half the man's skull, his brain oozed out on the wet sand of the ditch. His body twitched back and forth for about ten seconds and then stiffened out. A howl of protest roared from the receding mass of prisoners. More guards came up, pointed their rifles at us. Pointing to the dead soldier, Bassieux said, "Take this piece of garbage out of here!"

A man close to us fell to the ground and cried. "Oh God, why have you forsaken us?" Two thin forms tugged at him, finally getting him up from the vile sandy ground and back into the prison yard.

On cue, a drizzly rain began and added to the gloomy picture of men, on the brink of freedom, cruelly called back to the chains of bondage. Seth, Isaiah, and I returned to Buckeye Manor, a mess now down to three members—us.

We sat in our tent and surveyed the tools and materials left by our friends of the 123rd Ohio. The clay stove at the end of the tent still had some coals burning from cooking our breakfast rations. The poles for picket duty laid along the walls. A few books like Victor Hugo's *Les Miserables* showed through some cloth wrappings. Six blankets lay folded in the corner. This was a treasure trove.

How could we hang onto these items with only three of us? Distress fell upon the faces of Isaiah and Seth. I covered my face with my hand to hide the tears welling up. Finally, I took a deep breath, exhaled, and exclaimed.

"The first thing we need to do now is to find some dependable men to fill out our mess. I don't want to wait for the Rebs to squad us out and put us with just anybody. We have a good tent and a good setup. We're now in the same situation as the 123rd when we first met them. We have learned from them—we can survive if we get some good men to join us." Isaiah bowed his head and started praying.

Seth came over to me, looked at the prayerful Isaiah, scratched his head, and said, "Where do we start? Who can we look for? Have you met anybody out there that you can trust?" I felt the tremendous weight of leadership descend on me as Seth looked at me for an answer. Isaiah, who had finished his prayer, also gazed at me looking like a student trying to understand an esteemed teacher.

"Well, we will have to start searching right away before the raiders figure out we're ripe for the picking." Seth and Isaiah drew closer.

At this moment, a very thin man in ragged clothing approached the tent opening. Thinking him a potential thief, Seth rushed to meet him, grabbing one of the poles.

"Now wait a minute there Seth Hall—don't you recognize me? I'm James Barker of your very own company—Company F, 82nd Ohio. I marched behind you many a mile. Don't you recognize me?"

All three of us leaned forward, closely examining the thin man before us. "James Barker! Why you old dog!" Seth yelled with delight. Sure enough, it was our comrade in the 82nd. Waiting outside the tent, we discovered six more men, very ragged and thin. Barker limped over to them.

"These men are also with the 82nd, all captured at Gettysburg."

"James, where did you boys get captured?" Seth inspected James as if he was a long lost brother.

"We got swamped by the Johnnies out in the field at Gettysburg when our flank collapsed." He put his hand on a tall thin man with a slanted smile showing through a scraggly beard. I stepped closer to the man, that grin looked familiar.

"Bushey Thomas, is that you?" I could not believe my eyes.

"The one and only," said Bushey who then named off the other five men from the 82nd Ohio. I did not know them as they came from other companies.

I continued to stare at Bushey. I remembered him as stocky but this man was gaunt and thin. However, Bushey's dancing blue eyes and the wry twist to his mouth identified him as one of the best storytellers in company F. "Bushey, you look a mite thin!"

Bushey eyed us carefully, paused, and then spoke with a smirk. "While you boys lived high on the hog in this here tent, we've been a bit closer to nature. The Rebs took our blankets and clothes and gave us these rags. They've been downright hostile, I tell you. I get the impression that they don't care much for us."

I cracked a smile. "Well, Bushey, you have found a home now! I can't believe we did not come across you boys sooner in this prison yard?"

"I don't believe my own mother would recognize me now," said Bushey. He raised a skinny arm and pointed to some missing teeth. "And I don't figure we ran in the same social circles," he said looking at our tent and the blankets inside.

After we embraced and entered the tent, I asked our new messmates, "How did you find us?" After he looked at the stove, James Barker replied.

"Well, I was standing beside Seth there when he began hollering about the 82nd Ohio at old Bassieux. I tried to say something but you all moved around so much I couldn't keep up. We finally followed you to your tent here."

"Well praise the Lord!" exclaimed Isaiah. "We just lost our new friends from the 123rd Ohio and now we get old friends from the 82nd! Praise be!"

Seth smiled and shook his head. "I don't understand it but ...." Bushey interrupted.

"Hey, you got anything to eat?" Seth reached under one of the blankets and brought out a piece of bacon wrapped in a cloth and then cut it into seven pieces. Our new messmates were mesmerized.

"Oh Lordy, Lordy!" exclaimed Bushey as he chewed on the bacon. "We have not had any cooked meat since we got to this cursed place—only that damned corn meal and pea soup." Bushey savored every chew. "Those damned raiders took any meat soon as we got it. We were too weak to fight off those sons of bitches." The others chimed in with other horror stories. Looking at them, Isaiah, Seth, and I realized how fortunate we had been to find Bates and the 123rd Ohio men.

Isaiah, obviously offended by Bushey's language, still interjected. "I believe this calls for a prayer of thanksgiving and an entreaty for Divine help." Nobody objected and we all bowed our heads while Isaiah asked God to help our new band of brothers survive Belle Island. After the prayer, Isaiah led us in a hymn "Blest be the tie that binds." Not a man was silent.

Thus began the second edition of The Buckeye Manor. Composed now only of the 82nd Ohio, our first priority was to bring our messmates back to health. Seth, Isaiah, and I cut down on our own food and gave it to our new friends. Gradually they regained their strength.

Next, we taught them how to defend our tent and the valuable tools and items it contained. Two men always stayed at the tent when others went away. We combined our rations at mealtime just like we had done with the 123rd.

Although it was sometimes difficult, we held our own as the numbers of prisoners increased on the cramped island prison. We estimated that more than eight thousand prisoners inhabited the camp at the end of the summer. It was hard even finding a place to sit down. More perplexing, what were we going to do with the cold of winter approaching?

The fall months brought increased rumors of exchange. At first, we got excited, remembering how good it was for our friends of the 123rd Ohio to get their freedom. However, with each disappointment, our resolve to merely survive took precedence over our cravings for freedom.

Many prisoners talked incessantly of escaping but such efforts invariably failed and resulted in the men being horribly punished. We decided that if an opportunity presented itself for escape, we would oblige but we did not actively plan or dig tunnels. Still the shrinking rations and our shriveling supply of cash was a problem. In October, a solution presented itself.

The autumn sun turned the river into a golden glittering ribbon between ranks of red, yellow, and orange trees. Leaves fell into the river swirling down like little tops. Into this beauty, came the raw drum beat announcing another camp search by the Rebel guards. We picked up what we could carry and hurried out through the gate while the guards searched our tents. After the search, Bassieux stopped the prisoners at the gate as Seth, Isaiah, and I tried to hurry up and get back to our tent.

"I want to see a Private Hiram Terman of the 82nd Ohio." I looked at Seth and Isaiah and saw blank faces covered with concern.

"Terman, are you here?" I stepped forward ready to take whatever fate awaited me. Seth and Isaiah walked through the gate, glancing back.

"I'm Terman."

"Private, I have an order here from Richmond for me to place you on the crew bringing in rations." I slowly relaxed as he looked at me quizzically. "Why you Private?" *Be careful Terman.* Before I could answer, a guard came up and asked Bassieux where to put some new prisoners.

"Hold on there, Jones." He turned to me and then glanced at the new prisoners who were making a fuss. "Private, this means you are to go outside and help bring in rations. Here is a pass. Remember, you are honor bound not to escape. Do you agree to this?"

"Yes sir."

"Come to the north gate here after rations and the guard will show you what to do."

I knew the chance to get extra rations and supplies with this job was a godsend. Bassieux handed me my pass and I hurried back to join my messmates. I found Seth and Isaiah busy evicting two men trying to grab our tent.

"Sorry boys, this tent is already occupied," said Seth to the belligerent duo.

"Twarnt nobody in here when we came by, its ours now," said a dark haired man with a bandanna around his neck. The rest of the Buckeye Manor came up with clubs in hand.

"My friends here will vouch that this tent is already taken! Now move along!" The two men left immediately. I showed Seth and Isaiah the pass from Bassieux. Their eyes widened as I told them what I would be doing.

"Well, old Carlotta came through after all, didn't she?" said Seth as he rather sheepishly slapped me on the shoulder.

Isaiah chimed in. "Old Jim Thompson of the Michigan mess over there has a job like that and his whole tent gets on real well. Hiram, this really is a blessing! Thank you Lord!"

Right after rations were handed out, I went to the north gate, and showed the guard my pass from Bassieux. He took me to where the rations crew was getting a wagon ready to go over the bridge from the island to get supplies from Manchester. A young slave drove the wagon and cast a wary glance at me as I sat beside him on the front seat. Four other prisoners who were old hands at the job lounged on the wagon bed, chuckling, and telling jokes.

"You a new one? Ain't seen you befo'," said the young Negro.

"Yeah, just got my pass today. You'll have to show me what to do, partner," I said slapping the slave on the shoulder. The young black man flashed me a broad smile. I noticed a scowl from the men in the wagon.

"Getting' a little friendly with that coon ain't ya Jack?" I ignored the comment and looked at the man beside me. "What's your name?"

"They calls me Jim. Who are you?"

"Hiram."

"Well Hiram, just do what I does and you will get on just fine. Much better here than in that terrible prison yard."

When we arrived at the warehouse one of the other prisoners, a tall man with a dark face and rough beard, came up to me. He pushed me with his elbow and leaned close.

"Don't let the Rebs see you talking to a slave all chummy-like. They'll kick your ass right back into that prison pen. Just do your job, got my drift?" He gave a wry smile to his friend who smiled and nodded.

Bags of flour, peas, sweet potatoes, and buckets of meat were lined up on the floor of the warehouse. We lifted these onto the wagon and then made our way back to the island. One of the prisoners grabbed the seat beside Jim and I sat in the wagon. After we were out of site of the warehouse, the other prisoners reached into the buckets, pulled out pieces of meat and sweet potatoes and put them in their pockets.

"Hurry up Hiram, get yours before we get to the camp," urged the tall man. The others pointed to the supplies in agreement. I thought about this, then grabbed two big pieces of meat and put them in my coat pockets. "That's it," said the tall man. "The guards know we do this—its our payment for doing the work." Jim looked at me, started to hum, and shook his head ever so slightly. I secretly returned the meat to the buckets.

When we got to the gates of the prison pen, the guards told us to unload the items next to the cookhouse. After unloading, the guards approached us. "You boys only took two pieces apiece, right?" The other prisoners nodded, looked at me with a grin, and walked through the gates. When I approached, the guard looked me over carefully. "You're new on the crew, ain't you Yank?" He circled around me. "Got any meat on ya? Cause if you do, you're in for it."

He then searched me and found nothing. "Hey, you're a good fella. Most of the new ones get caught right off." He slapped me on the shoulder. "Well, next time you *can* take two pieces. Now you know how we keep the Yankee trash off the rations crew." I walked toward the gate not impressed about their selection process.

I turned to see Jim smiling at me as he whipped the horse and pulled the wagon away. Jim and I became good friends. I told him often about Ohio and the Underground Railroad stop in Richland County.

True to their word, the guards allowed me to bring two extra pieces of meat into our mess each day. I also brought in pieces of wood, metal, wire, nails, spikes and other useful objects that I found on our trips out of the camp. I even carried in clothes and blankets brought into Richmond from the Christian Sanitary Commission. As autumn turned into the winter, these kept us alive.

Sometimes I saw guards take these clothes and blankets for their own use thus depriving some poor prisoners of these precious items. I also watched guards open boxes sent from families desperately trying to sustain a captured husband, brother, or son. I saw hams, fruits, canned goods, and other items confiscated. If money was sent, there was little chance of it getting through. The lack of news from home was almost unbearable for those worried about wives, children, or relatives, themselves struggling to get by.

The Confederates charged two dollars Federal to send mail and we doubted if it ever left camp. For this reason, I did not even try to contact my family. I hoped that the woman in Gettysburg was able to notify them.

During the fall and winter months more prisoners crowded into the camp reducing rations to a fraction of what they were when we arrived. The extra rations and items I secured from my outside work proved to be lifesavers. We also made traps and caught some of the rats that came around our tent at night. The little morsels of meat added a lot to a stew.

All of us became astute at trading for needed items at the market and with the guards. Trading with the guards was a tricky process and we did this only when we had no other alternatives.

Prisoners in need constantly begged us for food. The number of destitute men was so great and the misery so intense in the increasingly cold days of winter that we soon were overrun with cold, freezing, miserable suffering men. The Buckeye Manor Mess was conflicted with how to deal with this human tragedy.

One night as we huddled in our tent around our small earthen stove, Seth told a starving and cold prisoner to leave, we were "plumb out of everything". Isaiah could not take this.

"How can we call ourselves civilized and Christian men? We have to help those who come to us. We are no better than the raiders if we let these wretches starve and freeze." Isaiah left in search of the man as the rest of us settled in for the night. Isaiah's comments seared my soul and I could not sleep.

When Isaiah returned from giving the man his food, Seth and two other men of our mess raised their weary heads from the "spooned" sleeping formation that we had adopted with the falling temperatures. Seth, coughing intermittently, finally spoke with hesitant but forceful words.

"What choice do we have? If we give away our clothes and food, we freeze and starve. We hardly survive as it is. We're in a hell of a fix here."

"Well, I couldn't let that poor soul die!" The rest of us moved over and let Isaiah lie down near the stove. We took turns being near this warm giver of life and the order was strictly followed—except for tonight. "Hell of a fix!" muttered Seth as he gave up his coveted position near the stove and let a shivering Isaiah lie down.

The next morning a Union officer named Dow, a prisoner at Libby, came over to the island and began distributing clothing from the Sanitary Commission. I was on the crew that helped hand out the precious items. I made sure that Isaiah got one of the best coats.

More and more Union prisoners were added to the island every month. They told us how General U. S. Grant was pushing Lee's army farther into Virginia. "Old Grant just keeps attackin', he's like an old dog that won't let go of Lee's leg," said a gray-bearded sergeant from Indiana.

"Yeah, and look at the number of us he's killing off in the process," said a man to his side, recently captured from Grant's army.

In November, I estimated over nine thousand hapless men were on Belle Island. As tents, space, and rations decreased, quarreling and fighting erupted almost every day and night. Among the new prisoners were many conscripts, bounty jumpers, and malcontents so the raiders increased in number.

Under the evil leadership of men like Willie Collins, these brutes became more brazen, attacking men at any place and any time of day. Collins was a big, stocky Pennsylvania bounty jumper used to fighting in the streets. Only those prisoners organized in a group were passed over by these predatory animals. The Buckeye Manor was not on their list of acceptable prey.

Even our captors became sickened by the depredations of the raiders. On one occasion, a guard shot a raider as he tried to make off with a pair of shoes from a sick and dying prisoner. The camp broke out into loud cheering as the thief fell dead on the lice ridden sand and the shoes were returned to the suffering prisoner.

The man did not hold on to his shoes for long. As he slowly died from typhoid fever, a prisoner sat beside him like a vulture. Right after his last breath, the scavenger took his shoes. Many diseases such as typhoid and small pox threatened us, flowing like invisible deadly mists of pestilence from man to unsuspecting man.

In early December, we looked across the river and saw fires break out in Richmond close to the Tredegar Iron Works. We also heard the rumble of shouting from crowds gathering on the streets up the hill in the city.

"What's going on over there across the river?" asked a man standing by a guard.

"None of your damned business, Yank. Get back away from the deadline or I'll plug your miserable hide!"

"Ooh, the Rebs are getting touchy. Something's going on over there and the Confederates don't like it," said Seth as he watched the red glow of buildings on fire emanate from Richmond.

I learned from the warehouse workers the next day that food was getting scarce for even the citizens of Richmond and riots were breaking out, mainly among women unable to afford bread for their families. The warehouse worker then added. "No way in hell that we can continue to feed all you Yankees like this." He grudgingly pushed a sack of sweet potatoes across to me. "Somethin's gotta change soon."

On a winter, afternoon rumors of exchange fell like snowflakes and filtered into the tent of the Buckeye Manor, 82nd Ohio edition. We were skirmishing with graybacks, searching every seam of our clothing and blankets for the despised parasites. Isaiah, now very thin and gaunt from giving away his rations, smashed a louse between his thumbnails. His voice had changed with his worsening condition, becoming low and scratchy.

" Things have got to get better for us. Exchange is coming. The Rebs can't even feed their own people in Richmond!" Seth, reeling from a bout of diarrhea and dysentery, painfully adjusted his aching body.

"Isaiah, what makes you think things will get any different for us? The Rebs will just take away what little we get now!" Pointing to some frozen stiff dead bodies laying by the ditch, he groaned and continued. "Lord, if Hiram did not bring in extra food, we would be like those poor slobs out there by the ditch!" Seth cramped over with pain. "Hiram, see if you can get something for these screamers next time you go out."

"There's no medicine any place," I said as I watched Seth writhe in pain as he tried to break gas. "I'll see if I can find some of that red rooted plant. I don't know what else I can get you, Seth." Isaiah, coughing, feebly raised his voice.

"One of the boys in the Michigan mess said that eating clay with a little powdered charcoal helped." I walked over by Seth and felt his forehead that was hot and sweaty. He moaned as he spoke.

"Clay? Where did he find any dirt not saturated with shit in this place?" A thought came to me.

"There's a band of pure clay on the hill where the battery sits across the river. I'll see if I can grab a hand full today when we go across the bridge to Manchester." Amazingly, this concoction of clay with charcoal ashes from the stove helped Seth with his cramping on the first dose. I sold the mixture in the market calling it "gut plug".

In late February, prisoners arrived from a failed Union raid whose mission was to rescue us. Ironically, the rescuers now became those needing liberation. This failed raid and a successful breakout by about one hundred Union officers from Libby Prison sparked the flames of fear and anger across Richmond.

On one of my trips to Manchester, I heard a man by the warehouse door talking to two friends. "We can't have those filthy Yanks around Richmond, there's just too many of 'em. Got to either exchange or send them somewhar's else."

The animosity grew almost hourly between our captors and us. We threatened to break out in mass if not fed and they pointed more cannons at us in the yard. To add to the frenzy, an informer foiled a planned breakout and the severe punishment of the recaptured infuriated the prisoners further. Later, Bassicux's pet dog was killed and eaten by some of the prisoners, which set the tensions even higher.

The real threat of a mass breakout by the prisoners in Richmond and Belle Island prompted a visit to our miserable prison by Rebel President Jefferson Davis and his staff in early February. We could see his mansion across the river and for many nights had taunted his family with patriotic Union songs. A favorite song was "Rally Round The Flag" and we prisoners were adept at emphasizing the verse "down with the traitor, up with the stars". Singing took our mind off our suffering, calmed us down, and was common at everything from card games to prayer meetings.

Confederate President Davis's demeanor was anything but calm upon seeing the discontented throngs of prisoners. As he passed, his presence was like a torch in front of dry hay. Foul remarks crackled out of the conflagration of skeletons like sparks from a grassfire.

The stress on the Rebel president's face was conspicuous as he often turned to his staff with a puzzled look and said, "What can we do with all these men? What can we do with these damned Yankee prisoners?"

"Sumpter's almost ready sir, just a few more days," said one of his staff.

Nodding his head, Davis left and returned across the James to Richmond. Soon trains began to assemble in Richmond and Manchester and it became obvious that we were going to be moved. Moved, but where? Rumors of an exchange again spread through camp.

On a cold day in late February a man came to our tent screaming, "We're going to Georgia! We're going to Georgia! The Rebs are taking us to Savannah to meet our fleet anchored there! We're going to Georgia to be exchanged!"

The ten men of the Buckeye Manor huddled in our tent. Seth, draped in his blanket and looking like a bony Indian squaw, spoke up first. "Why are we going all the way to Georgia to be exchanged when City Point is just up the river? I don't understand it. It's got to be another Rebel trick. We better talk this over, boys."

We then tried to form a strategy for the upcoming journey, wherever it would take us. How can we stay together? What items would we need to take? How could we hide them from Rebels (due to my position on the food crew we still had over one hundred dollars of greenbacks plus many useful items)? Would we try to escape?

Sometimes our voices lifted high with talk of being exchanged and boarding a steamer out of Savannah. At other times, our tone sunk to despair as we envisioned another prison camp.

Bushey Thomas, always looking for the bright side, said, "Hey boys, if we are going south its got to be warmer than this frozen wet slice of sand in this blasted river!" The rest of the Buckeye Manor managed a low laugh. The chuckle I emitted hurt the back of my frozen throat and the smile hurt my cold cheeks.

We spent our last night on Belle Island spooned up in our tent. I was unable to keep warm in my position farthest from the stove. Like I had done on many previous nights, I got up, walked around, waved my arms, slapped my chest, and exercised to build up body heat. After achieving a small modicum of comfort, I looked up into the moonlight bathing a dirty and cold Belle Island. The moans of other suffering prisoners echoed around me, a choir of the dying.

Suddenly my spirit elevated to the clearer air above the filth of the prison pen. Without words, my entreaties were made. *Why Lord, was I here? How did I come to a place of such suffering? Am I going to die? How can I live? Will you be with me in the days ahead?* My skinny hand felt my bony face. I was thin and gaunt but wiry, tough, and strong. I was in despair but something in me was determined, confident.

My eyes lowered from the warm, golden glow of the moon to the cold, dark rushing waters of the James River. I returned to our tent and joined the "warm pile" of my comrades strangely content in all this pain.

Such was the dilemma that haunted our minds the next morning as we trudged in four ranks through an early morning fog across the bridge to Manchester along with four hundred of the oldest prisoners. Seth had again maneuvered our band of ten so that we were front and center as the names of the 82nd Ohio were called to board the boxcars of a train, our fate unknown. We were among the first groups to leave.

CHAPTER 15
THE COLD PRISON TRAIN SOUTH TO GEORGIA

The guards examined us closely as we walked up to the train. The wooden, rickety, and ramshackle boxcars stood like wheeled coffins on the tracks that would take us to our next destination. A cold winter wind blew across our faces. I wondered aloud to Seth and Isaiah about my doubts on how these vehicles could make the journey.

"I've ridden some pretty bad trains but these could be the worst! God, what's next for us?" Putting a bony hand on my back, Seth tried to console me.

"Well, Hiram, it beats that march from Pennsylvania to Staunton—at least we will be riding and not walking. There's no way I could do that trip now." Isaiah came up close.

"God will provide, Hiram. We will make it. He has not let us down yet."

"I for one would like a little bit better accommodations! My Lord, Isaiah, you can see God's hand in the most miserable of situations!" Undaunted, a smile came across the thin face of Isaiah as Bushey came up, shaking his head.

"Well, Jonah had to travel in the belly of a whale. I guess we can ride in those cars." Even Seth smiled, brushing aside his long, scraggly hair as he surveyed the scene more thoroughly, ever taking in information for the next strategic move.

We had hidden our money in the lining of our Testaments instead of internally at the ends of our intestines. We concluded that the length of this journey prohibited our first strategy of concealment.

"Did you ever see a Reb search a Bible?" said Bushey. "Let's lay up our treasures in the Word." I had never seen a Bible searched but fear gripped me as enemy sergeants scrutinized us from head to toe as we stood in front of the ramshackle cars.

Because it was so cold, they let us keep our clothing and blankets issued by the Christian Sanitary Commission. Sadly, many poor prisoners had traded these for food and shook violently from exposure. We forcibly prohibited Isaiah from giving his blanket away. "No, by God, we need every one," yelled James Barker as he and others pushed Isaiah and his blanket to the middle of our group.

"Where's the locomotive?" yelled a man in front of me. We stretched our necks to see both ends of the train. A connection on the south would confirm we were going to Georgia; if on the north, maybe to nearby Union lines in that direction.

A collective moan rolled from us when a wheezing engine with steam leaking out of its boiler made its connection on the south, jolting the line of sixteen cars. As the hitches on each car clanked, we pondered our fate.

The engine blew a weak high-pitched whistle out of its leaky metallic lungs as the first group of sixty men trudged up the gangplank and into the first car. Each car had a guard positioned on the front roof and one by the sliding door.

We had maneuvered about seventy men back from the front of the line so all ten of us were able to enter the second car. Seth, ever calculating our best interests, yelled that the car was full when only forty men had entered. The Rebel sergeant did not dispute this and directed the next bunch to the next car. This deception gave us some room to sit down, a luxury the fully packed cars did not enjoy. The Rebel guard by the door scanned the group as if counting but then grinned, relaxed, and commenced to hand out some cornbread and hardtack for the first leg of the journey.

We left Richmond about noon and headed south toward Petersburg, Virginia. I saw the countryside through a crack in the boards that not only provided a view but air to breathe. We huddled together to keep warm.

At Petersburg, a crowd gathered to get a look at the "dirty Yanks" and gave us a dose of the typical Virginian hospitality. Taunts of "serves ya right you filthy heathens" trailed behind us as the train slowly traveled along jerking behind the rickety old locomotive. The guard by the door, an older man with a stooped back, seemed embarrassed by the shouting.

We arrived in Gaston, North Carolina in the afternoon. Here the reception was much more kind, the fires of secession did not burn as hot here. Groups of young women tossed apples and cakes into the boxcars. This did more harm than good. The men acted like starving dogs, trampling on weaker prisoners on the floor in their attempt to get at the food. Some of us tried to help the guard calm the melee but were unsuccessful. "Oh Lordy, Lordy, Lordy," repeated the guard as he looked over the wretched scene.

After all the apples were greedily secured and the snarling animals retreated, we found a man dead on the floor, blood coming out of his mouth from being trampled. The ribs of his frail frame had been easily crushed. His corpse lay among us until we got to Raleigh, North Carolina in the evening. Here we got off the train and camped in a woods while we waited for another train to take us further south the next morning. Our guard gently pulled out the dead man. "I'll take care of him," he said to Seth as he pulled the thin corpse out of the car.

Large fires were built all around us so that escape was difficult. Seth walked about trying to find a dim corner but came back discouraged after witnessing a man shot down in his attempt to flee into the outer darkness. Seth gnawed on a hardtack as he recounted this scene.

"That fellow was so light that the ball carried him along about ten yards! I'd like to get out of this but it's too risky here, maybe we will get another chance further along."

"Are your teeth hurting Seth?" I asked. He nodded as he opened his mouth and revealed some bloody gums.

"Even if we did get out, where would we go? Nobody is going to help us down here." Isaiah, hearing Seth's whispering, came near.

"There are Unionists out there and slaves have helped escaped Federals. We must try to escape some time! If I would have known what was coming, I sure would have tried harder on the way south from Gettysburg." A sad look clouded his face.

Seth noticed it. "Lord, we can't cry over that now, Isaiah. Sure, we should have done it back there—our best chance was in that fog—but, Lord, who knew what was coming? I sure didn't!"

James Barker made his way through the tightly packed prisoners and sat down beside Isaiah.

"Maybe this Georgia pen will be better," said James trying to cheer Isaiah. "Some of the guards said that there's a stream running through it and that there are little cabins to live in—sounds a sight better than Belle Island."

"Don't count on it Jimmy," cautioned Bushey as he sat on the spongy pine needles of the clearing. "The Rebs are as miserable as we are—look at those guards." He pointed at a skinny Confederate without shoes. "If those are our landlords, boys, I don't see the lap of luxury ahead." Bushey lay flat on the forest floor. "Hey, these pine needles aren't bad if only I could stop my teeth from chattering!"

Other members of our group of ten joined us and formed a close circle. We huddled close against each other in the cold North Carolina night. The guards cast shadows on us as they walked in front of the crackling flames of the fires. Off in the distance in the silence of the night, an owl hooted to its mate, cementing bonds of avian matrimony, their concerns and worlds completely different from ours.

Several shots rang out in the night as we slept. "Look, those boys are making a run for it," said a soldier near us pointing out into the night. He went up the bank to get a closer look. "Oh no, the Rebs shot 'em down! Oh, no."

A golden sun broke the morning to reveal some slaves burying some dead prisoners in a small opening in the woods. "Are those the men shot last night?" whispered Isaiah.

"Those and some others that died on the train coming down here," replied Seth. "Remember the poor soul trampled in our car? There he lies on that bank." We sat in silence looking at his corpse beside the expanding ditch being dug by the slaves. Isaiah broke the silence.

"What a pity! The man survived Gettysburg and the horrors of Belle Island to be trampled by his own comrades scrambling for apples tossed into our car by young girls! Now there he is, unknown to his family, without a coffin, naked to the soil in a nameless grave near the railroad depot in Raleigh, North Carolina. Not a good death, not a good death at all!"

Soon another train from Raleigh came out of the rising sun in the east, it's stack exhaust blackened the brightness of the morning. A cold breeze revealed not another boxcar but platform cars open to the air, in line behind the belching locomotive. Guards sat at each corner. Jumping to freedom flashed into my mind as I walked up the plank.

Seth, without hesitation, led us to the front right corner next to a lanky tobacco chewing Rebel guard. The guard, an older man, carried a smooth bore musket, deadly at close range but inaccurate beyond thirty yards, like a shotgun. About sixty prisoners crowded onto the car and sat down, each man looked longingly out into the distance. The old guard cleared his throat after spitting a brown wad onto the ground.

"Now you Yanks listen up. We know some of you'uns wants to jump and make a break for it off this yar flat car. You better know that ole Jake, Clem, Jasper, and I are crack shots even with these old flintlocks." He patted the stock that had a line of marks carved into the dark and stained wood. "After we get movin', nobody moves or gets up or we'll plug you faster than a whistle. If you need to go, just use the cracks in the floor." All four of the guards grinned, took their positions, and, in sequence, spit into the crisp early morning air.

As the train pulled out of Raleigh, storm clouds crept up the horizon, following the rising sun like a large dark curtain.

The rest of the morning passed without event even though escape was on every prisoner's mind. Isaiah, Seth, and I huddled together in our blankets relishing the cold but clean air. The smoke from the locomotive floated above the trailing cars like a cape. A hot spark landed on my face as the train struggled up a hill. Isaiah fidgeted, looked furtively out into countryside and to the edges of the railroad track flanked with thick brush and trees. With an eye on the guards, he leaned close to Seth.

"This may be our only chance to escape, Seth. On the next train, we'll probably be back in boxcars. What do you think?" Seth looked around, his face full of anxiety. The guard, Ole Jake, tapped Seth with his foot.

"Thinking of jumpin' are ya boy? Well, I wouldn't. We ain't missed but a few times. Those we nicked or missed have all been tracked down by the hounds. They ain't a pretty sight after those dogs has chewed on 'em. But go ahead and try if'n ya got the grits for it."

One of the prisoners in the middle suddenly stood as the train reduced speed, straining up the incline. The man in blue leaped like a great bird from the slow moving train. A shot rang out. Blood and tissue from his abdomen spattered on our faces as the bird fluttered to the ground. Straining our necks, we saw him thrashing on the rocks of the rail bed.

A loud cry of protest rose from the prisoners. The other guards raised their guns as Jasper reloaded his flintlock. Old Jake stood up and yelled, his voice barely audible above the screeching of the wheels.

"Whose next? Who's the next stupid hero out there?" Seth, Isaiah, and I looked at each other in shock as we wiped the blood and bits of flesh off our clothing. Seth, shaking, motioned us closer to him.

"The only sure way to get off this car is for everybody to jump at once! How are we going to get that to happen? There's got to be a better way." Isaiah, visibly discouraged, bowed his head and prayed as Jasper carved another notch on his gun. Closing my eyes, I silently joined Isaiah. *Please Lord—show us what to do.*

Later, as darkness fell, three men did jump at once. One was shot and killed but the other two hit the ground, rolled into the brush and disappeared into the night. A cheer rose from the car. "Good luck boys!" yelled a prisoner next to us.

After the noise settled down, Ole Jake mumbled, "Dogs will get 'em, always do."

At Salisbury, North Carolina, our train stopped near a prison. As we sat in the darkness, a sour stench wafted over us. A prisoner in back of me nudged a man next to him. "Smells a lot like Belle, don't it fellers?"

"All the Reb pens smell," said his friend. A rustle at the front of the car drew our attention as a guard led about ten prisoners away. "What's going on? Where are they taking those boys?" asked Isaiah.

"Probably over to that prison pen. Must be taking some of us at each stop." Seth scratched his chin as he looked around. "Hiram, Isaiah, let's stay together no matter what. If they take one of us, they gits us all by God!" After about two hours, a freight train pulled up and we were loaded, as Isaiah predicted, into a boxcar.

This time the car was cleaner having hauled freight rather than cattle. One guard sat on the roof and two others rode in the car with us, sitting on a plank that ran in front of the sliding door.

These men were not home guards like the ones on the platform car. They had the look of regulars, soldiers from the front. Some of our boys opened conversations with them and discovered they were former prisoners of war having been exchanged from Union prisons. While clear about their duty as guards, they obviously identified with us. They even shared their food and filled some of our canteens when the train stopped for taking on fuel and water.

As the train moved along through the night, the moonlight filtered through the cracks and illuminated the face of one of the Confederates. I had seen this man somewhere before but where? Intermittently, his eyes met mine and lingered. Scenes of a steep hill flashed through my mind. McDowell! McDowell! That man is Sam Parker the Rebel that I nearly stepped on. It has to be him! He was with the 12th Georgia—it's got to be him! I leaned over to Seth who was trying to sleep, his head rolling back and forth with the rocking of the car.

"Seth, I know that guard over there. He is the one I told you about at McDowell, the Reb I nearly stepped on coming down that hill. That's him, I'm sure of it." Seth carefully eyed the Rebel who was now focused on us. I waved my hand, smiled, and mouthed, "remember me?"

Sam Parker slowly raised himself up from the plank, leaning mostly on one leg. He looked carefully at me and then grinned broadly, his smile cutting across a thick beard, revealing wide gaps in his teeth. I carefully made my way over to him, stepping over some men sitting on the floor. The rocking of the car made it difficult to hold my balance and I nearly fell into Sam as I neared the door. The other guard, a thin man with a yellow feather in his slouch hat, quickly stood and raised his gun. Sam quickly spoke.

"It's all right Theodore, I know this Yank. He put a tourniquet on my leg way back at McDowell when old Stonewall was still alive and we was fightin' with General Allegheny Johnson. What was your name again? German?"

"No, Terman, with a T, Hiram Terman." With this, the other guard spoke up.

"Well I will be dadburned, shot, plugged, and roasted! I know you too! I'm Theodore Comfort. You shot me with a spent ball at McDowell. Remember?" I could not believe it and gaped open-mouthed, unable to speak. I nodded my head and managed to ask what had happened since McDowell.

"Both Sam and I was captured there by Milroy. Sam here lost his leg and now has a wooden one. I was exchanged after some pretty rough treatment too, but we both got back to the old 12th Georgia." A momentary look of empathy crossed his face as his eyes steadied on mine. "Now I am heading south to head off old Sherman and Sam here is heading toward the new prison at Camp Sumpter." I looked at Sam's lower torso, envisioned the belt I applied to his leg and asked.

"Sam, you lost your leg? That wound did not look that bad. What happened?"

"Well, Hiram, after you left some of your Yankee friends came along and hauled my butt down to your camp. I was throwed into a wagon and hustled back with y'all to Franklin where I laid for a couple of days. A Yankee surgeon finally came around, said I had gangrene and took off my leg above the knee here." Sam lifted his pant leg revealing a wooden shaft. "After I was exchanged in Staunton, I have been on guard duty ever since. Now I am heading down to that new pen for you Yanks down in Sumpter County Georgia. It's right close to my home in Americus." The train rocked and jerked on the uneven rails, causing us to bump against each other. "Hiram, how did you get ketched?"

"Caught the first day at Gettysburg. You Rebs outnumbered us real quick and chased us back into the town where me and my two pards over there was captured." Sam looked across the moonlit car to see Seth and Isaiah who feebly waved and strained to hear what we were saying.

"The 12th Georgia was right there in front of you in Dole's brigade! Have you been a prisoner since way back in July?" Sam seemed incredulous. "Where were you kept?"

"Belle Island—until we got on this train."

"My God, Hiram, no wonder you look like a bean pole! Belle is a hellhole during the winter." The irony of being pitied by the enemy welled up in me. Tears wet my eyes as Sam and Theodore looked up and down my scrawny frame.

I pointed out the other members of the Buckeye Manor, 82nd Ohio edition. We talked throughout the night and next day, recounting battles and trying to figure out if we could have seen each other across that deadly space familiar to all veteran soldiers on both sides. The experience awed me. Meeting Sam and Theodore on a train to a prison in Georgia—talking and laughing about death and dying with the enemy. Other prisoners looked on with a quizzical fascination.

The train stopped at regular intervals to be refueled with cordwood (I saw no coal) and to fill up with water for the steam engine. At each stop, a band of Negroes pumped water into the locomotive and loaded firewood. While we waited at a small depot, two men rose up and starting pushing their way to the door. "Hey boys, this shit pot is full." Reaching the door, they threw the foul mixture out into the darkness. The smell of urine and excrement filled the frosty air.

We shivered through the cold damp nights and ached for the warmth of the sun in the morning. This long, cold train ride tortured us and we yearned for the train to get to its final destination. Finally, we passed through Charlotte, then stopped at Columbia, South Carolina.

The well-kept appearance of Columbia, the capital of South Carolina, surprised me. Many fine buildings lined the streets and well-dressed people stood around the railroad depot. The women raised dainty handkerchiefs to their faces as they turned and gawked. Off in the distance I saw flat cars loaded with cotton along the sidetracks. Small groups of mulatto women tried to come up around the cars to sell us food but the guards kept them away much to our dismay.

Sam and Theodore looked like they wanted to help us but they had to behave like the other guards or they would have gotten in trouble. The women could not have sold much anyhow as most of the prisoners had no money. As my stomach growled in hunger, I felt for my New Testament and its precious lining of green.

Later that evening, we crossed a high railroad bridge spanning a river. Sam and Theodore worriedly examined the bridge below. "This is the one that the Yankees fired last month," said Sam. The comment created a silence that amplified the thumping of the wheels against the rails of the repaired bridge. The creaking of the bridge timbers made us feel like we could at any second fall into the dark cold waters below. A collective sigh of relief rose from us as we reached the solidness of land. Relieved, I fell asleep as our train rattled into Georgia.

The warm rays of the morning sun found the prison train near Augusta, Georgia where we were to board another train. We were herded from the train to a depot dock were a Rebel officer with a red sash around a portly waist paced back and forth, looking down at us from the platform. "I know you poor prisoners want to go back home but the problem is your government." Walking back and forth, he stopped periodically, slapped his hands in frustration, and continued his diatribe.

"Your General Butler will not consent to exchange y'all without requiring us to give back the Nigras we ferreted out of your army! We can't do that! No, sir! No way in hell that we're going to trade slaves for soldiers!"

Some of the prisoners started to yell curses about Butler. Isaiah, though weak like the rest of us, yelled out at the cursing men.

"Don't you men know why we are fighting this war? If slavery is not wrong, nothing is wrong! What good is it to save the Union if the curse of slavery survives to rot out its insides!"

At this, the Rebel officer yelled loudly at the guards. "Strike that man down! Break his damn abolitionist skull, by God!" Before this could be done, Isaiah disappeared in the mass like a twig going down a whirlpool. The guards stopped looking when it became clear no one would give him up. Isaiah surfaced near me after uttering "thank you" to the men who hid him.

A prisoner with a bleeding gash on his arm begged a guard for some quinine. "Sorry Yank, we ain't got quinine thanks to your damn blockade. All's we got is this here ground root."

A form of local herbal medicine was manufactured in Augusta within view of the railroad depot. The supply of any kind of conventional medicine, especially quinine, was almost nonexistent. Looking at the man with his still bleeding arm, Isaiah remarked. "It's bad enough to be a prisoner but being one in the land of the starving— Lord, what will we do?"

Two women tried to approach and give us food but the guards stopped them. A man with them then threw us two old cans stuffed with tobacco plugs. I looked up to see Sam Parker motion to pick them up and hide them. Seth leaned against me and said, "The cans will come in handy and we can trade the tobacco."

"God bless those women and that man," said Isaiah.

"Amen," said Seth as he put one of the cans in his pocket.

We left Augusta about noon and soon entered rolling hills covered with pines. As the sun settled in the west, we stopped at a small town depot where we were herded into a low area next to the tracks. The guards then gave us some hardtack and a small piece of bacon. Later Sam Parker walked by us, carefully looking around. "Hiram, you best bed down. We are going to stay here till morning." The red clay beneath our feet afforded little comfort.

The guards took up stations all around us and built large fires which they kept going through the night. We saw the hobbling figure of Sam Parker on the bank above us but there was no sign of Theodore Comfort.

In the dark silence of the early morning, several prisoners from the middle of our pack attempted to escape. These unfortunates were shot as they ran up the bank hoping to dive into the outer darkness. They hardly made a sound. "They must have been hit solid and not winged," said a man to our left.

The next morning the bodies lay in plain view of us on the bank. One showed a chest wound and the other was shot in the head, his open mouth and eyes pressed against the wet Georgia clay. "Poor suckers, but some of the boys did get away," said a prisoner in front of us.

We watched some slaves drag the bodies off and start to dig a grave in a clearing. Up on the bank three prisoners returned to our group. Each of the men had been beaten and their faces were swollen.

"How far did you get? How did you get captured?" The questions flew around these men like bees as the guards pushed them back into us.

"We got to the edge of town and the whole place came at us with knives, pitch forks, and who knows what else," recounted one of the three as he picked a broken tooth out of his mouth.

About ten in the morning, we were loaded onto a new set of boxcars. Theodore Comfort was gone but wooden-legged Sam Parker remained in our car. He really was going to go to our new prison with us. This thought comforted me although I doubted how much Sam could do for us.

The new guard who stood beside Sam was very talkative and complained about having no chewing tobacco. We traded tobacco plugs to him for Confederate dollars.

About noon, we went through Milledgeville, the capital of Georgia. Well-kept homes and the appearance of prosperity greeted our inquiring eyes. Well-dressed men and women stared at us as our train rattled by the depot. White gloved delicate hands began covering dainty mouths. Aghast, the top of Southern society now surveyed the unfortunate effluent of the war flow down the tracks.

About the middle of the afternoon on February 27, 1864, our train of misery pulled up to a small railroad depot in the middle of a pine forest. The locomotive relaxed after its long struggle, slowed, and finally stopped, releasing steam. Sam

Parker braced his wooden leg, pulled open the door, and said, "Here we are boys. This is Andersonville, your new home!"

Present day view of the railroad depot at Andersonville, Georgia.

Andersonville prison yard viewed from a fort on the south hill. The Ohio monument is just above the replica of the North gate.

CHAPTER 16
INTO THE GATES OF ANDERSONVILLE

The Rebel guard Sam Parker grasped the door railing, thumped his behind unceremoniously to the floor of the boxcar, and let out a groan. He then slid out, his pants sliding up, revealing his wooden leg. Landing on the ground, Sam teetered for a moment on the bank of the railroad bed. Regaining his balance with his musket, he then turned and shouted. His words came from lips hidden deep in his thick beard. "Come on you Yanks, tumble out of there, and start lining up in four ranks. We're going to count you off and put you in squads. You boys from Belle Isle, you know what to do. Right smart now, let's move!"

After days in the crowded stinking car, we were ready to get out. We were stiff and barely able to move. "Hey boys, come over and lift me up. My crazy legs just won't move," yelled an Ohio sergeant in the back of the car. Immediately, four thin comrades came to his aid. "I'm a sight lighter now than before Belle, I tell ya, but my oh my, so are you boys! I hope the grub is better here."

"Can't be much worse than at Belle," came a bitter reply from two thin soldiers as they made their way down the gangplank in front of me. I stepped out of the car to a bright sun; a cool breeze carried the smell of pine and sawed lumber. Isaiah, Seth, and I hobbled down the plank and fell in tightly with the rest of the Buckeye Manor. Raising our eyes to the west, we saw the open and bare prison pen about one thousand paces away. The prisoners began to grumble.

"That is just an open field like a hog pen! Where are the little cabins for us to stay in?" Jaws dropped as more eyes viewed the distant stockade.

"Are they just going herd us into that open field?" said another man crying. The guards now forced us to the front of the railroad depot where we counted off.

"Stay together," growled Seth. "We must get into the same squad." Other prisoners wondered why we all hunched together and moved in mass, like the sections of a centipede. A prisoner inquired as we passed him.

"You boys all family, brothers maybe?"

After counting off, the 82nd Ohio got into the first detachment, second hundred, first mess. We joined men captured from the 26th Wisconsin, a German regiment taken with us at Gettysburg.

The guards formed a double line along the thousand-foot path that led to the large, fenced prison. Sam Parker stood about a third of the way down the line. Their bayonets sparkled in the rays of the afternoon sun producing a glistening, shiny path to the stockade. Beyond them, I saw two huge gates on either side of a small stream that went into the prison.

We gathered in ranks forming a rectangle that drooped and sagged with sick men. The stronger propped up the weaker; sometimes both fell in a pitiful heap. A slim, bearded, distinguished looking Rebel officer came out of the railroad depot and, from his perch on the dock, scanned the prisoners. One of his sergeants then shouted.

"All right you prisoners, keep in ranks, and hush up!" A sea of shallow eyes and open mouths slowly turned and focused in on the commandant of the prison.

"Men of the Federal army, my name is Lieutenant Colonel Alexander Persons and I am in command here at Camp Sumpter. I know that most of you are thirsty and hungry from your long ride and it won't be long before we will give you some rations. There is a stream in the prison yard over there and you can refresh yourselves there shortly."

The skinny heads turned to look at the distant prison pen, longing for the food and water to come. "As you know, we fully expect to exchange you men in the near future as soon as details can be worked out with your government." A low groan flowed out of the emaciated men before him. We had heard this exchange business before and discounted it.

Ignoring the moans, Persons continued. "In the meantime, you will have to make do in the prison here. Each squad of men will be given a place on the grounds. You must return to this place every morning for roll call and to get your rations. Severe punishment will result if you fail to do this. We have only a few tents, not enough for all of you. If you do not get a tent, you can make shelters from the available wood and brush on the grounds. We will give each squad what cooking utensils we have but realize we cannot give you much. Our own soldiers are desperately doing without and, alas, so will you. Now men, please make your way to the stockade."

A low murmur arose in the group. Isaiah leaned close and whispered. "That Reb seemed a lot better than Bassieux. Maybe things will be better here, huh Hiram?" Before I could say anything, a guard came up and shouted. "Now get going you damn Yankees. By god, if you don't move I'm goin' to stick your butts!" Moving forward, I glanced at Isaiah.

"Isaiah, I really doubt it."

Slowly, the ragged procession of prisoners moved toward the stockade gate, dissecting the lines of guards. The Buckeye Manor was near the front of the line. Sam Parker watched me closely with a strange mixture of empathy and duty. He, like the other guards, waved his bayonet for us to move along.

The afternoon sun illuminated the stark outlines of the approaching prison pen. The two gates of the stockade grabbed my attention. The north gate was on the left of the stream and the south gate was on the right. We crossed a small bridge, walked along the stockade wall, and then halted before the north gate. Here we lingered while several Rebel sergeants examined us. Seth nervously fingered his Bible. *That must be a new experience.*

Sentinels in square boxes on either side of the huge gate peered down at us, their shouldered muskets made them look like vultures on a roost. The large gate swung open, screeching, into a chamber with closed inner gates leading into the prison interior. Here the Rebel sergeants searched pairs of prisoners before turning them into the prison yard.

One of the Rebels grabbed at the blanket and rubber ground cloth of a man in front of me. The prison commandant reprimanded the guard. "Let the man keep his blankets—it is winter". This surprised us as we had seen these things taken at Belle Island. The man drew the blankets to his chest and hurried forward through the inner gate, not waiting for a change of mind from our captors. Seth and I stepped forward.

The Rebel sergeant felt my blanket roll and noted my tin cans, railroad spikes, metal scraps and other things I had picked up at various stops. He shook his head. "This Yank's a damn pack rat". Next, he examined my Bible, quickly opening and closing it. The sixty dollars in greenbacks so carefully secreted at Belle Island eluded him. *Thank you Lord.*

"It's good you got the scriptures with ya Yank, you'll need 'em in here."

Next, the guard examined Seth who clasped his Bible tightly.

"You a Christian too?"

"Oh yes sir, born and bred, a Baptist," answered Seth as the guard circled around him. Satisfied that Seth had nothing he wanted, he motioned us up to the gate. Next came Isaiah also gripping his Bible.

"Hey, Jim, these darn bluebellies got more Bibles than the whole 55th Georgia and 26th Alabama combined! Now don't that surprise the dickens out of ya?" Laughing he pushed Isaiah and Bushey Thomas forward, next to us by the inner gate.

Seth edged closer to me. At this final threshold, I expected a god of the underworld to rise up, open his mouth, and gulp us down into to the lower vortices of hell.

The door opened and revealed a stockade about fifteen acres in size. It was littered with pine limbs left over from cutting trees for the walls. Only three of the walls were up, the end wall to the right (south) of us was not finished and revealed a larger creek and pine forest in the distance. A battery of cannons with artillerymen stood in this opening. We stepped forward to where guards directed squads to various parts of the prison grounds.

A tall guard with a crooked mouth and large nose approached us as we examined the expansive opening. He told us to go up the middle of the north slope to make our shelter. He warned us against going too close to the opening on the south slope.

"Don't you boys go past those stakes or those cannons will cut you to pieces."

I saw slaves chopping and dragging logs. The shouts of the overseers urged them to work harder. I felt as if we were in a large open theatre watching an act from *Uncle Tom's Cabin*.

"There's what we came down here to stop," said a balding prisoner with thick eyebrows off to my left.

A small stream bounded by a marsh meandered across the middle of the grounds. From this stream, a rather steep slope rose up to the left or north end of the stockade and another long bank extended to the south to where the slaves were working on the wall. There were about five hundred prisoners in the prison. All were busy constructing shelters and making fires for the cool night to come.

We waited for the rest of our squad then went to the stream and quenched our thirst. The water was somewhat muddy but was drinkable. We then made our way to the middle of the north end of the prison to examine what would be our new home.

The Germans quickly separated from us and started talking in their native language. We watched them for a short while. They pointed this way and that and eventually organized into subgroups of three or four men each. Each subgroup began constructing a shelter, gathering pine branches and making poles on which to spread their blankets. Mesmerized, the Buckeye Manor stood and watched our busy neighbors until Seth clapped his hands and stepped in front of us.

"Well boys, we had better get our heads together and figure out what we need to do here. The sun is going down and its getting cold!" We decided to first get a fire started and cook our rations of bacon, black peas, and cornmeal. We were old hands at this from our days at Belle Island.

After eating, the ten of us in the Buckeye Manor sat in a circle around the fire. Off to our right, the Germans settled into their individual shelters. Across the prison, small fires pierced the darkness as the cold and heavy dew of the Georgia night settled in around us.

Huddling under a tent made from the four rubber ground cloths and blankets we shared, the ten of us discussed what should be done regarding shelter and how to survive in this place. The pitch pine fire snapped and crackled in the middle of our group. The smoke burned our eyes and made our faces black.

"Damned if you don't look like a nigra, Hiram," said Seth as he coughed and waved the smoke away from his eyes.

"Looks like we all better get used to being black," laughed Bushey Thomas. Seth smiled, his white eyes shining against his dark, smudged face.

Having survived Belle Island, we had a wealth of experience among us and the discussion became lively. As we talked we instinctively moved in sequence so that each man received warmth from the fire and from his fellows.

His profile outlined against the light of the fire, Seth addressed the 82nd Ohio at Andersonville. "We have to move quickly to get our hands on the wood that is available in the camp now. You know damn well that more prisoners are going to be coming in by the trainload, just like at Belle Island. We need to act now to build our shelter and get supplies! It's survival of the "firstest"!" Not a man among us disagreed but Isaiah.

"Seth, I know we need to take care of ourselves but what about other prisoners? We cannot just go out, grab, and hoard everything." Seth's expression became noticeably agitated.

"Isaiah, didn't Belle Island teach you a thing? You are not back in your little church in Ohio; you are in a hellhole of a Rebel prison camp where every scrap of food and canteen of water means life or death. Wake up for Christ's sake!" Isaiah rose to his feet and stood before the fire, the flames illuminating a calm and confident face.

"For the sake of our Lord! Men, what will become of us if we let this wicked place drag us down to our evil natures? Can we live with ourselves if we survive at the expense of others? No, I say! Let us take the higher road! Besides, we never know when we will need help. We host 'angels unaware' sometimes." Heads nodded and some of the 82nd Ohio at Andersonville even muttered a subtle "Amen". Others found themselves deep in the complexities of a moral dilemma that would unfold at daylight.

As the North Star highlighted itself on the handle of the Big Dipper in the clear night sky, we fell asleep. Each of us evaluated in his mind the conversation that had just transpired. The survival of our bodies and souls was uncertain.

The morning of February 28, 1864 dawned gray and misty over the cold, damp prison ground at Andersonville. The rains of March were already threatening. A Confederate drummer intruded on our sleep and beckoned us to the roll call at the North gate. We lined up by detachments and messes, each man responding to the call of the enemy sergeant as he called off our names. All were present and accounted for so we were able to immediately receive morning rations.

If a man had been missing, the Union sergeant of our detachment would have to hunt him down. If the man could not be found, much of the day would be spent standing in line and our food allotment may be cut or reduced. The Rebels thus highlighted the predicament of self versus the group. Escape and your comrades suffered. Stay and you endured the misery of Andersonville. The rations were brought to the camp in a wagon in the morning and late afternoon.

After cooking and eating breakfast, the Buckeye Manor began immediately building a circular hut with three sections resembling the pieces of a pie. Each section was big enough to shelter three men. The center could sleep one man for a total of ten. The sandy soil was scooped into raised benches for bunks and pine boughs provided bed mats.

Brush left over from making the stockade was plentiful and the prisoners were low in number so every man was able to find what he needed. Some men did not engage in shelter building but most did. Using railroad spikes we had picked up, we whittled pine logs for the walls of our hut or shabang and plastered the spaces between the logs with clay from the bank by the stream.

As I was bringing clay up to the hut on a flat piece of wood, I noticed Isaiah helping a young soldier push poles into the ground so he could make himself a small tent with his blanket. After plastering a section, I went down to lend a hand.

The soldier was just a young boy, a courier who carried messages between commanders on the battlefield. A huge scar was on his forehead. A tree branch knocked him off his horse near enemy lines. He had been captured at Williamsport as Lee made his retreat south from Gettysburg.

He was by himself at Andersonville until Isaiah found him. In a few minutes, his shebang was up and he found shade from the late morning sun. Before leaving him, Isaiah told him to find someone from his regiment and to get into a group. "Son, you can't survive in here by yourself. Now first thing, son, go out and find somebody!" The boy shook his head and said he would but first he wanted to get some rest.

We discovered that the red Georgia clay made good pots and more importantly bricks. When dried in the sun our clay molds became hard and we used these to build a central stove and to strengthen the walls of our hut. Pine logs were used to frame the roof and again clay was used to seal the cracks. During heavy rains, we put our ground cloths on the roof to shed excessive water that might leak through the clay.

In a matter of days, the Buckeye Manor house was completed. A substantial structure, it impressed many a fellow prisoner. "You fellows got a right smart shebang there, almost like a castle," said a man hobbling by on a crutch. I felt the twinge of "the dilemma" we felt at Belle Island.

Our building was well thought out. It provided shelter, shade from the sun, and was open to the breezes from any direction. The circular shape allowed us to watch from all sides for any attacks like those of the raiders at Belle Island. We had indeed learned our lessons from that terrible place.

After the first week at Andersonville, I noticed some of the raiders from Belle Island walking about the camp. We talked to our neighbors and made a protection alliance with the Germans of the 26th Wisconsin and an Illinois regiment off to our left. They too had survived Belle Island and knew of the importance of this kind of bond.

Our early arrival and access to a good campsite, wood, and other resources was a major advantage over the later arrivals. In the days that followed, about four hundred new prisoners were coming in each day and the wood was disappearing fast. By early spring, most of the logs were gone and even tree stumps were being removed. Any green plants on the grounds were pulled and eaten and frequent March rains made the prison bare and muddy. Our elevated location on the middle of the north slope allowed us to stay fairly dry but other prisoners were destitute. The 'dilemma" grew stronger.

Isaiah was often gone for a whole day and we knew where he was—helping destitute men find shelter and substance. On occasion I and others from the Buckeye Manor, 82nd Ohio edition would go out with him. There was no shortage of men alone and in desperate circumstances. Because he often shared his rations, Isaiah was becoming thin, even more than the rest of us.

As at Belle Island, the rations were inadequate in quantity and quality to sustain health. The corn meal was rough, unbolted, and still contained the husks and cob. Eating it irritated the digestive system and caused bleeding in the stool. The black peas were wormy and the meat often spoiled to where it could not be eaten. Water from the stream grew more contaminated from the wastes from the growing numbers of prisoners and run off from the Rebel camps upstream. It was imperative that we supplement our diet with other items from a sutler allowed into Andersonville and from the marketplace that developed just like at Belle.

The market was on the large central street through the middle of Andersonville. Almost anything could be purchased since the guards and local residents looked on the growing numbers of prisoners in Andersonville as an outlet for goods. Vegetables such as sweet potatoes and onions were highly prized for preventing scurvy. Federal greenbacks were greatly valued. One greenback was worth up to five or even ten dollars of Confederate currency depending on the supply.

Our stash of greenbacks was carefully hidden in our shelter in hollow clay bricks. We were careful in getting it out; usually done only at night. Having money made you a prime target for thieves and raiders. Belle Island had taught us well in this regard.

Before the native plants disappeared on the prison grounds, Isaiah and I had gathered up a good store of pine bark, sassafras roots, sage, laurel roots, mints and other plants that my Indian great grandmother had taught me were good for medicinal use and for making tea.

We also gathered these plants when we went outside the stockade on wood gathering details. A guard had to go out with about ten prisoners for this purpose and we did this with Sam Parker as often as we could. Sam let us roam quite widely and for longer periods than other guards.

We kept careful watch for Sam Parker's appearance on the stockade wall. The word of "Sam's at the gate" signaled the 82nd Ohio of possibilities for some trading or wood gathering outside the stockade. While he had to be careful (we often heard Sam rebuke us with a long oath), we knew he was an ally.

If Sam was on duty at night, I often received the gift of an onion, sweet potato, or some Confederate bills thrown at me concealed in a ball of clay as I walked by his station at an appointed time. These gifts were lifesavers and I often thanked God that I stopped on that hillside at McDowell to help a wounded Confederate soldier.

To supplement these gifts from Sam and our paltry rations, I dried strips of the medicinal plants and bartered them for vegetables in the market. I soon became known as "Mansfield medicine man" and many prisoners came to our shelter or shebang for a remedy for indigestion, diarrhea, dysentery, or the many other maladies that increased as the prison population grew.

As the numbers rose, we began to see men die in considerable numbers just as at Belle Island. The dead were hauled out to near the South gate and laid in a row. From here the bodies were carried by friends of the deceased to a "dead house" to be taken to a nearby graveyard and buried by slaves and burial teams of prisoners.

One day in March, James Barker of our Buckeye Manor came back from being on a burial detail. He had broken out in a cold sweat and was vomiting. Through his wrenching, he was able to talk.

"Boys, I never saw such sights as I saw today, even at Belle. Some of those dead men were actually rotten they had been left so long. The skin came off as you tried to move them. Lord knows what foul contagions I got from being out there. If you can get out of it, don't ever get on a burial detachment. The cabin bed, double rations, and even the whiskey they give you are not worth it."

With a groan, he crawled to his bed of now dry and crackly pine needles and tried to sleep despite constant shivering, diarrhea, and dry heaves. We tried to get James down to the sinks at the east end of the stockade stream when he had an attack but found that he could not make it. Eventually we dug a hole by the hut for his use.

This practice was distained by the neighboring messes because it fouled the grounds. "Can't he hold it till the sinks?" asked a German soldier of the 26th Wisconsin.

"Not hardly Fritz! Let's see how you do when you get the screamers."

His thirst became severe over the next days. The pure rainwater we had collected in our clay pots was soon exhausted and we went to the Stockade stream for more. The stream was by now contaminated by the growing number of prisoners and unsanitary conditions but was the only water we had to give him. It only hastened his demise.

All of our attempts at finding a cure were to no avail. Clay tablets, pine bark, sassafras, and other concoctions failed. We thought about taking him to the hospital tent on the far south end of the stockade but he would not go. We had all heard how the hospital was the worst place to go, everyone taken there seemed to wind up dead.

Within a week, we carried James Barker's body to the south gate where he himself awaited burial while others assumed his prior duties. As Seth and I stood over his body guarding it from others who wanted to take it out, our sadness almost overwhelmed us. This was the first death experienced by the Buckeye Manor. We had all survived the severe test of the winter at Belle Island, had built a good shelter here at Andersonville, had been able to get vegetables, and thought ourselves as rather well off compared to many others. The stiffened body and yellow, pallid face of James destroyed any thoughts of invincibility and death became a real possibility for all of us.

As we waited for the gates to open and allow us to take James out, we saw a new group of prisoners arrive at the north gate. Seth watched them stand aghast at what they saw in the pen. Some raiders then attacked these "fresh fish" and the stunned men lost their blankets and knapsacks. Seth erupted.

"Oh Lordy, can you believe that? When will they stop bringing in more prisoners? Don't they know that we're filling this hellhole up? The men are attacking each other and you can't even find a place to lay down anymore without getting stepped on. My God, Hiram the place stinks so much that you can't breathe!"

Our attention shifted to a guard opening the south gate. Seth murmured to me under his breath. "It's about time that bastard opened that gate. I can't wait to feel a little breeze. You grab old Jim by the legs, I'll get his arms."

The weight of the dead body pulled against our weakness and it was quite a struggle crossing through the gate to the open ground outside the stockade. The guard kept a close eye on us as we placed James beside other corpses in the dead house, a shabby pole structure with pine branches for a roof. The putrid smell of the place was overpowering. The guard came up to us with a cloth over his face that he briefly removed as he spoke.

"Well, you boys got anything to trade for a few minutes to pick up some firewood?" I pulled out a brass button that I had traded some sassafras tea for at the market.

"Will this get us ten minutes in that brush pile over there?" The guard looked carefully at the button that had an eagle shining in the sun. "That's a right smart hen on this one. Yeah, you boys git on over there now and don't take too long!" Before long Seth and I had an armload of branches and we made our way back into the stockade. Other men were now carrying their dead friends out to the dead house.

As we passed back through the gate, I grabbed the branches tightly as we made our way through the masses. Thin, bony arms snatched at our firewood breaking off pieces as we walked back to our hut. Exhausted, I stooped down, entered our shelter, and dropped the branches by the clay brick stove. The cooler, darkened interior of the hut gave some relief as I laid down on the sand bunk and closed my eyes.

I had by now learned to remove myself mentally from the misery of the prison by forcing my mind into a lightheaded numbness or dreamlike state. I placed myself into the camps at Kenton or Grafton or into the march to Gettysburg; never at home in Ohio as the contrast in emotions was too great. The constant murmur of the camp gradually retreated as I lost consciousness.

We figured that the pen at Andersonville could hold about ten thousand men. Going into the last week of March we were getting close to that number and still new prisoners came in daily. No longer were we able to walk around the grounds without jostling against other prisoners. Painful memories from Belle Island convinced us that the Rebels were sure to pack us in even more, especially now that Grant and Lee were rumored to be hard at it again in Virginia. As Bushey Thomas often said, "Belle Island taught him what it must be like to be a sardine. There were ten thousand of us fish in that six acre tin can of an island!"

Belle Island also taught us that safety and survival lay in having friends and a protective group. Individual prisoners without friends rarely survived, especially when conditions became severe and they were certainly headed that way. What would the future hold with Captain Henry Wirz, the new commandant of the prison at Andersonville?

Henry Wirz replaced Alexander Persons of the 55th Georgia who, with his regiment and the 26th Alabama, left to fight an ever-expanding Federal army. We actually appreciated Persons and the regular infantry troops. They were not overly belligerent and Persons let groups of prisoners frequently go out to collect wood despite the fact that some prisoners used this freedom to attempt escapes.

Wirz, on the other hand, came on as a more regimented, restrictive, and combative Rebel officer. He was an European with a noticeable accent. In appearance, he was slim and angular and appeared taller than his true height. He held his arms and shoulders in an odd way, as if some muscles did not work. Talk was that a bullet in the right arm in the Battle of Seven Pines had injured him. Every movement of his shoulders caused contortions on his face and it looked to me like he was in constant pain.

When angry he swore long oaths, especially at men who tried to escape. As March 1864 turned into April, Wirz's devotion to duty and the deteriorating foul, stinking situation of the Andersonville pen set up conditions for confrontation. Escape was now foremost in every man's mind.

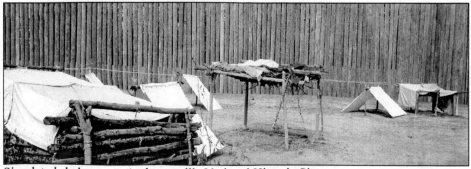

Simulated shabangs at Andersonville National Historic Site.

CHAPTER 17
ANDERSONVILLE'S WHIRLPOOL OF DEATH

Soon after his arrival in late March 1864, Captain Wirz changed the way prisoners were counted and divided into messes. Under the new system, each detachment was made up of two hundred seventy prisoners, each of these then had three nineties and each ninety had three messes of thirty. We were in the second detachment, second ninety or detachment 2.2.

This recounting and reorganizing of ten thousand prisoners occurred just when untrained Georgia Reserves of young boys, old men, and soldiers unable to serve in the field were replacing regular Confederate infantry soldiers at the guard posts. During our wood gathering details Sam Parker told us that all able bodied men were needed for fronts in Virginia, Tennessee, and other battles erupting throughout the South. Sam said he was worried that some of the young guards may have short fuses and that we should be careful.

To add to the confusion and uncertainty, Rebel sergeants counted and recounted, sometimes taking all morning. Rations were delayed. Weakened prisoners fainted in the hot sun and men became sick and death rates increased. Prisoners became increasingly desperate and tried to escape by any means possible, mostly by walking away from wood gathering details or by tunneling under the walls. All of this infuriated Wirz who wanted an orderly and tightly run prison camp with all men accounted for and duly recorded.

As numbers of prisoners grew, food and supplies became harder to procure. Rebel quartermasters cut back on meat and amounts of cornmeal. Reduced rations fueled more discontent. Starving men became frantic. Escape attempts by tunneling increased.

Men absent from roll counts slogged through the swamps with bloodhounds and hired man hunters on their trails. Most were caught, put in chains, and thrown back into the prison. Others were put in stocks where they lay exposed to the weather, unable to move. Furthermore, food was withheld from the detachments of the men who escaped from the stockade. An air of fear and anger spread through the prison as spring moved into summer.

Escape was certainly on the minds of the Buckeye Manor but we were perplexed. Isaiah started the conversation as we sat in the humid and damp shade of our hut near the end of April.

"We have to try to escape. It's our duty as soldiers! I know of a tunnel being dug by some Pennsylvania coal miners over by the east wall. They could use our help." To this some would nod ascent but others like Seth replied with caution.

"Isaiah, didn't you see those poor souls in the chain gangs and in the stocks? Those bloodhounds are good at tracking down Yankee hides and the boys are all bit up by those dogs." A pair of prisoners dragging a ball and chain trudged by our shelter. "Besides, we're in the middle of Georgia. Where can you go in these swamps?" Each of us surveyed the prison around us. "No, we best figure out how to survive 'till we get exchanged or Union cavalry raids get us out. These Reb guards will run at the first sign of Union horseflesh and carbines."

Bushey Thomas, rubbing the back of his head, remarked. "Can you imagine what it would be like to be ten feet underground in a tunnel and then have the thing cave in on you? It happened to a Massachusetts soldier named O'Brien. By the time they dug him out, he had suffocated to death. His mouth was full of dirt from screamin' for help!"

Thus, while escape was in our hearts, caution ruled our minds as we grew accustomed to the monotony of roll calls, collecting rations, trying to cook and prepare meals, and the ranting of Captain Wirz.

One early May morning as we stood at roll call in the rain going through a third recount, Isaiah, weakened by giving too many of his rations away, fainted. Wirz immediately recognized the gap in the line and rode his gray horse up to where Seth and I were trying to revive Isaiah.

"Get up you damned Yankee and get back in line!" Seth looked up at Wirz with a scowl that would fry eggs.

"You blasted fool, can't you see he has fainted!" Wirz then called over a guard who was a mere boy, maybe fifteen years old.

"If dis man says one more word, shoot him! I vill have order in this prison!" The boy grimaced as he clumsily pulled back the hammer of an old smoothbore musket. He then laboriously aimed it at Seth. I quickly put my hand on Seth's shoulder and said, "Let's pick him up and hold him. You grab his right arm and I'll get his left."

As we raised Isaiah, his limp legs solidified and he regained consciousness. Coughing, he then righted himself and stood in line. Wirz sneered at us and waved his hand at the guard. The boy exhaled in relief, lowered his gun, and released the hammer. Smiling to his comrades, he then walked back to his former position.

The prisoners around us murmured their disgust. Isaiah's good heart and deeds were well known and an affront to him was an insult to them all. Finally, the count was finished and rations, meager as they were, reached our famished hands.

More crowding in late May agitated the discontent that pervaded the prison grounds. Nearly twenty thousand prisoners now inhabited the cramped space of Andersonville. The constant bumping and physical contact stressed every man who straightaway wanted to get out. Plans of escape were on everyone's agenda.

Prayer meetings sprang up around the camp like mushrooms. Men heretofore brazen and callous about religious things began to fear death and sought salvation. Sermons and hymns could be heard around the stockade almost every evening. Petitions to the Lord for rescue rode every prayer.

Groups of men began to dig shafts and side tunnels for escape. The Rebels, who reportedly had spies roaming among us, tried to ferret out any organized strategies for a break out. Wirz especially feared a mass run at the gates or walls and aimed cannons filled with canister and grapeshot on the prison grounds. To remind us of the deadly consequences of a charge on the walls, he occasionally fired a shell over the grounds.

He also established a no-man's land around the inside of the prison demarcated by a deadline of boards nailed to poles set in the ground about nineteen feet inside the walls. Any prisoner in that space (or even reaching into it) was liable to be shot by the guards. Not only did this deadline add another means of dying, it also made the overcrowding worse by taking away space. Those who had set up comfortable quarters next to the shaded walls now had to move to the interior.

Selfishness and self-preservation vanquished morality and produced thievery and a general atmosphere of violence. Evil increased its grip on Andersonville and wickedness flourished along with hoards of flies, lice, and mosquitoes. As new groups of prisoners entered the stockade, this whirlpool of misery twisted and spun, sucking more and more men into the depths of hell itself.

June brought rainy steamy days that became relentlessly oppressive in the foul prison pen where any breeze was blocked by the high stockade walls. A trip outside was worth almost any price and prisoners fought over who could carry dead or wounded men outside to the dead house or hospital.

The overcrowding produced horribly unsanitary conditions, especially along the stockade creek. The sinks overflowed with excrement, contaminating the upper reaches of the stream. Wounds exposed to this filth became gangrenous and arms, legs, fingers and toes rotted and dropped off living men, revealing raw nerves and bones. Maggot infested bodies littered the prison. The summer of 1864 witnessed the playing out of Darwin's theory of natural selection as the weak died and only the strong continued to endure the misery of Andersonville.

Those of us who survived seemed to be thin and wiry. Two of the taller men of the Buckeye Manor died in the extreme conditions of hot, wet weather and scant rations. We who survived could barely carry the dysentery-riddled bodies of these farm boys from Ohio to the south gate. Those who kept cleaner and could get along on less food and water somehow persisted. There were now seven of us in our hut in the middle of a mass of tents on the upper north slope.

From our higher vantage point, we could see almost the entire prison including the forts and buildings outside the stockade. The camp of the raiders on the southwest side of the prison was the focus of our group one hot afternoon in mid-June. Seth, after silently watching the raider camp for some minutes, remarked.

"Hiram, remember what you said about the rats in your barn in Ohio?" After using an old dirty rag to wipe sweat off my forehead, I murmured a feeble "yeah".

"Those raiders over there are the mean, tough rats. They band together and take everything they need from the rest of us who just squeal and run away."

At that moment, some men down by the swamp stirred and shouts of "murder, murder, and thief" pierced the steamy air. Three large men ran away from the commotion, quickly crossed the bridge over stockade creek, and then casually walked up to the raider camp. Cheers and backslapping greeted the thieves who waved blankets and watches in the air. Seth gritted his teeth.

"Good God, look at those thievin' raiders! How can we put up with that? Those sons of perdition have got to be stopped!" Realizing the importance of this comment, the rest of the Buckeye Manor stirred from their slumber and focused on the area that Seth was so intently observing.

The man who the raiders attacked was now at the north gate angrily beckoning the guard. We could hear his cries, as he demanded to see Wirz. Soon the man left the stockade accompanied by a Rebel officer. Isaiah, shading his eyes with his hand, stared at the doors of the gate that were now closing. Turning to us, he asked.

"Where is that man going? How did he get out of the gate so quick? Do you suppose he will get to see Wirz? Do you think anything will be done about the raiders?"

No one in our group had the energy to speculate further. Hardly anyone in the stockade did anything until the hot sun mercifully descended behind the horizon. As we reclined on our bunks, the grinding monotony of the stockade reclaimed the seven soldiers of the Buckeye Manor.

In our hut, we were much better off than the masses that surrounded us. Most prisoners were under flimsy tents or makeshift shabangs. Some had no shelter at all, the heat relentlessly removing life from their burned bodies.

With evening came a hard rain and we refilled our clay vessels with runoff from the roof. As we picked lice off each other and swatted mosquitoes, we questioned whether we should sleep on our ground cloths or put them on the roof to shed the abundant amounts of water coming down in waves from the heavens. It had rained almost every day in June. Isaiah had kept a diary in the pages of his Bible that revealed twenty-one straight days of rain.

Small drips of muddy water formed and ran down the inside of the roof as the moisture dissolved the clay between the pine logs. I decided to go outside and place my rubber blanket on the roof since I did not want to repack the spaces with clay. I could not imagine having the strength to do that job again.

As I exited the door, I bumped into Isaiah who was carrying a man in his arms. The flashes of lightning revealed the unconscious limp body of the young courier we had helped earlier. Isaiah was barely able to speak to me as he struggled up to the entrance of our hut.

Forgetting my mission to cover the roof, I helped Isaiah pull the boy into the hut out of the rain. The eyes of the rest of the Buckeye Manor were on Isaiah.

"I found this boy lying in his shebang almost drowning. I would like to add him to our mess if the rest of you agree." I disrupted a long silence.

"We certainly have room in the hut now." As Isaiah placed the man on the center bunk, Seth questioned him.

"Isaiah, do you think we can save every poor wretch out there?"

Isaiah carefully caressed the boy's forehead and felt his neck for signs of life. Finding a weak pulse, he looked at Seth. "No, Seth, just this one life tonight." Seth took a deep breath, exhaled, and slowly approached the boy. Seth paused over the boy as a lightning flash revealed his young face, amazingly peaceful, almost childlike.

"What's his name, regiment?" Isaiah said he did not know his name. "You don't even know his name? What's your connection with him?" Exhausted, Isaiah closed his eyes and then calmly spoke.

"I met him earlier and his face came into my mind tonight as I slept. I felt that he was in trouble so I got up and went to his shebang." Isaiah looked like he would faint but continued. "I found him drowning, unconscious. It was surely a sign from God."

Seth clapped his hands and then ran his fingers through his straggly hair. He then moved to his bunk where we heard him mutter. "Why not, the more the merrier!"

I heated a bowl of my sassafras tea and spooned it slowly into the young courier. The brew warmed his blood and got it coursing again. The next day we found him conscious and awake. His name was Richard Cummings and he was the son of a prominent New York congressional representative.

He had not been able to find any men from his regiment and was still alone. He most certainly would have died if Isaiah had not brought him to our hut. Tears ran down the boy's pine pitch darkened face as he repeatedly thanked and blessed us for saving his life. The Buckeye Manor was now up to eight members.

The last week of April had brought Andersonville a group of two thousand "fresh fish" that changed the economic and social fabric of the prison. These were the "Plymouth Brethren", a group of well-equipped and fancily dressed soldiers captured by the Rebels at a fort in North Carolina.

These men had made special surrender arrangements with their captors that allowed them to keep their knapsacks, equipment, and money. The Rebels honored this agreement and into Andersonville came an infusion of money and items heretofore unseen in the market place. Watches, pots and pans, knives, spoons, blankets, writing utensils—the variety of materials in their knapsacks seemed limitless.

Convinced that they would not be in this "despicable place" more than a few weeks before being exchanged, the Plymouth Brethren readily traded these items for food and extra rations. We were amazed that only a few astute men in their group realized that they had better hang on to items that might be needed for an extended stay. Old prisoners like us realized that exchange was an improbable dream and that grinding day-to-day survival was what really mattered.

A surprise came to us in late June when Richard Cummings recognized one of these men as his cousin and left us to take up residence with the Plymouth Brethren. Richard later proved to be an "angel unawares" as he brought us a large metal cooking pan for our mess. This bonus of an item from the Plymouth Brethren allowed us to better combine our rations of meal, peas, bacon, and bartered vegetables to make a stew.

The pot was an obvious blessing and caused much introspection and discussion in the Buckeye Manor around many a meal. We debated repeatedly whether we should help other destitute men around us. Bushey Thomas said the pan in front of us argued strongly that we should. Others thought our connection with Richard and the pan was just a fortunate but improbable outcome of a foolhardy practice.

The 'dilemma" was the subject of a discussion on another night in late June. Seth was stirring a stew cooking in the large metal pan. The rains had mercifully stopped and the night was clear and moonlit.

"Well, it worked out with Richard but you fellows see my point, don't you? How can we take any more men into our mess? We will be swamped and all of us will starve."

Seth lowered his carved wooden spoon into the pan for a bit more stew. A shot rang out. His hand jerked spilling some of the precious brew onto the ground. We peered out of the hut into the darkness and could only see the glowing light of the fires lighting the perimeter of the stockade. A guard was standing on the wall with his rifle pointed downward.

Bushey, after a long silence, remarked. "Another fellow exchanged and paroled to the heavenly shores!" I followed with a question.

"I wonder if he was trying to get some of the cleaner water where the stream enters the pen? I can't believe they would shoot a man for reaching into the deadline for some water but I've seen four men shot in that area!" Seth shook his head.

"I bet the poor wretch walked into the deadline on purpose hoping to end his suffering." This comment caused us all to consider the condition we were in at this hellish place.

By the end of June, almost thirty thousand prisoners were crammed into the prison. Disease was rampant and the hospital, which had been moved from inside the prison to the outside, overflowed with sick and dying men. Surgeons were without medicines due to the Union blockade of Southern ports.

Rations, already too small, were cut in half. The only way we survived was to use our greenbacks to buy food at the market. Those without money starved. The dead pile at the south gate numbered over fifty, sometimes near a hundred.

Men became even more frantic with hunger. For more food, some turned into spies for Wirz and reported the locations of tunnels or informed guards about attempts to escape. A mass escape plan was foiled when Wirz learned of it and threatened to fire canister and grapeshot if a rush on the walls or gates was attempted. Spies or traitors who were caught by the other prisoners had their heads half-shaved or were tattooed with two T's standing for "tunnel traitor". These "half-shaves" did not survive long unless the Rebels took them outside.

Some desperate prisoners accepted offers to join the Confederate army in exchange for food and clothing. Not many did this, an impressive credit to our patriotism given the absolute misery that men were under. "Death before dishonor!

Death before dishonor!" chanted a group of prisoners at a Confederate officer trying to recruit more skeletons.

Others committed suicide by stepping over the deadline. Young boys barely able to peer over the walls of the pigeon roosts shot these miserable men.

One afternoon as I walked along the deadline, I saw a young guard go into shock after shooting a one-legged and insane prisoner called Chickamauga. Chickamauga was suspected of being the spy who revealed the mass escape plan. His isolation and destitute circumstances evidently caused him to lose his mind and cross the deadline.

After shooting the man, the young guard just stared at the corpse, becoming almost catatonic. He did not respond at all to the jeering crowd protesting his action. I moved closer careful not to get too near the deadline.

Sam Parker, who occupied the next guard station or pigeon roost, climbed up to the boy's guard post, his wooden leg produced a noticeable thump. Sam glanced at me before placing his hand on the boy's back.

"Son, if you didn't shoot that poor wretch you might have been shot yourself. Ain't no way a boy your age should be in a place like this. I pray to God that this war ends before too long and we both can get out of here."

The young guard gradually took his stare off the now stiffening corpse of Chickamauga and found the eyes of Sam Parker. Wiping a tear from his cheek, he shouldered his musket. Sam gave me a glance and shook his head. I reciprocated in kind.

Sadly, the raiders recruited more and more Union soldiers ready to sell their souls by killing and robbing their fellow prisoners. Attacks by these brutes became commonplace in June. We estimated that there were almost one thousand raiders generally located on the southwest side of the prison. Bands of club wielding brutes roamed the grounds robbing men suspected of having money or other items the raiders desired. This was often done at night where the thieves would communicate by whistling when they selected their prey.

Frightful were the nights when this eerie whistling suddenly roused us to attention and caused the hair to stand up on the napes of our necks. Grabbing his club and peering out of the hut into the blackness, Seth remarked one night. "These damned vultures are our own men, our own men damn it! How can Union soldiers be such fiends?"

Isaiah had a ready answer. "We are all fiends by nature, Seth. It's by the grace of God that we control it."

For the most part, the raiders avoided groups such as ours that were vigilant and well prepared against their predations. They mostly attacked the weak, defenseless, and new arrivals that were lured to where they could be overwhelmed in the now packed stockade.

The enlarging of the stockade at the north end, about twenty paces away from our hut, marked the beginning of the month of July. Ten more acres of unsoiled ground with tree stumps was made available and all detachments numbered above forty-eight were instructed to pull up stakes and move as quickly as possible to the new area.

About thirteen thousand prisoners moved through a large hole made in the old north wall in about two hours. So fierce was the stampede that some prisoners were trampled to death unable to get out of the way.

Opening this hole in the wall of the stockade released a valve on the human steam boiler of Andersonville. While the stockade was still crowded, the moving of the thirteen thousand prisoners to the new space allowed us to now walk around without having to push and shove and have constant contact. It also supplied us with a needed supply of wood.

As soon as night fell, the prisoners on both sides of the old wall began tearing it down. Like ants removing sticks from an anthill, the logs disappeared one by one. Groups of thin, emaciated men performed miraculous feats of strength, loosening logs buried five feet in the soil and dragging them away. By the next day, the entire wall was gone and the new ten acres lay open to the old original seventeen making a total area now of about twenty seven acres.

The Buckeye Manor secured a whole log that we took turns chipping into bundles of firewood using a railroad spike. We traded some of these bundles in the market for sweet potatoes, green ears of corn, blackberries, and sumac berries that helped prevent scurvy. Prisoners all around us were losing teeth from disintegrating gums and leg muscles were involuntarily contracting so that a man could not walk.

Contracting scurvy was a serious matter and all of us were acutely aware of its symptoms. A sour mash beer made from fermented corn meal was also sold in the market as a scurvy cure but we invested solely in vegetables, a proven preventative for a host of maladies.

More difficult to come by for the majority of prisoners was a cure for the robbing and mugging of the raiders. The number of attacks in June going into July was unacceptable. Men were now being attacked, robbed, and killed in broad daylight as well as at night. An organized resistance began taking form all over the camp.

In our area of the stockade, the first call to action came at a prayer meeting. Seth, Isaiah, and I were some of the first men to volunteer to be part of a large force of men dedicated to identifying and capturing thieves, flankers, and raiders. We were called the regulators, a type of police force. Memories of being in the provost guard for General Sigel coursed through my mind.

An Illinois sergeant named Limber Jim became the leader of the regulators. Limber Jim and a number of other sergeants had communicated with Captain Wirz and convinced him to help subdue and keep under guard men known to be thieves and raiders who would then be given a trial and meted out punishment. We were convinced that this would be the best way to end the misery of the raiders.

Anything that restored order was favored by Wirz and with his help the scoundrels were gathered up during the last week of June and the first week of July.

At the orders of Limber Jim, a tall and lanky man with a fetching personality, the Buckeye Manor grabbed our poles and headed for the south bank where the bulk of the raiders resided in rather plush style on stolen food and other items. As we approached the raiders, the same fear that I experienced on the battlefield gripped me. The raiders were in much better physical shape than us and their line of clubs and knives was daunting.

We, however, possessed the added strength and determination of the righteous cause that fueled our anger. Seth, Isaiah, and I along with a growing group of other men attacked on the left flank of the raider line. In five minutes their defense, held together only by selfishness and greed, broke. We used our poles to knock down and hold seven raiders trying to escape after the front of the raider line dissolved. Each of these brutes snarled at us like rabid animals, threatening to cut our throats once this "farce was over".

The swelling number of prisoners plus the Rebel guards soon overwhelmed the resistance of the raiders and the result for the thieves and murderers was far from being a farce. The ringleaders plus over two hundred known thieves were soon put under guard in the holding areas of the gates to the stockade.

Credit must be given to Wirz and the Rebel guards for helping to achieve this successful outcome. Wirz, ever careful of the mass escape, nevertheless, had his artillery guns loaded and ready should anything but the capture of the raiders transpire.

Over the next few days, a trial by jury was given to the raiders. Six of the ringleaders were sentenced to death by hanging and the two hundred others convicted of crimes were to run a gauntlet. One by one, the raiders were released from the prison gate doors to run through a double line of club wielding and fisted prisoners. The blows killed many of the thieves while others were able to run the line of death and limp out into the stockade to disappear among the chanting throngs to nurse their injuries.

After this, the six leaders of the raiders with hands tied behind their backs were led up to the gallows. Three Rebel guards beat drums playing the death march in the background. One of the condemned men tried to escape by running through the masses down across the swamp. He became mired in the filthy mess and was eventually led back to the gallows. A Catholic priest from Savannah who had been unselfishly helping dying prisoners, then pleaded for their lives saying that all of us in these terrible conditions deserved mercy and a second chance. Those men who endured without attacking their fellows listened but drowned out the priest's words with repeating chants. "No, hang em! No, hang em!"

Finally, a silence came over the grim scene. The six men were then allowed to say any last words. A couple of them broke down from their bravado and lamented their ways. They claimed that they were good men once but had fallen in with the wrong crowd and had given vent to their desires and lost their sense of morality. They asked for forgiveness. My thoughts briefly went back to the preacher at Camp Simon Kenton and his short sermon. Others were stoically silent, saying nothing. Two of the raiders snarled and cursed the men who put them into this situation telling everybody to "go to hell".

"You will soon be there" was the response of Seth who with Isaiah and me stood about thirty yards off to the west of the gallows.

Isaiah had a sad but angry look on his face as he murmured, "God's will, God's will". Surveying the rest of the Buckeye Manor revealed demeanors ranging from anticipation to disbelief. A sense of profound unrest settled into my stomach as I watched the noose go around the neck of Willie Collins who stood on the end of the gallows closest to us.

Meal bags were placed over their heads. I jerked as the planks were pulled out from under the men and the ropes stretched and strained, squeaking under the weight of the men.

Willie Collins had jumped at just this moment and his weight snapped the rope. As he hit the ground and rolled, the bag came off his head. The poor brute then looked up from the ground and witnessed the others gasp and strain as the taut ropes slowly strangled his partners in crime. Their legs straightened and shook as life leaped from their convulsing bodies. Collins blubbered like a man possessed.

"Please fellows, God has spared my life. Don't put me up there again!" As two of the regulators lifted him, he tried to drop to the ground to secure seconds to his miserable life. One of the men lifting him then spoke.

"Ah, come on Willie. Stand up and take your medicine. You killed and robbed and it's done. You're going to hang. Don't look at these others. It just makes it worse." Indeed, it was if the worst of the raiders was given this psychological torture before his own bout with strangulation was to begin. Soon, mercifully, his huge lifeless body swung beside the others. After twenty minutes, the bodies of the hanged men were lowered to the ground and left in position on the filthy clay of the south bank at Andersonville.

Prisoners filed by them for hours until darkness fell on the horrific scene and the bodies were removed to be buried apart from the other soldiers who died at Andersonville. Prisoners needing firewood quickly removed the wood from the gallows and soon more fires than usual flared up in the cool, damp Georgia night. The Buckeye Manor did not sleep well but the nightmare of the raiders was at an end. The regulators, now numbering about twelve hundred, formed a police force that maintained a relative if somewhat arbitrary sense of justice in the camp.

Soon the monotony and misery that was the essence of our reality came back into our consciousness. The relentless challenges of survival resumed as the days of July sizzled and burned in slow progression from sunrise to sunset.

The relentless march south of Union forces in the summer of 1864 exposed more Federals to capture and increased the numbers of new Union prisoners coming into the camp. Some of these new prisoners were from regiments now fighting in the state of Georgia, soldiers under General William Tecumseh Sherman. They brought hope that the war may be ending but dashed any anticipation of a prisoner exchange.

One new prisoner from Sherman's troops, on hearing our complaints about the government abandoning us, exclaimed. "Exchange? Grant and old Abe will have nothing of it. The paroled Rebs from our prisons are soon right back in the field while our men are almost dead when returned to our lines. The worst sticking point is that Negro soldiers captured are kilt outright or sent back into slavery, not even put up for exchange. No, I don't see much chance of exchange."

Indeed, one day we observed a local plantation owner come into the camp with an old gray bearded slave who walked behind him, head bowed. The portly southerner closely surveyed some of the colored troops captured in recent battles in Florida. The black troops turned to him full bore and looked him fiercely in the eye as he and the old slave walked with a group of Rebel guards in front of them. The proud look of the colored troops infuriated the slave owner who suddenly stopped and pointed out a black sergeant standing erectly off to his left.

"Moses, do you know that negra standing over thar?" The old slave slowly walked over to the sergeant and returned to the plantation owner who was slapping a whip handle into his hand.

"Sho enough, massa, dat one dere is massa Jones slave, sho enough is. He ran off last plantin' time." With this the Rebel guards seized the protesting colored soldier and handed him over to the slave owner and his men who waited outside of the south gate. Absolute anger and pain marked the faces of the colored sergeant's comrades as they watched him get shoved and whipped again into the darkness of slavery.

Another black officer stepped forward at this time and addressed his men. He was a handsome man, tall and slim, with a distinguished manner. With well-formed words, he assured his men that "vengeance was the Lord's and the evil just witnessed would be repaid with full measure, and even now, the sword of the Lord was in the land."

Meanwhile, the pale horse of pestilence and hunger was roaming Andersonville as the hot unbearable days of summer and reduced rations squeezed life out of the miserable prisoners. This led some of our men to write up a petition to President Lincoln detailing our terrible state of affairs and demanding that we be exchanged. Wirz even agreed to let some of our men leave to take this letter to Washington.

Not very many men, including the Buckeye Manor, felt comfortable signing this document. Isaiah felt that our government had reasons for leaving us at Andersonville. Bushey Thomas said that "some lice free clothes and a taste of some meat and vegetables" would go a long way in helping his understanding of the matter.

Seth could not understand why some cavalry units from the Union forces were not sent to free us. "If Sherman is in Georgia, freeing the prisoners at Andersonville would give him a lot of extra man power."

Evidently, the Rebels agreed with him as they worked feverishly building an additional stockade wall and earthworks for defense. They also placed more artillery to defend an attack that they were sure was to come any day.

News of that day came to us in early August with the arrival of captured cavalry troops of Union General Stoneman. They had been captured in Macon by Rebel forces in a failed attempt to attack Andersonville. Even Stoneman was captured in the attempted raid.

Our two hopes of salvation were to be exchanged or freed by Union cavalry attacking the stockade and rescuing us. While rumors of exchange circulated constantly, nobody took them seriously. The failed raid depressed our spirits even more than the thirst and hunger that constantly pulled us down.

The fetid grip of death tightened around Andersonville even more firmly in August. Each day the dead house received over one hundred prisoners, every corpse a grim reminder of our own tenuous hold on life. Each of us in the Buckeye Manor now realized that our lives now hung on our ability to avoid the pestilence that pervaded the prison pen.

The pitiful and poisonous conditions were even noted by the Confederate government who sent a military surgeon named Chandler to inspect the prison. He saw Andersonville at its worst. Rations had again been cut. Disease, vermin and starvation threatened every prisoner; none escaped the ravages of the filthy pen.

Our number in the Buckeye Manor was reduced by three more due to the ravages of a fever that caused our comrades to first convulse with heat, then go mad with pain, and finally collapse. I tried every remedy I had from sumac berries to sassafras to laurel root but nothing worked. As Isaiah, Seth, and I dragged the three brave soldiers of the 82nd Ohio to the south gate, Dr. Chandler noticed our pitiful condition and came up to us.

"How long have you men been in prison?" asked the Rebel doctor.

"Since our capture at Gettysburg July 1—first at Belle Island and now here," I replied. His jaw dropped as he beheld our thin and gaunt appearance. Calling his assistant over, he motioned to him to record our names, regiment, and capture dates on a ledger sheet.

"My God, you have been in prison over a year? You men will be the first to go in the coming exchange at Savannah. Just hang on a few more weeks." He then left shaking his head and disgustingly repeating, "This is a reproach, a reproach to the Confederacy!"

The days of August were not only hot but clean water could not even be bought at the market. Wells had been dug in the new area of the stockade but the water was as undrinkable as the putrid Stockade Creek. As we lay in our hut, we often looked at our dry clay pots just to stir the memory of the rainwater that we used to have available. All of us showed the telltale signs of scurvy, tight leg muscles and bleeding gums.

Even Seth attended our prayer meetings where mournful entreaties were made every night to the Almighty for deliverance.

On a day in early August, our prayers were answered. A massive cloudbank formed in the late afternoon over the prison, the lightning flashed, and the winds blew as if out of the mouth of God. Torrents of rain came rushing down and in minutes the stockade creek and swamp were filled with rushing waters that mounded up against the west and east walls of the prison. As we watched from our position high on the north slope, the west stockade wall collapsed followed by the east wall. The accumulated stench of thirty thousand prisoners was swept away in minutes.

Through the waves of rain, we saw the Rebel guards form battle lines around the openings in the walls. In the forts, artillery teams quickly staffed their guns. The suddenness and severity of the storm did not allow for any organized mass attempt at escape. A few prisoners tried to ride the floating logs out of the prison but they were captured by the guards and returned to captivity. Most of us bathed in the rain and restored our water supplies.

As I collected water off the roof into our clay pots, I saw Isaiah and Seth, both with their arms outstretched towards the heavens. Isaiah was weeping; his tears joined the raindrops that ran down his cheeks. Seth was wiping his body with a wet rag, murmuring, "Thank you Lord, thank you Lord." Had the profane but close friend of mine finally received a convincing demonstration of the existence of the Almighty?

Noticing my penetrating stare, Seth slowly dropped his arms, composed himself, and came with Isaiah, who was still weeping, over to near the hut where I stood. Placing his left hand on my back and his right on Isaiah's head, he embraced us. No words came from his lips but his message penetrated our hearts.

As the refreshing rain let up, we went into our hut and began singing *Amazing Grace*. Our feeble voices joined thousands of others from all around the camp. Our singing mixed with the sounds of Rebels and slaves working zealously throughout the night and over the next few days to rebuild the walls and washed out areas of the stockade.

The storm left a lasting blessing to us in the form of a new spring that formed near the north gate just inside the dead line. The Rebels built a trough to convey this life-giving water to the prisoners. Thousands stood in line for hours to get a refreshing drink from this new source of water. Before long, the name of Providence Spring was given to this vital source of water that no doubt saved hundreds if not thousands of lives.

This was not the only improvement that came to the prison as we went into the middle part of August. For some reason, Captain Wirz took sick and went to Macon to recover. In his absence, an officer named Davis took command and immediately instituted measures to clean up the stockade. Conditions improved and better rations were also provided. The weather at night became more pleasant and sleep helped many a prisoner to recover. However, record numbers of men continued to get sick and die. The struggles of prison life finally laid Isaiah low.

As the sounds of slaves and multitudes of workers building a new wall around the original stockade filled the days and nights, our friend Isaiah lay on his bunk struggling to stay alive. Like the others who died previously, he became feverish and hot, shaking with chills and then losing consciousness. Seth, Bushey, and I took turns attending to Isaiah's needs. We brought him water and shared our rations. We bathed him and cleaned up his bouts of diarrhea. We were the last of the Buckeye Manor and we did not want to lose another life. Isaiah had a strong constitution and gradually showed signs of recovery but he could not walk and was totally dependent on us.

With September came new and serious rumors of parole and exchange. Captain Wirz returned and our hopes again sank. The only good news was that Sherman had captured Atlanta and the end of the war seemed closer. We learned this through a Rebel guard who late at night on September 4 called out "post number ten and all's well and Atlanta's goin' to hell." After this pronouncement, the stockade literally pulsed with excitement as nearly comatose prisoners suddenly found new vigor.

Over the next days, Rebel officers called together the various detachments and told them to get ready to board the trains to the coastal port of Savannah to meet Union ships that would take us home. A new energy swept through the camp as the dead literally sprang to life. We were to be one of the first detachments to leave and immediately began gathering up items that we thought we might need.

Isaiah watched us from his bunk, his eyes alternately closing and opening in weakness, as the rest of us excitedly prepared for the short train trip to Savannah. Seth went over to Isaiah and put his hand on his warm forehead.

"Hang on, Isaiah. We are finally going to get out of this, er ah, prison. I almost said damn, didn't I, Isaiah?" The sick man managed a slight smile. "Well, I am turning a new leaf, the Lord willing, and you, me, Hiram, and Bushey will even form a new kind of church back there in Ohio. What should we call it? Let me see here." He looked at the rest of us who bore a resemblance to a circle of vultures eyeing two skeletons. Bushey began laughing.

"Isaiah is a Hard Shell Baptist, ain't he?" Isaiah gave a short moan. "And Hiram, you and I are Presbyterians and Seth there, well, he is a new convert. Why don't we call ourselves Hard Pressed New Baptists?" Realizing that this was the first time I could remember hearing laughter anywhere in Andersonville, I replied.

"I certainly agree with the hard pressed part!" After a few seconds, our laughter turned to silence as we noticed that Isaiah had again lost consciousness. Seth came over close to me and began whispering.

"Hiram, you know the Rebs are only going to allow able bodied men to leave for Savannah. Our side won't exchange anybody who can't make their own way on board those Union ships. Those who can't walk are going to have to stay behind. If Isaiah can't get up on his feet, what are we going to do?" Bushey overheard us and leaned up close.

"If he can't walk, we will carry him between us. The Rebs will never know he's being carried if we get into the middle of a crowd." This sounded like a good plan and we talked the rest of the night about Savannah, the Union ships, and the details on how to get our good friend carried out of Andersonville. The thought of leaving him for the surgeons in the wretched hospital was not an option.

Inside Andersonville 1864 *(Library of Congress)*.

The isolated graves of the six leaders of the raiders.

View of Andersonville from sinks to Ohio monument top right. The monument to Providence Spring is visible in the upper left center of the photo. The raiders were hung on the slope to the left.

The Ohio monument at Andersonville.

The author with Andersonville historian Kevin Frye at a replica of the north gate at Andersonville.

CHAPTER 18
OUT OF ANDERSONVILLE

The rhythmic cadence of a lone drum pierced the cool, dank darkness of early morning at Andersonville. The moon kept the rising sun at bay. The beat mingled with the groaning misery of multitudes strewn on the sordid soil. The gates then swung open and the creaking sound of the huge hinges hailed the first detachments of prisoners to make their way out of the filthy prison and to the railroad depot to board the boxcars to Savannah.

It was September 8, 1864. Rumors about Sherman and his whereabouts ran through the moonlit camp like rabbits. Confederate officers worried and fretted about what would happen if the armies of Sherman liberated the starving angry throng pulsating within the stockade. In the stillness, I heard a Rebel officer talking outside our hut.

"This Yankee scum would rape and pillage our womenfolk from here to Atlanta! These prisoners must be moved!" Before long, orders went forth to call out the prisoners and load the trains. A blonde private from New York ran screaming through the camp.

"Exchange! Exchange! Boys we're going to be exchanged!" The clamor stirred us from our hungry stupors born from months of slow starvation. In an instant, we understood what was happening outside our hut.

"Hallelujah, the great getting up morning is finally here!" yelled Seth as he lifted his skinny frame, groaned, and felt his way through the dark hut. Light from huge fires along the path to the railroad depot weakly penetrated the door of our hut. "Hurry! Get up! We don't want flankers to rob us of our place. Praise the Lord, Hiram I really do feel like a new man!"

Bushey groaned and grumbled, stretching his taut arms and legs. "Well Seth, you must feel better than you look!" He then tried to move but his body faltered.

"Tarnation! Leave it to the Rebs to get us out of here in the middle of the night! Do you think we will need this large pan that Richard Cummings gave us?"

I tied together the ends of my blanket roll in which I had placed a spoon, tin cup, and my Bible given to me at Kenton by the preacher. This book and I had come a long way indeed. It sustained me and promised to do more. Five greenbacks hid between its leather covers. After feeling for these again, I responded to Bushey.

"I don't think the Rebs will keep us too long before sending us to the Union steamers, do you?" Bushey sat down on his bunk and began scratching his beard while fingering the large pan. It had cooked our food, collected water, and in no small way helped us survive in the rawness that was Andersonville. Men risked their lives for a spoon, let alone a large pan.

"What if the Rebs send us to another pen? Blast it Hiram! You know that just may happen. How many times have the Johnnies told us one thing and done another?"

Isaiah started to moan which was unusual. Even in the misery of his sickness, he was stoic and quiet. Bushey and I moved over to him. Seth stayed by the door watching the multitudes of prisoners now moving toward the gates. The light of the Georgia moon and the fires around the prison revealed Isaiah's face. His lips were moving and we strained to hear his feeble words, formed with great difficulty. He took large breaths between each phrase.

"You should take the pan... but you'd better... leave me. I can't move my legs... and I can't stand up." At this point, he tried to move and only his arms responded. He now groaned loudly in pain. "Dear friends... I can't make it." Tears ran down his ashen face as he strained to raise his head.

"Hiram, my Bible... it's in... in my coat pocket." He pointed a feeble finger to his things. I found the Bible, which had a gold chain dangling from it. The sight of the Book seemed to strengthen him. "Would you give it to my family in Lucas? I have written some messages in the margins for them. There's also a few dollars hidden in the covers." He pointed again at his Bible. "Could you put the gold chain with the cross around my neck?" I opened the Bible to the page marked by the gold chain. Psalm 140, verse 12 was highlighted with a pencil mark barely visible in the dim light.

I know the Lord will maintain the cause of the afflicted and the right of the poor.

I raised his head and put the chain around his neck. Feeling the cross on his chest, he fell back, a faint smile on his face.

Seth came over and knelt beside us. "Hiram, we have to get going! " Our hearts were in our throats as we contemplated the situation before us. We knew it would be impossible to get Isaiah by the Rebel guards who were now checking the first detachment at the gates. "The guards are running the men through in double file making sure only able-bodied men go to the boxcars," said Bushey peering out through the door. The pain was palpable, fear marked our faces.

Isaiah's eyes opened and he placed his hand on mine. "It's all right, boys. You have to go. The Lord is standing by me. I am not alone. Now please go."

I put Isaiah's Bible in my coat pocket next to my own. I then held Isaiah's hand. My eyes filled with tears. I could barely get out the words that I would take care of his Bible and would look up his family.

Seth lowered himself beside Isaiah and put his hand under our friend's head and looked intently at the man he had argued with so many times. Seth's hard featured face softened with a gentle smile. "Thank you my friend for standing by me." Placing his hand on Isaiah's, he continued. "If I don't see you down here, I'll see you up there." Isaiah opened his eyes and with great difficulty, whispered.

"His love endures forever." He then fainted, his breathing irregular.

With tears in our eyes and lumps in our throats, we watched his chest raise and lower. In the distance, we heard the call for our detachment. I turned back for a last glimpse of my friend. His eyes were closed but he was still breathing. The small gold cross on his chest shown like a star as I walked away.

I swallowed hard and followed the forms of Seth and Bushey through the darkness and down the slope toward the gate. All around me, men rose like ghosts from a shadowy graveyard, formed amorphous groups, and hobbled toward the stockade entrance, a gateway that promised liberty and blessed relief.

As we approached the stockade gate, I saw Sam Parker in the line of guards. Beside him stood one of the Rebel surgeons. From my place in line, I told Sam about Isaiah, pointing in the direction of our hut. He said "we will do what we can" and the surgeon made a notation in a ledger.

Seth, Bushey, and I now trudged, heavy hearted, along the same path that we walked back in February. This time we were minus seven brave men of the 82nd Ohio who stepped with us into the darkness of Andersonville. The Georgia autumn moon shown overhead and illuminated our path. A thin, slumped man sitting on a horse came into my view.

Captain Wirz sat on his mount just before the steps leading up to the depot platform which in the night sky reminded me of a gallows. The flames of a nearby fire revealed his head and drooping shoulders. His cold steel eyes appeared lifeless, hollow as he watched the prisoners climb the stairs and board the cars. An essence of death enveloped him as if the misery of the stockade had flowed over the walls and into his soul. Seeing us, his voice cracked with a heavy accent, "You Yankees von't be coming back here, dat's for damn sure!"

A man back of me replied, "We sure as hell won't, by God!"

Our boxcar was soon packed with more than sixty men. The coughing and retching of sick men filled the air as the train filled with its human cargo. Two guards sat on the roof and two more by the door. Seth wondered aloud. "Why so many guards? Who is going to try to escape when Union ships await us? Something is not right about this." Bushey fingered the metal pan that he had decided to bring along.

In the sultry darkness of early morning, our train of pitiful prisoners left the prison. As the morning twilight brightened, I looked out the cracks between the boards and bid Andersonville farewell and lost consciousness. About noon, I woke as we neared the outskirts of the city of Savannah. Lowland swamps crept up against mounds with tall spreading trees. Old, shabby passenger cars sat along the railroad sidings and overflowed with hundreds of refugees, probably fleeing the fighting around Atlanta.

Further into the city, I noticed church steeples, large square houses, and tree-lined streets. Tufts of moss draped down from stately oaks and added a lace-like magnificence to this beautiful city.

Before long, the train stopped and we stepped out of the boxcars onto a platform at the Savannah railroad station. Soldiers in homespun butternut uniforms stood along a pathway to a stockade just constructed. Mounds of soil, new logs, and piles of brush lay all around.

"Another damned prison pen," moaned Bushey. The day was clear and sunny and we smelled the ocean in the distance but our spirits dragged the ground. We were not headed to any Union ships.

Crowds of onlookers gathered to see the next shipment of Yankees. As we came into view, a collective gasp arose from the crowd. "Could those be men? The poor wretches are walking skeletons!" Soon women with baskets of bread and fruits gathered around the gates of the new prison. Several prisoners, mad with hunger, tried to reach these baskets but were restrained by the guards.

"Let the poor wretches have something to eat!" yelled a woman with a white bonnet. A guard yelled at her as he pushed a prisoner back in line.

"The Yanks will be fed inside. Give your bread to the guard at the gate!" Frantic and feeling dizzy, we moved into line and, like bewildered children, walked to our new home.

Again, the Buckeye Manor was among the first into the prison. We walked a bridge over a large water-filled moat. A tall water tower stood at one end of the moat. The large gate reminded me of the one at Andersonville but this stockade was smaller, about ten acres in size. The old Savannah jail formed the north wall and shadowed a cluster of tents and shanties.

After getting our detachment assignment, Seth, Bushey, and I shuffled off to one of the shanties. We selected one with a slanted roof located on higher ground. We knew the importance of drainage after Andersonville. While Bushey stayed with the hut, Seth and I gathered any wood or branches that we could find. Next, we took Bushey's pan to a water pump on the north side of the prison.

The desire to bathe rivaled our thirst and hunger. Our skin itched from the filth of the boxcars. We made a fire, heated water, and each of us took a refreshing sponge bath. Thank God for that pan. In a short while, we heard the call to form up to receive rations.

Much to our surprise, the prison commandant, an officer named Anderson, gave us larger portions of cornbread, biscuits, and bacon. Bushey, after eating a piece of sizzling bacon, patted his stomach. "This is the first time I can remember my belly being out far enough for me to pat it!"

Later in the afternoon, some Masons from Savannah gave us more food as well as clothing and blankets. The generosity of this fraternity impressed us. For a southern organization to treat enemy soldiers this well was awe-inspiring. One of the Masons even gave us a small ham when Bushey flattered him by saying he "would join this here group of Masons first thing when he got back to Ohio".

Even though the September nights were cold, the food in our stomachs warmed our souls. How good it felt to lessen the pangs of hunger that had been our companion for many months! Now, when would we be exchanged? Rumors were heard every day but no arrangements for exchange took place. Gradually we accepted that we were in for another prison stay. *God, how much longer?* It was difficult to know. From the captured soldiers of Sherman's troops we knew the Union army was pressing through Georgia.

"The Confederacy was done for! Do not despair! Your day of liberation is near and at the gates!" So said a burly sergeant from Ohio recently captured at Macon. We found out from him that the 82nd Ohio was in the area and that some might even be prisoners now. "I heard some 82nd Ohio boys were captured at Peach Tree Creek." We kept an eye out for any from that point onward.

More Andersonville prisoners kept coming into this small prison. We questioned each new group about Isaiah but no one knew anything. The last trainload said that only five thousand men now remained there. A sergeant from Illinois saw the concern on our faces. "Things at Andersonville are a heap better now without the crowding. The rations are better and the surgeons are able to treat more prisoners. Even ole Wirz is less mean. Maybe your friend survived."

This gave us hope but seeing Isaiah alone in that hut, struggling for breath, haunted our minds and weighed on our hearts. Seth often remarked, "I should have stayed with him! How could I have left him alone?" I rationalized we had to go; the Rebels would not allow us to stay behind. This did not help. Our sense of guilt was too strong. We had let a friend down. Fervently did we pray God to forgive us and miraculously rescue Isaiah Rinehart.

Death also stalked the grounds at Savannah. Toward the end of September, the weather turned damp and cold. Crowding increased as more prisoners came into camp. Men weakened by months of imprisonment under the roughest of conditions finally gave out. The first few days of October found all three of us lying in our shanty delirious from high fevers. The cold and constant shivering had drained our meager resources. We were at the end of hope; death seemed desirable.

Seth descended into a deep depression. He murmured unintelligible phrases that sounded like a mixture between swearing and hymn singing. His constant banter wore on our nerves until Bushey and I lapsed into our own unconsciousness.

In a daze of delirium, I remember a man coming into our hut. He gave each of us water and food, no doubt saving the remnants of the Buckeye Manor. I never discovered the name of our "angel of mercy". I am not even sure he existed outside of my mind.

I was the first to recover and looked about me. Bushey and Seth lay still on the cold dirt. *Were they alive?* I needed to get water. Bushey's pan was in the corner of the shanty. I crawled over to it. It was half full of water! *How in the world? Who?* I drank voraciously and then I moved over to Bushey and wetted his lips with a rag. He groaned and turned his head, opening one eye. "Hiram, is that the best you can do? I could use something I could swallow." He was returning to normal.

Seth was in a worse condition. He had to recover spiritually and physically, both soul and body had yet to reconcile.

At the end of a week, Seth opened his eyes. Although weak and thin, he no longer struggled with depression but had a peaceful look on his face. "Brothers, I have seen the glory beyond!" He pointed to his heart. "We need not worry about Isaiah. I now know what he was talking about. He will be all right." Seth's calmness flowed to us like a warm breeze as we stared at him with wonderment.

The overcrowding on the small, ten-acre prison became severe by the first week of October. Bushey estimated that over ten thousand prisoners crammed its boundaries. Even the guards became ill in increasing numbers. Prison officials looked over the prison from the stockade guard posts with handkerchiefs to their faces.

Conditions became as bad as at Andersonville and the Confederate officers got into open arguments about what to do with the growing numbers of prisoners. I heard two argue as I stood near a guard post.

"If Sherman comes here, these prisoners will rise up and kill us on the spot. We have got to move these Yankees away from here!"

Recently captured soldiers told us that Sherman was close by and their best guesses had him coming toward Savannah. Rumors spread throughout the camp that we were again going to move.

On October 11 in the late afternoon, our detachment was called to the gate. When asked where we were going, the Rebel officers told us the usual refrain. "You boys are going to be exchanged just as soon as we get the agreements authorized."

After hearing this, Bushey exclaimed, "If I had a damn greenback for every time we heard that exchange line, I could outfit a regiment myself. Hell, I could outfit a brigade!" Seth smiled at Bushey and told him to stop swearing.

After counting off, we made our way back to the railroad station. Again, women gathered to give us bread, apples, and sweet potatoes. This time the guards let the women get closer. An older woman trailed by a small child gave me a loaf of bread as I walked to the train.

"Here soldier, take this. This awful war is almost played out. I hope you boys get to see your families soon. I am so sorry that you had to go through this down here in Savannah." After handing me the loaf, she stroked the head of her granddaughter who watched the terrible events through large brown eyes. "Come on, Sarah honey, let's go home. This is what glorious war is like!"

These citizens of Savannah were either very kind hearted or Unionist in sentiments, perhaps a little of both. The food they gave us supplemented the reduced supply of cornbread and bacon provided by the Rebels for our journey to who knows where.

We moved toward the awaiting boxcars. We again were among the first prisoners to board. Bushey sat down and looked out between the boards. "My God, where are they taking us now?"

Seth looked at Bushey then at me. "God only knows brothers, but we can handle it." He then approached the guard by the door. "Hey Gramps, where are you Rebs taking us now?"

Guarding the door was an old Confederate dressed in a butternut shirt and ragged pants. His shoes were wrapped with rags and he had a patch over one eye. "Why, you boys are going to Millen to Camp Lawton, 'bout ninety miles to the north of here."

"Are we going to be exchanged there?" asked Bushey with a smirk. The one-eyed guard gave him a wry smile. Bushey shook his head.

"Oh, but it's a fer piece better than here. It's bigger, almost forty acres, and has trees and a nice spring-fed stream of clean water." At this, all three of us shook our heads.

"Yanks, I'm a tellin' ya the truth! I am a preacher man and I taint lyin' to you'uns!" This stirred our hopes but little as we did not believe anything our captors said, even a preacher with a patch over his eye. Who knows, we may even be going back to Andersonville. The thought boiled up within me as I slumped on the cold, dirty floor. Once the train got moving, we all three wrapped up in a blanket and huddled together in the corner of the boxcar.

We were snuggled up like animals in a den. This caused me to remember three hibernating groundhogs that I dug up one winter in Ohio while setting a fence post. When I nudged the animals with my hand, they barely moved and were as cold as rocks. I pushed them back into their burrow to continue their deep sleep waiting on the arrival of spring. I wondered if we would ever see another spring from our winter of captivity. Nearly fifteen months of prison had just about broken us.

It was not long before the rocking of the boxcar caused us, like hibernating groundhogs, to fall into a stupor. Neither the other prisoners nor the jerking of the train awoke us. The three remaining members of the Buckeye Manor were alive but barely.

We arrived at Camp Lawton around daylight. A cold halo crowned the rising sun as it struggled up the horizon. The boxcar stopped with a violent shudder and some of the rickety cars even came unhitched, so tenuous was their grip on each other.

I awoke and opened my heavy eyelids. Cracks in the ceiling of the boxcar admitted the probing rays of the low-set winter sun. A knothole in the board next to me revealed a number of rough looking huts and cabins in a thick forest of pines. This was evidently another railroad depot and the end of our journey.

I tried to wake Bushey and Seth but both did not move. As the other prisoners began to leave the car, they stepped on Bushey's foot. He let out a yell. Seth tried to get to his feet. "I can't move! My legs—they don't move! Oh Lord, what am I going to do?" Bushey and I carried him out of the boxcar onto the platform.

Seth, not used to being dependent on anyone, mumbled on and on. "I don't know what's wrong with me. I've never had to be carried anywhere in my life. What's wrong with my crazy legs?"

Seeing how embarrassed he was, I tried to calm him. "Seth, after what we've been through it's a wonder we're alive, let alone walkin'. Just relax, we'll take care of you until you get your strength again." Seth smiled and shook his head and I could feel his fingers tighten on my shoulder.

Off in the distance through the trees, about half a mile away, we saw the walls of the stockade and other structures partially hidden by the forest. We trudged toward an opening at the end of the tree-lined path. We could hardly carry ourselves let alone Seth.

We emerged from the pines into an open area and a large fort with cannons overlooked the stockade. To our left were many houses and wall tents. By the looks of them, I guessed them to be officer's quarters. Guards stood by the doors and men in gray uniforms went in and out.

About one hundred feet away from us we saw a large Negro man on his knees before a Rebel officer. The slave's top front teeth were missing. He was begging for his life while the officer walked around him with a whip, slapping the handle in his hand and saying, "No Rufus, No! You know'd better than to try to run to the Yankee lines." We passed this drama without knowing its outcome and headed around the corner of the stockade to a large gate, not unlike the one at Andersonville.

A single large gate was on the south wall of this large forty-acre prison. The stockade walls were freshly hewn logs and were somewhat taller and straighter than at Andersonville. Tall trees raised their pointed heads above the walls.

Bushey, tired from carrying Seth, paused. "Leave it to the Rebs to give us shade trees in the winter and none in the summer!" Seth raised his head. I could feel him stiffen and straighten at the mention of the trees.

"Trees? Thank God for trees at anytime, anywhere. Don't you remember how we wanted those trees the damned raiders had at Andersonville?" He grimaced after hearing himself swear again. "Well, boys, let's get a look at our new home."

Trying to lighten the load, Seth tried several times to walk but his legs would not bear his weight. As he leaned on us, he kept repeating, "I'm sorry boys. I hate being a burden. God bless you Hiram, God bless you Bushey!"

To this Bushey replied grinning. "Shut up Seth, tomorrow you get to carry us!" Another prisoner, seeing Bushey struggle with his pan as he carried Seth, asked if he could carry it. "Oh no," said Bushey fully recognizing the survival value of the pan. "I'll manage just fine!"

The man passed and stared at the pan, even turning his head a second time to get a last look. Bushey waved his hand at the man to keep moving, then looked at me. "I had better keep an eye out for him. That rascal will steal this the first chance he gets."

"If he needs it, let him have it," said Seth. We almost dropped him.

We followed the path around the corner of the stockade. I looked up and saw guards in the pigeon roosts. Soon we reached the large gate that was the only entrance to the stockade.

A Rebel sergeant scanned our meager belongings. Rubbing his stubby jaw, he remarked. "Well you boys are a sorry sight, that's for damned sure!" He then spat on the ground through a gap between teeth stained dark brown from a lifetime of tobacco chewing. "We shan't be keepin' y'all too long, I hope you'uns enjoys the accommodations."

Bushey, Seth, and I prepared our souls for another Andersonville as we stood before the gate. The sergeant motioned two young guards to swing open the heavy structure. The large doors creaked and revealed—not a hoard of skeletons, not begging lice ridden prisoners—but a path lined with trees to a bridge over a stream. Our mouths dropped and Bushey, never at a loss for words, could do nothing but exclaim "Well I'll be! Well I'll be!"

Seth raised up and seemed to be resurrected. The clear stream flowed from our right or east through a grove of trees and exited the stockade on the left. To the far north across the stream, lay a campground consisting of a few tents and shanties. Mounds of soil undulated in the distance—probably earthen huts. The stream was much larger than the mere rivulet at Andersonville and there was no swamp. This was a much better place.

Awestruck by the stream, Seth suddenly found his legs and started to hobble away from us, sometimes crawling on all fours. Reaching the stream, he turned and shouted. "We can take a bath! Look at that clear water! This must be over four feet deep!"

The line of prisoners bunched up at the stream like a string of ants at a sugar lump. A short, burly Rebel sergeant with a gray beard then addressed us. "All right you Yanks, now look here! Thar's a bunch of huts and tents up yonder but they's already occupied by your pards that came in yesterday. You can use the brush and branches layin' around to make yourselves a place but I'd get up thar in a hurry."

He waved to the guards to draw back and open up the path over the bridge. We tried to pick up Seth but he was already hobbling across the bridge. We caught up with him as he collapsed on the other side of the stream.

Carrying Seth, we trudged up the slope past many tree stumps to the north end. Here we sat Seth down on a stump on a piece of higher ground. "It won't be long before I will get my legs back. I can feel it," said Seth as he surveyed the spot for our new home. Bushey and I began gathering branches for a hut.

A long time ago in Ohio, my great grandmother taught me how to make a teepee. We were out for a walk and had come across some brush my father cleared from a field. "Hiram, these branches are just right for making a fine Indian home. Would you like to see how?" In my mind's eye, I remembered how we did it.

"Bushey, let's make an Indian tepee like my great grandmother showed me."

"A what?" replied Bushey.

"Don't argue with him, Bushey," said Seth. "Hiram's great grandmother has saved our butts many times."

We arranged the branches in the shape of an inverted cone. We then used our rubber blankets as the roof and then piled soil against the branches forming the walls. In the middle, we made a fire pit. After about six hours, the shelter was finished.

Surveying our work brought back memories of the larger round hut at Andersonville. Who was in it now? Was one of its occupants Isaiah? His unknown fate gnawed at our insides.

We heard a report that one of the last trains out of Andersonville had jumped the track and many prisoners were killed just a short way past the railroad depot. Upon hearing this, Seth exclaimed. "Isaiah, Isaiah, would God do that to you?" Neither Bushey nor I had an answer.

Even though the October days were cool and the brook waters cold, we took baths in the stream. On a bright sunny day, even Seth felt good enough to try it. We helped him down to the stream, passing other prisoners who were trying the water with their feet but then backing off.

"After that sewer at Andersonville, I have got to get into that water!" declared Seth as he peeled off his ragged shirt and edged into the cold water, gritting his teeth. "Oh Lordy this is cold!" he proclaimed as he sank beneath the water in a swirling pool. Bushey and I edged up to the stream waiting for Seth to rise. Nothing.

"Where is he?" yelled Bushey in a panic. Suddenly Seth rose to the surface. His eyes were closed and his face blue. We jumped in and hauled him back to the hut, built a fire, and warmed up a pan of water. The warm water invigorated Seth who gradually regained his color and humor. "To everything there is a season and it's too cold for that stream. Oh, that beautiful stream." Seth stopped talking as a shiver shook his thin body. "I guess I will have to settle for that…that damn pan of yours Bushey."

Bushey laughed and said "Now Seth, don't swear at my pan!"

Seth chuckled and slid onto his bed of pine needles. "Wake me when rations are called." He then covered up with his blanket and fell asleep in the warmth of the afternoon sun.

Rations, even though Union troops were severing Confederate railways, were better than at Andersonville. We heard about the Yankee raids from the prison commandant, a Captain Vowles, who often came into the camp on Sundays and talked to us prisoners. Vowles was a quiet and tolerant man who seemed to sway with the winds of opinion.

"Men, I know you would like more food but the Yankees have cut our railroad lines. We will give you what we can but you must blame your own army for the shortages." This was news with a double edge.

Wrapped in our blankets and sitting close to the fire in our tepee, we debated this dilemma. Bushey edged closer to the fire then backed off when the flames almost ignited his blanket. "Lordy, I want to eat but I am glad that Sherman is getting close too." Ever looking to turn a phrase, Bushey smiled. "It's kind of like huntin' for bear meat, you want the varmint around your place but then again you don't."

We smiled but realized that our survival in this prison was razor thin. Could we hang on until Sherman took Georgia and liberated us? Would we die of starvation at the hand of our liberator? Time was running out as winter approached.

The cold and rainy weather made all of us sick with bad chest colds. Our hacking joined the incessant coughing of other prisoners. "This camp sounds like a consumption choir," said Bushey.

Prisoners without shelters really had a hard time of it. Men walked around with phlegm dripping from their noses and mouths. Their skin became yellow and their eyes sank into the skull. The cold turned many men into babbling idiots. One man wandered around incessantly yelling "Jesus Christ! Jesus Christ! Jesus Christ!"

"Reminds me of Belle Island," said Seth as he fed some more sticks into the fire. "The only difference is here we have more wood." The number of graves at Camp Lawton grew, sometimes reaching twenty per day.

As a tribute to Isaiah, we tried to help one dying prisoner near us on cold nights. We called our undertakings of mercy "Mission Isaiah". However, we could not help all who needed it and "the dilemma" faced us many times. No permanent additions were added to our group of three. Our shelter was too small.

As the cold weather and spreading disease became more severe at Camp Lawton, men began to break. The Confederates encouraged these men to accept paroles and work for them in return for increased rations, shelter, and clothing. The Rebs needed everything from shoemakers to accountants. Men who accepted these paroles were called "galvanized Yankees" if the jobs benefited the Rebels and not the prisoners. Jobs that helped feed or shelter prisoners such as being a cook or hospital attendant were coveted.

On a cold day in late October when our food and wood was gone, a guard asked "Is there a Private Hiram Terman here?" I crawled out of our teepee and weakly replied, "I'm Terman."

He asked if I would help with hauling and distributing rations to the camp since I had done this at Belle Island. For some reason, this record followed me to Millen but had not benefited us at Andersonville. As happened at Belle, this gave us added food and wood.

In early November, the Confederates tried harder to recruit Union prisoners for their army. They offered not only food, clothing, money, but also even land after the war. Desperate, some men finally relented. They rationalized the act by saying they would desert at the first chance. I saw one of these "galvanized Rebels" brought back to the camp after trying this tactic. His name was Isaac.

Isaac was from Kentucky, a border state with mixed allegiances. After being taken out of camp by the Rebs, Isaac came back among us about a week later. We were standing in line to get rations. Everywhere he went, friend and foe shunned him.

Destitute, he climbed up on a stump and yelled. "How can you blame me for trying to live? I was starving and cold. My God boys, how can you hold this against me? I was going to go over to our lines first chance I got but the Rebs caught me. How can you blame a fellow for that?" His pleas went unanswered. On Election Day, Issaac's corpse laid at the gate awaiting the next burial party.

On November 8, the Rebels decided to collect ballots from the prisoners to see how they would vote for President. The Rebel officers gave speech after speech about how our government and Abraham Lincoln had abandoned us. They were anxious to see if their strategy was working.

Bushey was excited as he picked up his ballot and the stub of a pencil. "Well, Hiram, I'm voting for ole Abe. That man is our hope for victory." A man next to him rose up and pointed his finger at Bushey.

"Victory? Ain't nobody going to win this war. It's been nothing but blood and guts, killing and being killed and for what? Now we're rotting in this prison and do you think Lincoln gives a damn? Hell no, I'm voting for McClellan. Little Mac is the only general I knew that cared a damn for his men. If he was President, we wouldn't be here." Seth entered the conversation.

"I don't care how you vote, but don't drag our President in the dirt. Back in Ohio, we have people called Copperheads that want us to give up, let the South have its slaves, and do what they want with them. Did you see that Negro begging for his life as we came in? How can we let that sort of thing go on?" I could have sworn it was Isaiah speaking.

A voice came from the background. "That Negro was hung and he is still hanging from the gallows. I saw it when I came in. When the wind is right, you can still smell the stink."

"Good Lord!" said Seth, shaking his head and glaring at the Rebel officers.

The Confederate officer counting the votes took off his hat, scratched his head, and shrugged his shoulders. Next, he slammed his fist on the table and exclaimed "The most of them voted for that gorilla Lincoln!"

The officer standing by him was stunned. "No, by Gawd, that cain't be so!" No doubt, he thought all their speeches would bring better results. This sent a chill through the Rebels who now realized that even suffering prisoners longing for exchange and home, still stood by their government and its President.

Back in our hut, politics was the topic of discussion. Bushey asked Seth whom he voted for and Seth refused to answer. "Did you vote for McClellan? How could you vote against ole Abe?" Seth, a veteran of his battles with Isaiah, had learned diplomacy well. "Bushey, the secrecy of my vote is protected by the constitution even here at Camp Lawton. I ain't telling you how I voted."

Frustrated, Bushey then turned on me. "Hiram, you voted for Lincoln, didn't you?" Not wanting to reveal my vote any more than Seth, I used a different tactic, diversion.

"Bushey, tell us why you voted for Lincoln." His eyes brightened as he leaned closer to the fire pit. The blazing light in the tepee turned his face red and reflected gold from his eyes.

"I have always been a Lincoln man. If we save the Union and stop what we saw with that slave… why all this blood, all this suffering, it's worth it by God!" Seth and I offered a hearty "Amen".

Our votes remained a secret as we listened to the sounds of the prison late into the night. Unlike the horrid sounds of Andersonville nights, the predominant sound here was the rustling of the wind through the tall pines. As I dozed off, I contemplated our discussion.

I voted for Lincoln but I was more confused and of two minds about the war now than when I first joined the Federal army. The bloody, scarred hand of war and its violence, suffering, and deprivation had scorched my soul. The prison camp showed me man's unfathomable potential for evil as well as good. They were cruel but effective teachers.

In the morning after roll call, I walked down by the stream to wash. A crowd gathered in the middle of the stockade by the sutler's shanty where a Confederate officer stood on a platform to address us prisoners. An older portly man with gray hair and smiling eyes, he wore a clean and neat Confederate uniform with a yellow sash across his chest. He gave another long speech about how our government had refused all their offers of exchange and was the reason for our suffering. Why did we cling to our unreasonable devotion to Abraham Lincoln? His voice droned as he went on and on about how we had been abandoned.

My mind wandered. I evaluated where I had been and where I was now. I recognized that I now saw the issues of war, killing, suffering, and destruction from other perspectives. Being in the South and seeing enemy soldiers up close had affected me. I was less motivated by a desire for glory and adoration. True honor came from the ability to persevere, to hold to one's humanity in the most severe conditions. I no longer was a youth enamored by war's illusions but a man refined and tested, hardened by war's realities. I learned not to seek control over events but to adapt to them, to look for opportunity in the most improbable of circumstances. Friends and faith in God proved to be of great value. In the midst of suffering, I felt good about my transformation.

A change in cadence in the Rebel officer's voice regained my attention.

"Well, men, what do you say?" Adjusting his yellow sash and gray hat, he began to rock back and forth, his hands behind his back. "You can end your suffering now, this hour, yea this very minute. You can have new clothes, be fed, and be on your way to a new future in the grand Confederacy. Just step forward and sign the enlistment ledger."

The general in gray then surveyed the ranks of prisoners in front of him with a hopeful smile. An uneasy silence turned into a rumbling murmur, which spread across the Union prisoners. After a few minutes, a Massachusetts sergeant with a blood stained shirt limped forward. Turning his back to the Rebel general, he faced his men who immediately stood to attention.

"Men of the 51st Massachusetts! Attention! About face! March! One two, one, two!" The men marched away. A chain reaction began as other units performed the same tactic. Company after company of stooped and suffering men now stood erect and marched away leaving the Confederate general dumbfounded. Soon I too turned and marched back to our hut with Seth and Bushey on my right and left.

"By God, this is what honor means," said Bushey as we returned to our hut. This revelation reinvigorated us. We needed the boost. Winter was at the doorstep.

President Abraham Lincoln *(Library of Congress)*.

Views of monument at Andersonville National Historic Site cemetery.
"Turn you to the stronghold, ye prisoners of hope!" Zechariah 9:12.

CHAPTER 19
THE END OF TRIBULATION

The middle of November brought cold weather and snow to Camp Lawton. While watching the cottony flakes fall, Seth mused as he shivered. "Boys, can you believe we were captured in July at Gettysburg and now we are sitting here watching the snow fly almost a year and a half later? Lordy, Lordy, what we have endured!" He looked at me as I unwrapped a piece of moldy bacon I secured outside the gates. "Hiram, if you didn't have that outside parole job...I don't see how we could make it."

The increased rations and wood supply I secured on my visits outside the prison were blessings but we were very concerned about the winter. Could we hang on?

The war just had to end sometime. On November 19, another rainy, cold day, I saw signs that the end was near. As I passed through the gate to work outside of the stockade, I saw slaves and soldiers hurriedly packing supplies and moving equipment. Courier after courier came riding up to the Confederate headquarters.

I was loading a wagon near headquarters when I saw General Winder, the Confederate general in charge of all the prison camps, rush into the building. We had seen Winder a few times at Andersonville arguing with Captain Wirz. He was a big man with a full head of hair and a permanent scowl on his face. A rough man with a mean reputation, he was agitated.

As I loaded bags of meal, I overheard a conversation between two Rebel soldiers standing by the mules at the front of the wagon. Covered by dirty capes of sewed together rags, they had their backs to me.

"Shepherd, I can't believe we're going to move all these prisoners out of here when we just finished building the dern place!"

"Blast it Henry! Don't ya know Sherman is about to grab us and all these Yank prisoners! Those cussed Yanks are breathin' down our necks and Winder wants these prisoners out of here fast!"

"Where are we gonna take 'em?"

"Most likely to Savannah, I'd reckon. Look yonder, the first train's a'comin' into camp."

"Sho' nuff, Shepherd. Look, there's another train coming behind it. Something sure is in the mix."

After heaving the final bag of meal onto the wagon, I looked down the tracks and could see the smoke of the approaching locomotives. *Good Lord, are we going to get out of here? Oh, dear God, make it so! Could it be that the day of our release is almost here?*

That night, as we sat around the fire in our hut sipping on a watery stew, Bushey, Seth, and I discussed what I had heard. Seth held his bony hands up to the fire and then started rubbing his stubby, bearded jaw. In his sickness, Seth had lost most of his front teeth and his gums were bleeding. His advancing scurvy made us anxious. He spit a mixture of saliva and blood into the fire that sizzled before he spoke.

"Hiram, your sure about them Rebs movin' us out? Who do you figure they'll take first? Walkers or sick? I could go either way, I tell ya."

Managing a slight chuckle, Bushey said, "We all look like scarecrows and thin ones at that!" Bushey then leaned forward, his thick beard profiled against the light of the fire.

"Hiram, I bet they will take the ones that can walk first, just like they did at Andersonville. We had better get there looking pretty spry, don't you think?" I gazed into the fire hoping for a wise reply.

"One of the Johnnies said that the first bunch out would most likely go to Savannah. I bet that is where the exchange will take place and will be the quickest way home. Our detachment was the first out of Andersonville and Savannah so we should be first out of here." Bushey turned his backside to the fire.

"All we can do is be ready when that drum starts beating." Seth then closed his eyes. "Good Lord, please take us home tomorrow. I don't think I can stand many more of these cold, wet nights." As he turned another side to the fire, steam rose from his damp clothes.

I moved to the door and looked out over Camp Lawton, fires flickered around the outside of the prison. The Rebels were moving back and forth in front of the fires. I called Seth to the door. "We had better get ready to go tomorrow morning," said Seth.

The morning of November 20 dawned cold and rainy and we awoke wet, cold, and stiff. Seth rolled over and examined his feet wrapped in a rag and up against a pile of rocks. He reached down and rubbed his toes. "Ouch, my toes are purple again and it hurts to touch them. I wish the rocks would stay warm longer. I forgot to stoke the fire and my feet paid the price." This strategy kept us alive many nights and it was ironic we let the fire die out this last night.

As the hazy light of morning filtered through the drizzle and over the east wall of the stockade, we heard a drumbeat and an engine whistle off in the distance. Could this be the day? We had been disappointed so many times before. Keeping our emotions in check was agonizing. The bustling outside our tepee refocused our attention. A Pennsylvania private heralded our spirits.

"Get up boys, we're going to move. Uncle Billy is marching through Georgia and the Rebs are moving us out."

Bushey picked up his pan and had a troubled look on his face. "Good Lord, what do I do with this pan? Are we goin' to God's country or just another prison?" Seth hobbled up to Bushey, took the pan, and threw it out of the hut. It rattled along striking a running soldier who stopped immediately and picked it up.

"Well, there it goes," said Bushey fatalistically. Seth walked up beside him, a determined and irascible look on his face.

"I just ain't got another stay in one of these Rebel prisons in me. This time..." He started to sob. "This time we are going home...one way or another...we are going home! Damn that pan anyway."

The drum began to beat. The Rebel sergeants called out the first seven detachments and that included us. About fifteen hundred men now made their way down to the stream near the sutler's shanty. Because we knew the Union army was close, a look of cautious optimism was on each man's face as we gathered, the stronger helping the weak.

We then divided into our separate units, men teetered and leaned on each other as we waited for what the Rebels had to tell us. In the distance, we heard a locomotive pumping as it built up power. Our spirits rose with the floating clouds of steam. If we could just hang on a little longer. The cold pierced our hearts and the blustering winds taunted us. *"You boys are just about done. You'll never make it to those cars."*

A Rebel officer got up on a platform. We strained to hear his every word.

"Prisoners, we're moving you to other sites in preparation for exchange." A rumble of anticipation went through us. The officer coughed and cleared his throat.

"The sick, wounded, and men whose terms of enlistment expire by the end of December will now be taken to Savannah."

The Rebel stopped and stroked his mustache. One prisoner in the front line fell down and began to cry.

"The rest of you will be going to other prisons in Florence or Charleston to await your paroles." A loud, worried groan arose from the prisoners. "Only men going to Savannah should leave the prison today. The rest of you should prepare to leave at the next roll call."

A sense of confusion spread and men began to get angry. "We will now select and load the sick and wounded followed by men whose enlistments expire in December." Teams of Rebel soldiers began circulating among the detachments, shoving men into groups, hurrying them along with their muskets.

A look of fear came over our faces. Seth turned to us, his eyes troubled. "Bushey, when did you enlist? I joined up in March "62."

"February of "62," replied Bushey.

"Hiram?"

"Dec..., Dec..., December "61," I said with a stuttering, stiff voice.

I realized the implications. The Buckeye Manor was going to be split up. I was going alone to Savannah today and Seth and Bushey were going later to Florence or Charleston. Seth's jaw dropped and Bushey closed his eyes in disbelief. "My pan, my pan...." Our worst fear, separation, was upon us.

A wave of unrest moved across the crowd of prisoners. Men began questioning each other trying to determine who would stay and who would leave. Behind me, two soldiers from Indiana chattered. "Johnny, you signed up in December, didn't you?"

"Hell, I don't know. I think it was December."

"Well, what did you tell the Rebs when we came in here?"

As we tried to figure out what do to, Rebel soldiers started collecting the sick and wounded. "Herschel, here's one. Bring over that stretcher and take this Yank to the ambulance over there. Private Hanks, get me another stretcher over here!"

Some prisoners around us feigned lameness and others moaned and whimpered as if feverish. Some of these men were carried off when we knew them to be mobile and able to walk.

"Hey, he ain't sick but I am," yelled a man lying on the ground.

A Rebel sergeant took a quick look at us. "You is walkin' all right, ain't cha?" Seth limped up to him and showed his missing teeth and bloody gums. "Ye gads, you look poorly but you is walkin' Yank." He waved us out of the way and walked to a man laying on the ground. "Now here's one, you two boys pick this one here up and take him to that wagon over yonder."

I looked anxiously at the officer at the head of our detachment who was paging through a list of names.

Seth put his hand on my shoulder. "Hiram, it looks like you will be getting back to Ohio before us." He looked over to Bushey who was rubbing the back of his head and wandering about aimlessly. "Bushey and I are headed for another blasted prison." His voice was broken by a weak sob. "Could you take this letter to my family. They live just south of Ashland. Tell them I will try everything to make it out of here, but if I don't, well... it's in the letter." He squeezed my shoulder and then began wiping tears from his eyes.

Bushey came up and pulled out a small cloth bag with a drawstring. "Give this to my parents in Shelby. Tell my father I am sorry for all the things I told him when I left." Tears also ran down his face. I put my arms around both of them. We hugged each other, shaking with emotion. My voice cracked as I felt time was running out.

"You boys will get out of here. Sherman's right next-door. The war is almost over. Just don't give up hope." Seth nodded his head and looked at Bushey. "I just hope we can stay together." Bushey clapped his hands together in frustration.

"But we ain't got no more pan!"

I patted Bushey on the back and then turned my attention to the Reb officer who was calling off names. He was a tall man with glasses and a dark well trimmed beard. After every declaration, he looked up to see if the prisoner he called was present and then marked off the name on his ledger.

"Private Hiram Terman, 82nd Ohio".

Picking up my blanket roll, I looked back at Seth and Bushey as I moved away toward the gate. "You two will make it. I will see you both back in Ohio! Goodbye, my friends!"

Walking across the bridge of the brook, I joined a line of prisoners now making their way to the single opening out of the stockade. Some were wounded and alone, hobbling along with a determined look.

I passed two men, one helping the other. "Clyde, now don't walk too fast. My toes are numb from the cold last night and I can't feel 'em!"

"Come on, Burt, you don't have to feel them to walk with them."

After passing these two, I turned to look behind me. Seth and Bushey blurred into the mass of prisoners standing on the north slope as I got farther away. Soon I went through the gate and was now walking along the half-mile path to the railroad station. I stopped for the two hobbling men now right behind me.

"Clyde, now slow down, damn your hide. We'll get there."

"Burt, by God, if you don't keep up, we'll lose our places. Now come on you old cow."

I was now near the opening to the woods and could see a corpse dangling from a gallows. Carrion crows flew around the hanging skeleton. *Oh my Lord, this is the Negro we saw coming in...the devils hanged him!* The stench met my nostrils and sickened me, making me dizzy. I stumbled over a root and hit the ground covered with pine needles.

"Watch your step there soldier. You don't want to give out now. Here let me help you up." A balding man with thick eyebrows put his hard bony hand under my armpit and lifted. The sight of the hanging Negro caused me to stare. "Terrible, ain't it? How could a man do that to another human being?" The man shook his head. "Guess that's why we're down here, blamed if it ain't."

I regained my balance and started to walk again. The man nodded to me and continued ahead. "Thank you, much obliged," I said as I dusted myself and hobbled on. The ghastly gallows mercifully disappeared behind a thick stand of pines.

I could now see a line of cars extending far back on the tracks. Further, another train chugged in the distance. *Many men were going to Savannah today.*

Soon I reached the train station and I could see the commandant of Camp Lawton standing on the platform surrounded by a ring of men vying for his attention.

"But I should be next to go," yelled a man as I passed the group and headed to an open boxcar that was swallowing up men in front of me. I was the last one to get on the car and took a position by the door close to one of the Rebel guards.

He was the same one-eyed preacher that was on the boxcar that brought us to Millen. We recognized each other instantly.

"How did you like Lawton? I told you it was a good prison, didn't I?"

"Ain't no such thing as a good prison," I replied gruffly. I began hacking as my chest cold was getting worse. Other prisoners moved away from me fearing the contagion in my chest. Eventually I fell on the floor where I looked up at the preacher through teary, swollen eyes. He appeared to be genuinely concerned and I tried to continue the conversation. "It was better than Andersonville, you're right about that Reverend." He smiled as he adjusted the patch on his eye. "The cold was tough on us, got this darn cold," I said coughing.

"You look played out." He moved a few prisoners and cleared a spot next to him. "Here, have a seat by me at the door, you'll breathe better." I crawled to the spot and sat at his feet. "Thanks," I replied feeling somewhat sheepish.

He knelt lower, coming close to my head. I could smell a strong scent of chewing tobacco. "Had to leave your friends behind, did you? Weren't there three of you hangin' on to each other in the car coming here from Savannah?"

"My friends are still back at the prison, they are going to Florence or Charleston. I got to leave early because my enlistment runs out before theirs."

"Charleston is being shelled by the Yanks in the harbor and Florence is a real hellhole. Hope they don't go those places!" My heart sank. "But you, my boy, you are heading for exchange. The Yankee boats are in the harbor at Savannah, shore nuff! I seen 'em there couple days ago."

Trying to return his concern for me, I asked him about his future.

"What's ahead for you preacher?"

"Oh, I spec I'll be ridin' this yar car back and forth for quite a spell deliverin' you Yanks. A passle of your sick and wounded have been goin' to Savannah for days. After that, with Sherman breathin' down our necks I spec I will be on the lines around Savannah." Leaning closer, he whispered with a wink and a furtive look over his shoulder. "That is, unless I skedaddle!"

I looked at him with surprise. "Don't be battin' those Yankee eyes at me. Ain't nothin' wrong with a man getting back to his sufferin' family when he cain't do no more good by stayin'. No, ain't nothin' wrong with that!"

The preacher got up abruptly and walked out of the door answering a call from an officer. I then lay my head on the wall of the boxcar and closed my eyes. Chewing a sprig of dried mint, I wondered what would happen to Bushey and Seth.

By late afternoon, the train was filled and ready to leave. My one-eyed friend stepped back through the door and took his position. "Won't be long now soldier, won't be long till you see those ships I was a'tellin' you 'bout."

The whistle then blew and the preacher closed the door to the boxcar. With a jerk, the train got under way. I strained to get a last glimpse of the prison where Seth and Bushey remained but my view out through the crack in the door was blocked by pine trees. They gradually became a green blur as the train picked up speed on its way to Savannah.

The man next to me gave me a poke. He was rather heavy set which struck me as unusual in this world of skeletons. His face was round with a large nose and close-set eyes. With a loud voice, he laughed raucously, and other prisoners looked in our direction as he spoke. "Hey bub, got any tobacco plugs for a greenback or two?" I shook my head. "Where are you from?"

"Ohio."

"Oh, you're a damn buckeye, ha, ha! I'm from N'Yaark myself." He paused and looked around at the others responding to his loud voice. "What are you blokes lookin' at, mind your own business I say! Damn wretches. Hell, I could not spend another day in that pigpen. Good thing the guards could be bought off or I would still be there."

This got my attention.

"You bribed your way out of Lawton?" He looked surprised.

"Well hell yes, didn't you? I gave that fool guard by the bridge a five spot and he hustled me right into line. Just kept walking and got into this car smooth as silk."

"You got out of there for five dollars!" I was in a state of shock and felt sick to my stomach.

"Well hell yes, everything in the "Cornfederacy" runs on bribes now, don't you know. I heard even the damn commandant could be bought off." I started to cough and gasp for breath. "You don't look so good partner. You all right?" I turned away disgusted as he started moving back through the car to another man that he recognized. "Hey, Scatwell, I'll be damned! Did the Rebs catch you at that whore house too?"

For five lousy dollars! Five dollars and scum like this fellow got out while Seth and Bushey go to some prison camp to rot and die. And poor Isaiah, where was he? God, where are you when such things go on? Thoughts of my sister who died at the age of ten and the mother I barely knew before she died crossed my mind. *God, do you even exist?* I was outraged, nauseous, confused and anxious. Gradually exhaustion convinced my heavy heart to sleep.

Late in the evening, the train from Millen crawled into Savannah and we sat still at the railroad depot. In the haze of the gaslights, I could see though the crack in the door soldiers and civilians hurrying along the streets and around buildings. Fear was on the face of the city. The preacher, looking through the door, looked at me and said, "You can tell the hot breath of Sherman's army is near, sho' nuff can." After saying this, he stared at the darkness for a long time, fingering his musket.

Women with bread and sweet potatoes, that staple of the local agriculture, soon gathered at the rail station. They handed these to us prisoners as we again made our way into the Savannah stockade to await further orders regarding our exchange. The cool breezes off the ocean promised the scent of freedom. It was if the Union ships were fragrant flowers floating on the harbor's waves.

I moved toward the area of the stockade where Bushey, Seth, and I stayed before leaving for Millen. How different I felt being alone in the clutches of a prison. Every man that I passed was a stranger. Memories of seeing lone men at Belle Island and Andersonville crossed my mind. The remembrance of the joys of being a member of the Buckeye Manor brought intense feelings of guilt. As I walked past groups of soldiers, I envied the clusters of friends busily planning. "When we leave tomorrow, let's not get separated, Ben. Let's move as a group, no wandering off."

I felt bad for all those men we saw at Belle and Andersonville who were without friends, alone—for I now was one of them. Fortunate for me, I only had to spend one more night in the prison. If I were alone facing the long days of agony that we had just gone through, I would be a candidate for the dead house for sure.

In the drizzly darkness, illuminated by locomotive lanterns placed on the walls around the prison, I saw the outlines of the shanty that Bushey, Seth, and I had shared during our brief stay at Savannah. Drawing closer, I could see that the small hut was occupied.

Oh no! What now? I would have to spend the night out in the open. Could I survive a winter's night without a fire? The November winds were chilly, wet, and laden with the promise of the season's first snow and I was at the end of my resistance. How ironic it would be to freeze to death after surviving all this time only to die on the last day with freedom just over the horizon. *Oh God, just one more night.*

Turning away from the entrance of the hut, I looked for a protected spot to sit down, curl up in my blanket, and survive the wintry night. My spirits were low and depression was my companion. I coughed and clinched my teeth at the thought of the brute on the train buying his way out of Millen for five dollars while my friends were still there. *Damn son of a bitch. Forgive me Lord.*

The wind picked up, the rain went through my blanket with ease. The chill and cold that claimed my body now frightened me. A pit formed in my stomach and chills ran up my spine, nauseating me. *Oh God, you haven't brought me this far to die now?*

I could not survive out here in the open. I must get to a shelter. With reluctance, I went to the entrance of the hut that I once called home and beckoned its two occupants.

"Friends, I wonder if I might come in, I fear I will freeze to death without shelter. I hate to die tonight with exchange coming tomorrow." There was a stirring and two thin forms crawled into the dim light. A voice, crackly and strained but vaguely familiar, stirred my heart.

"Hiram? Hiram? Is that you Hiram?" Unrestrained joy blew the chill out my bones as I now recognized the features of Seth and off to his side the bearded face of Bushey! My mouth gaped and I drew a deep breath.

"How did you.....? How did you get here?" My ecstasy overcame my confusion and I flew to their open arms and embraced them in a triad of delight and relief. We danced around in a circle. Other prisoners came around.

"What's going on here? Are you boys brothers?"

Ignoring the host of onlookers building around us, I finally asked. "I thought you two were back at Millen or on your way to some other prison." After our emotion drained, we began to sort things out. Seth began the story.

"After you left for the train, the Rebs asked for all those who were prisoners for more than nine months." Bushey tried to speak but was stopped by Seth's continuing enthusiasm. "Well, Bushey and I were the first ones to step out. We then marched to the cars next to the locomotive. The other cars were all full."

Bushey jumped in. "When we got here, we looked all over for you. Nothin', no sign of you. We thought you might have gone to Florence or Charleston, we didn't know nothing!"

Seth patted me on the shoulder as he led me inside to a small fire. "Well, I decided to go to our old hut and hope to blazes you would show up. We had to use a couple of greenbacks to get two fellows to move to another shanty and let us have it."

Bushey, bursting with questions butted in. "Where were you, Hiram?"

"I was in a car in the middle of the train with some of the most miserable scum you ever saw. How did you get here before me?" My mind made the connection quickly. "Since you were near the locomotive, you were unloaded first." Bushey put his arms around both of us.

"Well, the main thing is that the Buckeye Manor is together again. Lord Almighty! We are together again." Sadness suddenly settled on his face. "All we need now is for Isaiah to show up!"

"Good Lord willing, he will," said Seth as he poked the struggling flames of the fire that was going out. Eventually the fire flamed up and the warmth of its blaze soothed us and our spirits. We now awaited the sunrise and the birth of our liberty.

Sleep came only in short intervals for us. Judging by the commotion around camp, it was the same for all the other prisoners awaiting this most anticipated of all days. As the morning sun poked through gathering rain clouds, drums began to beat calling us to leave this final time. Hoards of men, some barely able to move, made their way to the open gate. A cold rain pelted down. "This is appropriate," mused Seth looking up at the sky. "Every time…every damn time, a storm comes up."

We were in the front lines of the group with those longest in captivity. Bushey, Seth, and I locked arms as we walked along. We were not going to be separated again.

In the distance through the cold rainy haze, we saw hundreds of ambulances and men with stretchers. The Rebels first transported sick prisoners down toward the dock on the Savannah River. We heard the whistles of Rebel transport ships as they took load after load of prisoners to the harbor beyond Fort Pulaski where Union ships awaited.

A soldier beside me raised his thin arm and pointed to the chain of ambulances. "That's the sick exchange. I hear they have been loading for the last three days and are just finishing up today. I hope there are plenty of ships out there for us prisoners. What is today anyhow?"

A bespectacled soldier with tousled curly brown hair answered. "November 21. We should be in Annapolis in six days if all goes right." He shivered and shook his wet head. "Good Lord, what's taking so long? I hate just standing here in this cold rain."

Indeed, indeed! All of us felt like iron filings being pulled by those magnificent magnets off in the distance, those beautiful Union ships. Finally, finally, we began to move out through the gates and down the streets to the dock. The citizens along the street showered comments into our ranks, some lifted us. "Bon voyage! You poor men are finally going home! Bon voyage!"

Sometimes a bitter storm of words struck like lightning. "Go home you Yankee scum! Go back to your thieving homes! I hope you all die just at your filthy doorsteps!" These barbs flashed and disappeared like so many bursting bubbles. We were going home!

Around a bend and down a slope and soon the Rebel transport ships met our tearful eyes. The ramshackle boats took Bushey aback. "My God look at those rickety things. Will those hold together for us?"

Seth put his hand on Bushey's shoulder. "If those trains we rode held together, these boats should do just fine. Don't worry, Bushey, we'll make it." The Rebel transports looked like floating sheds tacked together with wire and string. Jets of steam came out of their sides and black smoke belched out of the tall stacks of these ramshackle boats. No matter, all they had to do was make a short trip down the Savannah River to the harbor. Just a little bit more to go.

The crew on the transport that we boarded were ragged, barefoot, and scampered around the deck like rats. They hovered around the hissing boilers like flies, hitting the pipes with wrenches while throwing wood into the fires. The swirling waters of the Savannah River provoked thoughts of crossing the Ohio River at Bellaire, a lifetime ago. The span of my time in this war seemed immense and the experiences born unbelievable.

A dark thought entered my mind. *Was I only dreaming this and would I wake up on the filthy sand of Andersonville?* I shook and shivered. *Oh Lord no, this was really happening!* The Rebel transport was now away from shore and on its way to the ocean down the wide river.

Near the shore there appeared to be floating barrels or structures resembling them. "Torpedoes," said a tall toothless man with a deep voice and pointed nose off to my right. "Hit one of those and we blow sky high!" He started to cry and laughed with a maniacal giggle. "Wouldn't that be the worst thing? Survive Andersonville only to be killed on a boat going home!"

"Oh please, Jimmy, don't say such things now," came a voice from the background. Every thought of being snagged at this late hour felt like a burning coal on my consciousness.

Soon the mouth of the river opened and we flowed into the harbor. A vast armada of ships, each with a Union flag fluttering in the breeze, appeared on the shining waters. I wept, my tears joined the cold rain running down my face and tasted of salt as they passed my cracked lips. Men near me fainted into the arms of their comrades.

"Come on Robert, don't give out now, not now for Lordy sakes!" I felt the arms of Bushey and Seth around my back. We hugged each other and whelped with unintelligible sounds as the grimy Rebel transport pulled up alongside of a shining ship with the name "New York" emblazoned on its bow.

On deck, a small band played "Rally Round the Flag" as we ascended the gangplank and put our feet on the firm and clean decks of the steamer. As soon as his blistered, cut feet hit the new decks, Seth raised hands heavenward and shouted. "Glory, Glory, Glory Hallelujah!" Bushey, tears in his eyes, grabbed my arm.

"Hiram, we made it, Lord Almighty, we made it!" He wiped his eyes with his dirty sleeve. A gray smudge of Georgia clay came off on his cheek. "And we did it with honor, did it with honor." The smudge dissolved in the rain and dripped to the floor.

We were next led to a large pot of soup protected by a line of sailors. Thin prisoners charged into these men trying to get at the soup. Holding a man tenderly to his chest, a surgeon gently addressed us.

"Not too much, boys, not too much food all at once. You must eat slowly or you will kill yourselves." To the sailors, he again repeated. "Make the poor boys eat it slowly. Too much at a time will kill them."

It was all I could do to eat the thick soup and soft biscuit according to orders. My whole digestive system convulsed and threatened to leap out my throat with the first bites. Seth murmured repeatedly, "This is so good, this is so good."

After we calmed our hunger pangs, we went in groups to a bath area where we removed our old tattered clothes and tried to get free of the pitch pine that had blackened our bodies and souls. Before the stewards took our old clothing to burn in the ship's boilers, I removed a patch of my old shirt as a memento. Bushey laughed. "Hiram, what are you doing?"

"This will help me remember." Bushey shook his head as he threw his clothes onto the floor. Seth came up with a new shirt and pants for me.

"These will make a new man of you Hiram." I took the new clothing and inhaled the cleanliness. The new shirt and pants felt like a tent on my thin frame. The belt was too big for my thin waist. We returned to the deck of the ship to see more of this grand exchange.

With food in our stomachs and clean clothes, we felt resurrected.

Holding on to the guardrail, we saw a Rebel transport receiving Confederate prisoners of war from a Union ship. The men on board that ship looked very much like us and they appeared just as relieved to get off the Union ship and onto the dirty Rebel boat. Seth, Bushey, and I silently watched this scene for a minute or two when Bushey remarked.

"Home for them was hell for us, wasn't it boys? I bet our camps weren't no picnic either but I sure would rather have been in them than Andersonville!" A soldier with a thick beard, sunken eyes, and small head to our rear replied immediately.

"No place could have been worse than Andersonville!"

After our ship was full, it made its way out of the harbor to the open sea. Standing by the railing, I could see small whales breaking the waves, their bottle shaped noses and smiling faces piercing the blue waters. They were the picture of freedom and liberty, going where they please, doing what they will. I could not imagine a more stark contrast to what we had been through.

The next day the weather cleared and a bright sun parted the clouds. As our ship continued its way north along the coast, a chaplain called for a time of thanksgiving. Those of us who were able met in the late afternoon on the deck. The sun sat on the horizon and looked like a bright dot on a shelf of shimmering water. Seth remarked pensively, "Looks like a period at the end of a sentence, doesn't it."

The chaplain reminded me of Preacher Sams back in Rome. A smile was on his round moon of a face as he looked across his audience of thin, gaunt prisoners.

"In keeping with President Lincoln's 1863 declaration of the last Thursday in November as a day of Thanksgiving (this was news to us), I would humbly ask you to give thanks to God for bringing you men out of darkness to the bright light of liberty. I take my text from the prophet Isaiah, chapter 9, verse 2." Opening a well-worn leather Bible, he began to read. *Those who dwelt in the land of the shadow of death, Upon them a light has shined.* When he looked up and saw our expressions, his voice choked, he began to weep, and he could not continue.

Andersonville cemetery. Nearly 45,000 men stepped into the darkness of Andersonville and approximately 12,913 died there. Clara Barton helped identify the dead after the war using a list kept by Dorence Atwater while he was a paroled prisoner.

CHAPTER 20
HE WHO WAS LOST IS NOW FOUND

On the afternoon of November 27, right on schedule, we arrived at Annapolis, Maryland and pulled up to the docks of the Naval Academy. The sun shown like a golden emerald in a bright blue sky. Even though sick from bouts of seasickness, Seth, Bushey, and I were among the first to limp up the gangplank and on to the dock. Union officers and surgeons immediately met us, their mouths aghast as their eyes probed our thin frames.

A doctor in a white coat put his hand on my shoulder. "Welcome home son. What's your name and regiment?"

"Private Hiram Terman, 82nd Ohio sir."

"Lord only knows what you have been through but we'll do our best to bring you back to health. Orderly, take this man over to the ambulatory group." Seth, Bushey, and I went over to a line of men who could walk.

A large band on the grounds of the impressive military academy began playing "Hail Columbia" as we walked to a large cafeteria. As bad as I felt, chills ran up my spine and the hair on my neck stood on end.

My appetite was strangely small and I ate reduced portions of the boiled ham, potatoes, and other vegetables given us. Seventeen months of being on a Rebel prison diet had reset my digestive system and it would take some time for things to come back to normal.

After being examined by the doctors and giving our information to the clerks, we were directed to the nearby College Green Barracks where we were given beds along with writing materials. Every man who could write was so engaged. Men who could not write dictated their exceptional tales to others who could.

The Barracks resounded with chanting souls each telling stories of incredible courage and survival to families not seen in years. As I picked up the writing implement, I noticed that my finger was not much thicker than the pen. I did not recognize my own body. What about my mind? Who was it now writing home to Rome, Ohio?

Annapolis, Maryland
November 27, 1864
Dear Family,

I am alive! I hope you knew about my capture at Gettysburg and my being a prisoner of war. We told a woman in Gettysburg to let you know. I hope she did. If not, well, I am alive; skinny and thin, but alive! Isaiah Rinehart and Seth Hall were captured with me. Seth is here with me now but Isaiah, well, he may be dead, we don't know for sure. We had to leave him at Andersonville, which was awful hard for us. We pray that he may show up here somewhere, maybe in a hospital.

I was not able to get a letter out even though I tried many times. I'm sorry if you did not know whether I was dead or alive. We were marched from Gettysburg south to Staunton and then put on a train to Richmond where we were kept on an island in the James River known as Belle Island until February. It was tough especially in the winter but we found good friends to help us survive, some from the 123rd Ohio and later a bunch from the 82nd showed up. We called ourselves the Buckeye Manor. We were then put on trains and taken south to Georgia to a place called Andersonville that was terrible in the extreme. I am sad to say that a bunch of us died there. Isaiah *might still be there. He was too sick to leave with us. It was not bad at first but the Rebs just kept crowding more and more prisoners into a little area and it became filthy. Food was terrible, and well, I will tell you more when I get back to Rome. From Andersonville, we were sent to Savannah to a small prison for a few weeks. It became packed and then they sent us to Camp Lawton about 90 miles away. Lawton was cold and wet but better than Andersonville. From there, we went back to Savannah to catch steamers to where we are now at Annapolis. I should be back around Christmas or early January. I am done with this war. God be praised. I will see you soon.*

Your son,

Hiram

After writing our letters and dropping them in a post office box, we slept on the clean bed sheets and soft mattresses like men deprived of sleep for centuries.

The next day we were taken to Camp Parole, a military camp about two or three miles from the Naval Academy to begin final processing. After getting the necessary passes and payroll vouchers, we were put into barracks with many other recovering prisoners. The government determined that I should get one hundred dollars in back pay. I would not go through it again for millions!

Periodically surgeons and attendants came around and examined us as we slowly gained back our health. Before long, we were able to move around Camp Parole and visit with others who had come through the same ordeals as we did. Stories abounded. Especially interesting were the tales of escape attempts.

One night as we sat around our bunks, a soldier with scars on his arm that looked like bite marks told his story.

"It was night when we got out of the tunnel at Andersonville, and boys, was I glad to get out of that hole." He closed his eyes and shivered. "Now just you boys think of it. You are ten feet down in a dark tunnel that you can barely squeeze through. It's pitch dark, sand falling all around, and no air." The circle of listeners drew closer. "All of a sudden, you get caught. My God, you can't move. You strain with all of your might. *Lord, Lord, help me* you yell inside because you don't want the Rebs to hear you." We leaned even closer. "Finally you break loose, crawl like the dickens... and finally you see a dim light at the end of the tunnel. You gasp for air trying to keep from fainting. Woo eee! Makes your skin creep, doesn't it, boys?"

"Go on Clint, tell us what happened after you got out," yelled a man from the back of the room.

"How did you get those bite marks?" This question came from a man with a scar on his cheek.

"Hold on there Donald, I'll get there. Well, after we got out we hoofed it through the woods to the river. Boys, that was tough getting through all that swampy brush. You remember that swamp?"

"Yeah, yeah, what happened at the river, Clint?"

"Well, Lawrence, that cussed Turner and his bloodhounds was waiting there for us. One of the dogs jumped up and grabbed my arm and wouldn't let go. The hairy devil just kept grindin' his jaws, tried to saw my arm off! I tell ya fellas, it hurt like hell. With my free hand I grabbed that dog and damned near tore out his windpipe!" Clint jerked violently. "The cussed hound howled like a banshee and by God, it let go, by God it let go!"

"Is that where you got those scars, Clint?" asked the man next to him.

"You betcha, Tim! I bled like a stuck hog. That dog-hunter Turner then clubbed me on the back of the head. Next thing I knew, I was in the stocks with old Wirz staring down at me. Liked to die in those stocks, terrible I tell ya. We didn't tunnel no more after that."

From what I could tell, only a few who escaped the stockades made it back to our lines. Most were caught and suffered dearly when returned to the prison. As I listened to Clint's tale, I wondered if we could have escaped on the retreat march south from Gettysburg. *Oh my, what we could have avoided!*

Those of us in the barracks at Camp Parole were the fortunate ones. When we visited the Naval Academy, we saw a vast hospital for the thousands of the Sick Exchange. The men we saw were in bad condition and sadly, many who had survived the prison camps now died. Family members took some away for funerals at home but most were buried in the academy cemetery, far from the family churchyards and friendly environs of the place of their birth and growing up. This was far better than the many, many soldiers who died on battlefields, in camps, and worst of all, in prisons and whose whereabouts are only known to God.

Was Isaiah one of these? He deserved better.

One night in the middle of December, a strong impulse to search the hospitals came into my dreams and woke me. I found Seth and Bushey in the same state of mind. "Remember Isaiah was always having visions? Well, I just had one. I bet he is here, we just have to find him." Excited by our similar thoughts, we decided to visit the sick the next day to see where our group intuition would lead us.

After making our way back to Annapolis, we entered the largest building on the Naval Academy. Rows of sick and wounded men filled room after room. We stopped at a large desk where a busy clerk asked what we wanted and did not even look up. "Do you have anything on Isaiah Rinehart, 82nd Ohio, Company F, a sick prisoner at Andersonville, there around September 8, 1864 or thereabouts?"

The bespectacled clerk, a clean-shaven officer with a thin goatee, fingered through scattered boxes of forms like a dog burying a bone. Frustrated, he removed his glasses and shook his head. "Can't find him. We've had so many men come in with no information about them. They are so sick and many were unable to speak." He looked up at us and his jaw dropped. Seeing our thin, bony, and emaciated appearance, his facial expression became suddenly sallow. He knew that we did indeed understand, at the deepest level.

"I'm sorry men but we do not have any record on an Isaiah Rinehart at this time. However, if he came in on the Sick Exchange he may be here. Check back in a few days, I might be able to tell you more. For now, you can check with the clerks at the various buildings to see if you can find him."

Every day for the rest of our stay at Camp Parole, we went from hospital to hospital but could find no sign of Isaiah. We talked to some prisoners who were at Andersonville after we left there but no one knew anything. The agony within us grew larger with each shake of the head or empty reply. Not even the Christmas celebrations lifted our gloom.

Finally, December 26, the morning of our departure for Columbus and Camp Chase, came and we boarded the train at the Annapolis depot. Bushey and Seth had thirty-day furloughs after which they would have to return to the regiment. I was to be mustered out in Columbus, my three year term of service finished.

For Hiram Terman, the war, was almost done.

What happened to Isaiah? Did he die at Andersonville and was his thin body stacked like cord wood in the dead house and then buried with the other thousands who died there? Or, did he miraculously survive? Would we ever see him again?

These were the thoughts that filled our minds as we waited among hundreds of other soldiers for trains to take us home.

We knew the war caused many, many people to live without answers and we were not alone in our grief. As the train pulled out of Annapolis, Bushey, Seth, and I looked out the window at the disappearing buildings for as long as we could, the hospitals holding our gazes. Was Isaiah in one of those disappearing buildings now growing smaller in the distance? Soon, our strained necks gave out and our eyes and thoughts turned to the future as the train chugged along toward Baltimore where we then caught a train to Columbus, Ohio.

After two days journey, we arrived at the rail station in Columbus and then were taken to Camp Chase. Seth and Bushey, since they were still on active duty, had to stay there a little while. I was to be mustered out.

In the few minutes we had before their sergeant called them into line, we embraced, cried, and laughed and in some of the most powerful emotions I have ever felt, relived the tremendous events we had survived. Seth, holding my head between his bony hands, said my name repeatedly.

"Hiram, Hiram, Hiram. What words are there…you know, don't you, you know."

"Yes, Seth, I know."

With promises to keep in touch, we parted in a misty rain. As I headed off to the camp headquarters for my final processing, Bushey yelled out. "We'll look for you at your hut in Ohio, Hiram." As Bushey and Seth merged into the blue lines of their regiment, thoughts of our joyful meeting in Savannah flashed through my mind and a lump lodged in my throat.

When an officer handed me my muster-out sheet and final pay, a wrenching took place in my mind and body that must have been evident. The clerk, a neatly dressed man with a close trimmed beard named Wickes, smiled at me, shook my hand, and said, "The country thanks you for your service soldier, now Godspeed to you as you make your way home." Carrying a small bag with all my possessions, I boarded a carriage that took me to the Columbus railroad station to meet the train to Mansfield.

Standing at the station, I replayed the sights, sounds and emotions of that first train ride from Salem (now renamed Shiloh after the famous battle—Ohio had too many towns named Salem). Reaching into my pocket, I felt the scrap of my shirt I wore at Andersonville. It seemed to smolder between my fingers and seared my mind. *Good Lord, how did I make it?*

I was now a different person. I felt honorable. Not honor due to praise that comes from winning battles or performing heroic deeds in front of generals. Indeed, that kind of glory had eluded me. No medals, no battlefield promotions. My name was buried in anonymity with thousands of others both living and dead. But my friends and I knew.

I had survived disease, long marches, battles, and horrible prison camps. I had kept my humanity in the most vile conditions. Not alone but with friends of the deepest kind who knew me and I them. While I was weakened in body, my spirit was strong. Like a tree growing in the wind, the gusts of war and prison had bent but not broken my spirit. I was braced by the Almighty and with strengths that only come from surviving tests of the severest kind; the kind that could bring you down, and indeed had broken many men. My head, though I slouched from weakness, was held high on that third day of January, 1865 as I waited at the Columbus rail station to head north to Mansfield and home.

As I sat on the platform, a black man walked in front of me and confidently took a seat to my left. He did not act at all like the constantly slouching and bowing contrabands that frequently showed up in our camps down South. He sat erect and looked longingly down the track. I noticed scars on his neck that extended down under a white cotton shirt. I saw these brands of an overseer on slaves in the South and on those that had escaped to Ohio. I felt his pain, as one prisoner knows another.

His eyes brightened as a distant train came into view. It came from the south. He got up and paced the platform as the train pulled into the station. It slowed and stopped, the brakes engaging, the engine releasing jets of steam. Memories of the loud screeching brakes of Rebel trains in Staunton flashed through my mind. I clinched my teeth.

Soon a Negro woman and two children exited the car. The woman carried a young boy of about three and a girl of ten tagged along by her side. The man let out a cry and ran up to them, hugging them and smothering the children with kisses. "Sarah, oh Sarah, how long, how long? Welcome home, welcome to our new home." His wife was a slim woman with sharp features. She and the children melted into his strong arms.

"Benjamin, how we have waited for dis day, oh praise da Lord!" This reunion touched my heart. Tears welled up in my eyes as the terrible sight of the gallows at Camp Lawton intruded on my thoughts.

As this family turned to leave the platform, the young girl looked at me and asked her father, "Who is dat man dere?" Mortified, the former slave drew his long lost daughter close as he looked at me, his back straight and his head held high.

"Dat man, child, is a Union soldier come back from the war. He is the reason you and your mamma and brother were on dat dere train and not on da plantation no more. Dank you sir, Dank you."

I could not talk, pent up feelings within me bound my voice. I did manage to smile and nod which was enough. I waved again as they walked down the depot steps. They walked by a number of carriages to an old rickety wagon on the edge of the lot. Hitched to the wagon was an old mule, long worn out by pulling cannons on many a battlefield, its hips and shoulder blades shadowing protruding ribs. As I watched the wagon slowly pull away wondering when the mule would drop, I could not help but wonder. What would the new birth of freedom produce for this just liberated people?

Eventually the rest of the passengers got off and the train left the station, leaving me alone. As I sat there, I reached into my pack for some food and Isaiah's Bible fell out as I removed an apple. I picked it up. The name of my friend was on the bottom right corner. *Isaiah, where are you?*

A strong desire to open the Bible overcame me. I hesitated because I was sure there were things in there only his family should see. As my fingers passed along the clay stained edges, the pages parted and Psalm 69 revealed its words, verses 33 to 36. The words cut into my doubts and soothed my spirit. I, like the country, was neither healed nor whole but the storm was almost past and even now the seeds of reconciliation swelled in the blood-dampened soil.

For the Lord hears the needy, and does not despise His who are prisoners. Let heaven and earth praise Him. The seas and everything that moves in them. For God will save Zion and build the cities of Judah. That they may dwell there and possess it. And the descendants of His servants will inherit it.

The author at the farm owned by Hiram Terman after the war.

The author and his brother Don at the cemetery in Rome, Ohio.
"Hiram, did I get it right? I'll ask again on the shore of eternity."

HISTORICAL NOTES AND ACKNOWLEDGEMENTS

The Oath

I do hereby acknowledge to have volunteered this ___ day of _____, ____ to serve as a soldier in the Army of the United States of America, for the period of three years, unless sooner discharged by the proper authority: Do also agree to accept such bounty, pay, rations, and clothing, as are, or may be, established by law for volunteers. And I _____ do solemnly swear, that I will bear true faith and allegiance to the United States of America and that I will serve them honestly and faithfully against all their enemies or opposers whomsoever; and that I will observe and obey the orders of the President of the United States, and the orders of officers appointed over me, according to the Rules and Articles of War.

Approximately two million Union and one million Confederate soldiers crossed the threshold into the maelstrom of the Civil War and each has a tale of camps, marches, battles, or even prison confinement. The story for this book is that of my great uncle, Private Hiram Terman of the 82nd Ohio Infantry, who after surviving the war and the prison camps, returned to farming and lived to the ripe old age of 84, dying in 1926. I not only wanted to recount historical facts but actually relive his experiences, perhaps the quintessential aspiration of any writer of a historical novel. Unfortunately, I found no written materials by Hiram himself. It was left to my mind's eye and imagination to relive what happened to him, the richness of his Civil War experiences.

Here lay the challenge. How could I reach back beyond the years and accurately create the world of a Civil War soldier and how would I respond if I were he?

I first searched the memories of my father's stories, some of which were written down. To these I added the accounts of relatives and older residents who knew of Hiram and his family. I found a cousin, Mary Stone, who knew of anecdotal stories about Hiram and she had found Hiram's grave near Rome, Ohio. I also talked to one of the oldest residents of nearby Greenwich, Ohio who delivered propane to the Terman farm then owned by Hiram's son, Harry, a bachelor. He related how the son and his father were known as quiet, humble people involved in the community but he did not recall any accounts of Hiram's Civil War experiences. Some citizens of Rome knew of the Terman family and remembered them as dependable stalwarts of the community. Hiram is recorded in the history of Richland County as a member of a committee for the location and burial of itinerant soldiers of the Civil War. He is also mentioned as single handedly stopping a threatening grass fire, saving nearby buildings.

Many of the family stories did not match with the records. My father, for instance, said that Hiram had lost a leg at Gettysburg but none of the records supported this claim. Such is the task of the historian but I did not have only a historical task. I had to discover how to transform my thoughts and tendencies into a reasonable facsimile of Hiram.

First-hand accounts are best for this and I am indebted to Richard Fink of Kenton, Ohio, site of Hiram's first training experience at Camp Simon Kenton. Richard sent me copies of Hiram's military records from the National Archives, letters from soldiers, reports of officers, and magazine and newspaper accounts on the 82nd Ohio from his extensive collection. He also reviewed the manuscript. Without his help, this book would be a lot less rich in its historical details.

As the ancestors of Civil War soldiers can readily attest, there is no substitute for standing where Hiram stood at McDowell and Cross Keys, in the sunken road at Manassas, on the western flank of the 11th Corps at Chancellorsville, in the fields north of Gettysburg, on the low sands of Belle Island, or where the raiders were hung at Andersonville. Along with finding a grave, this is the literal essence, the Holy Grail, sought by those seeking to relive the Civil War experience of their ancestors. Many thanks to Civil War Trails for maps and signs—we stopped at many a signpost erected by this organization (see www.civilwartrails.org).

Visits to the battlegrounds and prisons are the backbone of this book. Crysta Stanton of the Highland Historical Society at McDowell, Virginia, introduced me to my favorite battlefield, the site of Hiram's first engagement. The Village of McDowell, the Hull house museum, the Presbyterian church with bricks initialed by soldiers, and the slopes of the battlefield are almost untouched by commercialism. The same can be said of the battleground at Cross Keys. Standing at the Union Church across from a Civil War cemetery, a broad vista presents itself and I could easily imagine Hiram's company on the far left, descending down into the boiling cauldron of combat.

Our visit to the heart of Civil War Virginia was made special by a reunion with Don Roth, an old college friend and baseball teammate at Spring Arbor University living in Locust Grove, right next to the Chancellorsville battlefield. Many thanks, Don, for helping us search out the paths of the 82nd Ohio at Cedar Mountain, Chancellorsville, and Manassas. These visits plus the trip to Gettysburg where Hiram was captured were informative and powerful. With the help of maps supplied by the Civil War Trails organization and other research materials, it was often possible to locate where the 82nd Ohio and even Company F might have been located. Special thanks go to the staffs at Manassas (John Reid), Chancellorsville, and Gettysburg (John Heiser) who not only supplied information but critically reviewed relevant chapters in my rough drafts.

To get inside the minds of soldiers in camp, on marches, and in battle I devoured diaries and firsthand accounts such as *For Country, Cause, and Leader: The Civil War Journal of Charles B. Haydon* by Stephen W. Sears, and *Eye of the Storm* by Private Robert Knox Sneden. The accounts of soldiers in *Voices of the Civil War* by Time-Life inspired many of the events and encounters I wrote about, as did the eyewitness accounts of Captain Alfred Lee of the 82nd Ohio. He recorded in detail events from the earliest campaign in West Virginia to Gettysburg where Captain Lee was wounded and Hiram was captured. *Buckeye Blood: Ohio at Gettysburg* by Richard Baumgartner and *Retreat from Gettysburg* by Kent Masterson Brown provided many facts and fueled my imagination about this, the greatest of all battles in the Civil War.

Recreating Hiram's prison experiences was a challenge. The unadorned and undeveloped grassy prison yard at Belle Island produced a strange set of emotions; ironically, its elemental state increased its poignancy. Many thanks to Mike Gorman and his web site on Belle Island for information on that infamous Confederate prison.

My three visits to Andersonville were powerful. Kevin Frye, an historian at Andersonville, shared his insights as we walked around that well-known Rebel prison with copies of Hiram's prisoner of war records in our hands. The awareness that nearly thirteen thousand prisoners died there moved me. The chance finding of two of Hiram's 82nd Ohio comrades in the large cemetery amazed me. One of these, Milo Carpenter, could be related to my wife—what are the chances? Kevin's web site on Andersonville is a treasure trove and his review of this book was invaluable.

Searches of the Internet supplied a vast set of resources such as county histories, maps, photographs, drawings, and Civil War period writings. Many thanks to Hal Jespersen for access to his fine maps of troop movements. Noteworthy in this regard was the *Library of Congress* web site and the online access to public domain historical documents provided by Google Books. A partial list used in this book includes *Johnny Reb and Billy Yank* by Alexander Hunter, *Battles and Leaders of the Civil War, Official Records of the Rebellion,* and a regimental history of the 123rd Ohio as well as many firsthand accounts by Civil War veterans. Of note here are John L. Ransom (*Andersonville Diary)*; H. M. Davidson (*Fourteen Months in Southern Prisons*); G. A. Sabre (*Nineteen Months a Prisoner of War*), S. M. Durfur (*Over the Dead Line*), L. Long (*Twelve Months in Andersonville*) and John McElroy (*Andersonville: A Story of Rebel Military Prisons*). Important treatises include *Prisoners of War and Military Prisons* by A. B. Isham, H. M. Davidson, and H. B. Furness.

Ovid Futch's well-regarded book on Andersonville helped separate fact from fiction as did the directly transcribed daily journal of Eugene Forbes (Styple, William B., ed. *Death Before Dishonor: The Andersonville Diary of Eugene Forbes*). As for getting the human drama, the classic novel *Andersonville* by McKinley Kantor literally dragged me into the darkness of that horrible place.

The well-regarded *Civil War Times* magazine provided varied insights into the Civil War period as did the acclaimed books by Bruce Catton, James McPherson, and Shelby Foote. Earl Hess's *The Union Soldier in Battle: Enduring the Ordeal of Combat* facilitated the reliving of battlefield experiences. Mark Noll's book, *The Civil War as a Theological Crisis,* Steven E. Woodworth's *While God is Marching On,* and J. O. Lehman and S. M. Nolt's *Mennonites, Amish, and the American Civil War* helped with theological aspects of the Civil War. The encounters with Mennonites and the debates between Seth and Isaiah have their roots here.

Forays with my brother Don and his wife June through cemeteries, museums, and genealogical collections near Shiloh (formerly named Salem where Hiram enlisted) and Mansfield, Ohio (my birthplace) provided a sense of place in my quest to understand Private Terman's family and hometown communities. Along with Hiram's grave, we located the original farmstead belonging to Hiram and his immediate family near the town of Rome, Ohio, Blooming Grove Township. The old barn clearly identified the farm with bold letters still readable "The Terman Farm 1869".

A private visit to the Sailors and Soldiers Museum in Mansfield, Ohio where Hiram may have visited as a G.A.R. veteran was noteworthy because it was there I discovered a picture of Hiram's mother labeled "Mrs. John Terman, early settler of Richland County". Special thanks to Dr. George Findlayson.

A visit with the staff at the Old Jail Museum in Warrenton, Virginia uncovered what it was like for the 82nd Ohio as they skirmished along the Rappahannock River before Second Bull Run. A fascinating tour through the Museum of the Civil War Soldier in Petersburg, Virginia, particularly the experience of being in a virtual battle, helped me better visualize what Civil War combat might have been like for Hiram. I can still hear the whizzing of Minnie balls and the whir of shell fragments.

Research trips to libraries with extensive Civil War collections such as the one at Hillsdale College in Hillsdale, Michigan provided access to a wide array of books from historical accounts to novels. A statue of a Civil War soldier at the entrance to Hillsdale's campus gives witness to the many young men from Hillsdale College that served in the Civil War.

Another monument to the *Sultana* sits in the city park of Hillsdale. This poignant and strangely underreported tragedy suggested to me the route that poor Isaiah could take to get home from Andersonville. As incredible as it sounds, this explosion on the Mississippi River really did happen, and Isaiah's journey home is the subject of my next Civil War novel.

It was also in this small Michigan town near the home of my wife's parents that I went to breakfast many times at the Finish Line Restaurant to meet with Albert Castel, noted Civil War author and his circle of retired college and university historians. The conversations provided good testing grounds for my ideas. My most asked questions? What would it have been like for Hiram in this or that situation? What would I have felt if I had been him?

Castel's book, *Tom Taylor's Civil War*, where the author filled in gaps in a soldier's wartime letters was an inspiration for this undertaking. Furthermore, Albert grew up near Wichita; close to my present home in Hillsboro, Kansas. This was just one of the many chance meetings that accompanied the writing of this book. Like Hiram, Isaiah, and Seth, I was amazed at the serendipity of events.

Viewing and methodically reviewing the extensive media on the Civil War allowed me to better visualize the details of the Civil War experience. Especially valuable in this regard were the video series on the *Civil War* by Ken Burns, the History Channel episodes of *Civil War Journal*, and movies such as *The Blue and the Gray, Shenandoah, Andersonville, The Andersonville Trial, Glory, Gettysburg, God's and Generals, Cold Mountain,* and the classic *The Red Badge of Courage*. These dramatized experiences helped me feel some of the basic emotions. Stonewall Jackson's "you are the first brigade" speech in *God's and Generals* is a good example.

The classic Civil War novel by Stephen Crane, *The Red Badge of Courage* and Joseph Kirkland's Civil War era novel, *The Captain of Company K*, gave me a look into the nature of conversations that took place between soldiers as did recent books by Michael Shaara *(The Killer Angels),* Jeff Shaara *(Gods and Generals)*, and John Jakes *(North and South* and *Love and War)*.

Attending and videotaping several reenactments of Civil War battles helped in writing battle scenes as did interviews with participants. Civil war reenactors showed up at many places in my travels including a family reunion in Ohio. I treasure the comments of this very astute group.

Finally, I thank all those not previously mentioned who helped me research, write, and edit this book. I gratefully acknowledge Dr. Neil Veydt, Dr. C. Richard Terman, Dr. William Terman, Craig Swain, Dan Reigle, Melinda Nikkel, Dr. Hugh Siefken, John Siefken, Patrick Shulze, Viola Gossen, Ben Wiens, Lyle Faurot, Marcella Bruce, Robin Ottoson, Bruce Plank, Rosella Epp, John Dick, Joel Klaassen, Dr. Bill Kostlevy, Dr. Richard Kyle, Gari-Anne Patzwald, and many others who encouraged me. All errors, of course, are mine. Finally, I thank my wife, Jan, who was by my side on this journey. Without her, no book would exist.

For an author produced audio book, image and video DVD, and other media and information associated with this book and other books by Max Terman, email me at maxt@tabor.edu or visit http://home.southwind.net/~mjterman.

82!
To The

YOUNG MEN
AND THE MIDDLE AGED!

The undersigned have received authority from the Governor to organize the

82d

REGIMENT,
and rendezvous at
CAMP

SIMON KENTON,

near Kenton, Hardin County, Ohio.

We earnestly call upon all patriotic citizens to lend their influence to fill up this Regiment; in order that it may be ready for service as soon as possible. The loyal army of the Nation is in danger of being overpowered by the superior numbers of the enemy, and the Rebellion, as a consequence, prolonged. Will not the able-bodied men of the country promptly step forward in this, the hour of their Country's great necessity and peril?

Recruits will be Uniformed and subsisted forthwith, and paid from the date of their enlistment.

The pay of a Soldier ranges from $13, to $21 a month independent of Clothing and Rations. He will also be entitled to and receive

$100,00

BOUNTY

at the end of his term of enlistment, together with a Land Warrant for

160

ACRES OF LAND!

Every care will be taken of the health and comfort of Soldiers under our command.

For further particulars, as to the appointment of Recruiting Officers, and other matters connected with the organization of the Regiment, apply to either of the undersigned.
Col. JAMES CANTWELL, Kenton, O.,
Lt. Col. B.R. DURFEE, Marion, O.,
Maj. J.S. ROBINSON, Kenton, O.
Kenton, Ohio, Nov. 1, 1861.

☞ One full Company will report here tomorrow for the 82d regiment. Another Company will immediately commence forming here, and those who wish to enter the service, should come forward without delay, as this will probably be the last and best Company formed in Hardin County. Come right along.

Recruiting poster for the 82nd Ohio (courtesy of Richard Fink).

Colonel James Cantwell and Major James Robinson of the 82nd Ohio *(courtesy of Richard Fink)*.

Corporal Sam Armstrong *(U. S. Army Military History Institute)* and General Robert Milroy *(Library of Congress)*.

Cross Keys battleground (*Library of Congress*). Union losses (killed, wounded, and missing) 625.

Cedar Mountain battleground (*Library of Congress*). Union losses (killed, wounded, and missing) 1400.

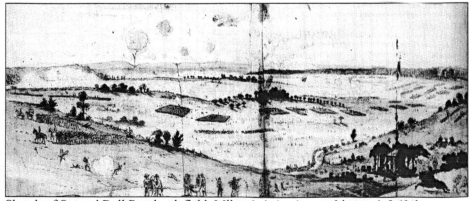

Sketch of Second Bull Run battlefield, Milroy's brigade marching on left (*Library of Congress*). Union losses (killed, wounded, and missing) 14,800 August 28-30.

Chancellorsville battleground, the Chancellor house ruins (*Library of Congress*). Union losses (killed, wounded, and missing) 16,030.

Gettysburg battleground where Hiram was captured July 1, 1863 (*Library of Congress*). Union losses (killed, wounded, and missing) 23,186.

Painting of Gettysburg battlefield. Hiram was probably kept as a prisoner west of town over the ridge (*Library of Congress*).

Belle Island where Hiram was prisoner July 1863 to February 1864 *(Library of Congress).*

Andersonville where Hiram was imprisoned February to September 1864. Shown are shabangs and the deadline (*Library of Congress*).

Andersonville when rations were distributed (*Library of Congress*). Does the prisoner in the lower center of the photo have a pan?

Drawing of Camp Lawton at Millen, Georgia where Hiram stayed until November, 1864 (*Battles and Leaders of the Civil War*).

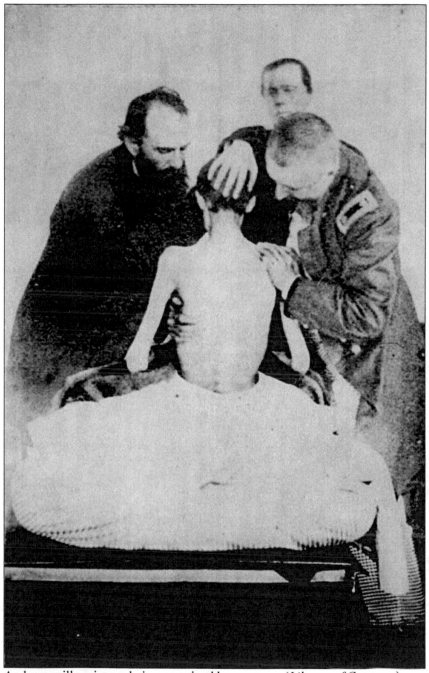

Andersonville prisoner being examined by surgeons (*Library of Congress*).

238

Painting of Camp Parole, Annapolis, Maryland where Hiram recuperated until January, 1865 (*Library of Congress*).

Painting of Camp Chase in Columbus, Ohio where Hiram finally left for home (*Library of Congress*).

"These struggling tides of life which seem
In wayward aimless course to tend
Are eddies of a mighty stream
Which moves to its appointed end."
-William Cullen Bryant, "Thanatopsis"

The name, rank, fate, enlistment date and age of the 82nd Ohio soldiers captured at Gettysburg and sent to Andersonville (courtesy of Kevin Frye, Andersonville National Historic Site). Some names may have similar but different spellings in the records.

Branigan, John, Private, died 5/8/1864, 12/5/1861, 29

Cahill, David, Private, survived, 12/16/1861, 18

Karpenter, Milo, Corporal, died 3/4/1864, 12/9/1861, 25

Cole, Benjamin, Private, died 7/18/1864, not recorded

Folk, William, Private, died 8/14/1864, not recorded

Hall, S., Private, survived, not recorded

Kellough, Samuel, Private, survived, 10/22/1861, 29

Roose, Henry, Private, survived, 11/15/1861, 23

Smith, Horace, Sergeant, died 3/14/1864, 11/15/1861, 23

Tallman, Benjamin, Private, died, 12/14/1861, 21

Terman, Hiram, Private, survived, 12/26/1861, 20

West, Jonathan, Private, died 6/1864, 4/13/1862, 35

Grave markers of two of Hiram's comrades who died at Andersonville.

"Now, though numberless fates of death beset us
Which no mortal can escape or avoid
Let us go forward together, and either
We shall give honor to one another
Or another to us."
-Homer

Union soldiers in camp *(Library of Congress)*. Private Hiram Terman's story is but one of many. As we near the 150 year anniversary of the Civil War, may the telling of his help tell them all.

82nd OHIO—The regiment was mustered into the United States service December 31, 1861, at Kenton, Ohio, broke camp there January 25, 1862, crossed the Ohio River, and on January 27th went into camp at Grafton, (West) Virginia. The 82nd Regiment fought in the battles of McDowell, Cross Keys, Cedar Mountain, Second Battle of Bull Run, Chancellorsville, Gettysburg, Wauhatchie, and Mission Ridge. Skirmishes included: Franklin, Virginia; Port Republic; Freeman's Ford; Rappahannock Ford; Sulphur Springs, and Waterloo Bridge. The regiment marched over 2,500 miles and saw much hard service. The 82nd Ohio was particularly unfortunate in the loss of officers, losing 16 officers killed or mortally wounded. One of the most respected regiments in the Civil War, it numbered over 2,300 names on its rolls. (Source: *Whitelaw Reid (1867). Ohio in the War*)

TERMAN, HIRAM—was born in Richland County, Ohio on the 8th of May, 1842; passing away on December 10, 1926. He has always resided here, with the exception of three years and two months, which time he served in the late war; he enlisted in December, 1861, on the 26th day, and was mustered out on the 4th of January, 1865; he was a member of Co. F, 82d O. V. I.. He participated in all the battles the regiment was called upon to engage in, until the battle Gettysburg, on the 1st of July, when he was taken prisoner, and remained as such for a period of over seventeen months; was first taken to Belle Island; thence to Andersonville; from there to Savannah, and thence to Annapolis, from where he was paroled. Mr. Terman is a farmer by occupation, and has always followed that. In the year 1868, he was married to Miss Nancy J. Boals; they have two children, Walter B. and Harry W. (Source: *History of Richland County, Ohio*)